APRISMO

*The Ideas and Doctrines
of Victor Raúl Haya de la Torre*

APRISMO

The Ideas and Doctrines
of Víctor Raúl Haya de la Torre

SELECTED, EDITED, AND TRANSLATED BY
ROBERT J. ALEXANDER

The Kent State University Press

Copyright © 1973 by Robert J. Alexander.
All rights reserved.
ISBN 0-87338-125-4.
Library of Congress Catalog Card Number 78-181083.
Manufactured in the United States of America.
First printing.

Dedicated to Tony

PREFACE

RELATIVELY LITTLE OF THE WRITING OF LATIN AMERICAN POLITI-
cal thinkers and leaders is available in English. This contributes
considerably to the widespread belief in this country that the Latin
Americans have had very little of interest to offer to the world of
political ideas and theories. However, such is not the case. Long
before most of the rest of the world was much concerned with the
now fashionable problems of political and economic development,
Latin American political theorists and politicians were wrestling with
these issues. They evolved important notions concerning the nature
of the development process, its difficulties, and how it should be initiated. Some of these ideas now have general currency not only in all of
the "third world," but even among those concerned in the "developed"
countries. Indeed, some of the ideas are now so widely current that
their Latin American origins of a generation or more ago have been
all but forgotten.

One of the seminal Latin American theorists and authors in this
area is Víctor Raúl Haya de la Torre. Now over seventy-five years
old, he has been writing about the problems of the economic and
political emergence of Latin America for five decades, has been active
in his country's national political life for half a century, and has been
head of its largest political party for over forty years. Haya's name is
familiar to anyone who has the least interest in Latin American affairs.
Almost none of his published work, however, is available to those
unable to read Spanish. Aside from a few articles which Haya has
written for United States periodicals and the pioneering work of Dr.
Harry Kantor on the ideology of the Aprista movement, which contains liberal quotes from Haya's works, almost nothing written by
him has appeared in English.

The present volume brings together selections from his publications on the principal subjects of his major concern. There has been no attempt here to reproduce everything that he has written. Many of the passages in his numerous books have been journalistic observations and comments on contemporary events, most of which are interesting in themselves but do not represent lasting contributions to the political thought and evolution of Latin America. I have concentrated on those portions of Haya's work which seem to have lasting importance, either in putting forth original ideas and syntheses, or in influencing the thinking and programs of the parties and political leaders in the hemisphere. I have tried to present Haya's most important statements on several representative topics but at the same time have tried to avoid unnecessary repetition. I have also attempted to show the development of various aspects of his ideas by generally arranging each section in chronological order. There are a few exceptions to this, where a selection gives an overall view providing a logical introduction or where one contains autobiographical material useful to an understanding of his ideas.

I have sought to translate and edit these selections in such a way as to render without distortion their content as Haya meant it. However, the translation of Haya's ideas into passable English has involved some difficulties. Most of his pieces were written for the press in various parts of Latin America. Particularly in the earlier years, these articles were written in a somewhat hurried style with a large number of incomplete sentences and other idiosyncracies. In most cases, these passages have been recast as complete sentences, except where the more informal form seems called for. I have also eliminated most of the underscoring and capitalization that Haya used exceedingly liberally in his earlier works. Haya's references to and quotations from other sources have not generally been traced to the original sources but have been translated or rendered as he quoted them. This has unfortunately been necessary since the citations given are often too vague to be effectively tracked down.

In being able to do this book, I owe various debts of gratitude to several people. First of all, I wish to thank Haya de la Torre himself for his cooperation in authorizing me to make this kind of a selection of his works available in English. Second, I must thank those who undertook the somewhat laborious job of typing the manuscript, Mrs. Emma Wenz and Mrs. J. H. Carman.

I owe a particularly great debt to Ms. Jo Zuppan. As editor of the manuscript for the Kent State University Press, she has done a remarkable job of "retranslating" my translations of Haya de la Torre's writing. Too often I had tended towards a literal rendition of his material, and she vastly improved my vocabulary, phrasing, and grammatical construction.

Finally, as always, I owe much to my wife Joan and my children Meg and Tony for their tolerance during long evenings and over weekends when they undoubtedly got tired of hearing the clicking of the typewriter and my muttering about some particularly difficult piece of translation.

New Brunswick, New Jersey
April 1972

CONTENTS

8. Internationalization of the Panama Canal

9. The Word Indoamerica

APRISMO

The Ideas and Doctrines
of Víctor Raúl Haya de la Torre

Introduction

VÍCTOR RAÚL HAYA DE LA TORRE IS CERTAINLY THE MOST IMPOR-
tant political philosopher and idealogist of the democratic left that
Latin America has had in the present century. He has not only been
the leader of one of the oldest and largest mass political parties in the
area—the *Partido Aprista Peruano*—for more than forty years, but
has been the pioneer in presenting economic and political ideas that
have subsequently received wide currency throughout the hemisphere.

Haya de la Torre began to write extensively in the 1920s.
With the rise of indigenous popular parties advocating basic social,
economic, and political change in their respective countries in the
1930s and 1940s, Haya's ideas became fundamental elements in the
programs of nearly a dozen national revolutionary parties. Subsequently, some of these ideas became part of the programs of some
of the more traditional parties, revamped and modernized, as well
as part of the programs of some of the new Christian Democratic
groups which have been gaining importance in recent years.

Haya de la Torre was born in Trujillo, in northern Peru, on
February 22, 1895. His family was one of the most distinguished in
that region, and ancestors on both sides had been active in the country's struggle for independence in the first decades of the nineteenth
century. Near Trujillo is Chan-Chan, seat of one of the great pre-Inca
civilizations of Peru. Through its gigantic ruins, Haya de la Torre
first became interested in and intrigued with the Indian antecedents
of his native country. Although his family was proud of its "pure"
European ancestry, Haya was struck with the similarity of some of
the sculptured heads at Chan-Chan with his own physiognomy. His
family was unable or unwilling to give him any acceptable explanation for this striking resemblance.

In his teens, Haya became associated with a group of young intellectuals of his native city, headed by Antenor Orrego, that was particularly concerned with the history and fate of the Peruvian Indians. Through this circle he learned a good deal about the people who made up two-thirds or more of the population of Peru. He also began to evolve his own ideas about the uniqueness of the Peruvian and general Latin American civilization, and its differences from that of Europe.

Haya as Student Leader

In 1917 Haya went to the University of San Marcos, in Lima, which prides itself on being the oldest still-functioning institution of higher learning in the Western Hemisphere. He arrived there at a period of considerable turbulence in Peruvian and Latin American affairs.

Haya had contacts, through his family connections, with Augusto B. Leguía, aspirant to the presidency, a somewhat liberal leader of the opposition. While studying at the university, Haya worked in the law office of a relative who was closely aligned with Leguía and, from that vantage point, entered into his first genuine contact with the practicalities of Peruvian politics, having the opportunity to observe some of the preparations for the coup d'état which ultimately brought Leguía to the presidency.

Meanwhile, Haya was very much involved in student politics at the university. Somewhat unexpectedly, this activity brought him quickly into the heart of general national political activity—and as it turned out, as a leader of the opposition to President Leguía.

In 1918 there began, at the University of Córdoba, in Argentina, a student movement which quickly spread throughout Latin America. This was the famous University Reform. The Reform was a movement of revolt against the traditional Latin American university, dominated as it still was by a classical orientation, virtually excluding study of the physical sciences and completely banning that of the social sciences. The students were also completely subordinated to conservatively minded faculty members.

The University Reform preached a number of ideas. It insisted on a thorough revision of the curriculum, changing the exclusive emphasis on philosophy and allied studies to include both the physical and social sciences. It advocated "university autonomy," meaning the granting to the institutions of higher learning freedom from govermental political influence and the provision of financial resources independent of the general government budget such as would assure that autonomy. It urged the opening of the universities to lower class youths. Student "co-government" of the university itself was also demanded with student participation in the governing bodies of the institution. Finally, the Reform urged that the university should be a revolutionary force in the general society, bringing about fundamental changes in the economy, society, and political life of the nation with the specific recommendation that the university do extension work in the community.

The students of San Marcos soon followed the lead of their Argentine counterparts. The first president of the Federation of Students of Peru, Hernando de Lavalle, moved cautiously, but he was soon succeeded, late in 1918, by Haya de la Torre, who took a militant stand in favor of the Reform.

Under Haya's leadership, the Peruvian Students' Federation showed a particular interest in taking the message of the Reform to the community at large. Haya and other student leaders entered into contact with the fledgling labor movement, which was generally under anarcho-syndicalist influence. Together, the student and trade union leaders organized a Popular University. This organization established adult education classes for labor union members and their families, generally in the headquarters of the trade unions. These courses not only included instruction in such utilitarian subjects as reading and writing, but also Peruvian and general history, economics, civic affairs, and current problems. The students also threw their influence behind the further extension of the trade union movement. Thus, Haya played a leading role in organizing the Federation of Textile Workers of Peru in 1919. He was one of the principal orators at their founding convention, and he continued to play a leading role in the federation as long as he remained in Peru.

President Leguía, however, soon became suspicious of the intentions of the student and trade union leaders. Although he had had a certain degree of popular support when he came to the presidency, Leguía soon started to govern with a heavy hand, and he suspected the "subversive" intentions of the student and labor leaders and their Popular University. For their part, they became increasingly hostile to the administration.

A crisis in student-government relations arose in May, 1923. At that time, President Leguía, in an apparent attempt to rally the support of the Church behind his regime, decided to "dedicate Peru to the Sacred Heart of Jesus." The student and trade union leaders, who were anti-clerical in their outlook, were strongly opposed to this move. They organized demonstrations against it, and as a result, Haya and other student leaders were arrested and, after being kept in prison for some time, were deported to Panama.

Haya's First Exile

For the next seven years, Haya de la Torre remained in exile. He travelled widely in Mexico and Central America, as well as in the United States and Europe. It was not possible for him to return to Peru until after the overthrow of the Leguía regime.

In Mexico, Haya studied at first hand the Mexican Revolution, the first of the great modern revolutions and, because it was indigenous, the movement which Haya was convinced would have the most to offer for the rest of the hemisphere. He talked with governmental leaders on all levels, became associated for a while with Jóse Vasconcelos, then Minister of Education, lectured at the University of Mexico, and did a great deal of thinking about the nature and implications of the Mexican Revolution.

It was in Mexico, too, that Haya began laying the foundations for what he hoped would become a hemisphere-wide, revolutionary political party. There on May 7, 1924, he and some other Latin American students established the *Alianza Popular Revolucionaria Americana* (American Popular Revolutionary Alliance—APRA). It was planned that branches of this new party would be established in each of the Latin American countries.

From Mexico, Haya de la Torre made his way to Europe for the first time, stopping in New York only long enough to embark on the S. S. *Esthonia*. He soon headed for the Soviet Union where he was greeted with considerable interest and enthusiasm as a young revolutionary who could be of great use to the Communist International in its plans for Latin America, if he could be won to the Communist banner. He visited and had extended conversations with such Soviet leaders as Trotsky, the founder of the Red Army and, in 1924, still a leading figure in the Soviet regime; Kalinin, titular president of the Soviet Union; Frunze, Trotsky's successor as Commissar for War; and Lunatcharsky, Commissar for Education, who showed a special interest in the Peruvian Popular University.

As a result of this visit, Haya came to the conclusion that the Communist International had nothing to offer Latin America. He found the Soviet leaders very ignorant of conditions—and even of the geography—of Latin America. He felt that they were seeking to apply more or less automatically to the Western Hemisphere the model of revolution which had served them in Russia, but which Haya felt was largely irrelevant for his part of the world.

After his visit to Russia, Haya spent the next two years in Western Europe. He studied for a time at Oxford University, among other things taking a course in economics from G. D. H. Cole. He also visited France, where he helped to organize a Paris branch of the APRA among Peruvian students, and where he got to know the Spanish philosopher Miguel de Unamuno; Switzerland, where he became acquainted with the French writer Romain Rolland; and Italy, where he saw at first hand the early period of the Fascist regime.

The culmination of Haya's first residence in Europe was the World Anti-Imperialist Congress, held in Brussels, Belgium, in February, 1927. A group of Apristas attended the meeting, which was organized and completely dominated by Communists from various parts of the world. There, the Apristas made clear their fundamental differences from the Communists, and in effect, war was declared between the two groups, a war which continues more than four decades later in the early 1970s. Haya and other Aprista delegates also made it clear in this Brussels meeting, to which Haya later frequently referred, that they disagreed with the Communists on several vital issues. They were opposed to the Communist concept of a worldwide revolutionary party directed from Moscow and argued that the Russian revolutionary model was not valid for Latin America. They emphasized that what was needed in the Western Hemisphere was a party with branches in each of the twenty countries, a party which would be uniquely Latin American and would seek solutions appropriate to the problems of the underdeveloped parts of the New World.

After the Brussels Congress, Haya returned to the United States. There he got to know socialists and liberals interested in Latin American affairs and gave lectures at Columbia University and the Institute of Politics at Williamstown, Massachusetts. He also gave a number of talks in different cities for the socialist-led League for Industrial Democracy, of which Norman Thomas and Harry Laidler were co-directors. It was from these early contacts, as well as writings by North Americans critical of United States imperialism in Latin America, that Haya undoubtedly became convinced that the Latin American

Anti-imperialists should seek support from and alliance with the liberal and socialist intellectuals of the United States.

Haya returned for a short visit to Mexico, after which he undertook a speaking tour of Central American universities. He met enthusiastic support from the students, but attitudes ranging from neutral to hostile from the governments of the area. In Panama he was unceremoniously deported, being put on a ship heading for Germany with nothing more than the clothes on his back.

Again in Europe, Haya continued his studies, this time at the University of Berlin. There he had contacts and long conversations with people in all the important political groups of the Weimar Republic. These included not only the Social Democrats and the Communists, but also the National Socialists or Nazis, who were then only a small minority group but were active among the students. Haya was not convinced by any of the advocates of what he considered to be European political movements and therefore inappropriate for the New World.

Haya was still in Europe when the dictatorship of Peruvian President Augusto B. Leguía was overthrown in September, 1930. The military junta that took over from Leguía refused to allow Haya's return until almost a year after Leguía's ouster. Meanwhile, Haya's student and trade union followers in Peru had organized the party about which he had been preaching for nearly a decade, the *Partido Aprista Peruano*. They rallied the support of the urban workers and many of the country's leading intellectuals, along with penetrating to some degree the Indian masses. Among the workers and the peasants, they established a network of Popular Universities, this time as subsidiary organizations of the Partido Aprista.

The Nature of the Aprista Party

The new Partido Aprista was a unique kind of political party. Right from the beginning, the founders gave it a form and content distinguishing it from all the other parties in Peru and in Latin America in general. During the next four decades, the Apristas remained the largest single civilian political force in Peru.

The party borrowed some of the outward trappings of the mass parties of Europe. It had its own hymn, "The Aprista Marseillaise." It had characteristic ways in which its members showed enthusiasm and support for orators at its public meetings: the waving of white handkerchiefs and hand clapping in a rhythmic three-clap staccato fashion, repeated over and over. When the occasion permitted, this three-beat rhythm was adapted to the blowing of automobile horns during parades and other party demonstrations.

But most characteristic of the Partido Aprista was its wide range of activities not directly associated with the vote-getting and parliamentary activities which were and still are the principal preoccupations of most Latin American parties. The party undertook intensive training activities to indoctrinate its members in party principles and ideas. Through the Gonzalez Prada Popular Universities, organized in each party branch as well as in the national headquarters in Lima, the widest range of "courses" were taught to party members and sympathizers, often by some of the country's leading intellectuals who offered their services free of charge. In addition, the party organized extensive social services; and each headquarters building had some kind of medical clinic, dental clinic, or blood bank, as well as a "popular restaurant" selling food at low prices—the national headquarters having all of these.

The wide range of party activities which is an inherent part of the Aprista Party organization can be judged by what was transpiring in the *Casa del Pueblo* in Lima during a week in July, 1971. Every evening that week, a class in business management met, attended by perhaps fifty people—organized for the purpose of training workers who might be chosen to become members of boards of directors in firms, under the program of the Military Government of President Juan Velasco for instituting worker participation in management. On one night there was a "colloquium" in which businessmen, trade unionists, and peasant leaders belonging to the party exchanged views on the current economic problems of the country. Another evening, Luis Alberto Sánchez, dean of Peruvian historians, gave a lecture on "America in the Eighteenth Century," one of a series he was offering on the history of America. On another, a psychologist met a session of his class on social psychology. On still another night, the National Executive Committee of the party had its regular weekly meeting.

Meanwhile, a chess tournament organized by the party was taking place every night of the week around some twenty chess tables set up in the main hall of the party headquarters. In what resembled an athletic field at the rear of the building, pickup basketball games took place every evening. Each night there were meetings of Aprista students, trade unionists, peasant leaders, and other specialized groups, to treat with the particular problems facing the party and its members in their respective fields.

Haya de la Torre was present most of the evenings of this week. In his office he met with a wide range of people, including party officials, students, a delegation from the Sugar Workers Federation, foreign visitors, and others. Such a wide range of activities has been characteristic of the Aprista Party whenever it has been legal during the last four decades.

From the beginning, the Aprista Party established a nationwide organization on a functional and hierarchical basis. On the national, regional, and local levels, there are separate party "commands," dealing with party activities in the trade unions, among the peasants, among students, in the cooperative field, as well as specialized party units dealing with training, finances, organization, and discipline. This functional organization borrowed much from the Communists and was in turn adopted by most of the "national revolutionary" parties, which became Apra's allies elsewhere in Latin America.

Party congresses on various levels are the highest bodies of the party. In between these meetings, however, the party executive committees have extensive power, directing the activities of the various functional units of the organization and laying down lines of policy for the party. A general secretary is in charge of the day-to-day operations of the organization. However, from his return to Peru in 1931, Haya de la Torre was recognized as *Jefe* or "chief" of the party, and during the next four decades his voice remained considerably more than just that of the first among equals.

The Apristas and the Sánchez Cerro Regime

The Apristas nominated Haya de la Torre for president in the elections scheduled for late 1931. Thus he returned home in August as a candidate. His reception in Talara, in northern Peru, where he first arrived, was ecstatic. The next few weeks were ones of furious activity. Haya toured the country by train, car, mule, and airplane, meeting with people from all segments of the population, speaking to huge and enthusiastic crowds, and getting to know the local leaders of his new party. There seemed to be little doubt about the Apristas being victorious over the candidate of the military junta which had overthrown Leguía, Colonel Luis Sánchez Cerro.

It was the supporters of Sánchez Cerro, however, not the supporters of Haya de la Torre, who counted the votes. The result was that the government candidate was credited with the victory, although the Apristas were recognized as having elected a substantial number of members to both houses of Congress. The immediate reaction of many Apristas was to attempt violent resistance to the Sánchez Cerro regime. However, Haya was instrumental in convincing his supporters not to attempt an insurrection, but to go on working towards the consolidation of the party's support among the great masses of the people. That way, the next time, the Apristas would be so strong that no regime would be able to deny their victory. His action on this occasion is characteristic of one attitude he has held throughout his political career: an opposition to violence.

For a few months, the Apristas were allowed to function legally, but the government of President Sánchez Cerro soon outlawed the Partido Aprista Peruano, had its congressmen removed, and arrested, on May 5, 1932, Haya de la Torre. In the trial that followed, Haya used the opportunity to expound upon his ideas and to discuss the transformation which the Apristas were seeking to bring about in Peru. He was sentenced to a long term in jail.

A little over two months after the arrest of Haya de la Torre, on July 7, 1932, an uprising of Apristas occurred in the city of Trujillo, his birthplace. The fighting between army units and the Apristas was extremely bitter. An unknown but certainly large number of Apristas were killed by the soldiers after they had surrendered. (The military claimed that the Apristas had also killed some soldiers taken prisoner by them.) This event drew a line of blood between the Peruvian Armed Forces and the Partido Aprista that has continued for forty years, bringing great tragedy to Peru and to the Apristas, in particular.

During the following months, the persecution of the Apristas became intense. However, this phase came to a sudden end on April 30, 1933, when President Sánchez Cerro was assassinated. The government accused the Apristas of this act. The Apristas have always denied organizing it, and Haya de la Torre's biographer, F. Cossio del Pomar, argues that it was Sánchez Cerro's successor, General Oscar Benavides, who was responsible for his elimination.

General Benavides promised the nation "peace and concord." To carry out his pledge, he released Haya de la Torre from jail, allowed the Aprista congressmen to return to their posts, and permitted the party's headquarters to reopen and the Apristas to resume legal activity. However, President Benavides honored his democratic commitments for only a few months, after which he again outlawed the Apristas and sought to jail their leaders.

Haya in Hiding

This time, Haya de la Torre escaped capture. He succeeded in staying in hiding for over a decade, until the Aprista Party was once more allowed to function openly in 1945. Haya was forced to change his place of hiding frequently, and sometimes his youthful Aprista body-guards exchanged shots with the police while Haya fled. Scores of private homes, and even monasteries, were temporary refuges during these long years. The Aprista underground continued to function, and one gathers that a surprisingly large number of Apristas must have known Haya's whereabouts at any given moment. (Benavides may also have shared this knowledge at least part of the time.) Thus, at one point, I sent a letter to Haya de la Torre, addressing it merely to "Lima, Peru," and received a reply from Haya a few months later.

The furtive clandestine life which Haya was forced to live during the 1935–1945 decade did not keep him from sending out of the country articles which were published in various other Latin American nations. Some of these articles appear in this volume.

With the approaching end of World War II, in which the Peru-vian government had supported the Allied cause in the name of the "defense of democracy," and with the expiration of the presidential term of President Manuel Prado (elected in 1939 to succeed Bena-vides), the government was forced to allow more or less free elections. President Prado did not go so far as to allow the Apristas to nominate their own presidential candidate, but he did legalize the Aprista party under the name *Partido del Pueblo*. Once again, the Aprista exiles were allowed to return, those in hiding (including Haya de la Torre) were permitted to come out into the open, and the party was free to renew full-scale activities.

The 1945–1948 Period

The Apristas threw their support behind a distinguished judge and diplomat, José Luis Bustamante y Rivero, who was running as the opposition nominee for president. They named their own candidates for the Chamber of Deputies and Senate. The Apristas were largely responsible for the election of Bustamante and won a majority in the Senate and a plurality in the Chamber.

From May, 1945, until October, 1948, the Aprista Party functioned normally. During most of this period, however, a very difficult political situation existed. In effect, there were two presidents of Peru. José Luis Bustamante y Rivero may have resided in the presidential palace and had the constitutional responsibilities of chief executive, but he was unable to govern effectively, according to constitutional prescription, without the support of Víctor Raúl Haya de la Torre, with his headquarters in the *Casa del Pueblo,* seat of the *Partido del Pueblo,* whose word was virtually law for the Aprista deputies, senators, and other public office holders.

Relations between Haya and the Apristas on the one hand, and President Bustamante on the other, reached a crisis during the last half of 1948. The Apristas, under Haya's instructions, boycotted the sessions of Congress for a considerable period, making it impossible for President Bustamante to pass his own legislative program. Finally, on October 3, 1948, a naval mutiny broke out in the harbor of Callao, near Lima, in which some dissident Apristas were involved. The party was faced with the question of whether or not it should mobilize its full force in support of this insurrection, an action which might possibly have given the Aprista Party full power for the first time. However, as in 1931, Haya de la Torre threw his decisive influence against such action. The results were disastrous for the Apristas. The naval mutiny was suppressed, and President Bustamante took advantage of the situation to outlaw them once again, on the grounds that they had launched the Callao movement.

The Haya de la Torre Asylum Case

Once again, the Aprista leaders were forced into hiding, exile, or complete silence. Haya de la Torre went into hiding and then, early in 1949, sought political asylum in the Embassy of the Republic of Colombia. With that action, Haya initiated one of the most bizarre diplomatic controversies in twentieth-century Latin American history. General Manuel Odría, who had overthrown President Bustamante a few weeks after the Callao mutiny and proclaimed himself president, refused to follow the normal procedure and to grant Haya safe conduct to go into exile. He insisted that Haya was guilty of common crimes and was not a political refugee. For its part, the Colombian Government insisted that it had given Haya refuge in its embassy because of his status as a leading political figure and continued to demand his safe conduct.

This controversy went on for five years. It would have been

ludicrous if it had not been so serious. The Peruvian Government built trenches around and virtually laid siege to the Colombian Embassy. As a result, the Colombians were forced to rent other quarters in which to carry on their normal diplomatic activities, leaving one Embassy official in the old building with Haya. Haya felt his life to be in danger and was careful to stay away from the Embassy windows, so that the troops outside could not shoot him.

The Haya de la Torre case became a cause célèbre. It was twice brought before the International Court of Justice in the Hague. The first time the Court decided that in spite of many volumes of evidence presented by the highly paid French lawyer on behalf of the Peruvian Government, the Odría regime had not proven that Haya was guilty of any common crime. Haya boasted subsequently that he was the only person ever to be declared innocent of any crime by the International Court. When the case came again before the Tribunal, on the Colombian plea that since Haya was a political refugee the Peruvian Government must give him a safe conduct to leave the country, the Court decided that this was a political issue which had to be resolved by negotiation between the two governments.

Finally, in 1954 a *modus vivendi* was worked out between the Peruvian and Colombian governments permitting Haya to leave the Embassy and go into exile. This denouement was reached because the issue was on the agenda of the Interamerican Conference which was to meet early in 1955 and the Odría regime found that it would be all alone on the issue.

Haya first went to Mexico, and then proceeded to Europe. He stayed there until the turn of the Peruvian political wheel of fortune again permitted him to return home freely in the middle of 1956.

The Apristas and the Second Prado Regime

In spite of its persecution by the Odría regime between 1948 and 1956, the Aprista Party had succeeded in maintaining some underground organization and a hold on the imagination and loyalty of many Peruvians. This became evident early in 1956 when, with the approach of new presidential elections, all potential candidates sought the backing of the Aprista Party.

Late in 1955 the Odría government had relaxed the dictatorship and allowed many of the Aprista exiles to return, although not Haya de la Torre himself. One of those returning was Ramiro Prialé, one of the earliest party leaders, who undertook the job of rebuilding the

Aprista organization. It was he who conducted the negotiations with the competing presidential candidates.

The nominee backed by President Odría was Hernando de Lavalle, Haya de la Torre's predecessor as President of the Federation of Students of Peru and by 1956 a prominent engineer. His principal rival seemed to be Fernando Belaúnde Terry, a former member of the Chamber of Deputies in the 1945–1948 period, when he had been an ally of the Apristas, and Dean of the School of Architecture at the University of San Marcos. The third, and most unlikely candidate was ex-President Manuel Prado.

The basic demand which Prialé made of all three candidates was that they legalize the Aprista Party once again. After long negotiations, General Odría refused to do this before the election, although candidate Lavalle agreed to do so if he were victorious with Aprista support. Although Belaúnde Terry was willing to promise legalization of the Aprista Party, the party leaders decided not to back him, for two understandable reasons. In the first place, they felt that if Belaúnde won, Odría would not allow him to take office. In the second place, they felt that Belaúnde and the forces organized in support of his independent presidential campaign constituted the first serious popular rival to the Apristas appearing on the scene since the Partido Aprista Peruano had been founded in 1930, and it seemed undesirable to give him support.

Finally, there was ex-President Prado. Although he was generally given little chance of winning, the Apristas negotiated with him. He readily agreed to push through Congress a law legalizing the Aprista Party as the first act of his new government, if he were elected. Thus, although Prado had kept the Apristas illegal in his previous period as president, the Apristas agreed to back him in 1956. As a result of this backing, Prado was elected.

With Prado's election, the Aprista Party was promptly legalized, and Haya returned home. In the six years that followed, he divided his time between Peru and Europe. Meanwhile, the Aprista Party gave critical but real assistance to the Prado government. Although the Apristas had few if any members of Congress, its support among the populace was of considerable importance to the president. It assured Prado of organized popular backing which he could not obtain on his own.

Many of those who had supported Haya and the Apristas in the past felt that his attitude towards Prado was a betrayal of what the

Apristas had stood for in the past. However, the Apristas reasoned that the essential thing from their and Peru's point of view was that regular and honest elections be held at the end of President Prado's term. They were convinced that they would win such elections. It was absolutely essential, therefore, that President Prado be allowed to complete his term and preside over the choice of his successor, and this he probably could not do if the Apristas were to go over to the opposition.

Hence, although the Prado regime was essentially conservative and did not seek to put into practice anything essential to the Aprista program—except political democracy—the Apristas backed it. In doing so, they lost the support of many of their "fellow-travellers," although the party organization and rank and file remained largely intact.

The 1962 Election

When the election of 1962 finally approached, the Apristas nominated Haya de la Torre for president. This was a risky decision on the party's part. The old Army-Aprista enmity continued and, by this time, had come to concentrate largely on the personality of Haya de la Torre. There was doubt in the minds of many Apristas whether, if Haya won, he would be allowed to take office. However, the rank and file of the party was exceedingly anxious that the wrong done to Haya thirty-one years before be rectified in 1962, and that their leader become the constitutional president of Peru.

If Haya had won by a very strong majority, he perhaps might have been able to take office. The United States Government, through President John Kennedy and Ambassador James Loeb, made it clear that they felt strongly that the military should recognize the election of whoever was victorious in the poll.

However, Haya did not get the 33⅓ percent of the popular vote needed under the constitution to be duly elected. Among the three major candidates—Haya, Fernando Belaúnde Terry, and ex-President Manuel Odría—he won a plurality, but not the required percentage. As a result, the election was thrown into Congress. There, the Apristas had elected enough members so that, with the backing of the small group of Christian Democrats, they could probably have secured his election. Nevertheless, Haya and other Aprista leaders were afraid that even if Congress elected him, the military would not permit him to take office. As a result, they entered into a series of somewhat frantic negotiations with the other two leading candidates. At one point, Haya agreed to withdraw from the race if that would save the constitutional succession.

The upshot of these negotiations was an agreement by Haya for the Apristas to back the candidacy of General Odría. Had this agreement been put into practice, it would in all likelihood have resulted in a split of major proportions in the Aprista ranks, since there was widespread opposition to it. The only excuse for this tentative agreement was that the Aprista leaders felt that the military would permit Odría to take office, the constitutional system would be preserved, and the Apristas would still have a chance to win in the following election.

However, Congress never got a chance to decide upon the presidency. The evening before the vote was to be taken, the military chiefs overthrew President Prado and cancelled the election, on the claim that it had been marked by widespread corruption on behalf of the Apristas, a charge which was never proven, although the military subsequently issued a "white book," listing their charges.

The United States reacted strongly to this coup. It withdrew its ambassador from Peru and held up all further economic aid to that country. Meanwhile, the Aprista-controlled *Confederación de Trabajadores del Peru* called a general strike against the military coup, which was only partially successful.

Finally, as a result of internal and international pressure, the military junta which had seized power agreed that within a year they would call new elections, in which all parties would be able to participate freely. The Apristas accepted this promise, agreeing to participate in these elections. The United States thereupon renewed diplomatic relations and aid. The military's decision to allow new elections was undoubtedly strengthened by the ouster of General Pérez Godoy, the first head of the junta.

The 1963 Election

The military junta was as good as its word, and almost exactly a year after the 1962 election, a new one was held. Again, the principal candidates were Haya de la Torre, Fernando Belaúnde Terry, and General Odría.

There is no question that Haya's candidacy in 1963 was a mistake both for Haya de la Torre and the Aprista Party. Although in 1962, popular pressure demanded Haya's nomination, and there was only a reasonable doubt about the military's allowing him to take power, the situation had changed in the following year. It was clear, in the light of the previous experience, that the Army was not going to permit Haya's inauguration as president. It was also reasonably clear that many who had voted for him in 1962 would not do so again, because they wanted the re-establishment of constitutional government, an eventuality which was highly unlikely if Haya was the victor.

Haya did not show the statesmanship which many expected of him in this 1963 election. It was clear even to many of the Aprista leaders that it was not in the interest of Haya, the party, or Peru for him to run again. Any other Aprista would have stood a better chance of winning and being able to take office, but Haya apparently would not concede this.

The Apristas and the Belaúnde Regime

The winner this time was Fernando Belaúnde Terry, who gained a substantial plurality although the Apristas challenged the authenticity of the election figures. Belaúnde assumed office shortly after his victory. In the following years, he carried out a program of agrarian reform, community development, diversification of the economy, and democratic constitutional government, which did not differ essentially from that which the Apristas had advocated for so long.

Nevertheless, the Apristas constituted the major part of the opposition during the Belaúnde administration. They formed an alliance with the parliamentary faction of the Odriista Party and with their help controlled Congress throughout this period.

However, several important Aprista initiatives became laws during the Belaúnde administration. They were the authors of the article of the Agrarian Reform Law which provided that land, which tenant farmers had been allowed by landlords to use, became the tenants' property immediately when the Agrarian Reform Bill became a law. They sponsored another law which provided for universal free education from primary school to the university level.

During the years of the Belaúnde administration, Haya de la Torre again divided his time between Peru and Europe. He had a connection with St. Catherine's College of Oxford University and spent considerable time there. In addition, he lectured widely throughout Western Europe. His grip upon the Aprista Party was somewhat relaxed, although he spent considerable periods in Peru and remained the party's most popular orator and an important adviser on party policy and program.

As the 1969 presidential election approached, the Apristas again named Haya de la Torre as the party's candidate. Their principal reason for doing so was the desire to avoid a split within their ranks, which they feared would result from any contest among other leaders for the nomination.

The victory of the Apristas in the 1969 election seemed virtually assured. All other parties had suffered serious splits: the Acción Popular of President Fernando Belaúnde, the Odrristas, the Christian Democrats, and the Communists. There were indications that President Belaúnde himself was ready to support Haya's candidacy.

The Velasco Military Dictatorship

However, the 1969 election was never held. Early in October, 1968, the Army overthrew President Belaúnde and seized power. This military regime was different from all of its predecessors. President Juan Velasco Alvarado declared it a "revolution," and the new regime began a process of change bringing substantial economic and social reforms. Virtually all large private landholdings were expropriated by the middle of 1972. A system of workers' participation in the management of industrial enterprises was also inaugurated, and the community development program launched by President Belaúnde was intensified.

Again, the Aprista Party was in the opposition. The October, 1968, coup was made as much against the Apristas as against President Belaúnde, as he himself pointed out. The military regime saw the Apristas as one of its major enemies, and many of the government's actions were designed to destroy Aprista influence among workers, peasants, and other elements of the population. However, the party continued to function. Although the government was very hostile to the Apristas, forcing their daily newspaper La Tribuna into bankruptcy, banning party street-corner meetings, and limiting severely other public demonstrations by the party, the Apristas continued the extensive cultural and social welfare programs which had always been a basic part of their activities.

During these rather bleak years of the military dictatorship since October, 1968, the Apristas have been considerably aided by the "mystique" that has developed about them over the years. They are convinced that no matter how difficult their current situation, their party is bound to bounce back once the situation changes. This opinion is shared by a large part of the populace. The Aprista Party, because of the many times it has been persecuted only to come back as strong as before, has acquired the reputation of being a phoenix, always capable of reconstituting itself from its ashes.

Haya de la Torre has spent most of his time in Peru since the advent of the latest military dictatorship there. He is functioning as the effective leader of his party. Except when on visits to the provinces, he spends five or six evenings a week at the Casa del Pueblo, the Aprista headquarters in Lima. There he conducts regular "colloquia" on current economic and political problems attended by hundreds of people each Thursday; he participates in executive committee meetings; he meets with innumerable party officials as well as visitors from the provinces and abroad.

Haya's Role

By some standards, Haya's political career has been an unsuccessful one. Although his party has been a major contender for power for over four decades, and although he himself has been an aspirant to the presidency of Peru for almost as long, neither he nor his party has ever come to power.

The reasons for the Apristas' failure to achieve what is presumably the objective of every political party, power, are numerous, and this is not the place to explore many of them. However, at least part of the failure of the Apristas is due to Haya's own weaknesses as a practical politician.

Haya has been characterized by what some call his vanity, others label his excessive personalism. Over the years, Haya has persisted in maintaining his unchallenged primacy as the indisputable leader of the Aprista Party. He has insisted not only on his "right" to be the party's presidential candidate, but also on his right to have the last word in virtually all party decisions of importance.

In part, his unique position has been due to the refusal of any other Aprista leader of significance to oppose Haya on any important issue. This attitude has undoubtedly stemmed from their vast respect for him as the chief architect of their party's philosophy and program, from their admiration for his steadfast continuation of the struggle in spite of exile, persecution, imprisonment, and other difficulties, and from a genuine personal affection for him.

Haya de la Torre's leadership of the Aprista Party has resulted from a number of other factors. First, Haya has been the major builder of the party's doctrine. Although other party leaders, such as the late Manuel Seoane and Luis Alberto Sánchez, have elaborated various aspects of the party's ideology, they were basically expanding or interpreting Haya's thoughts. The writings of Haya de la Torre have constituted the basic texts used in the party's intensive program of training and indoctrination of party members and leaders for forty years.

In addition, Haya's intellectual capacity and his breadth of knowledge of ideas have also been a source of strength as party leader. He has read very widely and has been personally acquainted with many of the intellectual and political leaders of the time, such as Miguel de Unamuno, Albert Einstein, Arnold Toynbee, Jawaharlal Nehru, and others. He thus has the respect of the other intellectuals constituting a major element in the leadership of the Aprista Party. It also has brought him admiration from, and has been a source of pride to, party members of less education.

Another source of power for Haya de la Torre within Aprista Party ranks has been his oratorical ability. He has been a powerful mass orator, capable of arousing vast enthusiasm and emotional response when addressing large crowds. On the other hand, he has been equally at home with small audiences towards whom he has tended to adopt a didactic air, almost more like a teacher than a party leader. Intermittently, whenever political conditions permitted, he has ranged the country speaking to large and small audiences, and personally visiting with party members and sympathizers throughout the nation.

Finally, during the decades in which he has been the Aprista Party leader, there has grown up a *"mistica"* around Haya de la Torre which gives him a stature in national politics not shared by anyone else. An example of the power of this mystique was shown during the period when the Apristas more or less allied with the Bustamante administration. During that period, the Aprista Party used its influence with the government to help Indian communities obtain the restoration of the lands stolen from them by neighboring landlords. On one such occasion, an Indian delegation that had walked hundreds of miles to Lima to present its case at Apra Party headquarters refused to turn over to party officials the documents which were the basis of their community's claim. They insisted on seeing *"Don Apra,"* that is, Haya de la Torre. When he appeared and as soon as they were convinced of his identity, the leader of the community's delegation pulled out of his stocking an old land deed for the community issued by an eighteenth-century king of Spain. Even these Indians from the far interior of the country had faith in *Don Apra,* Víctor Rául Haya de la Torre.

Haya's facial features have probably also been a political asset. Although supposedly descended from purely Spanish ancestors, his face is strongly reminiscent of the Inca forebearers of most contemporary Peruvians. With high cheekbones, a high, flat, ridged and beak-like nose, and a somewhat copper-toned skin, Haya bears more resemblance to the Indian than to the Spanish ancestors of his fellow countrymen.

Haya's strong physical constitution and ability to work hard and long has also been a prime element in assuring his predominance in the party leadership. When the party is legal and Haya is in the country, he often sits in on meetings of the National Executive Committee and other party committees. He also gives regular lectures and participates in the forums and discussions constituting a routine part of Aprista political activities.

However, Haya has not been content with remaining the principal source of doctrine and titular leader of the Aprista Party. He has usually also insisted on interfering extensively in the day-to-day maneuvering so essential to the conduct of practical politics. At this, he has not been an expert—we have already noted the disastrous effects of Haya's activity of this kind during the Bustamante administration, from 1945 to 1948.

As a practical politician, Haya has had several handicaps. He has been inept at petty maneuvering; he has not been sufficiently susceptible to the feelings and interests of others. Sometimes he has been indecisive at the wrong moment. But perhaps most important of all, he has been capable of being insulted—a luxury that politicians cannot afford, except when it is eminently convenient for them.

Haya's imperiousness and insistence upon his own way in the highest councils of the party has also been a negative aspect of his leadership. It has undoubtedly had the effect over the years of driving many brilliant leaders or potential leaders out of the party ranks, either into political neutrality or active hostility to the Aprista Party.

Finally, it should be noted that in spite of his wide popularity among large segments of the population, Haya de la Torre has been most unpopular with a group which is of decisive importance in Peruvian politics—the armed forces. Undoubtedly much of the Army's forty-year opposition to the Apra has been opposition to Víctor Raúl Haya de la Torre, personally. Had he not been the Aprista candidate in 1962, for instance, it is quite conceivable that the party might have been permitted to win the presidential election.

Basic Elements of Haya's Ideas

Haya's lasting contribution to Latin American politics has been more in the field of ideas, than in that of party leadership. He has presented and developed a number of the concepts adopted by the leaders of important political parties in many Latin American countries during the last three decades.

Perhaps the most fundamental of all the ideas in Haya's writings has been his insistence that Latin America must seek its own answers to its own problems. As a philosophical basis for this concept, he developed his theory of Historical Space-Time, according to which each continental people develops a view of the world and its own place in it, in terms of its own geographical "space" and its relationship to the space, and in terms of its own historical experience. This philosophical foundation of Haya's ideas constitutes the first section of the present volume.

In practical political terms, Haya applied this theory by rejecting the tradition of copying political institutions and party programs from those of Europe or the United States and was the first to attempt to organize a political party on the basis of this idea. Although he was not successful in organizing a Latin America-wide party such as he advocated in the 1920s, he did establish the Partido Aprista Peruano. This example has been followed in various other Latin American countries, as independent national parties rather than as branches of a regional group.

A second major concept put forward by Haya de la Torre was his insistence that this political party must be multi-class, rather than the kind of one-class organization advocated by the socialists and Communists. He argued that the Latin American proletariat was small and weak and that, furthermore, in the struggle over the principal issues facing the Latin American countries—the ending of the semi-feudal society characteristic of them and the confrontation with imperialism—the peasants and the middle class had as much at stake as the urban workers. The idea of a multi-class party became widely accepted by the democratic left in Latin America.

A third idea of primary importance which Haya first promulgated in the 1920s and continued to urge in the succeeding decades was his concept of how the Latin American countries should handle the problem of foreign investment. Haya rejected both the extreme attitude of those who argued that the Latin American countries so needed foreign capital that they should accept it whenever and wherever it came, and should do everything possible to entice it to come; and the opposite extreme of those who maintained that foreign capital was so dangerous to the sovereignty of Latin American countries that it should be rejected entirely.

Starting in the 1920s, Haya de la Torre argued that Lenin had been wrong in declaring that imperialism—the economic penetration of the highly industrialized countries in the underdeveloped ones—was "the highest stage of capitalism." That claim, said Haya, was characteristic of the European orientation of the orthodox Marxists. The fact was that imperialism for countries like those of Latin America was the beginning of capitalism, since it introduced modern capitalist institutions and industrialism into those countries for the first time. Hence, foreign investment in the Latin American countries was salutary and necessary.

However, Haya argued that capital from the highly developed countries needed to seek profitable investment in the underdeveloped ones at least as much as the underdeveloped nations needed to receive investments from the industrialized ones. This being so, Haya said that the Latin American countries should welcome foreign capital while establishing the conditions under which it should be accepted, and the sectors of the Latin American national economies in which it should be permitted. In any case, the Latin American countries should not allow foreign capital to be accompanied by political pressure or dictation from the industrialized nations. These ideas, too, have been widely accepted.

A fourth concept which Haya put forward against major opposition from other leftist elements in Latin America was that the Latin American nationalists and anti-imperialists should seek allies in the United States from the middle class liberals and socialists there. He rejected the Communist notion that the only possible allies in the United States for the struggle against U.S. imperialism in Latin America were the organized workers. He pointed out that it was middle class writers, professional people, and politicians who were the most effective critics of "dollar diplomacy" and United States interventionism in Latin America, and that it would be foolish for the Latin Americans to reject their support.

Undoubtedly this idea had much to do with the change in Haya de la Torre's general attitude towards the United States which took place in the late 1930s. In his writings at that time and in the years immediately afterwards, he seems to feel that the allies with whom he advocated that the Latin American anti-imperialists work had come to power in the United States under the Roosevelt Administration.

As in so many other things, Haya's attitude on this issue was followed by elements of the democratic left all over Latin America. In 1950, the cooperation between the liberals and socialists of the United States and various democratic leftist elements of Latin America was formalized with the establishment, at a conference in Havana, of the Inter American Association for Democracy and Freedom. Haya himself supported the IADF, which played an important role in arousing public opinion in the United States and Latin America over his long "incarceration" in the Colombian Embassy in Lima by the government of General Odría. Other Latin American figures such as Rómulo Betancourt, Eduardo Sánchez, Eduardo Frei, Víctor Paz Estenssoro, and others have been associated with the IADF.

During the Kennedy Administration, cooperation between the North American liberal community and the Latin American democratic left reached a high point. President Kennedy himself made it clear that his sympathies in Latin America were with the elements f the democratic left. It was the liberals of the United States and he Latin American democratic left who were principally responsible for elaborating the Alliance for Progress, as drawn up at the first Punta del Este Conference in July, 1961.

Another element in Haya's program and one which he did a good deal to popularize was that of Latin American unity. Haya has not been oblivious to the differences among the Latin American countries, but he has consistently argued that they have much more in common than they have to separate them, and that they form a natural community, vis-à-vis the rest of the world.

Since the foundation of APRA in Mexico in 1924, Haya de la Torre has been advocating the federation of the Latin American countries. He has frequently referred to *"nuestra gran patria,"* meaning the "fatherland" of Latin America and has referred to the individual nations as "provinces" of this greater nation. His original conception of APRA was that it should be a Latin American party, with branches in each of the countries. Each of these branches was to carry on, within its respective country, the struggle for the unification of Latin America. Haya's reason for such an international party was not only its common work for unity of the area, but his belief that these countries have common problems which could be resolved by a common program.

Haya's belief in and propaganda for Latin American unity has been reinforced in recent decades by political leaders in other parties favoring this same objective. However, these political efforts produced scant results until economic factors seemed to indicate that if Latin America did not begin to build a common front on economic issues, the whole area would suffer severely. Thus, in the late 1950s the establishment of a Latin American common market, or at least of a free trade area, began to be seriously discussed. The Latin American Free Trade Area was finally established in 1961.

Haya de la Torre gave his enthusiastic endorsement to the new LAFTA. He looked upon it as a welcome first step towards the final political federation of the area. He also enthusiastically supported the successful effort of the Aprista members of the Peruvian Congress to have that body take the lead in the establishment of the Latin American Parliament, of which Aprista Andrés Townsend Ezcurra became the first Secretary General.

A final element of Haya's program which has had influence throughout Latin America has been his advocacy of political democracy. From the inception of APRA, Haya has argued that profound social change in Latin America is consistent with political democracy. Although he has argued in favor of changing democratic institutions, particularly by adding an Economic Congress, composed of representatives of all of the important sectors of the economy, as an advisory body to the politically elected Congress, he has always been against any dictatorial type of regime.

In the late 1930s, Haya began to argue that political democracy was a key issue in Intra Latin American and Inter American relations. He maintained that a dictatorial regime in any one Latin American country was a menace to democracy in all of the rest. He also insisted that no real basis for friendly relations between Latin America and the United States was possible unless and until the non-intervention attitude established by the Good Neighbor Policy was accompanied by the suspension of United States friendship for Latin American dictatorial regimes.

In some of his writings on this subject during the World War II period, Haya put forth a suggestion which has gained certain currency in recent years. This is the notion that there should be some kind of multilateral intervention against the dictatorial regimes of the area. Although he did not spell out any details concerning this idea, except the establishment of some kind of civil liberties tribunal on a hemispheric basis, the idea was a fresh one at the time he presented it. In one form or another, it has been put forth by many other Latin American political leaders during the last decade.

Internationalization of the Panama Canal was one of the five fundamental points of the APRA program first announced in Mexico in 1924. Haya wrote about the question on various occasions but was unable to arouse a great degree of enthusiasm over the issue. Recently he has had to argue as much against Panamanian proponents of nationalization of the Canal by their country is against those who favor continued United States domination of it.

Another of Haya de la Torre's lost causes has been his battle for the use of the word *Indoamerica* to describe what is usually called *Latin America*. From the 1920s on, Haya wrote about this and regarded it for decades as a matter of considerable importance. However, in spite of the fact that the Peruvian Apristas generally use the word, it has not found popularity beyond the borders of Haya's native country.

Of course, the impact of Haya de la Torre's ideas has been greatest on his own country, and particularly on his own party, the Partido Aprista Peruano. In those periods when it has been able to function more or less normally, the P.A.P. has carried out extensive indoctrination of its members and lower-ranking leaders, and most of the material used for this has consisted of publications of Haya de la Torre.

Haya's Influence Outside of Peru

However, if Haya's influence did not extend beyond his own countrymen, its importance would be only relative. Such has not been the case. Parties similar to the Partido Aprista Peruano, which have incorporated into their programs Haya's ideas on the need for Latin American answers to Latin American problems, on a multi-class party, on controlled admission of foreign investment, and on the essential importance of political democracy have been established in various countries. These include the *Acción Democrática* in Venezuela, the *Liberación Nacional* in Costa Rica, the *Movimiento Nacionalista Rev-*

olucionario in Bolivia, the *Partido Febrerista* in Paraguay, the *Partido Revolucionario Dominicano* in the Dominican Republic, the *Mouvement Ouvrier Paysan* in Haiti, the Popular Democratic Party of Puerto Rico, and the *Autentico* and *Ortodoxo* parties of pre-Castro Cuba.

The leaders of most of these parties recognize an intellectual debt to Haya de la Torre and his pioneering presentation of the concepts and programs which they have made their own. There is ample indication of Haya's early influence on the leaders of some of these parties. For instance, a group of residents of Costa Rica sent Haya de la Torre a wire upon his arrival home in Peru in 1931, part of which said:

> In one of those years you were in Central America, presenting your apostolate of justice and Latin American liberation. Then we were immersed with your idealism, caught the contagion of your faith, and heard in yours a great voice of a continent anxious to seek its own destiny.

Two of the signers of this cable were Rómulo Betancourt and Raúl Leoni, later founders of the *Acción Democrática* Party of Venezuela.

In Cuba there existed for some years an Aprista Party, founded as a direct result of Haya's early propaganda tours around the hemisphere. With the formation of the *Partido Revolucionario Cubano* (Autentico), headed by Dr. Ramón Grau San Martín, in 1934, the Cuban Apristas merged with the Autenticos and had an important influence in molding that party's ideology. Victor Paz Estenssoro has assured me that the ideas of the Apristas in neighboring Peru had considerable influence on the thinking of the founders of Bolivia's *Movimiento Nacionalista Revolucionario*.

However, the influence of Haya's ideas has gone beyond these parties, which are closely allied with his own, and some of the other parties which he has influenced may well be unaware of the extent of their debt to him, since many of the things which he was the first to advocate have become the general property of all parties of the democratic left in Latin America.

Thus, Haya's stress on the uniqueness of Latin America, the need for the collaboration of various classes to bring about basic reforms, the way to handle foreign investment, and the compatibility of social change and political democracy has found wide currency in some of the more traditional parties that have sought to bring their programs more up-to-date. They have also found their way into the program of many of the Christian Democratic parties which have been growing in recent years, although there is no direct indication of Haya's writings having had direct influence in molding the philosophies or programs of those parties. Even parties and political leaders that rejected much of what Haya has advocated, have been influenced by some of his ideas. Thus, Juan Perón has stated that before he entered active politics, he had read some of the writings of Haya, had kept some of his books among those to which he made frequent reference, and that he had been particularly impressed by Haya's arguments in favor of Latin American unity.

The late Serafino Romualdi, in his autobiography, summed up the significance of the career and ideas of Víctor Raúl Haya de la Torre very clearly. He wrote:

> But then, was Haya's struggle in vain? Was he actually a defeated man? I do not think so. In forty years of struggle, suffering, bloodshed, exile, and underground work, Haya has given a new meaning, a new dimension to the concept of social revolution. He has kept it, in his own Peru, and elsewhere by the power of example, inside the boundaries of freedom; he and his movement have been the strongest bulwark that successfully resisted the infiltration and capture of the social-revolutionary concept by the Communist totalitarians. Peru is now considered by competent observers off the danger list. But where would Peru be today, I ask, if Haya de la Torre and his APRA Party had not been on the scene?"

PART ONE

Philosophy: Espacio-Tiempo-Histórico

THIS SECTION DEALS WITH THE PHILOSOPHICAL BASES OF HAYA DE LA Torre's political ideas and programs. For the most part, the selections are presented in chronological order, showing the evolution and development of Haya's theory of historical space-time. The one exception is the first selection, which is presented out of sequence because it offers interesting autobiographical information on how Haya arrived at his concept. As Haya de la Torre explains, he wondered as a boy in Trujillo, in northern Peru, where the Indian civilizations, the ruins of which he saw nearby, fitted into the history which he was learning at school. That essentially European-oriented scheme of the evolution of humanity did not seem to make allowance for the pre-Columbian Indians.

He found the first key to an answer to his question in the writings of Hegel and Marx, which he began to study seriously only after going into exile in 1923. It seemed to him that the dialectic, particularly as applied by Karl Marx—presenting history as a continuing clash of different civilizations and systems, out of which came new historical forms—made the history he knew a great deal more meaningful. However, both the Hegelian and Marxist dialectic suffered from two fundamental weaknesses, insofar as Haya was concerned. In the first place, they both ended in a concept of an "ultimate" static society, a denouement which seemed to conflict fundamentally with the very idea of the dialectic as an ever continuing and interminable process. In the second place, both Hegel and Marx viewed world history from a European focus. Thus, although considering himself a Marxist, Haya insisted that the Marxist dialectic itself had to be "negated," if it were to be applied to Latin America, and that out of this negation would arise a new historical system.

The essence of the inevitable negation of orthodox Marxism, Haya found in Einstein's idea of relativity. During his student days in Berlin in the mid-1920s, when Einstein was a professor there, Haya became his lifelong admirer and got to know him personally in the post World War II years. Haya felt that the Einsteinian theory of relativity, which stressed that all physical phenomena were relative and not absolute, and which viewed space and time as a continuum, a fourth dimension, was applicable to the study of history. It confirmed Haya's conviction that history differed, depending upon the point and time from which it was viewed.

In applying Einstein's theory of relativity to history, Haya argued that every people had a particular historical space-time from which it viewed its own history and that of mankind in general. This was a continuum of the physical space in which the people lived, as well as their conception and understanding of this space or "stage," and their own historical experiences and comprehension of them.

Haya's analysis bore out his long-held conviction that "universal" theories of history, based fundamentally on European experiences were not automatically applicable to Latin America. Thus, while he accepted basically the Marxist view of history as being a sequence of contradictions, he did not believe that the contradictions that had been characteristic of European history were the same as those in Latin American history. He cites only one example in this section—the different aspects which imperialism presents to Europe and to Latin America. In other discussions of Aprista political ideas, he also applies this concept to the Marxist doctrine concerning the role of the urban working class and other questions.

The key arguments of the theory of Espacio-Tiempo-Histórico (historical space-time) are presented in the second and third selections. In these, Haya also compares and contrasts his theory with those of Oswald Spengler and others who have also adopted a more or less relativist view of history.

The fourth piece deals principally with the integration of Haya's ideas into Toynbee's concept of civilizations arising out of the challenges which various human groups have faced and their particular responses to those challenges. Haya accepts this concept, but argues that the distinction between those people who have created a "civilization," in Toynbee's terms, and those that have not, is to be found in the development of, or in the failure to develop, a sense of historical space-time as Haya originally defined the concept. He goes on to study the challenges and responses met by the colonists who settled in North America and those who settled in Latin America. He finds that the North Americans have evolved a sense of historical space-time; but that, as yet, the Latin Americans have not, since they are still in the process of melding the concepts brought from Europe with those of the indigenous peoples. He ends by raising the possibility of the evolution of a single American civilization, in Toynbee's terms, incorporating both North and Latin America.

I

HISTORICAL SPACE-TIME

PERHAPS A BRIEF REFERENCE TO THE GENESIS OF MY THESIS OF HIS-
torical space-time is appropriate here. In looking back, I think that
it developed out of my first, adolescent, vague reflections on history
and chronology. Close to the Peruvian city where I was born, Trujillo,
the famous pre-Incan ruins of Chan-Chan, an extensive metropolis
of the so-called kingdom of Gran Chimú, still survive the passing of
the centuries. These vast ruins, situated in a wide and gently inclined
plain, extending from the foothills of the Andes to the Pacific coastal
beaches, offered me the first impressive vision of the Indoamerican
historical past. The legends of fabulous wealth and power, the golden
tradition of the treasure of the "Peje Chico," which García Gutiérrez
de Toledo seized with the aid of an Indian, and the numerous and
excellent pieces of early ceramics taken from graves also rich in arms
and utensils of bronze, adornments of silver and gold, rare rose-
colored shells, and fine textiles of brilliant colors, caused my first
amazement at the ruins of a culture chronologically located within
my high school history studies about which I was enthusiastic.

I still remember hearing the German archeological genius Max
Uhle, seated at my parent's table during one of his visits to Trujillo,
say that the antiquity of those ruins was much greater than that of the
empire of Manco Capac. The official history course of Inca Peru,
which was then given in the schools, indicated "between the ninth
and twelfth centuries of our era" as the probable period of the foundation of this powerful state, which later extended itself to a good part
of the continent, overcoming the Mochica civilization and destroying
the important city Chan-Chan. This increased my concern about *where*

Prologue from *Espacio-Tiempo-Histórico*, 1948.

and *when* the civilization indicated by those enormous ruins fitted into the historic world described in my clear and didactic textbook by the French author M. Ducoudray.

In the European time scheme of universal history, which delineates our understanding of that discipline, 1492 is the year of the Christian Era in which the Old World officially discovers the New. With that early morning in October, America is incorporated, with all of its profound past, into the general historical picture. The testimony of these ruins, however, suggests another dimension of time. It was not a *new* world as seen from my perspective. Chan-Chan was already in ruins when the Europeans arrived. It formed part of the very *old* world of America. How could it be new for those of us who looked at it *from here,* even though it was tor those who discovered it *from there?*

Solving this paradox of historical viewpoints was beyond my juvenile years. It remained relegated to my subconscious, perhaps, as a child keeps the pieces of a mechanical toy which he is unable to put together. But a secret doubt lingered and led me to consider skeptically all those social sciences written from a fixed European point of view which I later studied at the university, unwillingly following the universal plans and methods imposed by the cultural meridian of the Old World. The question always remained in the back of my mind: Where do the American civilizations fit into the European time scheme without conflicting with the reality of their own history?

When I visited Europe, a first reading of Hegel's Lessons of Philosophy or Universal History brought me welcome enlightenment. The American world didn't enter into the Hegelian interpretation. Hegel remained firmly and clearly in his European-German space and from there, like an astronomer in an observatory viewing only his own zodiacal hemisphere, uncovered the movement of the historic worlds. From his universe: "The sun rises in the East. The sun is light, is the simple universal reference to itself. . . . Universal History goes from East to West. Europe is absolutely the terminus of Universal History. Asia is the beginning. . . . History is not inscribed in a circle, but rather has a starting point, a definite East which is Asia."

Hegel was not interested in the American world, which was for him an immature continent: "This new world which is new not only relatively but absolutely, is so with respect to all of its characteristics, physical and political. . . . Everything which happens in America has its origin in Europe. . . . Consequently, America is the country of

the future. . . . More, as the country of the future it does not interest
us, since the philosopher does not make prophecies." Thus the talented
creater of the modern dialectic finishes his argument with the quietude
of dogma. In his universe that which is born, grows and dies; "child-
hood" is the Oriental world, "youth" is the Greek world, "the virile
age" is the Roman empire, and "old age"—the perfect maturity of
the spirit—"is necessarily double": the Mohametan and the German
world, according to him, "the empire of the true spirit."

He circumscribes his universe closely and *absolutely*—underscoring such an important concept and word—and indicates within
it the limits of what, with the classic and elegant Hegelian terminology,
he calls "the theater of universal history." Then, in the first lesson
of his interpretation, he claims that "the Philosophy of History is the
thinking consideration of History," and later, in his special introduction, leaves this suggestive apotegma: "Properly speaking, the history
of a people begins when this people becomes conscious."

One might add to these pronouncements—as a starting point
for these reflections—two citations expressive of the long-run Hegelian vision when he says: "Each people lives in such an individual
state that it must resolve and will always resolve it for itself alone—
Each people is in such a singular relationship that former relations
are never congruent with later ones, since the conditions are completely different. . . . The plastic material of history is something very
different from the supposition that Universal History represents the
idea of the spirit." He goes so far as to affirm: "The different spirits
of the peoples separate them in Space and in Time and in this respect
activate the natural connection, the connection between the spiritual
and the natural, the temperament, etc. . . ."

We recapitulate: If the philosophy of history, according to Hegel,
"is thinking consideration," and if the history of a people properly
speaking "commences when this people becomes conscious;" and if
the historical individuality of each people which constitutes what
Hegel calls "its spirit," "separates it in Space and in Time and in this
respect activates the natural connection between the spiritual and the
natural, the temperament, etc.," the legacy of the universal ideas that
the Hegelian philosophy of history left to the future of new forms of
his thinking was without doubt extraordinarily valuable. This was the
beginning of my first reflections on the relationship between the historical consciousness of a people and the *consciousness of its space
and of its time*. A formulation of these concepts in line with the new

ideas of scientific relativism brought about my first attempt at forming the thesis of historical space-time—history seen as being inseparable from the evolutionary movement of each people or social group within its gravitational field or stage of development. Thus it appears possible to locate the process of American history within a world framework of indivisible relative interpretations and of space-time determinants. Thus the integral division of the multiple universe of history appears more logical, in view of the many historical space-times which are offered as fields of observation.

The Hegelian interpretation of history, like its negation the Marxist dialectic, and like the "relativism" of Spengler, who defines and limits with the concept and word "Copernican" his cyclical and pessimistic conception of the "Decline of the West," are European and fix each of their historical analyses from an immovable angle of observation upon the historical "gravitational field" of the so-called Old World. The same thing happens with the other schools of the philosophy of history, idealist and materialist, spiritualist and rationalist and biological. All are European, and that fact sums up their limitation from our American angle of historical observation, as they must also appear limited for a relativist observer of history from another historical space-time, such as Asia, Oceania, or Africa. Indicative of this new awareness is the interesting book *Glimpses of World History* by Jawaharlal Nehru, which is an attempt at an interpretation of universal history from the Indian viewpoint.

The English historian Arnold J. Toynbee begins his monumental work *A Study of History* with this theme: "In whatever age of whatever society, the study of History, like other social activities is governed by the dominant tendencies of the time and the place." He maintains that it is not the nation nor humanity as a whole, but the civilizations of the various societies which constitute the intelligible field for the study of history. For Toynbee the limited national concept of history is "Copernican," and he formulates an interpretative theory of historical analysis subject to a relativist relationship of space-time. However, his field of observation is always European, although his new mode of observing historical processes implies a true revolution with respect to the classical, limited national conceptions or unlimited universal ones, without space-time relations. Ehrich Kahler points out in his interesting book *Man and Measure* that "the new Universal History as Spengler and Arnold J. Toynbee conceive of it, assumes a multiplicity of cultures, each in its own orbit, no one of which can be regarded as typical, all having in common only general characteristics of rise and fall, lines of History in line with laws of Nature." Morris Zucker, in a North American attempt to apply contemporary relativism to history, indicates textually that he uses the expression "Theory of Historical Field" as "an adaptation to our purposes of the great physical theory of electro-magnetic fields as it has been developed in the Theory of Relativity with its vast philosophical possibilities." Zucker is interested "principally in relativity for its concept of Field. . . . There is no instantaneity, but rather events take place in a defined field and are temporal by nature. . . . We maintain that Relativity marks as much the end of an era as the opening of the possibilities of a new one in the kingdom of thought."

Nevertheless, the differences between the Spenglerian and the Toynbeean and Zucker conceptions of historical interpretation—Newtonian relativist the first and Einsteinian relativity the other—and the thesis of historical space-time . . . are precisely delimited. They attempt to respond from a fresh viewpoint to that grave question which is presented penetratingly by Spengler when he writes: "And the great American cultures have been more or less ignored, under the pretext that they lack all connection—with what?"

On May 11, 1923, I published in the daily *El Tiempo* of Lima, a student polemical article attacking "the false concept of unquestioned truths and eternal principles in this hour of profound scientific revolution and of an irresistible relativist current, precursor of new and distinct fundamental affirmations of all kinds." In my book *El Antimperialismo y el Apra,* written in Mexico in 1928, I attempt a historical interpretation of the economic-social evolution of the peoples of Indoamerica, and I maintain, in Chapter VI, that Aprismo is "a methodical confrontation of the Indoamerican reality with the thesis which Marx postulated for Europe and as a result of the European reality in which he lived and studied in the middle of the last century." In Chapter VII, I emphasized that "our historical process has its own rhythm, its typical process, and its intransferable content." Later, in the same chapter, I add that "our economic time and space indicate to us a position and a way." And in the final chapter of the same book: "Observing closely the social and economic reality of Indoamerica, we cannot help but see a vast and new political problem *whose solution is not found in and cannot be adjusted to the known European ideological molds.*"

In the book *El Processo de Haya de La Torre,* there appears the judicial investigation to which I was submitted during my political imprisonment from 1932 to 1933. In those documents I reiterate this point of view in answering a specific question on the class struggle: "The struggle between capitalism and the proletariat does not have a world wide, but rather a relative meaning. It covers many aspects, brings about different problems, imposes different solutions."

This is, in summary, a brief resume of the origin and development of the theory of historical space-time, the philosophical basis of the Aprista doctrine. It answers the question that bothered me so much in the days of my turbulent youth: Where does the American world, our past and our present, fit into a logical scheme of history, one that would enable us to foretell our destiny?

II

PHILOSOPHICAL SYNOPSIS OF APRISMO

APRISMO ORIGINATES PHILOSOPHICALLY IN THE HISTORICAL DETER-minism of Marx and the Hegelian dialectic adopted by him for his conception of the world. It is inspired by the principle of Hegel: "Dialectic is the irresistible force before which nothing in things remains firm; it is the progressive determination inherent in thought itself and the result and negation of this. . . ." Or, in the more specific definition of Engels, "The dialectic is no more than the science of the general laws of movement and evolution of human society and thought."

Aprismo bases its norms for philosophical methodization on the dialectical principle of *the negation of the negation*. It thus recognizes the universal principle of eternal movement, change, and development —discovered by Heraclitus and each day proven by the progress of science—as a constant process of contradictions, negations, and continuity. However, Aprismo also recognizes in Marxism a philosophical school subject to the same law which it has discovered and perfected. In effect, whoever adopts Marxism as a philosophic norm cannot offer his doctrinary conclusions as inflexible dogmas. Since it is the product of human thought, it would be absurd to believe that Marxism is excluded from the dialectical process which rules all life. It is this characteristic and condition of philosophical Marxism that guarantees its continuity. Because a philosophy which keeps up with the evolution of the world can never be surpassed, it will be a live philosophy, in perpetual development, mobile and constantly renewed, like nature and history. To achieve its rhythm and surpass the transi-

"Sinopsis Filosófica del Aprismo," first published in *Claridad* de Buenos Aires in 1935, included as Chapter I in *Espacio-Tiempo-Histórico*.

tory and temporal nature of the static schools which get old and decay, the determinist dialectic must be negated in order to continue.

Engels clarified this idea when he said that

> to negate in the dialectic is not simply to annul or suppress. The process of Nature, scientifically verified, proves that negation doesn't destroy but rather continues and in its turn must also be negated. As in the algebraic case where a times $-a$, again multiplied by $-a$ gives a positive result elevated to a greater power, we obtain a similar result with the dialectic method of negations, affirmation, and continuity and progressive change.

Once these premises are established, ones which no Marxist can deny or refute, it is possible to take the next step and set forth another proposition. Because either Marxism is an inflexible dogma, immovable like an idol, or it is a living and mobile force; and in the latter case it is also subject, like the entire universe, to the law of the negation of the negation. From here we establish this new proposition: If Marxism is, like philosophy, "all a new conception of the world" (Plekhanov), a realist, materialist concept, based on the reality of the universe and of the material in nature and history, we must admit that this philosophical conception cannot ignore the incessant progress of science, the tenacious process of civilization, and the constant development of humanity and ideas.

This irrefutable dynamism is borne out in the recent revolution in two concepts essential in all philosophy: that of *time* and that of *space*. Contemporary relativism surpasses the Euclidian principles in the three dimensions of matter, of energy, and of gravity, and uncovers a fourth dimension of continuity called *space-time,* opening thus a new and vast horizon to human consciousness. And if Liebnitz defined time "as a drama of relations" and Hegel discovered "that the longitude of time—in history—is something completely relative," it is evident that our century confronts a new conception of time and of space, of matter and energy, and advances towards a notion and concept of the universe that was unsuspected until now. Time and space are two philosophic concepts strongly linked to the ideas of historical evolution and of human dominion over nature, that is to say, of social and economic reality. And Marx had to use for the formulation of his system those concepts of time and space predominant in his century, as he had to base his historical materialism on the scientific concept which his epoch had of matter.

We can ask ourselves now: Does the historical determinism of Marx stand up under a confrontation with modern relativism? Does the dialectical process of Marxism include an element as essential and transcendental as that which the postulates of relativism proclaim? This is exactly where the Aprista thesis raises the question of the negation and surpassing of Marxism. To the previous questions the answer must be affirmative. The application of relativism to historical determinism certainly creates a case of negation and dialectical continuity affecting the philosophy of Marx. Even more, it is exactly in the relativism of time and of space, applied to the Marxist interpretation of history, that one finds the basis of the Aprista philosophical norm. There is the dialectic line which both unites and separates orthodox Marxism and Aprismo.

Thus, as the dimension space-time has been definitively incorporated in the science of physics, the new philosophy must in turn consider this concept. Einstein, in his article "Space-Time" in the *Encyclopedia Britannica,* cites these words of Minkowsky: "From now on space in itself and time in itself merge like shadows and only a kind of union of the two preserves their independent existence." This union Einstein calls "Space-Time." Admitting this principle as the integral basis of a new geometric and physical concept of the universe, Philosophy must consider it and incorporate it. And although relativism has not yet formulated a philosophical system properly speaking, it is evident that its bases have been sketched. The fundamental principle—backed by a scientific verification—of relativism is this new concept of space-time which, accepted by general philosophy, can be applied to the philosophy of history.

It should be said that there is also a "historical space-time," consisting of the geographic location (objective field) and "the subjective time" (Ich-Zeit) which man conceives of in relation to that space; and of both in turn with a given rhythm of objective or "economic time" from which socially derives the "historic time." The geographical scene, basis of the concept of "historical space," is conditioned by all of the physical characteristics of each of the habitable regions of the planet and, in addition to this, by the distance between one region and another, especially the distance between the less civilized and those more advanced in their evolution who set the pace of progress. This separation is not only spatial, it is also distance in "historic time" not the time measured by clocks, but that "which is completely relative," according to Hegel, as previously noted. Thus, for example, the actual spatial distance between England and Greenland may be much less than that between England and Japan, but considered as a distance in history, in the evolution of historic time, England is much closer to Japan than to Greenland.

How do we measure this distance, or more properly speaking, this historic time? We start evidently from the subjective time (Ich-Zeit) which each man forms in response to his geographic space and the objective conditions of his individual and social life within this given space, or the specific economic time of his region. Darwin notes that in the Indoamerican pampas of the countries of the Plata he came across a gaucho who exclaimed, "How long the day is, señor." This is an expression of subjective time, determined by the objective conditions—geographic space, forms of life, work, etc. This notion of time is common, with slight variations, to the people living in similar conditions of development. The Indian of the Andes who walks patiently behind his llama, breaks the earth with primitive implements, and lives slowly, must also experience "the long day" and a long life. His sensations are spaced, made distant by monotony; and yesterday was as identical with today as today will be with tomorrow. As a result, he will apply and generalize to life his subjective notion of time, and its image or measurement, vague or precise, will be that of a slow rhythm.

But why of a slow rhythm? With relation to what measurement of rhythm do we venture to make this observation? Simply, with relation to the rhythm of the historic evolution marking the conditions of life and labor of the more developed peoples, for whom subjective time has another meaning. The man of the industrial city does not encounter this "long day." The industrial people have, therefore, another subjective notion (Ich-Zeit) of time, as we would say, aside from chronologic time; their economic time is the determinant of the social concept of historic time.

We thus see that the objective field or historical space—Hegel calls it a "stage of the theater of History"—determines the formation of an idea or concept of subjective time, which is variable in accord with the conditions of the social life achieved in this space and stage. But we see also that that variable concept of time is related to another more universal concept which established the relative velocity of the rhythm of historic time in the world. The gradations of this historic time measure the steps of the peoples in the evolution of their exercise of control over nature; not the history of isolated civilizations, but that of a general human advance over natural elements. This advance, as we know, is not located forever in a given space; it varies, changes, jumps from one geographic region to another, but it always has, in each epoch, a particular spatial zone where it is centered for an indefinite period in its incessant development (Egypt, Persia, Greece, Rome, etc.)

It is with relation to this maximum stage of development in each particular space that there appears the notion of "historical space-time." This term expresses the combination of relations among the people and their environment and the degree of dominion they exercise over their surroundings. *This combination of inseparable relations gives to history a measure of time inseparable from the conditions of space and permits the establishment of a new historical-philosophical point of view.*

From this new point of view, the historical determinism of Marx is not a rule that imposes itself in all latitudes. Admitting the relativist principle of historical space-time, we must recognize that the assessment of each social process within a given geographic area must be related to the process of other groups, all having as point of reference the rhythm of those most advanced, we might say of maximum velocity, remembering that in Physics, relativism is always related to the absolute measure of the velocity of light. But admitting also the relativist postulate that there are no parallel lines at great distances, we must recognize that parallelism in the development of peoples—a principle already sketched by Marx—is also relative in the vastness of history.

History considered in this way offers new perspectives to the observer and the philosopher. The spatial angle of observation cannot be excluded from the philosophy of history. The so-called historic laws and their universal application must be conditional upon the relativity of the viewpoint. Therefore, the history of the world, seen from the Indoamerican historical space-time will never be the same as that seen by a philosopher from the European historical space-time. In addition, we maintain that what is the "final stage" in Europe may be "first" in Indoamerica: While imperialism is in Europe the "ultimate" stage of capitalism, in Indoamerica—as affirmed in the Aprista thesis —it is the beginning stage. All the phenomena and problems which take off from this point determine a vast combination of forms which the philosophy of history, and also dialectical materialism, cannot negate. Consequently, there are here, among many, two points of view, two angles, two different planes which are relatively parallel; hence, the laws and principles conceived for one historical space-time do not correspond to those of another.

There is nothing more anti-dogmatic than relativism, which does not accept inflexible universal principles valid for all space-times. But there is nothing more dialectical either. Relativism strengthens and confirms the dialectic of Hegel which Marx adopted as his ingenious concept. Only relativism in the light of the dialectic, and the latter in the light of relativism, invalidates that absolute, incontrovertible, and fixed Marxism like a solid body seen through the Euclidian retina.

III

APRISMO, MARXISM, AND
HISTORICAL SPACE-TIME

SINCE, AFTER SEVERAL YEARS, THE THEORY OF HISTORICAL SPACE-time, first put forward in *Claridad* of Buenos Aires in 1935, has again engendered polemics, and since it is not possible to discuss it at length in the pages of a review such as *Hoy* of Santiago, allow me to summarize my points of view on the dialectic, Marxism, and historical space-time. Thus, in a summary fashion, I shall return to the theme of the philosophical bases of Aprismo, defending it with the same dialectic method used by the Orthodox of Moscow to attack it.

    I. Starting from the dialectical principles that contradictions are inseparable from all things and that the development of these contradictions constitutes the dynamic of all evolution, it is evident that ideas and ideological systems, including philosophies and world views, are subject to the processes which are the reflection and expression of those contradictions and, consequently, themselves evolve.

    II. Marxism, as a philosophical system and as a "conception of the world" (Plekhanov), is the expression of that universal process of contradictions inherent in and consubstantial with all things. "All movement is a dialectic process, a living contradiction" (Plekhanov). Marxism cannot remain outside of the laws of dialectics which direct the evolution of the Cosmos, Nature, and Society. In consequence, Marxism is also not outside the laws of dialectics that determine the evolutionary process of human thought and its scientific, artistic, and philosophical expressions.

    III. This universal process of evolution, determined by the con-

---

"Aprismo, Marxismo y Espacio-Tiempo Historico," August, 1942, first published in *Y Despues de la Querra Que?* 1946.

tradictions which, I repeat, are inherent in all things, is the very essence of the dialectic. "Contradiction is the root of all movement and of all life," writes Hegel, because "only when a thing has a contradiction within itself, does it evidence impulse and activity" (Wissenschaft der Logik-Lib. II). And that universal process of contradictions is fulfilled by what we know as the dialectical negation of negation and opposition of opposites.

iv. The dialectical negation "is not to say no" writes Engels in the *Anti-Duhring*. Consequently, to negate dialectically is not "to extend an act of defunction" to what is negated, which would be to kill, not to negate. It is to conserve and to surpass at the same time; it is to negate and to continue. And thus for Hegel, all process of the social evolution of history, of nature, and of science, which that thought reflects, is a succession of negations and processes of surpassing, determined by the fact that "all things are in themselves contradictory" (Hegel, *op. cit*).

v. The processes of the evolution of the Cosmos, of Nature, of Society, of Thought—of History, in a word—do not cease in our epoch. They continue to flow irresistibly. And the century in which we live is nothing more than a passing link in a moving chain of millenia, in perpetual advance, from the past to the future. No matter how distinguished may be the thought of outstanding men, no matter how extraordinary and influential may be their genius and vision, they always pass. As Heraclitus—the discoverer of development—passed, as Thales, Pythagoras, and Democritus; Plato and Aristotle; St. Thomas, Descartes, Spinoza, Bacon, Kant, and Hegel, as all of the great spirits who contributed to the discovery of the mysterious keys of the universe passed, so Marx will pass, and will also be negated and surpassed. This necessary development is not to depreciate his achievement, rather, it is his affirmation, but his affirmation in his space and in his time, as the historical continuity of his thought and of his work. The worth and contribution of every genius of science, of art, of technology, of philosophy, and of politics, always from his determining relativist space-time of immortality, is also affirmed in this manner.

Starting from these five points, Aprismo asks: How will Marxism pass, and how will it develop? How will it be negated and continued? To this we can suggest—always in summary—that passing, moving, and negating are not mechanistic and automatic but are *determined*. "Omnis determinatio est negatio" exclaims Spinoza. All determination is negation. Hegel says in his *Logic* (chap. 11), that this Spinozian problem is of "infinite importance." And Engels cites it, also in a eulogistic fashion, in the *Anti-Duhring,* as a precursor of the modern dialectic. Thus, for historical determinism, based on the inherent contradiction of all things that have within themselves the principle of their own negation, is produced the development of Marxism, which is negated and transformed, so as to be surpassed.

Supporting this argument, it is worth remembering what Engels writes in his criticism of Hegel:

> The ancient method of examination and of thought that Hegel calls the metaphysical method . . . had in its time a historical reason for existence. . . . The ancient metaphysics which considered a thing as totally determined, was born of a Natural Science which examined dead or living things as well as extinct ones. When this investigation had advanced sufficiently to permit decisive progress, that is, the transition from the systematic examination of completed transformation to these things in nature itself, there also sounded then in the philosophical field the hour of death for metaphysical science. In fact, if until the eighteenth century the natural sciences were a science which was eminently that of collecting—the science of finished things—in the nineteenth century, it is transformed into a science which coordinates, the science of the processes of the origin and of the evolution of things and of the chain which links in one great whole all natural processes. (*L. Feuerbach and the End of German Classic Philosophy,* Chap. IV.)

This quotation sets forth in brief what Einstein and Infeld say in their book *The Evolution of Physics:* "Philosophical generalization must be based on scientific results" (New York: 1938, p. 55). That is, philosophy is the expression, reflection, and summation of those results; therefore, *in each epoch philosophy has its historical reason for existence based on the science of its time.* Thus, Hegel could not advance further than the limits of the discoveries and scientific conclusions of his century.

However, Marxism also has its own historical reason for existence and cannot advance further than the discoveries and scientific conclusions of its time. Not being *prophecy,* but a science and a system of reality, Marxism also cannot be congealed, nor can it close the direct paths of negations and the obsolescence of the future, since science and philosophy continue ever to advance. This is our central thesis.

In stating that Marx conceived of the world as a series of *processes* and not as a collection of stationary objects, and in indicating the paths of dialectical examination and explanation of these processes of each concept, Engels announces that thus "will be terminated forever the pretense of definitive solutions" and "eternal truths." He then adds this significant comment: "We should never forget the necessary limitations of our knowledge." Certainly those limitations of knowledge are the unpassable frontiers of the scientific advances of each epoch, and that is, in the case we are analyzing, the limits of Marxism since—and we repeat—"Omnis determinatio es negatio."

The advance of science has not stopped nor should it have stopped since the nineteenth century. No matter how enlightening was the combination of discoveries of that illustrious century, ours continues in the astonishing progress of science and opens unsuspected and grandiose perspectives for the future. The science of today surpasses each day the achievements of the past. It demonstrates with its development what it will become in the centuries ahead. "There are no eternal theories in science. It always happens that some of the facts predicted by a theory are not proven by experiments. Each theory has a period of gradual development and triumph, after which it can experience a rapid decay" (Einstein and Infeld, *op. cit.* p. 77).

If there is no eternity in the theories of science, neither are there any in philosophy, which is the sum of the scientific laws. The greatest concepts arise, reach their culminating point, and being surpassed by others, fade. Each has its historical reason for existence, its place and its epoch, but the development of human thought is continuous. Thus, like all sciences, Marxism cannot be a supernatural exception to this law which it has done so much to substantiate.

All right then, what are the fundamental characteristics of contemporary scientific evolution?

Here are the words, which I have often cited, of a great scientist of our era:

> A century of which only a third has passed has been witness to two great revolutions in Physical Science. These are linked to the words Relativity and Quantum and have obliged the physicist of today to look at nature with a group of ideas very different from that which was in vogue in the nineteenth century. . . . The old Philosophy had ceased to be valid by the end of the nineteenth century. . . . The physics of the twentieth century is

developing a new Philosophy. (James H. Jeans "The *New
Bases of Science,* Spanish Edition, Calpe, Chap. I., pp. 11–12.)

This revolutionary period in physics brings to the scientific world a
new conception of matter, of energy, of movement, of gravity, and
of electromagnetic fields. Furthermore, with a new geometry, it denies
the three dimensions of Euclid, incorporating the principle of a fourth
dimension; and thus appears a category of thought, the continuum
of space-time, which cannot be separated from an observed physical
phenomenon.

The twentieth century presents, then, a new conception of the
scientific fundamentals of philosophy. The mathematical and physical
sciences on which were based many great philosophical generaliza-
tions are being revised. The classic geometry is being negated. Consequently, "Space by itself and Time by itself pass into oblivion and only
a kind of union between both, will conserve their independent existence" (Minkowski, cited by Eddington in *Space-Time and Gravity,*
Calpe, p. 51).

It is not difficult, then to accept this argument: If there has been
produced a true revolution in the fundamental concepts of science,
it must be projected into philosophy. Further, if this revolution includes the concept of matter—to the point that the theory of relativity
has established that neither mass nor movement, not the extension
in space can be labelled true primary qualities "of matter" (Jeans,
op. cit. pp. 21–22)—we are face to face with a new revolutionary
conception of philosophic materialism. We are confronted with a new
system of relations between thought and matter. Furthermore, the
new continuum of space-time is already an undeniable mental category. "Today, the theory of Einstein explains a large number of natural phenomena, and no fact of nature is known which contradicts it"
says Jeans (*op. cit.,* p. 49). Also, Eddington gives us a summary
expression of the new relativist understanding: "Give me material
and movement, said Descartes, and I shall construct the Universe."
The mind inverts these terms: "Give me the Universe (a Universe
in which there exist relationships), and I shall construct material and
movement" (Eddington, *op. cit.,* p. 274). There derives from this
new and stupendous discovery of the sciences a distinctive way of
seeing the world. In the new scientific categories, philosophy has to
find new bases. This is true also of the philosophy of history, since

isn't the essential element of history the relationship of space and time in the social sphere?

Aprismo applies, then, the new scientific and philosophical concept of space-time to the philosophy of history. Also, it seeks within this an examination of the objective conditions of the social reality of Indoamerica and an interpretation of its historical development. It does not accept, needless to say, the interpretation of our reality from Europe but demands one from the Indoamerican historical space-time. It rejects immediately the European division of world history into Ancient, Medieval, and Modern, subject to the chronology of the Old World. The Old World has its own historical-time, inseparable from its space. Consequently, this division of history is not "universal." It is "universal European" and is conceived of from the point of view of its own reality and for itself. But, with the eyes of America, and from American soil that is no longer colonial, our historical antiquity does not coincide with European historical antiquity, chronologically, nor is its Middle Ages ours. Thus, when the orthodox Marxist asserts from the industrial European historical space-time that "imperialism is the superior or final stage of capitalism," the Indoamerican Aprista replies "superior or final there, but here, where capitalism comes to us in the form of imperialism, it is the first stage." History demonstrates this, and one need do nothing more than investigate the process of our incipient industrialism.

Each historical space-time forms a system of cultural coordinates, a geographical stage and a historical experience which determines a relationship of thought and development which is inseparable from the spatial concept and chronology. Each space-time is the expression of a degree of collective consciousness capable of observing, comprehending, and distinguishing, as a historical dimension, its own field of social development. Thus, if a people only arrive at cultural adulthood when it achieves a consciousness of its peculiar process of economic and social development, this adulthood is only complete when it discovers, with the passage of history, the unique and interconnected nature of its own space-time. This is the philosophical basis of the Aprista interpretation of the Indoamerican People-Continent.*

---

* This term was the title of the major work (*Pueblo-Continente*, Editorial Ercilla, Santiago de Chile, 1939) of Haya's mentor, friend, and political associate, Antenor Orrego.

LIBERATION OF THE INDOAMERICAN MIND

PERHAPS THE FUNDAMENTAL CONCEPT OF THE PHILOSOPHY OF THE Aprista movement, as a definition of a mental set, would be that which has frequently and variously been expressed with the slogan "liberation of the Indoamerican mind from the intellectual dictates of Europe." However, this thesis has often been misunderstood. Some interpreters and commentators, completely unacquainted with our ideology, have imagined and believed that this affirmation of independence implies a challenging arrogance towards what we owe to Western culture. Others, perhaps more sympathetic, have come to identify us with that anachronistic reactionary tendency that would proclaim a utopian return to the aboriginal past, and attribute to us the fantasy of a renaissance of the social and political structures of the Incas, Aztecs, Chibchas, and Mayas.

I must, therefore, begin this chapter with a brief clarification of our position. Thus the reader will have a version—albeit synoptic— of the motivations of Aprismo. He will also know that the point of departure for the postulate "liberation of the Indoamerican mind from the intellectual and cultural dictates of Europe" is based as much on the historical reality of the social, economic, and psychological development of the peoples of this continent as on the evidence of the radical transformation of the world of our epoch.

Whoever would wish to understand the fundamentals of the Aprista basic historical interpretation of the Indoamerican reality will have to record the underlying importance in our ideology of the *location* of the observer with regard to the observed phenomena. This

---

"Espacio-Tiempo-Histórico," *Cuadernos Americanos,* May–June, 1945, and included as Chapter II of *Espacio-Tiempo-Histórico.*

application of the scientific principles of modern relativism to the philosophy of history brought me to promulgate—starting some years ago—the thesis of historical space-time.

There is a statement by Jean Bodin, the talented French political theorist of the sixteenth century, which is admirable for its simplicity and profundity: "la permiere utilité de l'histoire est de servir a la politique." It is well to remember this if one does not consider history as an immovable accumulation of dates, episodes, and facts, deprived of its dynamic function as the experience of society in action. Because history is not merely the memory of the world, but is something more —its very consciousness. History is not only a zealous and detailed memory, catalogued and inert, but is an intelligent and creative expression, the vital plasma of new social organisms to come. For this reason, history is inseparable from politics as is demonstrated by the great jurist in *Les Six Livres de la Republique*. And for this reason, too, history is inseparable from *its* space and from *its* time. And together they—inseparable from each other—complete the relativist concept which adds a new and illuminating dimension to the modern dialectic explanation of historical phenomena.

Dead history, separated and isolated from its space-time, does not exist, then. Consequently, there are no "dessicated" historical phenomena existing apart from time and place. Furthermore, each historical development is interpreted according to the point of view of the observer. And the philosophy of history—the "coordinates" or historical field of observation of which has been, until today, European space-time—must make relative its hierarchy of values and move from the cultural longitude and latitude which indicate a fixed and absolute position.

The easy and usual classification of history into ancient, medieval and modern will serve as an example. Can we consider this accurate, and of worldwide application, from the historical space-time of China, India, Australia, or from our own American angle? It is undeniable that the observed phenomena which bring about this historic division are absolutely limited to Europe and hence, for us, *relativized*. This classification can be imposed as a universal measurement of chronological time from the cultural coordinate or historical field of Europe, so long as Europe was the zero meridian of world development. It can be accepted as an imperious colonial norm by those social groups only beginning to form their own historical consciousness. But as their understanding broadens, this universal European classification loses its applicability. Any attempt to prolong or impose it leads to disturbing mental confusion and falsifies the bases for an authentic consciousness of the historic world.

There is not, then, a single ancient history nor one antiquity and one middle and modern age, but rather as many similar periods as there are social and cultural processes which consistently develop historical continuity. And since one might think that this thesis borders upon the ambitious construction of Spengler, it is necessary to define its modest autonomy. In another essay I have shown more fully this distinction so here it is enough to note that Spengler has always been, above all, *a stationary European observer.* In imposing a new cyclical movement strictly parallel to cultural developments, attributing to "groups of morphological affinity a rigorously symmetrical structure," he rejects the static, "durable and universal" classification of historical development which "must be thought of in parts." He makes of his philosophy what he calls "an attempt to predict History." Divorcing it of all Euclidian character and from a "relative-historical" angle, he contemplates it from the immovable height of his Faustian thought. For Spengler "Time is a counter concept of Space": the latter, "the form of what is felt"; the former, "the form of feeling."

The reader will remember the enlightening introduction to *The Decline of the West* because it gives us the key to the Spenglerian concept and the hierarchy of his relativism. When he negates the European scheme of history—middle ages and modern—he says to us, "I call it the *Ptolomaic System* of History and consider as *the Copernican Discovery* in the field of History, the new system which this book proposes; a system in which antiquity and the West appear together with India, Babylonia, China, Egypt, the Arab culture, and the Mexican culture." With this announcement, Spengler appears certainly as a relativist, but—and it is necessary to repeat this—*not* in the Einsteinian sense. His thesis derives from *the negation of the universe of Ptolomy by the conception of Copernicus applied to history.* It is thus that we can compare the difference which exists between this Spenglerian relativism and ours, with that which separates, in the physical sciences, the Copernican relativism of Galileo-Newton from the contemporary relativism of Einstein. They are precisely reversed. And because the historical relativism of Spengler is Copernican—as he himself proclaims—and derives from the already outdated concepts of time, space, and movement as absolute and autonomous phenomena, the conclusions of *The Decline of the West* are limited and fatalistic. For Spengler, "cultures are organisms and world-history is their biography." His historical universe terminates then with the agony of the Faustian culture which he observes from his German coordinate of German vision. It is thus immobile.

Spenglerian relativism is therefore anti-dialectic, prophetic, and quietist. His exegesis appears frequently artificial, forced, and in spite of his brilliance and the profundity of his poetic imagination, his conclusions and prognostications are skeptical and predetermined. *The Decline of the West* cannot be—as the author himself recognizes— "eternal and universal" truth. It appears rather to be the bold and grandiose German response to *his* West. But from *ours,* from any non-European historical space-time and from the moving basis of relativist and non-Copernican observation, the exegesis of the past, the estimate of the present, and the road of the future, take on a different aspect in our thinking.

It is necessary to assert, then, that the first Aprista postulate is relativity applied to history and the new mode of interpreting history as a vast universal coordination of processes, each inseparable from its own space-time and movement. It should also be noted here that time and space, separately, do not fully explain the classical geographic and chronological expressions amalgamated in the new concept, *historical space-time,. . .* And that the vital interdependence of teluric, ethnic, social, economic, cultural, and psychological factors which act and influence one another, form a dynamic continuity constituting a philosophical category which could be qualified as the historical fourth dimension.

With the fundamental concept of our philosophy thus summarized, the second element may be considered as the result of the incorporation of this relativist dynamism of history into the determinist dialectic, where it becomes a negation and continuation of the dialectical processes.

It is necessary here to refer to Hegel, the great forerunner of the philosophy of history and the creator of the modern dialectic. And to Marx, who within the dialectic postulated the negation of Hegelian historic idealism and the determinant affirmation of scientific materialism. . . . We must say only that the *thesis of historical space-time originates in turn from the dialectic negation of Marxist philosophy,* taking into account that the conclusions of Marxist doctrine are also, from their points of reference, exclusively European, seen and judged from an immobile point of observation.

/

Because of this immobility of the observer, when Marxism is applied as a worldwide praxis to other historical space-times, it falls within a dogmatically closed limit. And it is important to record here that all immobility and dogmatism are anti-dialectic in the Hegelian-Marxist philosophy, the essential basis of which is the principle of eternal change, of unanimous flux, of the negation of the negation, that distant legacy of the precursing thought of Heraclitus.

Hegel says: "each Philosophy is the Philosophy of its epoch; it is a link in the whole chain of spiritual development which can only satisfy the interests of its time," thus setting forth here the principle of its own negation. But his philosophy of history, which is an immense processional movement of people and cultures towards the consciousness of liberty—"like links of a great chain"—comes to a static conclusion which cuts and paralyzes it. Hegel ends with the idea of the European—German—super-state and is brought to this point by his absolute idealism, which, deviating from flowing determinism, ends and congeals in dogmatic orthodoxy.

Marx negates this point in Hegel. He builds with the objective elements of his era upon the structure of the dialectic, divorced of all idealism, a revolutionary and universal "conception of the world," as Plekhanov calls it—that is, historical materialism. But Marx—for whom space and time are disjointed, absolute values—also ends statically in his new meridian of observation. From it he discovers other laws of social development conceived of as a sole and grandiose process which begins in primitive antiquity and ends in the era of the proletariat. Marx, like Hegel—although from a different angle and moment—is thus located within the European historical space-time. The philosophy of each of them is the philosophy of *his* epoch, riveted to its intransferable reality. In the world of the nineteenth century, the cultural and political expansion of the great world stages to other latitudes had only begun, and as a result, the philosophical concept of the universe and of space, of time, and of movement applied to history does not reach the scientific levels to which they are elevated by contemporary relativism, on the bases of a new geometry and a new physics.

Since the Marxist theory cannot be an anti-dialectical "eternal truth," in the essence of its philosophy lies its negation. And this is, furthermore, its imperative to continue. To negate, dialectically, is not simply to deny. It is, at the same time, to *conserve and surpass.* Thus the universal validity of all historical-philosophical principles and doctrines becomes relativized by the modifications imposed by each space-time.

And the world continues its march. The universal and eternal is development, and history does not detain its own dialectical advance. The political-social stages expand, and new angles of observation open before the consciousness of men. History cannot be centralized in certain European poles. Its universal movement has *various speeds and various paths.* Everything develops, *but not in the same single way, nor with the same synchronized movement.*

Consequently, historical realities no longer form the links of a single "great chain." They are various, extending to an unlimited future. There may be, and there in fact are, among them points of contact, crossing, and proximity, but their parallelism is only relative. Their direction and their longitude cannot be identical. A similar historical-time—grade and rhythm of evolution, of culture, of organization, of psychology—is not applicable to all spaces. For time, space, and movement become inseparable in each observed reality. Thus, as there is a historical space-time which is European, there is another which is Chinese, others which are North and South African. There is a historical space-time for North America, and another for Indoamerica. We insist: there is no historical-time nor historical-space in isolation. There exist many peoples in the world that can offer relative simultaneity or similarity of temporal grades or stages of economic, political, and cultural development—in Asia, Oceania, in Indoamerica, and perhaps in the Balkans—but the similarity is modified by historical space which is not mere geographical location but which encompasses the conscious relation between man and his land, inseparable from his time category. On the other hand, there exist peoples in Asia and Africa whose spatial stage can be apparently almost undifferentiated from ours. However, what separates and distinguishes them is historical-time, which is not chronological and which, therefore, is not measured by calendars and watches.

Incorporating this relativist thesis in the dialectic of history, clarifies much in the disconcerting nature of a world as contradictory as that of today. Its contradictions not only assume a fully logical place and illuminate better the present world panorama, but they also acquire a new significance linking many phenomena which are inseparable from their space-times and which, in their turn, are also multiple. It is worthwhile to note now that this multiplicity, or variety, is not disarticulated or anarchic. It affirms a new and profound principle of universality. But the universal in history ceases to be the subjection of all its phenomena to an identical process, simultaneously and symmetrically regimented by the same determinants and from the same centers of irradiation. Such an *absolute* universalism does not explain —it is worth much to repeat it—the antagonisms of our contemporary world. Only a *relativist* universalism—derived from a finite universe, but unlimited, of four dimensions and conceived to be in constant expansion—enables one to see and comprehend lucidly the events of this new epoch. They cannot be separated from the *where* and *when* of their genesis, because upon this essential link depends *how* they are produced.

Simple examples of this relationship between universality and multiplicity, applied to social facts with the inseparable continuity of historical space-time, are the diverse forms and means of expressing and satisfying needs, customs, and cultural and political aspirations. For example, all people have to eat, but human hunger is satisfied in very different ways according to the customs, culture, class, psychology, and refinement of a people, as well as to their natural resources and climate. The universal needs of clothing, shelter, and spiritual expression are not satisfied identically in all parts of the world. Production by labor is an inescapable social imperative which is fulfilled in many diverse ways, too. Education, science, religion, and art provide further examples of variation in human progress and accomplishment. Thus, the way the state fulfills its functions, its social, economic, legal, and judical organization and, in general, the ends of man's physical and mental life are explained better in terms of the concept of historical space-time, since these multiple expressions and realizations of universal imperatives are transcended only by their coexistence, simultaneity, and variety within the unity of history. They must also be so in the relatively foreseeable future. Although the interdependence of peoples, accelerated by technology, brings the world ever nearer to *standardization,* it is important not to forget that by the yet unmodified laws of nature, the world and the men who inhabit it are still far from constituting an organic unity formed of identical elements. The systematization of its multiplicity and variety is, for now, a great and prolonged study.

The law of expansion, which displaces, aggrandizes, and transforms the stages of the peoples, indicates cultural cycles in those which, in spite of the more or less prolonged stages of negation across the centuries, fulfill the dialectic of development. What must be made

clear and always kept in mind is that historical-time is not chrono-
lôgical; that its movement and rhythm are different, and that, finally,
as has already been said, it is not transferable from place to place.
Thus, when there appears before the eyes of a fixed observer the illusion of continuity in the cultural life of the peoples, the fact is that
the old *does not die* but is displaced, by dialectical negation to another historical space-time. And here arises again the relation between
this concept and the dialectic of history, which thus becomes more
flexible and explainable, something which is very difficult to achieve
within a rigid and dogmatic itinerary, unilaterally predetermined.

Historical space-time explains also, in this way, the paradox of
the so-called "young peoples," who in reality are not young, but are
members and groups of old human races displaced from their former
context and established within a new system of relations, with a different spatial and temporal category, or who are renewed in their
own environment. There are not, in reality "young peoples" created
by spontaneous generation, but new or renovated historical space-
times. "Old China" and "Old Russia" are today peoples full of youth
and masters of a new and accelerated movement of development.
The "young" North American people is a conglomerate of the oldest
Indo-European races rejuvenated by a new and expanded historical
space-time. There is a new India which is announcing itself and is
approaching. Why not a New Europe? And why not a new Indoamerica, where the old Celto-Iberian-Arabic and African races enter into
contact with their contemporaries, the indigenous races?

This brief exposition should be rounded out by some questions
which arise as a corollary of it. What is the differentiation of these
historical space-times? What are their limits?

We respond that they, by a process of the political expansion
of the social world, become continental expressions. Not strictly geographical, in the circumscribed sense of the physical division of the
world in five habitable portions; but rather as "People-Continents,"
using the happy combination of words created by Antenor Orrego
for the title and theme of a suggestive book.

Are we limited here to geopolitics? Perhaps in some aspects. But
considered only in its general sense, the basic conception of Sir Hal-
ford Mackinder and not that of Rudolf Kjellen or Karl Haushofer;
since this new discipline, as is known, is not exclusively German. It
serves, furthermore—in passing, for the reference illustrative of ana-
logues and distinctions—the separation of concepts between geopoli-

tics and political geography; even though Frederich Ratzel in his
Seven Laws of Expansion seems to be a connection between both.
To note the difference is not useless, since it can be compared to that
between geographic space and chronological time, and the relativist
and dialectical concept of continuous historical space-time.

Geopolitics studies the relations between geography and the
development of peoples and states without taking into account the
relations of the individual and his environment. "As Marxism" writes
Strausz-Hupe, "has developed its dialectic and its attraction for the
radical masses in its materialist simplicity, in Geo-politics the social
and historical growth, that of religious and cultural aspirations of
humanity derive their only significance from the political struggle for
Space." It is worth noting, furthermore, that being definitely a *spatial*
study, of European origin, its "coordinate of observation" is Eurasian.
In the Old World is located the "continental heartland." And it is
Mackinder—who establishes that "each century has its own geographic perspective"—who is the first to demarcate "the Island of
the World" formed by Africa, Europe, and Asia. In that concept,
the importance of the Americas appears still secondary. "The three
so-called new continents are in area mere satellites of the old."

Perhaps when geopolitics can complete its evolution towards
systematization into an integral, *non-imperialist* science, it may be
able to find its relationship with the thesis of historical space-time, that
shows us a new *mode* of seeing and understanding history and the
present world from a non-European anthropo-socio-geographic point
of observation. But geopolitics specializes its action in obtaining from
the anthropo-socio-geographic reality the elements with which the
strong state, considered as a live organism which needs only "living
space," can fulfill its political ends. However, with the modification
in the spatial conditions of the world by the techniques of communications and instruments of war, geopolitics, which until today has been
a theory at the service of imperialism—will have to undertake a serious revision at the end of this war. But if it remains—displacing and
readjusting its objectives—it cannot elude history. And as interpretation, it cannot be observed from only one side of the world, from a
single historical coordinate or field.

The concept of historical space-time does not imply, then, the
exclusive linking of politics with the geography of certain vital zones
for the development of nations, but the conscious function of history in its sociological fulfillment, inseparable from each "People-

Continent." The North American professor and publicist William G. Fletcher, of Yale University, expounding the Aprista philosophy, writes:

> The history of the world and contemporary relations among states is seen in accord with two concepts: Historical Space and Historical Time. All political facts are relative and conditioned by those two factors. Historic Space signifies—in less imposing terms—the influence of Geography. Historical Time signifies the grade of economic, social, and political development within a country as conditioned by its geographical location, extension, form, and natural resources.

But Professor Fletcher not only offers a limited description of the significance of historical space and time, as if they are separate phenonoma, but he forgets that the essential element of this thesis is its category of "continuum" and its relationship with the theory of relativist physical space-time. Historical space is not only the influence of geography but the constant *teluric relationship* of land and man, which is a less material concept, is difficult to describe. That which is called the soul, consciousness, or spirit of a people—words only vaguely expressive of the cosmic profundity involved—also enter into the *teluric relationship* of man and his land, his landscape, his tradition, his art, his ethnic relationships, and his death. In sum, all the unconscious, conscious, and emotional ties to a particular region. It would have been better to say that "historical space" signifies the influence of socio-geography or of anthropo-socio-geography, if it is desired to submit it forcibly to a strict and technical-scientific definition. Because with the understanding of the sociological influence inherent in historical space there enters in the factor of social psychology which is a singularly important one to complete the vital and inseparable sense of historical time.

On the other hand, "historical time" does not only signify for Aprismo, as Professor Fletcher affirms, "the degree of economic, social, and political development within a country, conditioned by its geographical location, extension, farm resources, etc." There is something more: Historical time is not a mediation of periods as if it deals with a new chronology. It is, subjectively, the intuition and sense of individual and social time linked consciously and functionally to the way of living, working, thinking, and developing of a people. And, objectively, the expression of this mode of conceiving and using time, and of observing and interpreting time in the moving trajectory of historical evolution. Then, this characteristic of a historical time becomes clearly *inseparable from its space* and its movement. Thus the three constitute a "continuity" which cannot be sundered.

Brief illustrations should make this thesis easier to comprehend. The Egyptian, Mongolian, Mexican, and Incaic peoples, in different latitudes and climates, had an idea of time which was expressed in their religion, in their funeral cults, in their cycloptic monuments, in their slow productivity, in their passivity. If we compare, then, the time concept of our Indoamerican forebears, or of those of ancient Egypt, of Babylonia, and of China and India, with the more "presentist" idea of time in Ephesus, in Athens, in Carthage, and in Rome, it is indisputable that we perceive a *different grade of velocity,* of movement, and of rhythm which goes beyond chronological measurement. And as this is not a question of calendars, we *feel* that in the European Middle Ages the time concept was again long and extensive, until the maritime discoveries and the Renaissance gave it a new and more accelerated rhythm. These diverse modes of thinking about and experiencing time, of conceiving it, of valuing it, and of feeling it as a historical expression, are related to the expansive movement of peoples and to the acceleration of their methods of production, of exchange, of war, and of dominion, but are *inseparable determiners* of the stage on which they develop. An analysis such as one of "historical time," isolated from its space, is always incomplete and therefore false.

Thus in the social development of the world, we have come to this epoch, and we continue distinguishing various rhythms of historical time in the variety of anthropo-socio-geographic environments. The time concept possessed by a man of the United States or of industrial Europe and that of the Tibetan, the Hindu, or the Andean Quechua continue to be extremely different. But between these extreme poles *there are gradations.* Thus historical space-times can be distinguished not exclusively by countries—as Professor Fletcher mistakenly asserts—but rather by "People-Continents."

It is not necessary, as we have already explained, that a People-Continent be located in the whole extension of one of the five such geographic divisions. Here history in the service of politics, and the latter as a social expression, confer a new significance on the continental classifications. There are People-Continents which coincide geographically with their physical limits, such as the United States, Australia, and Indoamerica, but there are also those which form People Continents within vast zones of the hinterland, without oceanic boundaries. China is a People-Continent with its own historical space-time and so is Russia, even though it includes part of Europe and part of Asia. Western Europe is also a People-Continent as was the now dispersed Arabic world.

At this point we come to a final refutation of Professor Fletcher. Historical space-time, as its name indicates, is not an ahistorical concept. It doesn't exist without history. It can be said that it is not possible without *political consciousness,* that that is history.

For a historical space-time to become the determining factor in the dialectic history, it must exist not only as a geographic environment and the people who inhabit it—not only as a continent and political society in motion—but as the full living function of its social consciousness of historical occurrences. In other words, it must involve the psychological capacity of a social group to *understand* its history and *interpret it* in terms of its own reality.

In the same way that a physical phenomenon must be observed from a space and in a given time, a historical phenomenon is only comprehended when a people acquires the maturity of a social consciousness which equips it to be protagonist and interpreter of its own development and the development of the world. It is not sufficient then, for there merely to be a geographical environment and a race living there, for there to exist a unique historical space-time and a People-Continent. It is also necessary that there be a considerably advanced economic-social dynamism and a certain level of culture and relationship with the multiplicity of the other historical developments of the world.

Thus it is that the People-Continents transform the sum total of their historical experience, accumulated in the process of their cultural formation, into the psychological or mental qualities necessary for historical self-observation, self-assessment, and self-interpretation. In the same way that there are different levels of subjective understanding of time and of space—from the most elemental to the most complete and eminent—peoples do not quickly achieve by improvisation their historical consciousness or their use of political-social reason, but do so as the result of a prolonged process. For this reason, it is important to insist that where there is not history nor a consciousness of it—because it is still being formed or has been lost—there does not really exist historical space-time as a dialectic, and hence living and dynamic, process.

V

AMERICAN HISTORICAL SPACE-TIME

IT IS SEEN FROM THE THESIS OF TOYNBEE, CONCERNING THE GENESIS of civilizations, that they do not owe their origins in an isolated way to geographic or biological determinants. The "Challenges" to which man responds are physical and social. Further, in spite of one or another appearing predominant in certain cases, they are always the result of the interaction of both.

Thus, there are outstanding physical challenges: desiccation, in the rise of the civilizations of Egypt and Sumeria; great altitude, in the cordilleras, and the coastal desert, in the initiation of the Andean Civilization; floods and the extreme climatic contrasts of winter and summer, in the origin of Chinese Civilization; the sea, in the beginning of the Minoic Civilization; and the pervading tropical forest, in the advent of the Indian and Mayan Civilizations.

In addition, Toynbee enumerates the predominantly social challenges. The discovery of the Sumeric Society in the emergence of the Hittite and Babylonian Civilizations; the decline of the Minoic Society in the birth of Syriac Civilization; and the decline of the latter, in the fusion of the Iranian and Arabic Societies which created the Islamic Civilization; the exhaustion of the Chinese Society in the origin of the Far Eastern Civilization—its main body; the dissolution of the Indic Society in the beginnings of the Hindu Civilization; and the collapse of the Hellenistic Society in the appearance of the orthodox Christian and Byzantine.

When both challenges, the physical and the social, appear virtually simultaneously, Toynbee indicates the following: The civilizations

---

"Espacio-Tiempo-Histórico Americano" from *Toynbee Frente a los Panoramas de la Historica,* 1957.

of Korea and Japan confront geographically a new soil, and at the same time, the social contacts with the Far East, from the principal body of which they secede and transplant. The Hellenistic, Yucatan, and Mexican civilizations respond also to the challenge of harsh soils and to the disintegration of the preceding societies which were in one degree or another their predecessors: The Minoic in the Greek case, the Maya in that of Yucatan, Mexican, and Central American. The Orthodox Russian Civilization, descended from the Oriental Christian or Byzantine, is confronted also with a new territorial space and the relations with the principal body from which it breaks away. The Western Christian Civilization also responds to the physical challenge of another area—continental Europe—and the social challenge of the decadence of the Hellenistic Society. Later, that challenge expanded towards the newly discovered continents.

In all of these cases, the victorious encounter generating a civilization tenaciously overcomes adverse conditions. The Greek slogan with which Toynbee emblazons the second volume of his work is, in this respect, an expressive synthesis which may be translated as the beautiful is difficult or high quality involves hard work. Since, for the fulfillment of the *challenge-response* and for the creative realization of the "encounter," an unfavorable physical environment or the reactions in face of the human one, or both, are not sufficient. The civilizations are always caused by multiple factors.

Toynbee indicates how the process of challenge-response can be frustrated. He classifies two types of frustrated civilizations: the abortive and the arrested civilizations. Of the former he gives the examples of the Christian Civilization of the Far West, the Christian Civilization of the Far East, and the Scandinavian Civilization: The first arises "on the Celtic fringe," principally in Ireland, after the year 375 of our era, facing the *physical challenge* of a new soil and the double *social challenge* of the disintegration of the Hellenistic Society and of the development of the Western Christian Society. But the efforts of the Celts languished in the face of the dominating influence of the latter, and the increased ecclesiastical authority of Rome between the fifth and seventh centuries. Then as a result of the disastrous impact of the Viking invasions, which were repeated between the ninth and eleventh centuries, Ireland by the twelfth century had definitely come to be religiously a province of then powerful Christianity and politically a province of the English.

The second abortive civilization in the Toynbeean nomenclature emerges from the "chrysalis" of Nestorian Christianity, in the valley of the Oxus-Jaxartes. However, it succumbed when this region was incorporated in the Arabic Empire in the eighth century A.D. Finally, the third of this group is the Scandinavian Civilization, whose expansion during the eighth to eleventh centuries A.D. surpassed the Celtic advances. However, it failed, due to the interposition of the pagan Slavs, and because it was isolated by Western Christian Civilization. Born in Iceland, the Scandinavian Civilization lost its vitality when the Icelanders were converted to Christianity. Then, the Scandinavian kingdoms in Russia, Denmark, and Norway decayed successively under the influence of the Christian Civilization, which conquered and dislocated the Scandinavian Society, in spite of its remarkable triumphs in both literature and politics. Its first overseas conquest in Greenland in the tenth and eleventh centuries—which led to the first discovery of America—perished in the face of the then uncontrollable rigors of that physical environment.

Of the arrested civilizations, Toynbee enumerates five. The Polynesian, which in spite of its epical oceanic expansion, was finally immobilized by the invincible challenge of the *sea*. The Eskimo managed early inventions such as the kayak, the fishing harpoon, the dog-team, the igloo, lamps using blubber oil, and skins for the construction of tents, inventions that were nonetheless insufficient to provide a victorious civilization in the face of the *Arctic challenge*. That of the Nomads, essentially a "society without history," was notable for its achievements in domesticating animals, but like that of the Eskimo, was a society bound to the cycles of climate and vegetation although those typical of the steppes. The civilization of the Ottoman Osmalines, whose challenge-response was that of the passage from nomadism to settlement in a strange region, had to exercise dominion over virtually unconquerable communities rather than over animals; its *tour de force* was the severe organization of the Ottoman community on the basis of enslavement and the rigid maintenance of control over "human cattle." And finally, there was that of the Spartans, who faced the *social challenge of population growth* in reverse proportion to the increase of their means of subsistence—in the eighth century B.C.—which caused a policy of expansion. But its militarist spirit "kept the conquerors captive" and frustrated its own energies.

Thus, we can infer that all challenge-response sequences, which create a civilization, imply the achievement of a form of joint sovereignty between man and the space which serves as his stage, and a growing predominance over the social factors which resist and influence but at last submit to the innovating impulse of the society that is rising. That condominium brings about in the human group responding to the physical challenge the formation of a growing consciousness of its space; which results from the actions and reactions between the man and his enviroment. This consciousness of space, the definition, perfection, and elevation of which can be more or less rapid, is inseparable in its development from a consciousness of time. Here appears the transposition to the field of the philosophy of history of the Einsteinian theory of physical space-time, that is the space of four dimensions, of which the dimension of time becomes the stairway and diapason of the variable speed of reciprocal influences between man and the land about him, giving rise to a civilization. A civilization is inseparable from the environment in which it occurs, and this environment comes to be subjectively and objectively its dynamic and creative elan, its consciousness and its perspective.

Words written some years ago may clarify this proposition: "In order for a historical space-time to become determinant in the dialectic of history, there must exist not only the geographic area and the people that inhabit it; not only as a continent and the historical content in movement, but as a full living function of the social consciousness of the fact of history. In other words, the psychological capacity of a social group to realize its history and interpret it in terms of its own reality."

To the present definition of the social consciousness of historical space-time—arising from the acceptance of the *physical or human challenge* and the existence of a victorious *response* to it—can be added a figurative and clarifying parallel, not too forced, with the levels of evolution of a language and the consciousness of it which Cassirier classifies in three ascending steps—the onomatopeic, the intuitive, and the conceptual—of which "the first corresponds to the simple expression of what can be felt; the second to the comprehension of Space, Time and Numbers; and the third to the most eminent and pure forms of relationship."

It is true that Hegel says—in his watchful and profound preface to his *Philosophie der Geschichte*—"The History, properly speaking, of a people begins when this people becomes conscious of itself"— and offers a description of the origin and development of agriculture, which begins with the establishment of man in a given spatial area and determines the development of his concepts of time. This helps

to illuminate the dynamic of *challenge-response,* in function of the
rise of consciousness of historical space-time:

> . . . agriculture is established and with it are fixed the laws
> of life in common. The fertile soil produces by itself the transit
> to agriculture, from which immediately grows intelligence and
> foresight. Agriculture is regulated by the seasons of the year.
> The care of man is not reduced but rather extended in a long
> term basis. It is necessary to invent implements, and thus there
> arises the sagacity of inventions and art. Firm possession is
> established, property and law, and with this, the division of
> classes. The need for instruments and warehouses leads to a
> sedentary life and implies the necessity of staying attached to
> this soil. When this base is established, the determinants of
> property and law arise. And with this there is developed the
> possibility of a general government, and essentially of the rule
> of law. There arises in these countries great empires, and thus
> begins the foundation of powerful states.

This quotation, it must be underscored in passing, sounds more
like the materialist Marx than the idealist Hegel and shows the powerful influence of the rejected teacher on the heterodox disciple. But
it is pertinent and valid as an illustration of the thesis of historical
space-time, for Hegel sketches globally in his synthesis the development from pristine sedentary communities to the civilizing culmination
of a full consciousness of historical space-time. However, in it are recognized the levels of progress from the "simple expression of what
can be felt" in the words of Cassirier—that first response to "the
necessity of staying attached to this soil" mentioned by Hegel—to
the superior forms of relationship. It is perhaps not out of place to
paraphrase here the Hegelian dictum on the beginning of history,
which is that in civilizations this appears when a people rises to full
consciousness of its space-time. That is to say, when it goes beyond
its primordial relations with the fecund or infertile soil regulated by
the seasons of the year, and beyond those elemental and routine
notions of its space-time dimensions characteristic of all primitive
communities, and is able to pass on to the dynamic situation of civilizations impelled by the awakening of that consciousness.

When this is extinguished, when its network of relations is
broken, civilizations soften and decay: "Space-time loses its relationship with social consciousness, the human elements disperse and the
cultural determinant is extinguished." The scene is then left vacant

even though races and their vegetative needs survive; and the gravitational fields of history move on to other arenas, which acquire a historic consciousness of their space and their time until this consciousness becomes a predominant cultural expression. It is worth remembering here that Toynbee assigns to societies the name of *intelligible fields of history*.

We have said above that the thesis of historical space-time considers, like that of physics, both the subjective and the objective: a consciousness as well as a reality. Ortega y Gasset expressed three decades ago ideas on the theory of relativity which are worth repeating now:

> The theory of Einstein is a marvelous justification of the harmonic multiplicity of all points of view. Amplify this idea to the moral and the esthetic and we will have a new way of feeling History and life; . . . In place of seeing the non-European cultures as barbarous, we shall begin to respect them as ways of confronting the cosmos similar to ours. There is a Chinese perspective as justified as the Western perspective.

Here we must reiterate: as well as a "Chinese perspective"—or Hindu or Islamic or American—there exists a historical space-time consciousness of which one or another perspective is only a projection of an angle or way of seeing them. We must not only take into account how they are seen from the West, but how they view, from their space-time, the Westerners.

If the processes of history are obviously unthinking, without precise notions of space and time—not only because geography and chronology are "the eyes" of history—they are essentially linked to the new values which contemporary science provides to those concepts. Carrel, in the brilliant fifth chapter of the book which has made him world famous, notes how "although distinct from Space, Time is inseparable from it, both on the surface of the earth and in the rest of the universe; as much for the biologist as for the physicist." Herbert Dingle notes the distinction between Newtonian absolute space and absolute time, independent of one another—which had decisive influence in the philosophy of the eighteenth and nineteenth centuries— and the relativist space-time theory:

> For Newton, Space and Time were the theater upon which was present the drama of forces and movements. For Einstein, the

drama is mixed and confounded with the stage: The drama is the stage.

Thus, in the historical drama "of the stage" there are played out the double Toynbeean categories of obstacle and attack; of telluric or social environment which *challenge* and the human group which *responds;* of the soil which defies and the society on the way to the "dynamic situation of civilizations" which conquers or retreats, which dominates or perishes. The completion of the drama is thus: either the victory of the invincible environment which detains, or in the "happy ending," much less frequent, of the man who responds to the *challenge of space* and acquires and elevates a consciousness of it. But this *challenge-response* is inseparable from the consciousness of time, its protagonist; elemental and slow rather than stagnated, in the obscure primordial societies, and accelerated when civilizations begin "the march of history."

To complete this summary presentation of the thesis of historical space-time, and of the Toynbeean theory of *elan,* which impels the exceptional transformation of relatively static primitive societies into the dynamic situation of civilizations, it is right to point out that Toynbee has demonstrated that economic determinants are not omnipresent in this development. The fact, scientifically verified, that there are hundreds of pre-civilized communities of which not more than ten developed into civilizations, is a decisive argument in favor of the assertion of the illustrious British historian. Thus, the contrast between the universality of material needs, from which no society is exempt, and the rarity of the cases in which these needs appear as causes of the existence of a civilization, refutes, in this respect, the validity of the orthdox determining principles of historical materialism.

It is enough to reiterate that historical space-time does not presume an isolated or exclusive geo-climatic influence. Hegel has written about this, thinking of Montesquieu, and perhaps of Aristotle, a certain ironic observation referring "to the sweet Ionic heaven which is said to have produced Homer," and that it continues being the same "even though only Homer has come from the Ionic people." Nor is historical space-time—and this also has been demonstrated—a variation of circumscribed geopolitics, which is even further from our thesis. However, our thesis is not foreign to, even less contradicted by, the *challenge-response* categories of Toynbee, although it attempts a new causal explanation of the genesis of civilizations. Challenge and defiance promote the conceptual root of the Greek polemos: action and reaction, struggle, triumph, or defeat. But in the contest of man with his geographic space, each victory over the latter becomes a creative joint sovereignty, the affirmation of which results in a plastic synthesis of reciprocal influences. Thus, while man is defied and subjected by the still powerful surrounding natural forces, he must, to counteract them, discover and perfect technological methods: "invent implements," as Hegel puts it. Further, this first step of invention is not only imperative for the development of civilized societies, inventors of many implements and gadgets of basic use in the life of man, it happens that the difference between this comparative quietude of primitive societies and the dynamism of civilized ones is characterized by two different notions of space and time.

But it is not in these civilized societies that the consciousness of space-time achieves the most eminent forms of abstraction and people arrive at what we have called "their use of historical reason." The social consciousness of historical space-time evolves, is enriched and cleansed, from the most primitive forms which in the well-known didactic phrase is called "adaption to the environment," or vegetative life, without major changes, to the supreme expressions of culture and hegemony; from the beginning of the first struggles for territory by groups or tribes in a chosen area—embryonic *challenge-response* and stammering attempts at joint sovereignty between man and his space—up to the complete and expansive creations of civilization. These can rise to the hierarchy or universal churches, their culminating political step. Furthermore, there can also exist other civilizations; each of them distinguishable by their peculiar space-time consciousness.

* * * * *

The history of America, "very old and very modern," presents greater cases of physical and human challenge-response, which are ostensive examples of the formative process of consciousness of historical space-time, carried to the highest point of civilization. Toynbee classified two of ours among the original civilizations "without previous relations": the Mayan and the Andean. The first developed as a response to the geo-climatic challenge of the luxurious tropical forest; the second as a response to altitude—indeed a higher one than that of any other civilization—and to the sterile coastal deserts of the Pacific. The Mayan Civilization had a brilliant culmination but disintegrated with the overthrow of its universal state, whose First Emperor extended his dominion over a large part of Meso-America and probably extended his influence even further. From its decomposition there resulted the Yucatacan Civilization and the Mexican Civilization. This latter is the only one of the three which the Western conquerors found in full development; but— according to the observation of Toynbee—before it became a universal state, controlling all Central America, it was supplanted by the viceroyalty of New Spain.

In the south, the Andean Civilization included all of the former cultures of both the Amazonian and Pacific flanks of cordilleras and evolved to become a universal state, the Empire of the Incas. Its encounter with the invading Western Christian Civilization in the sixteenth century A.D. produced—as in the case of the Mexican Society—its collapse.

The Mayan Civilization responded to the challenge of the tropical jungle which the Central American man conquered victoriously, until, according to all conjectures, the jungle defeated him in the epilogue of splendid cultural achievement. The Yucatacan Civilization answered the physical challenge—as has been said—of the limy soil and the same jungle, and the social challenge of the disintegration of its "parent" society. The Mexican expanded towards the Central Plateau, responded to the geographic challenge of the new and more elevated soil, and the human one of the dauntless societies previously established there. The Andean Civilization established its firmest bases in the high cordillera, and from there dominated and absorbed the kingdom of the coast and founded an empire of great area—from Pasto to Maule—limited by the sea to the west and by the foothills leading to the low and hot Amazonian plain.

Far to the north of the dominions of the Mexican Civilization, above the broad and only sporadically populated deserts, lived other types of indigenous communities, organized in primitive tribes. Northern America, or the Atlantic sector of it where the European arrived, presented a scene very different from that in the territory of the kingdoms and empires of Mexico and the Andes. From these contrasting characteristics of geographic and human factors, which the Europeans confronted in establishing their colonies in the two Americas, can be inferred a complementary proposition of the Historical Space-Time Thesis.

Hegel, in a well-known generalization, wrote that while North America was colonized, South or Indo America was only conquered.

Insofar as that claim is true, it can serve as the basis for a brief analysis of the differences between the invasions of the Europeans in the New World, in terms of Toynbee's theory about challenge-response. To this we shall add an application of our thesis.

The physical challenge to which the colonizers of the North American zone responded, from which later arose their civilizing action, is that of extension. The English immigration moved in a lateral direction, without leaving the zone of the Northern hemisphere, and without encountering violent changes in soil or in climate. Nor did it clash with powerful, native politico-social organizations. "Neither in Virginia, nor anywhere in the colonies, were the English to discover, conquer, and loot Indian societies fabulously rich in rare treasures, such as the Spanish had found in Mexico or in Peru" (Charles and Mary Beard, *A Basic History of the United Staes,* Chap. III). From Merry Olde England, the Puritan Pilgrims went to New England, that is, to what was topographically and climatically like an extension of England. The colonizing population organized in corporations or commercial companies which, like that of Virginia, in 1606, "enjoyed all liberties, guarantees, and immunities," according to the Royal Charter; or like that of the "Mayflower Compact," in 1620, which formed "a civil political Body" for the purpose of making "just and equal laws" for the government of the Colony, whose members must use "their own liberties" (Beard, Appendix 1–2 and Chap. V).

Thus, the Anglo-Saxon emigration to North America—which was calculated between 1600 and 1770 at about 750,000 able bodied people, of whom "approximately two-thirds . . . belonged to families able to meet the cost of the journey and make a start of some kind in the new country. The other third composed of indentured servants, although lacking in money or property, had skills and talents which they could apply in making their way in 'a land of opportunity'" (Beards, *op. cit.,* Chap. II)—encountered a vast and fertile space. They merely had to adapt themselves to it. They did not encounter great differences in the seasons, nor in geographical characteristics, nor even in the view of the sky and its constellations. As a result, the primary task of the colonizer of North America was above all a reply to the *challenge of extension.* His historical consciousness, moved by a firm and rebellious religious faith and by a profound desire for freedom—fostered by the wide physical spaces—flourished from the first settlement of the Anglo-Saxons in the new lands of America, with their clear politico-social ideas of self-government, independence, and justice. Thus, their social consciousness of the North American historical space-time quickly emerged.

This space-time consciousness of the Northern European groups in North America was openly manifested in a persistent and progressive search for *territorial unity,* despite the often extreme disparity among the colonizing groups. To widen the space dominated, without disrupting it, is the true "manifest destiny" of their new historical sense.

North American colonization, then, was founded on the solid basis of agriculture, lumbering, and mining—not the mining of gold, which was to be discovered much later, but that of iron. The first cargo of ore was sent to England in 1608 by the Virginia colonists; and there too began the exploitation of tobacco and the Southern enslavement of the Negro. However, in New England and the Middle colonies —where slavery did not prosper—iron was worked actively before 1650, and the construction of ships for commerce came to be consequently one of the first flourishing industries.

The later conquest of the West involves the great adventure of the modern *conquest of distance* described by H. G. Wells in his famous book. The horse, the Conestoga wagon, the sailing ship, and the river barge were not enough for the advance of the colonizers across the vast forests, prairies, and deserts, in conflict here and there with the bitter resistance of the hostile but scattered Indian tribes. *To gain space by shortening time* became thus a spontaneous collective slogan for the survival and condominium of the North American people with their geographic milieu. This response stimulates, orients, and compels the rapid development of technical inventions and is the banner of accelerated evolution. It is the guiding political thought behind the actions of the United States in the forced retirement of the inconvenient Dutch and French neighbors, to the doubling of the size of the country by the Louisiana Purchase. Also in gaining Florida from Spain. Much later—1845, 1848, 1853—the expansion over Mexico added more than two and a half million square kilometers and confirmed the possession of fertile California. Later the purchase of Alaska from Russia provided for further expansion. And the North American People-Continent became defined within its boundaries.

However, to gain space by shortening time does not only mean, in the North American civilizing action, to take control of territory so as to keep inert a quantitatively vast area—as in the great Asian countries, or in Australia, Brazil, or in the Russia of the Czars, mere collectors of land—but to make it qualitatively dynamic, impressively fast. Thus the North American people define their historical velocity— their time—as the *raison d'être* of their national equilibrium, of their effort at hegemony. From this arises the growing creative power of their inventive technology—or their surpassing refinement and use of European inventions—characterized by an almost uninterrupted series of discoveries, destined directly or indirectly, to conquer their distances and to make more rapid their production, communications, and, in general, their way of living. From this arise, too, their early attempts to use the steam engine for river boats, weaving, milling, working metals, and the first patent for "a machine to make machines" given to David Wilkinson before 1800. There then follows a period of extraordinary technical victories: the railroad; modern navigation using the invention of the propeller, designed in Sweden; the mechanization of steelmaking; applications of electricity to the telegraph, telephone, illumination, and motor force; canals, tunnels, highways, bridges, and the "ferry boat"; concrete and steel applied to colossal vertical architecture; petroleum, asphalt, automobiles, linotype, typewriters, and calculating machines; machines for mixing, washing, freezing, voting, etc.; the movies, radio, television, atomic energy, and more—all inventions exhibiting high velocity. In contrast with the slow and precious techniques of other civilizations—the expertly and patiently worked arts and crafts, the monumental architecture of cathedrals and castles, the work of centuries in the slow development of Asia and Europe—the restless and willing North American spirit imposes upon its cultural expression a high degree of speed. Located in a virtually vacant continent, the manifest destiny of the dynamic unity of the continent influenced the national creative effort. This is the expression of its historical space-time.

Individual, social, religious, and political liberty along with a strong and actively joined territorial unity—under the emphatic and totalizing name of "America"—are the primary expressions of that North American manifest destiny, *E Pluribus Unum,* motive force of its galloping drive toward full civilization. The moneyed plutocracy, the "multimillionaire" appeared later; and to face him, their peculiar labor organizations. But, first there existed the free man, the citizen, and a coherent social unity built upon a democratic system of rights. The powerful economic interests of the slaveholders of the South were defeated by the robust principles and dominant tradition of liberty and unity. The Civil War not only defeated the secessionists with the banner of a high human right, that of freedom for the Negroes, but (and perhaps above all) saved the North American People-Continent from a dangerous division. In the accelerated rhythm of the North American historical space-time is ingrained its real essence; from basic work are raised all types of conduct, from these come the thought, science, and a pragmatic philosophy which "defines the truth as a principle of action." Thus, when the man of our epoch, coming from another European, Asiatic, or Indoamerican, space-time reality arrives in North America and submerges himself in it, he feels as if time has been accelerated: the result of a collective imposition of mind and action. Likewise, it is worth noting as a curiosity in passing— because it affects us—that the language of the slower and more backward neighbors to the South has found its way into the dictionaries and popular North American usage. They have adopted the Italian and Spanish word *pronto* and have chosen, as an ironic, pejorative contrast, the word *mañana* to allude to the Latin tendency to postpone and procrastinate.

In the field of recreation there has occurred a singularly expressive phenomenon: The movies increasingly attempt to gain and distract the imagination of the spectator, making it unnecessary for him to use his imagination at all. The North American cinema seldom uses the offstage scenes, so often found in classical theaters. It is virtually an antithesis of the Oriental theater, where the spectator must imagine much that goes on outside of his view. The humorous and comic movies—the admirable Walt Disney and his colleagues—attempt to anticipate everything imaginary, in the realms of possible and of the impossible, anxious to identify their audacious phantasy with that "illogical logic" of dreams, to use a strictly Freudian phrase. In it they combine movement, animation, color, alacrity, music, and the absurd in a new dimension of tempestuous and jubilant harmony. This sublimated way of gaining space and time extends to other levels and a great variety of forms in the North American diffusion of culture: in its journalism and its advertising; in its teaching; in its "business behavior"; in its university "campuses"; and in the abundant distribution of "micro-films," encyclopedic publications, and "digests" and abridgements on every subject, whether science, art, literature, technology, philosophy, or sex. . . .

That historical velocity which typifies North American civilization brings one to think, ingenuously and admiringly, of a vigorous "young people," of a "new race." But the "new" and the "young" in the North American comes only from his stage in and his consciousness of his space-time, inseparable from his civilizing energy and impetus. To verify this, remember that the people of the United States are descendants of the most ancient races of Europe and Africa. Its white population comes from the old Indo-European body, from the ever so ancient cultures of the Old World. From England, and other countries of the West—and a little of Africa and something of Asia— came the blood of that new nation, a People-Continent, full of juvenile vitality, in a recent migratory transfer which increases every day. But in the new space, there arises an inseparable, new, dynamic conception of time, and both bring about a distinct and accelerated continuity of social rhythm. Only 350 years ago did that uninterrupted process of migration begin and only a little more than 100 years ago did it take on massive proportions. In spite of that, in every moment of this period, whether in the last century or in this one, yesterday or today, the civilized man who became part of the North American community identified immediately with the high pressure and resolute pace of life. And when he turned his eyes to the space-time from which he had come, he viewed that pace, reduced and slow, from the broadened angle of his new historical dimension.

It is in this thesis—and it is worthwhile insisting on this—that rejuvenation is explained by the awakening of a particular space-time consciousness as the historical determinant. However, such a consciousness can also be produced without a people or race changing its geographic location. When this occurs, the people or the area becomes dynamic and is rejuvenated by a new conscious vision of its environment and the possibilities within it. Such brusque changes are like the "qualitative jumps" of the Hegelian dialectic. Raymond Aron, in affirming that in the concept of history "that which is decisive is the consciousness of the past and the willingness to define one's position in it," recognizes also that "in this sense, one understands the formula of Hegel: the only truly historic communities are those which work out a science of their development." Yes, but this is inseparable from a consciousness of the space-time which is defined, which is activated, which is accelerated; and which also can be attenuated and extinguished.

Islam and its rapid mobilization—in contrast with the initial slowness of Medieval Europe—developed a sudden consciousness of its historical space-time and from it came the imperative of its rapid expansion. The first centuries of its impulse and predominance, from the Indian Ocean to the Atlantic, are, however, as astonishing as its later slowing down and deterioration, in spite of no change in the area and the race which had realized such a magnificent cultural triumph. Also, in the old and enormous territory of Russia, the phlegmatic Slavic race was able to convert itself into the menacing "young Russia" by a renascent consciousness of its historical space-time, exalted and pugnacious. The imminent developments of China and India are also proof of the accelerated recuperation of rhythm of a space-time consciousness, once brilliantly manifest, and subsequently lost.

The historical drama of the geographic setting is something else, very different from that of the colonizers of North America, in the conquering efforts of the Spaniards and Portuguese which won the greater part of the New World. They—and this consideration of a geographic nature is not to be overlooked for a proper understanding— in their exploring had to cross diagonally towards the south, passing from one latitude to another, and confront, in an unknown land, *geoclimatic challenges* the rigor of which was unknown by the Anglo-Saxons who came to New England, and the same time to respond to *challenges of the social environment,* particularly that of the warlike resistance of old and populous national organizations. The obstinate Iberian adventurers met surprise and difficulty at every turn: the jungles, plains, and arduous deserts; the high altitudes with light and unbreathable air; the strange constellations in the southern skies; the fauna, the flora, and man.

Perhaps because of having to confront such obstacles and also because they were of another spirit, motives, religious creed, and country of origin from those of the rival colonizers of the North, the behavior and projections of those two epochal conquests diverged notably. The encounter of the Western Christian Civilization with the societies of America, therefore, has dissimilar appearance and historical results. The Iberian one, which covered an area including the Antilles, Mexico, Central, and South America, offers many inconfutible aspects, depending on the various geographic zones and the different levels of culture of the native social groups. These included everything from communities with the most rudimentary organization to completely organized civilizations. In terms of climates and topography, they varied from the low and humid tropical territories of unpassable jungles, to the highest, driest, and coldest mountain plateaus.

The unconnected events of the conquest of Indoamerica are the subjugation—due to a superiority in arms—of the great empires upon whose territories Spain established from the first half of the sixteenth century its major viceroyalties: Mexico and Peru. In these, as in the other lands submitted to Iberian control, a labor system based on the total servitude of the conquered peoples was established. Since the principal objective of the colonial enterprise was the discovery and exploitation of gold and silver, the agricultural economy in which the American societies had achieved extraordinary results ceased to be the basis of production for the new empire and was supplanted by a colonial form of feudal regime and an artificial centralized mercantilism, the basis of which was the mining of those incessantly exported precious metals.

These events explain why—and this is an outstanding example of the Spanish lack of foresight and the great defects of its improvised and unilateral economy in America—the natural products, such as the useful and then unique Peruvian fertilizer called "island guano," were not exported to Europe during the colonial period, in spite of having been invented and widely used in the efficient agrarian technology of the Incas. One can presume that if from the sixteenth or seventeenth centuries Spain had set out foresightedly to transform its agriculture and that of Europe with a monopoly and distribution of so powerful a fertilizer, a radical technological change of profound economic consequences would have resulted. At the same time, Spanish political influence would have achieved an imperial solidity and power of unforeseeable proportions; much greater and less ephemeral than that which a wealth of gold and silver gave Spain. This "revolution" in European agriculture came only in the nineteenth century, after the independence of Indoamerica—through the efforts of the Germans and British—when guano was considered along with electricity and steam one of the "marvels" of the epoch. It is well to note that many of the first chroniclers of the Conquest of America—it is enough to mention Garcilaso de la Vega—described in detail the methods of fertilization known since antiquity by the Peruvians and revealed the great importance of guano and the jealous governmental defense of the marine birds that produced it. But it was not exported to Europe for three centuries, until after the epochal visit to America of the sage Alexander von Humboldt. In the same way, the windmill—

in the sixteenth century one of the most necessary auxiliary machines of human labor—was not brought to America.

Only the aboriginal human beings—and in the torrid regions the imported Negro—were the exclusive and unpaid instrument of labor. The Iberian colonizer did not come to America to work the land or the mines with his hands, but to make millions of serfs and slaves work. The *repartimientos* and the *encomiendas* of Indians, which were characteristic of the feudal mode of the economy of the colony, resulted, as is known, in bitter struggles among the conquerors, in spite of royal ordinances which were issued in favor of the Indians.

In low and hot areas, such as those of the Caribbean, where the natives were exterminated in a few years, and in Brazil, where they were in short supply, Negroes replaced the Indians or were used as additional laborers. But in the high regions, inhospitable to the African, the inhabitant of the mountain had to be preserved for utilitarian purposes. There have been, and still are, mines in America, perhaps among the richest, where because of their altitude, no other man could work. This fact explains why the Indians of the mountains were those most protected by the Laws of the Indies, because their labor was irreplaceable.

The authoritarian politico-social regime imposed on the viceroyalties was in conformity with the economic one. Absolutism and privilege and the religious intolerance, regimented by the Inquisition, consolidated a rigid system of restrictions supported by force. No idea of liberty, no roots of local government could prosper in Iberian Colonial America. The jurisdictional divisions of government and of Church, many of them capriciously established, left a legacy of regional separatisms which later would give respectability to nationalist isolation, the greatest obstacle to the unification of our peoples. In contrast to the North American colonizers, those of this part of the hemisphere, under the pretext of great distances, separated instead of uniting. Spanish lack of foresight in this respect was even greater than that of the Portuguese, who in Brazil left the lesson of using great territorial areas as the basis of order and power.

Taking up once again the thesis of Toynbee, we can say that the response to the *physical and human challenges* which the Spanish conqueror encountered in America was only partial and is found still in the process of completion. As a result, the Indoamerican historical space-time is still more objective than subjective; more a prospect than a unanimous social consciousness, properly speaking. This advance towards definition is made with the uncertain rhythm of development, in which there are various velocities, necessarily converging toward a future fusion and unity.

Thus in Indoamerica there exist in juxtaposition all the levels of societal evolution, from the most elemental primitiveness to the organizational forms of the most progressive civilized life. In many cases, within each of the political boundaries which divide the Indo-american nation into twenty states, there exist in complete and perceptible divisions those various stages of social development. It is worthwhile reiterating here that he who travels from the city of Mexico to its most retarded Indian provinces, and even more from Rio de Janeiro, Buenos Aires, Lima, Bogotá, Caracas, or La Paz, towards the Amazonian area, sees everything from cities concentrating the modes of the civilized life of our century to tribal groups of a most incipient kind. It is as if by the roads of history one comes to the mysteries of pre-history, passing on the way each of the intermediate stages.

In spite of this, and underneath the space-time disparity, there exists a profound root of unity. Geography imposes its formidable challenge, but this, while dividing, also unifies. It is certain that the European and *criollo* of yesterday, and their contemporary descendants, struggled and still struggle to overcome the physical environment, and their victory has been and is relative. However, with the mountain, the jungle, and the desert unconquered, there remains the man who lives there, far from the average levels of modern culture, though already aware of them.

Over the heads of the semi-nude savages of the immense Amazonian jungle, scarcely explored by the missionaries of civilization, there frequently pass airplanes, even though the savages have not seen a cart pulled by a horse or oxen, a railroad, or an automobile. One can believe, therefore, that the great work of relating, educating, and incorporating those men into the centers of culture is what must be done, or rather that it is already under way. Its approach seems to be announced in the prodigious accomplishments of science and technology of our epoch, which will aid in overcoming those aspects of nature which are still unconquerable. This idea, developed from an opinion expressed by Einstein in a conversation with me in Princeton, in March, 1947, is a stimulating message: "In the impenetrable jungles of your America, or in the Polar tundras, the new atomic energy can carry out things which have not been possible with steam or with electricity."

The potential richness of the still unexploited American lands, their wide, unpopulated, but propitious spaces, and the proven adaptive capacity of the Indoamerican man, still virtually untouched by culture, offer guarantee and hope of the possibility of arousing their historical consciousness. For its definition, it is necessary to consider the strange time problem of our continent: the meeting of its two pasts. One proceeds from its unique origins in terms of physical reality and human content, the second comes from the other side of the world in the currents and influences of the Western Christian Civilization which has been implanted and is dominant here.

In fact, there is an American past which starts with its telluric formation, and includes in its mystery the origin of the American man, whose cultural apex, also past, was shown in those brilliant, extinct civilizations incorporated in the scheme of Toynbee in the hierarchy of those civilizations which have made history. As the tenacious investigations of the archaeologists and anthropologists verify and evaluate the greatness of these civilizations, there are growing from the obscure background of their unknown origins conjectures of other unknown preceding cultures. These present the pertinacious man of science grave and disquieting questions: Are the so-called "savage" inhabitants of the valleys of the Orinoco and Amazon the distant heirs of lost civilizations? What is the origin of the Mayas and what explains their great knowledge of astronomy and mathematics? When did men go up into and adapt to the Andean highlands to the point of becoming "a climatic-physiological variety of the human race," capable of creating a civilization between 3,000 and almost 5,000 meters above sea level? These and other unanswered questions, aroused by the monumental ruins recently discovered and the indecipherable inscriptions, the startling examples of art, the Inca quipus, the remains of San Agustin, of Chavín and Tiahuanaco, leave us, according to the eminent Indian archaeologist Julio Tello, "on the edge of an ocean which has never been navigated, and where those of us who consider ourselves to be most advanced are merely wading at the edges."

That Indoamerican past crosses in our developing historical consciousness with the other strong and fecund past of Western Civilization. From this merger arises one of the essential creators of our spiritual definition and of our collective psychology, which is today only dawning. However, simultaneously, there are appearing new determinants of that space-time consciousness in the cultural contributions of the present American: that which an intelligent Spanish writer has designated the "first cries" of an artistic definition of Indoamerica: the Mexican painters, the poetry of [Cesar] Vallejo and Garbriela Mistral. Many other names could be added to these. . . .

In describing the limits of the Western Christian Civilization, Toynbee extends its confines beyond the other hemisphere also called "Western." He thus includes the Americas. However, in the brief analysis contained in the second part of this chapter, we note the characteristics of the North American historical space-time, its own typology, and above all its unequalled rhythm. Taking that into account, the last question of this essay is based on the position of Toynbee concerning the civilizations which appear by separating from those that are their "principal body." Thus, if we consider to be in this category the origins of Orthodox Russia and those of Korea and Japan, we must ask: Will there not similarly be the advent of an American civilization as a branch in the process of separation from the Western Christian one?

With a reiteration of the words *in process of separation,* it would be enlightening to refer first to the name and significance of the probable historic question which is here being raised. Is there an American or New World Civilization, not North American nor of the United States, but an emerging civilization exempt from the colors, aspects, and circumstances of present economic and political conditions— which in history become transitory—and projected as an announcement and promise of the future?

To answer this question we can take the occasion to examine the American evolution starting with the civilization and conquest of the north and the south. This will offer the undeniable proof that upon arriving in the New World, Western Civilization, established there, but influenced by the geographic and human environment, began more or less quickly to become individual and to differentiate itself from its original nature.

Furthermore, to the probable objection contained in the well-known argument concerning religions and languages, considered as powerful links between Europe and America, it can be answered that such links have continued to exist for long periods between societies which have separated. Thus, Orthodox Catholicism continues to link the Greeks and Russians, in spite of the formal separation of the clergy, and Buddhism, as the trunk faith, unites the two separated branches of the civilizations of the Far East. Furthermore, if it is argued that the Indo-European languages dominant in America remain united, in spite of their notorious differences in accent, slang, and phrasing, again the question arises: Are not the vital movements and the preponderant influences of the environment stronger than these linguistic links or than those of race itself, because of the innumerable mixtures taking place in the Americas—even more in the South than in the North? That is to say, is not the consciousness that in being formed of space-time, the motif of the drama of our part of the World and the motif of our history, the most important?

We have already described some of the manifestations of the North American space-time consciousness, its rapid rate of life and labor, its activist and rapid creative capacity. We have compared it with the slower rhythm of European civilization. Transferring this parallel to Indoamerica, are there not greater similarities between the European rhythm and ours? The answer is affirmative. However, logic resists the idea that this will always remain the same. There are evident signs of a notable and progressive change in methodologies and habits throughout Indoamerica. Although this change could be called the effect of the brilliant North American civilizing velocity, it is in any case manifest. From this there arises an even graver doubt about our fatal North Americanization, summed up in the memorable and melancholic question of the poet: "How many millions of us men will be speaking English?"

But beyond all that is perishable or changing in the prolonged pathway of history—economic systems, political regimes, military predominance, imperialisms, and so on—and without failing to recognize the relative validity of the most fearful conjectures, it is possible to think a little philosophically with less pessimism. The pressing cultural influences have a more profound sense and radius. Even if Indoamerica, still divided and disoriented, is only beginning to achieve the coordination of its spiritual forces into a collective personality, the incessant increase of its population—comparatively much greater than that of North America—and the growing fusion of its component ethnic elements, announcing what in a happy phrase José Vasconcelos has called "the cosmic race," it is still logical to attempt other predictions. It is not impossible that, for example, in those already available evidences of our esthetic-social values—folklore, popular music, and dances, in the stylization of our artistic past, or in the superior creations of the innovative Indoamerican painting movement commencing in Mexico—there are already currents of influence projecting from our area towards North America. Nor can it be forgotten that in both Americas, in contrast to overpopulated Europe, whose power is fed by the required resources of colonialism, the vast and wealthy geographic space is still the vacant promised land of hundreds of millions of men yet to come. Those of today, on one or another side of our present cultural boundaries, will be only the distant precursors of that truly new world, the nature of which we do not suspect.

It is possible to transpose, finally, our known formula deduced from the contingent Inter-American economic and political reality of these days, to the lasting fields of the philosophy of history, and repeat that "the United States needs Indoamerica as much as it [Indoamerica] needs the United States." If this reciprocal necessity of relation is accepted as a premise, and is elevated to the cultural hierarchy inalienable for the genesis of a new civilization, it is not incongruent to consider the decisive factors distinguishing the contribution of the two Americas. Nor is it right to assert that the technological, positive, material predominance of the gigantic and rapid North American civilizing *tour de force* is insufficient to produce what Toynbee calls "a miracle" of a new society, autonomous, whole, and universal. The things which are lacking in it are outside of its dimension and appear within ours.

The American or New World Cvilization, if it is to be, must bring together the conceptual values of the *pronto* and the *mañana*—action and lassitude, rapidity and repose—but also, the deep roots of the past. It will have to perceive and confront the summits of the future without ceasing to pay attention to the multiple streams from the past which feed with eternal strength the "brusque mutations" of the "dynamic of civilizations." Thus, the question and hope remain intact.

PART TWO

Fundamentals of Aprismo

THIS SECTION DEALS WITH HAYA DE LA TORRE'S IDEAS ON THE nature and role of the Alianza Popular Revolucionaria Americana, or Aprista Party. Most of the selections presented here were written in the 1920s. The only exception is the first, taken from his book *Treinta Años del Aprismo* which presents his brief retrospective summary of the significance of Apra, written about thirty years after its formation. The second selection is the first, widely circulated public statement of the program and objectives of the Alianza, first published in English in the British periodical *The Labour Monthly* in 1926 and reprinted here from that source. The other selections are all taken from the book *El Antimperialismo y el Apra,* Haya de la Torre's major doctrinal work and one of his few books not consisting of collected articles. Chapters II through VI of that book are translated here.

The ideas set forth in this section are among the most important contributions which Haya de la Torre has made to Latin American practical politics. He describes in considerable detail the need for a specifically Latin American type of revolutionary party, and what the nature of that party should be. He argues that it must be a multiclass party, joining the urban workers, the peasants, and the middle class, all of whom suffer in one way or another from both imperialism and the semifeudal economies and societies then prevalent in the Latin American countries. He insists strongly that there is no room in Latin America for a purely workingclass party, such as that envisioned by the Socialists and Communists, because of the smallness and weakness of the urban proletariat, and because the initiative for fundamental change has not come from this class.

Haya de la Torre insists that the new multiclass party must concentrate its program upon three major struggles. It must give first priority to the fight against imperialism, a menace common to all of the countries, and this fight must be the basis of the espousal of Latin American economic nationalism.

However, the struggle against imperialism cannot be confined merely to protesting the specific acts of aggression of the imperialist powers in Latin America. Haya maintains that imperialism is essentially a phenomenon of economic penetration by the great industrial powers into the underdeveloped nations, and that it is able to function because of its alliance with and the ultimate subordination of the national oligarchies of Latin America, who control the political life and government of those countries. Therefore, the objective of the Aprista Party must be the seizure of power in each and all of the Latin American nations, because only through governmental control can the party strike at the economic roots of imperialism in the various countries. Thus, the second element in the program of the multiclass party must be the taking of political power away from the traditional oligarchies, and the subsequent destruction of the economic basis of the oligarchical class through the expropriation of its landholdings and their distribution on a cooperative basis to the landless peasantry. At the same time that it was expropriating the possessions of the traditional ruling class, the Aprista government would be nationalizing the holdings of the foreign firms which are the expression and essence of imperialism.

Finally, the multiclass Aprista Party must be dedicated to the economic and political unification of the Latin American, or Indoamerican, countries. Only if such unification is achieved will the countries of the area be strong enough to stand up as a group to the United States, and to avoid the repercussions and restrictions of freedom of action which the revolutionary government of Mexico, for instance, had experienced. As a result of this objective, it was necessary that the Aprista Party be a continental organization, with branches in each country, cooperating with one another to the greatest degree possible and rallying public opinion throughout the hemisphere in support of whichever one of the countries was under particular pressure from the United States or any other imperialist power.

The impact of this range of ideas has been very profound in Latin America. Although no continent-wide Aprista Party emerged, a series of parties espousing the Aprista ideals of a multiclass party dedicated to the struggle against imperialism, based on the assertion of economic nationalism and leading the fight for the destruction of the power of the traditional oligarchies, has developed in the region. In addition to these parties fully incorporating Haya's basic political concepts, a number of other political groups have also adopted some of them in conjunction with other ideas in their programs. Most of the Christian Democratic parties of recent years have stressed the multiclass idea, as well as the need for a joint effort on behalf of economic nationalism and the overthrow of oligarchical power, although they have probably borrowed more from the example of the Aprista-like parties than directly from Haya de la Torre's doctrines. Some of the older parties, such as the Liberal Party of Honduras have borrowed indirectly from Haya's ideas, through their contacts with the Aprista Party and its counterparts in Venezuela, Costa Rica, and the School of Democratic Orientation and Training maintained in Costa Rica by Apra, Accion Democratica, MNR, the Paraguayan Partido Febrerista and other allied parties.

I

FORERUNNERS OF APRISMO

APRISTA ANTI-IMPERIALISM HAS ITS PRECURSORS. THE DISTANT North American movement of Bryanism [Populism] of the turn of the century—promotor in the United States of civic campaigns—had repercussions at the time in this part of the hemisphere. Bryan brought up-to-date, or Americanized, with unusual semantics a terminology which more than thirty years later we made our own. Here in Indoamerica, young men of the brilliant intellectual generation of 1900, from both sides of the Rio de la Plata, were alert to the campaigns of Bryan and exalted Latin Americanism and achieved merited fame: José Enrique Rodó, José Ingenieros, Manuel Ugarte, Alfredo Palacios, Leopldo Lugones, Alberto Ghiraldo. Other fellow-countrymen, already famous in the field of letters, such as Rubén Darío, Enrique José Varona, Sanín Cano, Carlos Arturo Torres, Alejandro Korn, Amado Nervo, Enrique Molina, Pedro Henríquez Ureña, José Santos Chocano, José Vasconcelos, José M. Vargas Vila, and Antonio Caso, agreed with them in terms of the Bolivarian ideals of continental unity. Others followed them closely: Joaquín García Monge, Alfonso Reyes, Alberto Masferrer, Carlos Vicuña Fuentes, Emilio Frugoni, Omar Dengo, and many more.

Outstanding among them was the publicist and orator of Buenos Aires, Manuel Ugarte. Because of his rousing speech-making tours through the length of Indoamerica, he rejuvenated the unionist invocation of Bolívar—which had been denied by the militarists and the nineteenth-century criollo politicians—and foresaw the danger of North American imperial expansion. Undoubtedly much influenced

---

Excerpt from chapter on "El Antimperialismo Aprista" in *Treinta Años del Aprismo*.

by the crusades of Bryan—whose impressive notices, according to Ugarte's letter to me in 1926, aroused his enthusiasm in his adolescent years—Ugarte proposed to do the same here: tour our territory and admonish its people also about the risks of North American imperialism.

Ugarte—without understanding the basic economic significance of the imperialist phenomenon, in spite of his declared support of socialism, and without proposing to undertake the task of organizing a political force—was, nevertheless, correct, in his logical premise: that is, that the expansion of the United States has come about as an inevitable consequence of its power, and that power is a result of its continental unity. If the forty-eight North American states had been divided into an equal number of independent "fatherlands," "sovereign," each rivaling one another—with all their respective politicking militarisms and their jingoistic agitators—they would be no more powerful than are the weak Indoamerican states: weak because they are disunited. Or if the great slave holding plantation owners of the Southern United States had achieved through Lee and the North American reactionary militarism the secession which they sought with the Civil War of 1861 to 1865, that continental federation would not exist as a great power. Lincoln—symbol and chief of the civil government, representative of the Yankee democracy in arms—defeated Lee and his army defending an exploiting class. In defeating them, Lincoln not only imposed the abolition of slavery—in itself a significant human objective—but saved the North American unity, an objective which has been, for the republic of the North, a condition of liberty and democracy since independence.

During the first thirteen years of this century, Ugarte crossed the Indoamerican continent various times, calling for unity and demonstrating the inferior condition of the small, weak, "Balkanized" countries, in contrast to those continental, strong federated nations. He encountered applause and some resistance, but also, to a marked degree, warm sympathies from the students. Miguel de Unammuno—the best and most influential Spanish friend of our peoples—wrote him from Salamanca in 1906:

> It seems to me a splendid dream, your dream of a Latin American confederation, and bear in mind that when I call it a dream I do not wish to say that I consider it unfeasible in a more or less distant future. Dreams are often the precursors of realities.

The echoes of the message of Ugarte, however, fell on deaf ears when the flaming world of 1914 to 1918 closed a whole era and announced the advent of a new age. Then, with the University Reform, there arose in 1918 from the three-hundred-year-old classrooms of the University of Córdoba the most transcendant movement of intellectual renovation occurring in Indoamerica since Independence. A brave and intrepid generation in their twenties spoke to the Indoamerican students and workers in an unaccustomed language but one easily understood. It proclaimed "the sacred right of insurrection" and the watchword of sacrifice as "their best stimulation" and "the spiritual redemption of the young of America" as "its only recompense."

The University Reform, in essence the first cry of emancipation from our colonial mentality—herald of a new consciousness of Indoamerica—expressively called the old universities and their stagnant pedagogical methods spiritual viceroyalties. Against them—"secular refuge of the mediocre, support of the ignorant, sure hospitalization of the invalid"—arose the youth, searching for a way to a distinctly Indoamerican culture which had been closed by a university feudalism, that sustainer of the economic-social feudalism prevailing among our peoples. From that true student revolution, rapidly propagated throughout the continent, arose the doctrine that the mission of the reformed universities is to struggle against the social danger of the illiteracy of our masses and to secure the rights of the people to culture as the first step towards true democratic justice. The reform created the popular universities and inaugurated an epoch of growing student cooperation with the working classes and interest in their economic problems.

In Peru, where the movement achieved singular dimensions—provoking a transformation in the oligarchic teaching of the Universidad Mayor de San Marcos, bulwark of the Lima feudal plutocracy—its first victory culminated with the National Congress of Students of Cuzco in 1920. The Popular University was established and soon after honored with the name of Gonzalez Prada. In this university was molded a dynamic united front of laborers and intellectuals, which received a baptism of fire on May 23, 1923, and from its ranks came the founders of Apra.

II

THE UNIQUE MESSAGE OF APRISMO

BECAUSE APRISMO IS AN INTEGRAL DOCTRINE WHICH IS TRULY NEW and as such, in its beginning, used a new lexicon, it has been open to attack. This semantic and apparently weak phase of development provoked long and intense polemics over deciphering the confusions and errors which, innocently or premediatedly, have been circulated concerning our positions. We must remember that from its beginning, Aprismo presented new views of the social problems of Indoamerica. In the beginning, necessarily, the terminology then in vogue was used, that is, the jargon of those it was rebutting. This explains the compulsive nature of a long preliminary process of definition—which it would not be wrong to call semantic—of its basic concepts.

Aprismo can point to a peculiarity of origin distinguishing it from other similar movements and doctrines in Indoamerica. This is not only because of its characteristic of Bolivarian militancy—in this glorious name lies the foundation of our singular advocacy of continental unionism—but also to the singularity of its predecessors. These can be found in the vigorous youth movement which, in the period of 1918–1923, started and diffused in all our republics the University Reform. From this movement, we founders of Apra took vigorous ideas and transformed them into normative concepts: that of freeing our generation from the colonial mentality and of joining the intellectuals and workers to undertake together a bold effort of democratic civilization and to confederate our peoples and obtain for them economic justice, without loss of personal liberty.

Those two innovating objectives—never suggested until then by a political movement—necessarily outraged tradition and broke the

Introduction from *Treinta Años de Aprismo,* April, 1954.

foreign molds, jealously guarded and practiced, in a more or less deformed manner, by the criollo epigones of a culture partially transplanted, but not assimilated, in our schools and academies, as well as in governments, parliaments, and parties. The Aprista propositions linked, with logical correlation, in a polemic line that vassalage of intelligence and structure that had reduced these universities to mere schools repeating imported knowledge with the political imitations which were formed—on the right and the left—by our statesmen and leaders of opinion, utilizing theories brought from abroad.

Without these patterns and dies, it would have been unthinkable and even heretical in Indoamerica to conceive of or to attempt any assessment *from here,* and not *from Europe,* of our unique historical reality, of our exclusive sociological problem. Our continent was still the "country of reflection" alluded to by Hegel. On its soil there had been scions, shoots, and plantings—some accidental—of all the ideas, philosophic sects, literary novelties, and party tendencies from the Old World. Thus as we had nineteenth-century spokesmen for the utilitarianism of Bentham and Mill, of the Saintsimonian tendency, and the extensive positivist influence of Comte, of materialism in all of its forms, and of spiritualism of various kinds, we were also not without monarchists, jacobins, anarchists, and the rest. All with their respective heterodoxies and contradictors. In the same way, with the turn of the century and the world being set afire with the first great war, and through it Marxism being propagated, the Bolshevik echo was sounded, and shortly there swarmed alongside those influences the totalitarians, the racists, and the Jingoist corruptions. But all were always imitations. Consequently, what was necessary was an emergence from the European patterns, and an end to being mislead by their predetermined methods of thought.

This signifies how Aprismo negated Marx without resorting to European anti-Marxism and without reproducing the stereotyped confutations, and opposed Communism without declaring ourselves ultramontane or National Socialists. Of course, such a posture of complete independence was not understood. The most obvious and facile way to place us and to define us was to return to the foreign catalog and not give up the categories which had been learned there. If we objected to imperialism, we *must* be Communists; if we contradict Communism, we *must* be fascists. Beyond those immutable pigeonholes, "mental colonialism," hidden both in self-proclaimed "revolutionary" bands and in the ranks of reaction, could not permit any other alternatives.

It was more difficult for us to rebut logically another dilemma as simplistic and falacious as that. I refer to the handy sophism of attributing to our insurgency against the "mental colonialism" prevalent in Indoamerica, an intention of denigrating without exception the illustrious cultural values which Western Europe has transmitted to us. Thus in a manner similar to that which included us in the nomenclature of the social doctrines known in the great capitalist countries, they reasoned falsely in this case: to gain mental emancipation from Europe is to deny the culture which nourished us. They said this in almost exactly those words. Not only were we attacked by the loyal conservatives, supporters of the old transatlantic intellectual patronage, but also by their antagonists, renovators who, like the conservatives, were impassioned and equally indurate. Once again we exposed them and defied this attack on both flanks. For the one side, we opposed what was a splendid and imperishable lighthouse, and for the other an inheritance of a decadent society, loaded with unequaled trophies the supplantation of which they predicted with the aurora of a promising new order.

From this hopeful and optimistic angle José Carlos Mariátegui set straight, roundly and firmly, those who thought him Europeanized: "I think that there is no salvation for Indoamerica without the science and thought of Western Europe." In agreeing, we coincide in principle, but we place this on a relativist condition: yes, European science and thought, but only when "digested"—this a happy choice of words which is worth paraphrasing from the well-known philosopher Whitehead. That is to say, assimilated, metabolized by a dialectical process, flowing, something which comes and continues, and by a relation of space and time, which determines and transforms.

In the Nordic autumn of 1930, I wrote from Berlin a few succinct lines incidentally defining positions. I alluded to those who ignore or underestimate our distinction between unconditional acceptance of a transplanted culture, entirely exported and imposed on a dissimilar environment, and the recognition of it as one of the decisive precursory influences, for the development of something new and unique. All of this in laconic philosophical reference, with regard to our political organization and—it must be said—with the intentional dedication to those on the right and left, who execrate us as reprobates, irreverent before our European patrons. These expressions, included in an occasional note of commentary, published almost twenty-five years ago in Mexico, I humbly value like few others. Perhaps this is so because their backdrop adds significance: "They forget that Europe is Europe and America is America, and that in this epoch of relativism, the concepts of time and space, and the new one of space-time are revolutionizing all concepts, beginning with the concept of the universe itself."

These words explain the principal basis of the political philosophy of Aprismo and its indivisible link with the philosophy of history. If this cardinal relationship is forgotten or ignored, our program and our language become incomprehensible. The simple premise that "Europe is Europe and America is America" and that each demarcates different, distinct, four-dimensional fields of space-time—with their respective and inalienable grades of movement or rhythm of historic evolution—is our dialectical basis.

From this basis are derived concrete propositions which follow logically, corroborated also by simple reasoning dictated by common sense: If the problems of Europe and of America are different, their appropriate solutions must be different too. The proof of this truth coincides with that derived from a still wider vision of our cultural horizon, inseparable from the European one giving it birth; but dissimilar due to the transfer of the civilization of the Old World to the New, which in being separated, by the dynamic of its development "negates and continues" its antecedents:

"It is as dangerous to live imitating as it is to completely break with and simply deny all precedents. The biological, the vital, the profound, and renovating norm is to repeat the eternal teaching of nature, which drops its mature fruit, the born child, the dense egg, so that they follow only the upward line of life which by negations thus is emancipated and continues eternal."

To include and keep in mind this point of departure of the doctrine of Aprismo is to explain it all. The relevant fact about the social singularity of Indoamerica is that, for it, "the formulas of solution do not have any place and cannot be adjusted to the well-known European ideological molds." Thus, since 1928 it has been clearly stated: "The presentation of this problem, complex and characteristic, is the historical reason for the existence of Apra."

III

WHAT IS THE A.P.R.A.?

THE STRUGGLE ORGANIZED IN LATIN AMERICA AGAINST YANKEE IM-perialism, by means of an international united front of manual and intellectual workers with a program of common action, that is the A.P.R.A., the four initial letters of the following words: Alianza Popular Revolucionaria Americana (Popular Revolutionary American Alliance).

Its Program

The program of international action of the A.P.R.A has five general points which serve as a basis for the national sections: (1) Action of the countries of Latin America against Yankee Imperialism. (2) The political unity of Latin America. (3) The nationalization of land and industry. (4) The Internationalization of the Panama Canal. (5) The solidarity of all the oppressed people and classes of the world.

Its Organization

The A.P.R.A is a young organization formed by the young men of the new generation of manual and intellectual workers of Latin America. It was founded in 1924 and has organized sections in various countries in Latin America and also in Europe, where the number of anti-Imperialist Latin American students is pretty large. The principal sections of the A.P.R.A. are at present working in Mexico, Buenos Aires, Central America, Paris and other places in which for political reasons the action of these sections is not publicly allowed. A Central Executive Committee directs the action of all the sections.

The Labour Monthly [London], December, 1926, pp. 756–759; also included, in Spanish, in *El Antimperialism y el APRA* as "Que es el A.P.R.A.?"

The United Front

The A.P.R.A. organizes the great Latin American Anti Imperialist united front and works to include in its ranks all those who in one way or another have struggled and are still struggling against the North American danger in Latin America. Until 1923 this danger was regarded as a possible struggle of races—the Saxon and the Latin races—as a "conflict of cultures," or as a question of nationalism. From the "Gonzalez Prada" Popular University of Peru a new conception of the problem has arisen: the economic conception. In 1924 the First Pan American Anti Imperialist League was formed in Mexico and also the Latin American Union in Buenos Aires. The Anti Imperialist Leagues were the first endeavor of the international united front of workers, peasants and students against Yankee Imperialism. The Latin American Union was founded as the Anti Imperialist Frente Unico of the Intellectuals. As a matter of fact, the Anti Imperialist Leagues have no fixed political program, but only that of resistance to Imperialism, and the Latin American Union has simply intellectual activity. The A.P.R.A. was founded in 1924, with a program of revolutionary and political action, and it invites all the scattered forces to form themselves in a single united front.

The Class Struggle Against Imperialism

The history of the political and economic relations between Latin America and the United States, especially the experience of the Mexican Revolution, lead to the following conclusions:

(1) The governing classes of the Latin American countries—landowners, middle class or merchants—are allies of North American Imperialism.

(2) These classes have the political power in our countries, in exchange for a policy of concessions, of loans, of great operations which they—the capitalists, landowners or merchants and politicians of the Latin American dominant classes—share with Imperialism.

(3) As a result of this alliance the natural resources which form the riches of our countries are mortgaged or sold, and the working and agricultural classes are subjected to the most brutal servitude. Again, this alliance produces political events which result in the loss of national sovereignty; Panama, Nicaragua, Cuba, Santo Domingo, are really protectorates of the United States.

The International Struggle Against Imperialism

As the problem is common to all the Latin American countries, in which the dominant classes are allies of Imperialism in joint exploitation of the working classes, it is not an isolated or national question, but is international among the twenty Latin American republics. But the governing classes encourage divisions among these republics, assisting the Imperialist plan which fears Latin American unity (covering eight millions of square miles and about ninety millions of inhabitants). The governing classes stir up national feeling and national conflicts, as in the case of Peru against Chile, Brazil against Argentina, Ecuador and Colombia against Peru, etc. Every time that the United States intervenes as an "amicable mediator," they arrange matters purposely so that no definite settlement can be arrived at which might produce a principle of unification. The recent question of Tacna and Arica between Peru and Chile is the clearest demonstration of this policy of Imperialism.

Imperialism Cannot be Overthrown Without the
Political Unity of Latin America

The experience of history, especially that of Mexico, shows that the immense power of American Imperialism cannot be overthrown without the unity of the Latin American countries. Against this unity the national dominant classes, middle class, landowners, etc., whose political power is almost always buttressed by the agitation of nationalism or patriotism of countries hostile to their neighbors, are ranged. Consequently the overthrow of the governing classes is indispensable, political power must be captured by the workers, and Latin America must be united in a Federation of States. This is one of the great political objects of the A.P.R.A.

The Nationalization of Land and Industry as the
Sole Means of Combatting Imperialism

Within the capitalist system, and in accord with the dialectics of its historical process, Latin America would infallibly become a North American colony. The United States holdings of values in the world (The *New York Times,* June 27, 1926) are shown in the following table, exclusive of war debts:

United States holding in Asia $1,000,000,000
United States holding in Europe 2,000,000,000

United States holding in Australia 2,500,000,000
United States holding in Latin America ... 4,100,000,000

This introduction of capital into Latin America increases almost daily. From June to October, Imperialism has invested over $50,000,-000. The conflict between the United States and Mexico shows us that Mexico has not been able to nationalize the petroleum industry, which today is still dominated by the menace of a North American invasion in defence of the interests of the Standard Oil Co. (North American capital in Mexican petroleum $614,487,263). The "Enmienda Platt" of the Cuban Constitution and the cases of Santo Domingo, Panama, Nicaragua, Honduras and Hayti prove to us that national authority is lost in proportion as investments by Imperialism are accepted. The nationalization of land and industry under the direction of the producing classes is the sole means of maintaining the country's power, and is the correct policy for the countries of Latin America.

*Latin American Political Unity Pre Supposes the
Internationalization of the Panama Canal*

The Panama Canal in the power of the United States Government is one danger more to the sovereignty of Latin America. The program of the A.P.R.A. frankly proclaims the "internationalization of Panama." Dr. Alberto Ulloa, Professor of International Law in the University of San Marcos, Lima, Peru, writes in support of this thesis: "The Panama Canal must be internationalized . . . It is not possible to allow to the United States the exercise of supreme rule in Panama." (Open Letter to the President of the Federation of Students of Panama, June 1926).

Conclusion

The A.P.R.A. represents, therefore, a political organization struggling against Imperialism and against the national governing classes which are its auxiliaries and its allies in Latin America. The A.P.R.A is a united front of the toiling masses (workers, peasants, natives of the soil) united with students, intellectuals, revolutionaries, etc. The A.P.R.A. is an autonomous movement, completely Latin American, without foreign intervention or influences. It is the result of a spontaneous movement in defence of our countries in view of the experiences of Mexico, Central America, Panama and the Antilles, and the present position of Peru, Bolivia and Venezuela, where the policy of "penetration" by Imperialism is already keenly felt. For this our watchword is to be the following: "Against Yankee Imperialism, for the unity of the peoples of Latin America, for the realization of social justice."

IV

APRA AS A PARTY

THE PREVIOUS CHAPTER WAS WRITTEN ORIGINALLY IN ENGLISH FOR the political review *The Labour Monthly* of London and was published in December 1926. It has been reprinted many times in reviews and periodicals, both European and North American. Being so well known it serves as an easy point of departure for this summary analysis of the principles of Apra. However, since it was thought and written in a foreign language, using European terminology, I must, in presenting it in our language, explain and further develop the significance of some of its principal points, especially those referring to the Aprista concept of the state. The importance of this preliminary comment will become apparent later.

It is also necessary to refer to *The Labour Monthly* article in order to recount a little of the attitude of the Communists towards Apra, a quite inconsistent and contradictory one to be sure. My most sincere objective in writing these pages is to reorient the ideological polemic which the Communists have provoked with their negative criticism, taking care that the discussion does not deviate from the dialectical line. . . .

From the first moment, Apra appeared as "an autonomous movement, completely Latin American, without foreign intervention or influences," as that article clearly states. This declaration signifies, without doubt, that the new organization has not submitted to, nor is it ever going to submit to the Third, to the Second, or whatever other political International with European headquarters; and it thus defines its status as an Indoamerican nationalist and anti-imperialist movement.

"El Apra Como Partido," from El *Antimperialismo y el Apra,* Chapter II.

Now for a bit of history. At the beginning of the European autumn of 1926, while I was in Oxford, I received a friendly letter from Lozowsky, the president of the Red International of Trade Unions, or *Profintern,* who told me that after having read the article in *The Labour Monthly,* translated into Russian by a Moscow review "he gave welcome to the new organism." Lozowsky, with whom I had conversed on American social and economic problems during my visit to Russia in the summer of 1924, did not show any objection in his letter to the express declaration of Apra of its intention to form a party, or to its autonomous character, so clearly stated in what I have quoted above. He confined himself to explaining to me that he dissented from our plan of incorporating the intellectuals of both Americas in the movement, and especially the North Americans, maintaining that the anti-imperialist allies that the Indoamerican peoples should have in the United States should not be the bourgeois or petty-bourgeois intellectuals, but the workers. The letter of Lozowsky was, then, vague enough and repeated the well-known phrases of orthodox Marxism. It is worthwhile noting that Lozowsky wrote to me in English, a language which he recently learned under the instruction of a North American teacher, who served as intermediary during all of this correspondence.

I answered Lozowsky extensively and further developed some points already made in our chat in Moscow: the very peculiar characteristics of America, socially, economically, and politically; its complete difference from Europe; the need to focus on American problems, especially those of Indo or Latin America in all of their extension and complexity. I reiterated my sincere conviction that it is not possible to issue from Europe magic recipes for the solution of such problems, telling him that as much as I admired the knowledge of the new Russian rulers of their country's realities, I also noted their abysmal lack of accurate information about the reality of the Americas. I told him, furthermore, that these opinions, obtained personally from conversations with Lunacharsky, Frunze, Trotsky, and other Russian leaders, made me decide, after a serene and extensive visit to the great country of the Soviets, not to enter the Communist Party, because I did not believe that it would be the Third International that would resolve the serious and complex problems of Indoamerica. Then I answered his objections to the participation of intellectuals in the anti-imperialist struggle and told him my point of view about the mission of the middle classes and the participation of the

North American workers in the anti-imperialist struggle. . . . I presented Lozowsky with some facts about the conflict among imperialisms and their projections in the Indoamerican struggle for liberation from imperialism. In this direction—which included an allusion to Japan and interested Lozowsky more—the epistolary polemic was diverted, and it ceased one fine day. Some of those letters circulated in print during the World Congress of the Red International of Labor Unions in November of 1927 and appeared in the official, published versions of the congress. In them it was clear that Lozowsky, refuting my ideas and lamenting that I did not belong to the Communist ranks, nonetheless alluded with generosity to my capacity for presenting the problems of America and to my political sincerity. There also appeared Lozowsky's declaration of his opposition to the possibility that circulation of that letter in the congress should give rise to personal attacks by certain Latin American Communists. Then, the Peruvian delegate Portocarrero made an energetic defense of me. . . .

All these references, with the essential details, show that after the letter of Lozowsky—containing a frank welcome to the founding of Apra—the opinion changed. I understand that, convinced that we meant our declaration proclaiming Apra "an autonomous movement, completely Latin American, without foreign intervention and influences," the Communists lost all hope of capturing the new organization. Thus, Apra could not serve as an instrument of Communism.

The Aprista attitude was defined further—a little after my correspondence with Lozowsky—in the World Anti-imperialist Congress which met in February 1927 in the Palace of Egmont in Brussels. Apra was not officially invited, but as individuals we were specially asked to come along with some prominent Indoamerican intellectuals. The influence and control of the Communist Party was unconcealable in that assembly, which brought together the most illustrious figures of world leftism. In spite of strong Communist pressure and the atmosphere of easy optimism, prevalent in such assemblies, we maintained our ideological position and the character of Apra as an autonomous political organization tending towards becoming a party. Again the article in *The Labour Monthly* was commented upon. In the debates we opposed inclusion under the command of the World Anti-imperialist League which, we knew, would be an organization completely controlled by the Third International, not in the interest of the anti-imperialist struggle but for the service of Communism.

However, we cooperated sincerely in giving the congress the best constructive results. When a draft resolution by Julio Antonio Mella was unanimously rejected, I was charged with presenting another. I did so and it was approved in toto. On the sensitive point concerning the participation of the bourgeoisie and petty bourgeoisie in the anti-imperialist struggle, we posed the objections of Apra to the Communist slogans. That occasioned the most dramatic polemics of the congress. The Latin American delegation met in secret for five or six hours in an attempt to convince us. We maintained our reservations. Noting them, we signed the conclusions of the congress; and this fact appears in the official documents published in many languages.

Brussels, then, defined the Aprista theoretical line and established very clearly our differences with Communism. It was to be expected that from then on Apra was the target of bitter criticisms. For Communists there cannot exist any leftist party except one which is the official instrument of the Third International of Moscow, or Stalinist, orthodoxy. Every political organization that Moscow doesn't command must be execrated and fought. After the Congress of Brussels in 1927, this was true of Apra.

We should now discuss some of their more interesting and frequently repeated criticisms in order to refute them point by point. The most important, as might be expected, are directed particularly against Apra as "a political party."

In the former article, in dealing with the organization of Apra, it is stated: "The A.P.R.A. is a young organization formed by the young men of the new generation of manual and intellectual workers of Latin America. It was founded in 1924 and has organized sections in various countries in Latin America and also in Europe, where the number of anti-Imperialist Latin American students is pretty large."

Later on, in the concluding paragraph: "A.P.R.A. represents, therefore, a political organization struggling against Imperialism and against the national governing classes which are its auxiliaries and its allies in Latin America. The A.P.R.A. is a united front of the toiling masses (workers, peasants, natives of the soil) united with students, intellectuals, revolutionaries, etc."

Why must Apra be a political party? The answer is presented in summary fashion in the same article: "The experience of history, especially that of Mexico, shows that the immense power of American Imperialism cannot be overthrown without the unity of the Latin American countries. Against this unity the national dominant classes, middle class, landowners, etc., whose political power is almost always buttressed by the agitation of nationalism or patriotism of countries hostile to their neighbors, are ranged. Consequently the overthrow of the governing classes is indispensable, political power must be captured by the workers, and Latin America must be united in a Federation of States. This is one of the great political objects of the A.P.R.A."

Now, the Communist theoretical objections can be summarized thus:

1) Apra as an anti-imperialist united front is unnecessary because the same ends are served by the Pan American Anti-imperialist League, and 2) As a party it is also unnecessary because the Communist Parties already exist to fulfill the political task which Apra proposes to undertake.

The united front of the Anti-imperialist Leagues, dependencies of the Third International, only announce a program of resistance to imperialism. But resistance is not enough. To protect against the advances of the Yankee soldier in Nicaragua, or in any other Indoamerican victim of aggression, is only one aspect of the struggle against imperialism. Imperialism is essentially an economic phenomenon which takes to the political field to defend itself. In Europe, imperialism is "the last capitalist stage"—that is, the culmination of a succession of capitalist stages—which is characterized by the emigration or exportation of capital and the conquest of markets and of sources of raw materials in countries with incipient economies. But in Indoamerica what is in Europe "the last stage of capitalism" becomes the first. For our peoples, the capital which immigrates or is imported establishes the first stage of the modern capitalist age. In Indoamerica the economic and social history of Europe is not repeated step by step. In these countries the initiation of modern capitalism is begun with imperialist foreign capital. If we examine Indoamerican economic history, we shall discover this general characteristic: The immigrating capital introduces to our peoples the agriculture and mining stage of capitalist development. Furthermore, England—where capitalism first established its contemporary characteristics—has been the nation which initiated the exportation of capital. "Compared with other countries, British investments have acted as pioneers in the discovery and opening of new fields of development," says J. K. Hobson.

There has not occurred in our countries, then, the evolution as seen in the English, French, and German cases, where the bourgeoisies, well established as economic classes after a long period of growth, finally capture political power and defeat more or less violently the class representing feudalism. In Indoamerica we have not yet had time to create an autonomous and powerful national bourgeoisie, strong enough to displace the landowning classes—a vestige of Spanish colonial feudalism—which in the turmoil of Independence freed themselves from a politico-economic subjection to the metropoli and established their own power over the state. From the beginning of our incipient national bourgeoisies, which are like the accidental roots of our landowning classes, imperialism has existed in their midst, dominating them. In all of our countries before a more or less definitively national bourgeoisie develops, there enters immigrant capitalism, that is imperialism.

It is well known that in the modern economic process of some Indoamerican peoples, it is difficult to distinguish, at first glance, national capital from foreign capital and their lines of separation. However, if we look for the beginnings of the capital phenomenon, we shall encounter in every case almost always English or Yankee capital, in opposition to or in alliance with one another—usually in opposition—and around one, or the other, embryonic forms or small attempts to establish a true national capital. Our governing classes and the state—their political instrument of domination—in elemental or relatively advanced forms of organization, express loyally this Indoamerican characteristic of capitalism, coexisting in the great majority of our countries with the still undefeated power of the landlord class.

To struggle against imperialism in Indoamerica is not only to resist with shouts and protests every time that the foreign soldier, authorized or not by the powers of the intervened and impotent state, violates its sovereignty in accord with all or part of the dominant class. If we examine the history of Latin American imperialism, for example in the excellent book of Freeman and Nearing, *Dollar Diplomacy*, it will be seen that when Yankee soldiers have invaded our soil, they have always done so with the support of a treaty, or an agreement or with a formal invitation by the representatives of the invaded state. When those representatives, for whatever reason, have been hostile towards the measures adopted by the invader, they have been automatically relieved of control of public affairs, and have been replaced with more docile ones. It is not necessary to repeat—all of us Indoamericans know this well—that two-thirds of the force of imperialist power in our countries is based on the control that they exercise, directly or indirectly, on the powers of the state as a political instrument of domination.

The struggle against imperialism in Indoamerica is not only a struggle of mere resistance, of proclamations by committees, or of protests written on red paper.* The struggle is, above all, a politico-economic one. The instrument of the imperialist domination in our countries is the state, more or less defined as a political apparatus; it represents real power. Paraphrasing the founder of the Third International, we, the Indoamerican anti-imperialists, must maintain that *the fundamental question of the anti-imperialist struggle in Indoamerica is the question of power.*

The Pan American Anti-imperialist League, as an organization of simple anti-imperialist resistance or propaganda, is an organization of limited efficacy. We must first wrest the power over our peoples away from imperialism and in order to do that we need a political party. The Anti-imperialist Leagues, because they are so limited, are unnecessary and this explains—oh, how right is popular instinct—why they have virtually disappeared. The reply to our criticism of the innocuous nature of the leagues is not given in public for "tactical" reasons—an open secret—but they can be summed up thus: The leagues do not engage in political action because that is the function of the Communist Party.

This brings us back to the second theoretical objection: Apra as a party is unnecessary, because there already exist Communist Parties which fulfill the political objectives of Apra. It is also easy to answer this argument, which has been particularly pressed by the official Argentine Communists, who are the most orthodox in their arguments of all those hostile to Apra. We answer: The Communist Party is, first of all, a class party. The party or one of the parties—we cannot forget the socialists—of the working class. Furthermore, the Communist Party, in addition to being an exclusive class party, originating out of the economic conditions of Europe, which are very different from ours, is a single worldwide party—not a federation of parties—directed absolutely and in a completely centralized way from Moscow.

The countries of Indoamerica are not industrial countries. Our economies are basically agrarian or agrarian-mining. Look at the statistics. The proletariat is a minority, the complete minority, since it is only a nascent class. It is the peasant masses that predominate, giving a feudal or almost feudal cast to our nations. A party of the proletarian class alone is a party without possibilities of political success

---

* A jibe at the Communist origin of many such protests.

in these nations. We must not forget historical experience. In the three or four of our countries where Communist parties have been formed, we find cases such as Argentina. There the section of Third International, one of the oldest, has been split into two irreconcilable factions, whose struggle is tenacious and violent: "official" Communism and "labor" Communism. What is more important: Argentinian Communism split before having any representation in the Buenos Aires parliament after so many years.

In most of our countries, the lack of importance of the Communist Party does not have to be stressed in order to say that it is minimal. In Chile and Uruguay, the Communist Party has succeeded in getting representatives in congress, although the situation of those republics, especially that of Chile, reveals the failure of the influence of the Third International. The reason is economic; only in countries where industry is relatively important is it possible to find some weak manifestation of the possibilities of Communism. There is none in the more clearly agrarian peoples, for economic reasons.

It is in the agrarian countries that the young, small proletarian class needs allies in order to gain influence. "The alliance with the peasants is sufficient," say some optimists, repeating the Leninist European psalmody. However, without referring to the Indoamerican historical experience, because it is so obvious, we can recall that, in spite of their numerical power, the peasants in our countries need allies. Allies in addition to the working class. Thus, it is necessary to abandon the idea of a class party, exclusively Communist, and to recognize the need for a different type of revolutionary and anti-imperialist political party that is not a class party, but a party of a united front.

Before continuing, we must deal with another point of view referring to the lack of progress by the Communist Party in Indoamerica. The first thing that an attentive observer discovers in studying Russian political reality is the extraordinary capacity of their leaders, their solid preparation and intellectual solvency, and their detailed knowledge of the great problems of their country. The contrast with the *criollo** leaders is complete. In our republics there exists what Trotsky, in a memorable chapter of his polemics with Gorki, called a "revolutionary bohemia." In succession to the long necktie and flamboyant hat of the anarchist intellectual *against everything and against*

---

* Word meaning in this case national, Latin American.

everyone—our professional rebel—there is another, the arrogant, less picturesque and less esthetic, but no less exhibitionist, blustering, and ignorant Communist fellow traveller. Freud would find much to study and discover in this devotion to boastful pretensions by our improvised reformers of the universe. Among them, we have the well-known type of "revolutionary" bureaucrat: a person who has obtained the paid post of party secretary, a position he defends with ready-made phrases, with simplistic dogmatic speeches, while his "curve of happiness" rises, his bourgeois stomach enlarges, and he looks disdainfully at the "massman" who comes to him.

The false leadership of the criollo Communists has contributed a great deal to the rapid sinking of the Bolshevik ship in our seas. Meanwhile, the great majorities of the Indoamerican proletariat have not varied their direction. Our working class, to the degree that it is becoming class conscious, acquires an increasing sense of reality. It sees with sympathy, with admiration, and with curiosity the great social phenomenon of the Russian Revolution, but intuitively understands the great differences of milieu, of race, and of historical conditions. It comprehends, furthermore, the deep ethical and mental differences which separate the leaders of the Soviet effort from the great majority of the childish leaders of criollo Communism. The workers find the latter repulsive and do not follow them.

That contrast, which is recognized virtually by clairvoyance in our proletariat, is seen clearly in Russia itself. One senses this in conversations with the sincerely revolutionary workers and intellectuals, whether Communists or not, who have visited Moscow with clear vision. It is possible to affirm then, in spite of the conditions of our countries, that the Communist Party has not made progress, even relatively, among the working classes of these countries due to the evident incapacity of their leaders. This is despite the fact that, although one cannot accept the idea of a European Communist domination of Indoamerica in the near future, I believe that under intelligent direction, a large part of the proletarian masses, which today belong to the Socialist, Labor, and Radical parties of Mexico, Argentina, Chile, etc., in alliance with the middle classes, might be won, if only sentimentally and for a short while, to Communism. However, neither have the non-Communist parties of the left lost their workingclass masses, nor have the powerful political trade union organizations, representing a good number of workers, been undermined. The workers and peasant parties, including artisans and the middle class, and the trade union ranks continue as strong as ever in Buenos Aires, Santiago, Rio de Janeiro, Havana, and Mexico. Nor can it be said now that the workingclass masses follow the socialists or trade unionists from stupidity or ignorance. The workingclass masses are innocent of such charges, which apply rather to the criollo Communist leaders. Justice indicates this. . . . It is the Communist leaders, paralytically orthodox, who confirm the indisputable statement: *There are no good or bad peoples or masses; there are only good and bad leaders.*

On the other hand, the strictly centralized organization of the Communist Party does not permit its Moscow leaders to understand the faraway problems of America. Speaking on this theme during the Anti-imperialist Congress of Brussels with one of the Communists forming the great majority of that assembly, I was told that when the possibility of the recognition of the Soviet Republic by Uruguay was being discussed, it was officially suggested in Moscow that Kollontay, diplomatic representative in Mexico, should be named simultaneously to Montevideo because they were "neighboring countries." It was as if they were talking of Guatemala and El Salvador or Haiti and Santo Domingo.

It is understandable, furthermore, that the Russian leaders cannot have an intimate knowledge of all of the problems of the world. The relative success of the Communists in France is due to the indisputable intellectual quality of the French leaders. It is enough to hear them in the Chamber of Deputies in Paris to appreciate their great political capacity, their indisputably realistic spirit. The failure of Communism in England is due, also, to the fact that the Third International does not have any followers of importance who can take the leadership of the proletariat away from the Laborites.

One of the first things of which I became convinced in Moscow was the almost total ignorance which exists in Russia concerning Indoamerica. I had the chance of reading some original reports and of conversing with various leaders about the political and social situations in our countries. I repeat: The ignorance was almost absolute. During the World Communist Congress, in the summer of 1924, Zinovief,* President of the Third International, after a brief reference to the movement of Argentina and Chile, said something to the effect that

---

* One of the principal, old Bolshevik leaders of the Russian Revolution subsequently head of the Communist Party in Leningrad. Expelled from the Party as a result of his opposition to Stalin in the 1920s. One of the first victims of the Moscow purge trials in 1936.

"we know little or nothing of Latin America." In the face of the objection of Bertram Wolf, a Yankee intellectual,† who criticized this ignorance, the then idolized and now proscribed chief of Communism answered: "It is not our fault, it is that of our informants." I witnessed this dialogue from the press gallery.

Moscow's ignorance of our problems is not due only to the Russian Communists. Examine the programs of the Communists in America to see if any concrete reference to Yankee imperialism exists before 1923. In 1924, during the presidential elections of the United States, the Workers Party of America, or the Communist Party, presented as its candidate for the presidency their leader Foster.* The candidate announced his platform. Such a program should include all the points that might be offered by a candidate who can only put forth ideas. Nevertheless, not a single word about imperialism appeared in it. At that time our anti-imperialist movement was already under way. And yet, it is the Workers Party that insisted later on controlling the Anti-imperialist Leagues and still controls them under the supreme command of Mr. Manuel Gómez from New York.

In the meanwhile, imperialism has advanced triumphantly, to the point of having become an immediate danger for all of our peoples. Are we going to wait for the leaders of criollo Communism to be educated or to be transformed to the discovery finally of our reality, so that they can then direct us well? Or are we going to repeat with them the history of their previous phase of maneuvers and ill-advised actions which have not even approached success.

Will it be the Communist Party, directed from Moscow, that leads Indoamerica to its victory against imperialism? Let us reflect upon the map of the world, upon the history of our peoples, and on the consciousness of our reality. The answer, even of capable Communists, . . . the few realists attacked disparagingly by the rest as "rightists," "intellectuals," and "petit bourgeois," is negative. The Communist Party in Indoamerica lacks the force and the authority to direct the anti-imperialist struggle. Neither in the name of the Third

---

† Wolf was a United States Communist who spent some years in Mexico and was a delegate of the Mexican C. P. to the 1924 Comintern Congress. He became a leader of the "Lovestoneite" Communist splinter group after 1929. In recent years he has gained fame as a historian of the Russian Revolution.
* William Z. Foster, a trade union leader who joined the Communist Party in the early 1920s. He was Communist candidate for President in 1924 and 1928. He became president of the party in 1946 with the downfall of Earl Browder. He died in 1961.

International, nor in the name of its Pan American Anti-imperialist League, condemned to failure, can it do anything. The force of anti-imperialism in our peoples is older than the Third International and vaster than the exclusivisms of its class party. For a social class in Indoamerica to be capable of solely directing victoriously our peoples in their anti-imperialist struggle, it would have to achieve the conditions which Marx outlined for the effectiveness of the class control of a revolution: "For the emancipation of a people to coincide with the emanicipation of a given class within a bourgeois society, it is necessary that that class as such represent all of society." This, certainly, is not the case of our nascent proletarian class and is even less so of the feeble Communist Party in Indoamerica, which does not even represent that class. The anti-imperialist movement, which is and must be a movement with a united front, requires, therefore, a united political organization also. The Anti-imperialist Leagues are not enough—and the Communist party is too much.

Thus are refuted and dismissed the two central objections of criollo Communism to the role of Apra as the united front and Anti-imperialist Party of Indoamerica.

V

WHAT KIND OF PARTY IS APRA, AND WHAT CLASS DOES IT REPRESENT?

AN INDOAMERICAN ANTI-IMPERIALIST PARTY WITH A SENSE OF OUR social reality cannot be a single class party. Even less can it be organized along the lines of a European-model party. Less still, can it be a party subject to foreign direction. These are three arguments against the Communist objections discussed in the previous chapter. Furthermore, an Indoamerican anti-imperialist party with a sense of our social reality must be a national party of a united front, one which brings together all of the social classes menaced by imperialism. It must be, then, a party with its own realistic and efficient program and tactics, and with a national command. These objections favor the organization of Apra as a party.

Let us think about these statements:

Imperialism menaces others besides the proletarian class. Imperialism, which implies in all of our countries the arrival of the industrial capitalist era under the characteristic forms of economic penetration, brings with it the economic and social phenomena which capitalism produces in the countries of its origins: great industrial and agricultural concentration; a monopoly of the production and circulation of wealth; the progressive destruction or absorption of small capital, of small manufacturing, of small property, and of small commerce, and the formation of a truly proletarian industrial class.

We should note then, that the class first suffering the impact of capitalist imperialism in our countries is not the incipient working class, nor the poor peasant, nor the Indian. The worker in small indus-

---

"Que Clase de Partido y Partido de Que Clase es el Apra?" from *El Antimperialismo y el Apra,* Chapter III.

try and the independent artisans, in being employed by a new form of production backed with large amounts of capital, instead receives a more secure and higher wage which temporarily improves his conditions, and he becomes a member of the industrial proletariat. They sell their labor under better circumstances. The same thing happens to the poor peasant, the peon, and the Indian serf. Upon being proletarianized in a large manufacturing, mining, or agricultural enterprise, they almost always enjoy a temporary improvement in their welfare. They exchange their miserable wage of centavos or in kind for a higher one paid by their foreign master, who is always more powerful and richer than the national master. Thus imperialism in the newly developing countries is a determining factor in the formation and strengthening of a genuine modern proletarian class. This social phenomenon of the class structuring of our proletariat is subject to a spatial process as we shall note further on. It has its characteristic limitations, determined by the conditions and pecularities of the imperialist expansion over backward countries. The industrial proletariat which is being formed is, then, a new, young, weak class, fascinated with immediate gains, whose collective conscience only appears later to confront the implacable rigor of exploitation within the new system.

Since the great profit of imperialism is based on cheap labor, the wage paid the new worker, although greater than that which he received under previous conditions, is significantly less than that received by a worker in the industrial countries. When imperialist capital comes to our countries, it comes like the catechists of savages showing spangles and mirrors which attract the oppressed with transitory fascination. Thus the industrial proletarian class is formed during the first stage of imperialist penetration, but always under inferior economic conditions as compared to those of advanced proletarians.

For this reason, in addition to large capitalism bringing about an economic stage better than that of small capital, just as industrial capitalism is a superior stage to feudalism, the laboring masses who are transformed into a modern proletariat do not perceive the violence of the imperialist exploitation until much later. The type of modern imperialism, especially the North American variety, so advanced in its methods, only offers benefits and progress in the beginning.

Some of these characteristic contradictions of modern imperialism, whose vast and terrible proportions the nascent proletariat does not see in the beginning, have been previously mentioned. But the monopoly which imperialism imposes cannot avoid the destruction, the stagnation, and the regression of what we call generically the middle class. Thus, as industrial capitalism, upon appearing in the most highly developed countries reduces, absorbs, and proletarianizes the petty bourgeoisie of whom only a few are privileged to join the dominant class—imperialism subjugates or economically destroys the middle classes of the backward countries where it penetrates. The small capitalist, the small industrialist, the small rural and urban proprietor, the small miner, the small merchant, the intellectual, the white collar worker, among others, form the middle class whose interests are attacked by imperialism.

A very small segment of this middle class allies itself with imperialism and obtains advantages through becoming a cooperative aide and national front. Under the laws of competition and of monopoly controlling the existence of capitalism, the imperialist form—its culminating expression—destroys the incipient capitalists and proprietors, subjugates them, defeats them, and strangles them with the tentacles of the great trusts, when not under the yoke of banking credits and mortgages. The middle classes of our countries, as imperialism advances, see increasingly restricted the limits of their possible economic progress. They are subject classes which hope to join the dominant classes and are prevented by the imperialist barrier which is by itself the expression of a dominant class intolerant of rivals. Also within the imperialist countries themselves, and in the United States particularly, this phenomenon of paralyzation of progress of the middle classes is evident. In spite of the fact that they fulfill an economic function in the circulation and distribution of riches for small commerce, and constitute at the same time an ample sector of the market for national consumption, the impulse of the middle classes in the large countries is circumscribed in a vicious circle. It has lost already the possibility of increasing its economic power and converting itself into a bourgeois class. As capitalism is perfected and concentrated, the petty bourgeoisie finds inescapable the boundaries of being a dependent class.

In the countries of incipient economic development, the middle classes have a wider field of action. Allied or at war with the large landholding classes, the middle classes know that the future is theirs. For that reason, we see that at the end of the struggle for independence from Spain—which in effect turned over the control of the state to the great national landlords—the Indoamerican middle classes quickly learned the way to power and advanced towards the level of a well-defined national bourgeoisie. However, long before this transformation had been achieved, it was restrained by the entry of imperialism. The conquest of our economy is carried out from abroad, under an ultra-modern and all-powerful system. Upon its arrival, it hurts established interests, engages in irresistible competition, absorbs, and imposes. Thus, while imperialist penetration produces an upward movement of the working masses, who pass from semi-slavery and servitude, or from elemental forms of free labor, to become a proletariat, the middle classes suffer their first taste of defeat. They soon realize this, and reaction and protest are generated.

This is the economic explanation of why the first cries against imperialism in our countries have come from the middle classes, which are also our most cultured ones. In sentimental and purely lyrical forms, the precursors of anti-imperialist protest in Indoamerica have been genuine representatives of the middle classes. From their ranks appear the first agitators and the most determined and heroic soldiers of the initial anti-imperialist movement.

It would be vain to pretend to explain the historic fact that the Indoamerican working classes have not originated the movement of social protest against imperialism, simultaneously with the middle classes, for lack of pugnacity. It is well known that the uprisings of the workers and peasants in Indoamerica have been frequent and have a long history among us. But their protests have been directed against the visible exploitation, against the instruments of immediate oppression: the feudal master, the employer, the manager, the *cacique,** the foreman, or the government supporting them. Much later, and when imperialist exploitation made known its immense weight, our working classes understood the danger and discovered the true economic enemy. When the oppression of imperialism is felt in the form of national and political subjugation—by means of loans, concessions, dispersal of public property, through interventions and outright men-ace—reality demonstrates to them the need for a unification of forces with the middle classes that have already initiated the anti-imperialist struggle.

Would it be realistic, then, to reject the alliance of the middle classes with the working and peasant classes for the anti-imperialist struggle? Doubtlessly not. Should such an alliance, once formed, be limited to rhetorical protests, to a mere task of resistance, or to noisy

---

* A popular term for a local political leader, a machine politician.

agitation without a realistic plan of action? A negative answer is obvious. A merely formal alliance would become sterile. The middle
classes can carry out a valuable political role, as is demonstrated in
their cooperation with the Socialist parties of Argentina, Mexico, and
Brazil, among others. Furthermore, the middle classes that suffer
imperialist aggression at the cost of their own existence, have an interest in giving their protest substantial meaning. When the Communists
propose to link them to the anti-imperialist movement in the leagues,
but only for the purpose of protest and to prohibit them from political
action, there is sufficient cause to condemn the famous leagues to
prompt death. The middle classes would only thus take the chestnuts
from the fire. And there are many intelligent and capable people in
those classes capable of seeing through and disdaining, quite rightly,
such an ingenuous tactic! This tactic may be very Communist, very
European, and well learned from well-translated books—but it is
very stupid.

The oppressed middle classes displaced by imperialism want to
fight it, but they wish to do so politically from the ranks of a party
dedicated to that struggle, too. The historical task of an anti-imperialist
party consists, in the first place, of affirming the national sovereignty
by freeing it from the oppressors of the nation and capturing power
in order to carry out its liberating objectives. This is a difficult and
arduous task for which the aid of the middle classes, who would be
benefited by this liberating movement, is essential.

On various occasions I have alluded to the similarity of the Chinese anti-imperialist movement and our own anti-imperialist movement. In a speech given during a London meeting commemorating
the Chinese revolution on October 11, 1926, I noted that the only
anti-imperialist front with a similar origin is the Indoamerican, and
the only anti-imperialist party similar to the original Kuo Min Tang*
is the Apra. I insist on this parallel, in spite of necessary specific differences, remembering that the literal translation of *Kuo Min Tang*
in our language is National Popular Party. The words *popular* and

---

* The party founded by Sun Yat Sen, on the basis of republicanism, nationalism,
social reform, and democracy. It appealed to the middle classes as well as to
urban workers and peasants. Upon Sun Yat Sen's death in 1925, leadership
was assumed by Chiang Kai-Shek. At the time Haya wrote, the Kuo Min Tang
was leading a civil war, with wide popular support, against reactionary elements. Until 1927, when Chiang Kai Shek purged them, the Communists worked
in and with the Kuo Min Tang.

national, which clearly express the tendency of the united front of the Kuo Min Tang, belong also to the Aprista title.

The Kuo Min Tang was not founded as a class party, but as a bloc or united front of workers, peasants, and the middle classes, organized under the form and discipline of a party, with a program of concrete and propitious political action. Sun Yat Sen, one of the most illustrious creative spirits of our times, saw very clearly in his period that it was not possible to establish in China a purely class party, whether socialist, or, later, exclusively Communist. What was admirable in the political conception of Sun Yat Sen was his genius for realism—as much of a genius for China as the realism of Lenin was for Russia. Both created for their respective countries political forces adapted to their own surroundings. Both felt later—because of the geographic proximity and more or less notable psychological similarities between great sectors of their peoples—that those forces should be allied. But neither the Kuo Min Tang nor the Russian Bolshevik Party ever lost its own identity in this alliance when it was temporarily established. To have lost their individual identities would have been to confuse Russia with China and to surrender to the enemy which was, in China as in Russia, European imperialism and its class collaborators in each country.

Not only because of the really complicated characteristics of the imperialist phenomenon but also because of the ignorance of the working masses in the backward countries—an ignorance determined by the agrarian or feudal nature of their economy—an alliance with the intellectuals in the service of the anti-imperialist movement is necessary. The intellectuals in the agrarian countries belong almost completely to the middle class. In the revolutionary history of China and Russia, they have played a decisive function. The leaders of the Russian and Chinese revolutions were intellectuals, professors, economists, or writers. It would be stupid to deny the influence of the intellectual, or the left-wing university man—professor or student—in the liberating tasks of the modern world. Especially in the case of China, an agrarian country, the intellectuals have fulfilled and are fulfilling a memorable role in the struggle against imperialism.

In the Indoamerican countries, the function of the intellectuals has been and is definitive for the anti-imperialist struggle. Many may have surrendered their consciences to imperialism and reaction, but intellectuals of the middle class have also been the precursors of

our present organization, such as José Enrique Rodó* and Manuel
Ugarte,† José Vasoncelos,** Alfredo Palacios.†† José Ingenieros,***
the founder of the Unión Latinoamericana, today part of Apra, is
one of the most important sources of ideas that our cause has had,
in spite of being contemporaneous with many professional dema-
gogues of social revolution. In all of our America, the work of agitation
and of channeling the anti-imperialist currents has been undoubtedly
done by the new generation of intellectuals, who, proceeding from
the middle class, have clearly seen the tremendous problem and have
indicated the most certain ways of confronting it.

It has been ingenuous, lamentably ingenuous, for those propagandists of European revolutionary systems and tactics as a panacea
for our peoples to think that the phalanxes of Latin American anti-
imperialist intellectuals are going to accept the leagues as a paliative.
These intellectuals know full well that imperialism is an economic
phenomenon defended with political weapons and must be fought both
economically and politically. These propagandists argue that to fight
it effectively one must affiliate *velis nolis* to the Communist party,
whose recent pronouncements in favor of the anti-imperialist struggle
constitute one of the many aspects of their program of worldwide
action. But that is not for us. For us, the struggle against imperialism
is a question of life or death, a danger nearby, an inescapable menace.
The lessons of European Communism come to us too late, showing
us methods of defense which are primitive and strange. Our vanguard
of intellectuals may be lacking in orientation and method, but they
do not lack the clarity and realistic spirit to understand the kind of
discipline we need. Being somewhat conversant with our intellectuals
frees me from the need of elaborating further on this point.

---

* Rodó was an Uruguayan writer who was one of the first Latin Americans to
stress the dangers of "cultural" imperialism, alleging the superiority of Latin
American "spiritual" values over the "materialist" values of the Yankees.
† Ugarte was an Argentine writer and politician. Starting as a socialist, he
became a leading exponent of Latin American nationalism against United
States imperialism.
** Vasoncelos was the Mexican Minister of Education in the early 1920s. He
stressed the uniqueness of the supposed Latin American "race" which he saw
evolving.
†† Palacios was the first socialist deputy in Argentina. A lifelong Argentine
nationalist, he was expelled from the Socialist Party in 1915 for his nationalistic
attitudes. He returned to the party in 1930.
*** Ingenieros was the founder of sociology in Argentina. He also stressed the
racial uniqueness of the Latin Americans.

Since its founding, Apra as a united front party has incorporated the anti-imperialist intellectual. Just as it has incorporated the small capitalist, the small proprietor, the small merchant, the small miner, the artisan, the white collar worker, it has incorporated the intelligentsia, the student, the professor, the writer, the artist, and the school teacher. It has incorporated them without resistance or distinction, as allies in the struggle of worker and peasant, as "intellectual workers." So long as the state is the instrument of imperialist domination in our countries and while power sanctions oppression and national exploitation by foreign imperialist capitalism, all who suffer oppression and exploitation must unite to defeat the common enemy. The maximum program of Apra in its five fundamental slogans, indicates the stages of the great struggle in an effort to avoid—insofar as possible in history—opportunism and confusion.

We shall examine, once again, the program. Our first premise of anti-imperialism includes, as we have demonstrated previously, the middle class in its plan of struggle. Our second aim for the political and economic unity of the peoples of Indoamerica does not exclude the middle class either. Both postulates imply the taking of political power in order to achieve them. It is demonstrated that we are not going to obtain any possible political victory over imperialism without capturing political power, which today is the instrument of oppression, but which is also convertible by Apra into the means of liberation. In this political action for the overthrow of the oligarchic class that is the agent and accomplice of imperialism in our countries, we need above all the support of a united front. And the unification or confederation of Indoamerica, which cannot be accomplished by a single class, requires the organization of that front. Let us not forget reality! Unification, whether gradual, economic at first and political later, or all at once—the most difficult to achieve, but not for this the least desired—will have to be brought about, too, by the policy of a united front, by means of a disciplined and powerful party.

How long will this political task last? How much time will pass during which our party will have to continue struggling against the enemy, in a united front, having at its core the alliance of the workers of the city and the country with the middle classes and the intellectuals? To answer this question, it is necessary to think, if only superficially, of the geographic, ethnic, economic, social, political, cultural, and moral conditions of our peoples. After a rapid survey of the reality of Indoamerica, there is no reason to lose our optimism. Rather, we must remain stronger than ever; but we must reject honorably all the rhetorical fantasies which would embark us in the airplanes of hyperbole and carry us by explosions of demagoguery into regions of necromancy where it is enough to rub the magic lamp of desire for the world to be transformed.

Therefore, we must admit a possible objection: Everything is possible in the kingdoms of the uncontrollable and simplistic imagination! Let us presume automatically the unity of our peoples or even better—so as not to fall totally into the unlikely—let's suppose another possibility not so remote, that Apra by means of one of its national parties takes power in some of our countries and commences to exercise from its new bulwark all possible influence to fulfill its plan of continental anti-imperialist resistance and Indoamerican unification.

The political action of the united front would be more necessary than ever in this case. Imperialism will attack, directly or indirectly, but it will attack since in any country of our America where it loses political power, it will lose economic power. Thus, be it in Nicaragua, or Haiti, or Santo Domingo, imperialism will attack. Apra in that case will perhaps then lead the national united front into the field of war. Then the words which Sandino* speaks to the world today, we shall all repeat in the name of our menaced nation: "I am not Liberal or Conservative; I am only a defender of the sovereignty of my country." The united front in such a case would be political and military, and would become national in outlook. The struggle would take on more violent characteristics, but it would be another aspect of the same struggle against the same enemy. And for that struggle, so long as the enemy exists, the united front, as a party and as an army, will be indispensable.

But, let us suppose that there is no attack. We shall look at all the cases, to satisfy those who want to consider every conceivable possibility. . . . Let's suppose that Apra has gained political power in one of our countries, and dividing our political action into internal and external, we fully undertake the fulfillment of the third aim of our party: nationalization of the land and of industry. "There we shall break our spears!" shout the pseudo-orthodox. "How can the socialist

---

* Augusto Sandino was a Nicaraguan leader who led a guerrilla war against the United States Marines during the United States military intervention there in the middle 1920s. Sandino became a hero for anti-imperialists all over Latin America. He laid down arms when U.S. troops were withdrawn in 1932 but was murdered shortly thereafter.

program be conciliated with a party of united front? There you are lost! There Apra will fall!"

Since Apra is not an end but a means, its death would be welcomed and heroic funeral services will have to be demanded of the world, but only if it fulfills the glorious precursory role of federating the Indoamerican states after seizing power from the traitor classes or oligarchies which served imperialism. It would have lived sufficiently long if each of our hundred million fellow citizens—or however many there would be when this stupendous task was achieved—would have from Apra the heritage of their victorious flag as symbol of national liberation and unity. This accomplishment would surpass that of independence from Spain, since it would be our second great emancipation.

The realism of Apra, however, allows for all that and will prevent our premature death. The nationalization of wealth, and particularly defeudalization, is the first anti-imperialist weapon—the defensive weapon of national sovereignty—and the weapon of social justice comes thereafter. Imperialism, as an economic phenomenon, affects our wealth, captures it, dominates it, monopolizes it. Imperialism uses wealth to subjugate our peoples as nations and our workers as exploited classes. The first defensive attitude of our peoples must be the nationalization of the wealth wrested from imperialism. Then this wealth must be given to those who work and increase it for the common good: its progressive socialization under the control of the defensive state and by means of a vast system of cooperatives. This is the ideal.

But let us observe the European reality. Russia may serve us for an example. After all, Russia is the best and only example to refer to in this case.

What is the historical lesson of post-revolutionary Russia? The triumph of Marxist socialism? The total defeat of capitalism? Neither one nor the other. The leaders of Communism—it is enough to have read Marx and Engels to realize how true this is—have declared a thousand times that Russia is not yet a country where socialism is dominant. All admit that Russia *moves toward socialism*. It has been on this path for ten years of gigantic revolutionary effort, in which one must admire as much the realism for rectifying errors as the marvelous tenacity for persisting. While Russia announces the total advent of socialism, linked to the social transformation of all Europe, it gives us a clear and undeniable lesson: Russia is the first country of the world which has defeated capitalism in its imperialist form. It is the only complete victory so far, and the only historical experience of this kind in the whole world.

Ten years ago the Russian people, under the banners of the Bolshevik Party, defeated the remains of the Czarist regime and the unstable government of Kerensky, instruments of foreign imperialism and of the national classes allied to it. The first task has been, then, national liberation under the aegis of a powerful and disciplined revolutionary party of the working and peasant classes directed by intellectuals. The situation of Russia at the time of the revolution of 1917 was summed up very well in one of Trotsky's speeches: "either to decline definitively to the level of a colony or to recover in a socialist form, that is the alternative of our country." The Russian Communist party was victorious in its first nationalist revolutionary task: to capture the state, that instrument of foreign imperialism and its allies of the national bourgeoisie and feudal classes, and to cleanse the Soviet soil of all imperialist characteristics.

The second task of the Russian Communists was to nationalize and study the wealth. The maximum program could not be realized, and they attempted a minimum program. The first step, that of antiimperialist nationalization, was carried out by the nation being declared the only owner, and the state the exclusive controller of national wealth. The second step of nationalization—the total turning over of production to the producers and the elimination of the petty bourgeoisie and of small private property—has not been carried out even now. Lenin's "New Economic Policy" (NEP) detailed with opportunistic genius the maximum nationalization concerning land and industries. The economic alliance with the bourgeoisie dispossessed from power was a necessary modification. Russia, now free of imperialism, has maintained the system of the NEP for many years. The day will come in which socialism becomes operative in Russia. In the meanwhile it has been necessary to have a long process of state capitalism, which replaces, progressively, the NEP and fulfills the historic mission of industrializing the country, a task which the Russian bourgeoisie was only able to begin.

The lesson of modern Russia is: The country has been liberated from imperialism by the nationalization of industry, by the state monopoly of commerce, and by control over the entry of foreign capital. The "socialist form" is still distant. But the victory over imperialism has been practically achieved in accord with the necessities of the new proletarian state.

Indoamericans must take advantage of the experience of history, while avoiding servile imitation. The geographical, ethnic, economic, and political reality of Russia is very different from ours. However, there are things of universal value offering lessons and examples for all latitudes and for all times. Russia offers the world the first case of anti-imperialist economic liberation in contemporary history, along with all of the characteristics of an authentic national and social revolution. In order to carry it out, the Russian Socialist Party had to free itself from the Second International and take a name from its own language—Bolshevism—the literal meaning of which lacked all Marxist or European meaning before the revolution of 1917. The Russian leaders understand well the national imperative of their great revolution. Although its terminology is foreign to us, it is native to the Russian people. The revolution took national forms, and created its own lexicon. Many in our lands devoutly learn this lexicon and repeat it arrogantly. They don't realize that an understanding of the historical facts is needed so that we can learn from the Russian experience . . . and forget their lexicon so as to create our own.

Establishing the profound and numerous differences as well as noting the similarities of the general thesis in the cases of Russia and China and that of Indoamerica, Apra maintains the principle of the autonomous action of our peoples in their struggle against imperialism. Such autonomy takes advantage of the experiences of history, verifies them on our soil, and putting aside absurd criticisms, bases itself realistically on the dialectic of facts. As a result the united front anti-imperialist party which Apra proposes creates a vast Indoamerican national movement realistically undertaking the work of our emancipation from imperialism.

VI

APRA AS A SINGLE PARTY

Apra as a party of an Indoamerican nationalist united front is distinguished from all other parties of the left existing in our twenty republics in its objectives and its organization. We must remember that no party, without excepting even the Communists and socialists, has been previously formed in Indoamerica with the fundamental objective of carrying on the anti-imperialist struggle. The most advanced and modern parties have conceded to action against imperialism as a limited aspect, almost always theoretical and tangential to their doctrinary program. Insofar as organization is concerned, all of the Indoamerican parties of the left either circumscribe their action to the frontiers of their native country, or amplify it to the very limits of the planet. The Radical, Social Democratic, and Labor parties belong to the first classification. Isolated in an almost xenophobic localism, they have never had a vision of the continental problem; nor have they made their effects felt in distant geographical areas. Intimidated by chauvinisms or incapable of realizing the indestructible and undeniable relations of our countries to one another, they maintain an arrogant isolation. The others, the so-called parties of the extreme left, include too much. Subaltern sections of world organizations, they subordinate Indoamerican problems to those interesting more naturally the leaders of their parties. Logically, Europe is their objective. Outside of the old continent their political vision of the world becomes misty and vague. Generalization and simplification fill immense vacuums and lead to confusion and the absence of com-

---

"El Apra Como Un Solo Partido," from *El Antimperialism y el Apra,* Chapter IV.

mon sense. This occurs with the Communist sections of the Third International and with some sectors of the Second.

Between the former, excessively closed leftism and the other, so unlimitedly open, realism imposes a leftism of realistic inspiration and method coherent with the problems of Indoamerica. In the face of the local conception or the petty nationalism of the parties isolated in each republic—the antithesis of which is the worldwide projection of the international parties—Aprismo establishes as a synthesis: continental or Indoamerican action. It raises to the first political imperative the struggle against imperialism which, as we shall see later on, cannot be limited to each isolated country, or be confused with the worldwide struggle.

In the article which serves as the starting point of this exposition —"Que es el Apra?"—appear the following lines: "As the problem is common to all the Latin American countries in which the dominant classes are allies of Imperialism in joint exploitation of the working classes, it is not an isolated or national question, but is international among the twenty Latin American republics."

Then in the following paragraph: "The experience of history, especially that of Mexico, shows that the immense power of American Imperialism cannot be overthrown without the unity of the Latin American countries."

There is no historical experience, in truth, nearer or more useful for the Indoamericans than that which Mexico offers us. In my mind, the Mexican Revolution is *our revolution;* it is our most fertile trial ground of renovating experiment. Its correct actions and its errors, its failures and its successes, its contradictions and its constructive impulses must be the source of the most useful lessons for our peoples. We must remember that the Mexican Revolution has been a spontaneous movement, that it is necessary to examine it in all of its fascinating and sometimes terrible reality to understand that never was there more exactly applied the world "biological" to a revolution as in this case. Lombardo Toledano* has written correctly: "Whoever wishes

---

* Vicente Lombardo Toledano, an intellectual turned labor leader, had a checkered role in the Mexican Revolution. Starting out as a conservative, he became a leader of the first national labor confederation, the Confederación Regional Obrera Mexicana. When it broke up in the late 1920s, he headed a small dissident faction. In 1936, with the backing of President Lázaro Cárdenas, he took the lead in organizing the Confederación de Trabajadores de México. Subsequently, he became the key figure in the Communist Latin American Labor Apparatus. In 1948 he organized his own party, the Partido Popular Socialista.

to understand the Mexican Revolution must not fix his attention exclusively on the word or the deeds of the apparent leaders, military or civilian: The revolution has been made with their cooperation, but many times has had to move against their wishes."

At the gates of the most powerful and imperialist country of the world, Mexico has done in reality only what it has been permitted to do. Its revolutionary impulse, delayed or diverted many times, has been spontaneous and vigorous. The agents and short-sighted or corrupt leaders of imperialism have attempted to take advantage of it, but—as the native effort of a people wanting to free itself of all oppression—the Mexican Revolution conserves its extraordinary value of experience for America.

We must not forget, in the first place, that the Mexican Revolution was not made by the Communists. . . . It is not indispensable to be a Communist in order to be a revolutionary. The so-called "Mexican Bolshevism" is one of the many phrases made up out of whole cloth by the imperialist press and repeated by those who are ignorant or ill-intentioned. I remember that in one of my articles on Mexico published in the London review *Foreign Affairs* (1925), I quoted the words which appeared in the *New York World* article signed by a well-known American writer, Mr. Walter Lippmann:

> This revolution—the Mexican—which is frequently called Bolshevik and attributed by inaccurate writers to the Russian Communists, began and ended while the Czar was still on the throne of Russia. The new Mexican Constitution which incorporates the conquests of the revolution, went into effect on May 1, 1917, six months before Lenin took over the government of Russia.

Nor should we forget that Mexico in its revolutionary struggle for economic independence went as far as it could go alone. No isolated country of Indoamerica could have gone any further. That is the first lesson that the Mexican Revolution offers us. Its limitations and its defeats are characteristic of a people which struggles in isolation to free itself from imperialism under the formidable and nearby pressure of a great enemy. I would like to repeat some ideas of mine about the Mexican Revolution: "In Mexico, we encounter a spontaneous revolution, one even without a program, a revolution of instinct, one without science. Mexico would have fulfilled a mission for Latin America perhaps as great as that of Russia for the world, if its revolution had followed a program. But the Mexican Revolution has not had theoreticians or leaders. It has not been organized systematically in any way. It is a succession of marvelous improvisations, experiments, difficulties, saved by popular force, by the energetic and almost indomitable instinct of the peasant revolutionary. For this reason the Mexican Revolution is all the more admirable; because it has been made by ignorant men.

"But Mexico has not yet resolved many of its grave problems and runs the risk of falling either into stagnation or into retreat. All the spontaneous forces of the Mexican Revolution need orientation. Mexico has not yet tackled its industrial problem. Imperialism is now a terrible threat to Mexico, and it will only be saved from that threat either by instinct and rebellion or by a scientific study and more secure direction and understanding of its policies, which in this struggle cannot be separated from the revolutionary fate of the other Latin American peoples."

In the economic map of the world, Indoamerica is still a colonial or semi-colonial region. Until a few years ago there existed in some of our republics, particularly in the more advanced ones of South America, an illusion of economic independence. Particularly in the countries where British influence—restrained in its political effects by Yankee rivalry—had not been balanced or overcome by the latter, was this the case. Even the leftist revolutionary parties fell for the appearance of independence. They believed that each of those republics was, economically, like a European country, like England, like France, like Germany. They read and reread Marx in whole or in part and, wishing to apply foreign history, invented an "industrial revolution," a "dominant bourgeois class," and "the apparatus of the state," instrument of that class. The socialist literature of various of our countries is hilariously naive for the most part. For this reason, the political programs had little contact with reality and were deformed on this account to the point of being ridiculous.

When the Apristas asserted for the first time that "our countries are colonies or semi-colonies," there was misunderstanding and protest. When the new Indoamerican revolutionary generation launched its warnings about the danger of imperialism—already disfigured by other sentimentalist literature no less unreal nor less vague than that of the theoreticians of the left—we were made to confront fortresses of theses, doctrines, and rhetoric, and we produced fearful confusion. But our message was victorious from the beginning. José Ingenieros had led the way with a precursory admonition; then a phalanx of realistic young folk presented our peoples with exactly this problem. The programs of the leftists, especially those who pompously thought of themselves as the omniscient conductors of the social movement among our peoples, were as hidden as straw hats in a summer rain. Then they wished to catch up with us, but it was too late. The puppets of foreign ideology had had their arms and legs tied and could not move freely. The separation between them and us coincident with the separation of two epochs, two generations, marked clearly the limits of our field of battle from that of . . . the graveyard.*

This preliminary step was necessary. It was the infancy of our movement, with its consequent "disease of infancy," as Engels would say. But we had wisely isolated ourselves from the sick or we had piously buried the dead, and we went forward. Imperialism confronts our peoples today with questions which have obvious answers: Are you sure of your liberty? Are you really sovereign states?

"Our world lives an economic life which crosses political frontiers" (Prof. Achille Vilate, *The Economic Imperialism and International Relations in the Last Fity Years.* New York: the Macmillan Co., 1923, p. 165), and the first consequence of the growing economic domination of North American imperialism in our countries is a political one: *the problem of national liberty.* Are we in reality free peoples? A hundred years after the defeat of Spain and with our repeated celebration of that victory, it is difficult to think that once again we are slaves—more or less slaves. Many are irritated by the suspicion; and there are not lacking members of Cuban or Nicaraguan officialdom, for example, who are capable of fighting a duel in the name of the sacred honor of the fatherland, against anyone who dares to doubt their absolute national liberty, which they think is demonstrated by having their own flags, and a president of the republic with bands of office and decorations!

But again the admirable lesson of Mexico offers us a valuable example. The Mexican Revolution would have been the most advanced revolution of the epoch, perhaps, if it had not come up against imperialist pressure. Mexico has not held back for lack of revolutionary *elan.* It has held back for lack of material force to impose completely the conquests of the revolution. If any country of Indoamerica,

---

* Haya engages here in a pun, using "campo" to mean field of battle and also to mean cemetery.

whose people, in the name of its sovereign right to adopt the political
and social form which it thinks is to its advantage, or which it believes
to be in accord with justice, would attempt to do so, it would be faced
with the same disquieting question: Will the interests of North American imperialism permit this? The oligarchies or dominant classes, allied
with imperialism and its servants in the seats of power, will raise the
question. Washington will do so, in time, in accordance with the imperious statement of Mr. Hughes at the Congress of Havana,* which
no delegate fulfilled his duty by replying to: "As is natural, the United
States cannot renounce the right to defend the interests of its fellow
citizens," said the imperialist diplomat arrogantly. The criterion of
danger to these interests, and the criterion of the defense of the same,
is, like the Monroe Doctrine, and like everything in the policy of Pan
Americanism, to be interpreted unilaterally. It depends entirely on the
judgment of the United States. The history of Cuba, Santo Domingo,
Haiti, Honduras, Panama, and the fresh example in blood of the mar-
tyrs of Nicaragua, shows clearly to us the very debatable honor of
this judgment.

Our primary problem, then, is the problem of national liberty
menaced by the imperialism which will use violence against any political or social attempt for transformation that, in the judgment of the
Yankee empire, affects its interests. That problem is common to all
our countries. None can declare itself exempt from it. The economic
influence of North American imperialism in Indoamerica is well
known. Although it does not operate the same in a Caribbean country
as it does in Peru or Argentina, the influence exists and is growing.
The Anti-imperialist Congress of Brussels was obliged to support the
thesis of "the four sectors" in view of the impossibility of denying it.
The sector of Mexico and the Caribbean; the sector of the Bolivarian
republics; the sector of Chile and the republics of the Plata; and the
sector of Brazil, appear increasingly defined as zones of imperialist
economic and political influence, differentiated by gradations in tactics
in accord with the conditions in each zone.

The five billion dollars invested by Yankee capitalists in Indoamerica needs all possible security measures. That enormous capital
must increase under absolute guarantees of security and order. Any

* This refers to the Sixth Pan American Conference at which the United
States delegation made the most frank statement of the "right" of the United
States to intervene in the internal affairs of the Latin American countries to be
made at any such meeting.

menace against the tranquil exploitation of the working masses will be violently repressed. If the governments do not have sufficient force to guarantee the security of those billions of dollars invested, imperialism will put its armies and all-powerful fleet at the service of "the interests of its fellow citizens." Insofar as these investments are increasing—and they grow every day—the exigencies of Washington in the name of their security are increasingly great.

The day may come when in the name of the interests of its fellow citizens, whose defense cannot be renounced according to the declaration of Mr. Hughes—we repeat this once again—the United States will surround Indoamerica with walls of flame from its gigantic artillery. This would be an expensive undertaking. It is not done now because there is no need to employ so much money to defend five billions. When there are ten or twenty billion, or fifty billion, the North American position will change. Our peoples will then come to be a large Nicaragua. Then, our liberty or national sovereignty will become like the memories of youth of our grandmothers, the melancholy theme of afterdinner conversations.

Our first political task is consequently that of defending our sovereignty. In this defense no isolated country can be victorious. If the danger is common, an economic one with political projections, the defense also must be common. From this fact arises the elemental necessity for a party of frankly anti-imperialist orientation; a single Indoamerican party which has a definite plan for realistic defensive action. Such a party does not need interminable complicated programs. It is enough to have a brief and concise one which expresses the summary announcement of doctrine and common action.

Some people have been surprised by the extraordinarily laconic nature of the program of Apra. We have believed that the five points cover completely the major basic problems of Indoamerica. The application of these ideas or the way of realizing them in each country will be a question for the national program of the party which each people edit and sanction, and will be as ample as necessary. The program of Apra is applicable to any one of the Indoamerican countries. How will it be applied? This is a matter which depends on the conditions in each country. However, it can be taken as a basis of programs of national action as much in Brazil as in Costa Rica, Chile as in Haiti, Peru as in Honduras. The program, as we have seen, contains five points in logical order: Action against imperialism has a corollary the political unity of Indoamerica, which in turn—as a defense against the advances of the imperialism which seeks to seize our wealth—will nationalize the land and industry. The internationalization of the Panama Canal is the liberation of a means of the circulation of wealth indispensable for the free economic life of our peoples. "Pro mundi beneficio" is the slogan on the escutcheon of the little Panamanian republic. But the Latin phrase of its new republican banner has not been fulfilled in fact. The Panama Canal for the benefit of imperialism is an instrument of the domination of our countries and a great danger in case of war. Its internationalization would be imperative, therefore, for a complete victory over imperialism. For this reason, its internationalization is for us an Indoamerican economic and political necessity.

The fifth aim does not imply merely lyric generosity. Apra shares entirely the ideals of the liberation of all peoples and classes subjugated by imperialism all over the world. Our difference from the romantics of universal anti-imperialism, who wish to tie us to the cart of the freedom movements of India, China, or British Africa, comes from the fact that we believe historically that no politically independent region of the world is more menaced by imperialism than Indoamerica. It is enough to look at the statistics and economic geography. What is the greatest world power of our times? What is the country with greater possibilities as an empire in this epoch? No one would deny that it is the United States. Then, what is the region nearest to the United States, and—this is most important—the region in which the United States has invested the most capital? We shall look at a list of recent investments:

In Europe . . . . . . $4,400,000,000 (not including the war debts)
In Asia   100,000,000
In Canada   3,900,000,000
In Indoamerica . .   5,200,000,000

If we do not accept Hobson's humorous distinction that "Patriotism is the love for our own country, and Imperialism the love for more country," and if we look at the problem economically, we must recognize that the region of the world in gravest danger because of the nature of the imperialist aggressor is Indoamerica. The figures indicate this. Apra—in fundamental contradiction to the romantics of the anti-imperialist world—proclaims its most ample solidarity with the oppressed peoples and classes of the world, but proposes to commit itself to the historical job of freeing itself from the most monstrously aggressive power of our times, so as later to make practical its aid and cooperation with its subjugated brothers. It is even strategically logical that those who are nearest to the greatest imperialist power on the earth be the first to struggle: for ourselves and for the rest. It is naive and childish to offer aid to others in this hour so urgent for our own peoples. Or to ask aid when we well know that it cannot be given. To take a concrete case: Nicaragua.

When we see some self-named delegates, among whom only two or three really represented parts of Indoamerica, go to the World Congress of Brussels, which I have already mentioned, and be relegated to fourth place, under the control of criollo Communists, we must recognize once again—in spite of our attempts to be optimistic—that the hour has come to free our anti-imperialist movements from that ridiculous and useless subservience. It is necessary to see the role of our delegates in the European congresses, in Moscow, in Brussels, and in Paris, to understand exactly how false and stupid are these tourist excursions. The problem isn't there. There they look at us as picturesque representatives of exotic regions, and ask us in set phrases the area, population, and principal cities of our countries. We make such long voyages to give kindergarten geography lessons!

The practical results, the realistic consequences of all of this useless travel are nil insofar as the march of historic events in our countries is concerned. These meetings merely repeat the absurd comedy of the interbourgeois conferences of the Pan American type. Fearing any enemy so close, and with almost a hundred million inhabitants to defend and so many millions of square kilometers to salvage, we do not need to go to Europe to ask advice or to receive lessons in struggling. Without abandoning our fraternal solidarity with the rest of the oppressed world, and using all the factors which can serve the liberating cause, Apra, with a realistic outlook, proclaims the need for an exclusively Indoamerican action for the liberty of our countries. So long as the danger is as close to us as it is today, it is we who must confront it. Thus, paraphrasing the founder of the First International, we repeat: *The anti-imperialist emancipation of the Indoamerican peoples must be carried out by the Indoamerican peoples themselves.*

VII

THE UNITED FRONT OF APRA
AND ITS ALLIES

LET ME QUOTE FROM THE THIRD PART OF THE ARTICLE "QUE ES EL Apra": "The A.P.R.A. organizes the great Latin American Anti Imperialist united front and works to include in its ranks all those who in one way or another have struggled and are still struggling against the North American danger in Latin America."

Frequently we Apristas have been asked these questions: Is Apra a party or is it a united front? Can it be the two things at the same time?

Before answering we must finish quoting that paragraph: "The A.P.R.A. was founded in 1924, with a program of revolutionary and political action, and its invites all the scattered forces to form themselves in a single united front."

Apra is a party of alliance. This has been shown in discussing the basis of its structure in previous chapters. We have mentioned as a similar case the Chinese Popular National Party, the original Kuo Min Tang, which also has been a united front anti-imperialist party. We recall that even in the economically most advanced countries there are cases of parties of the left constituting vast organizations of a united front against the political domination of the exploiting class. The English Labour Party is a good example. Not only does it include workers and farmers; it includes in its front a vast sector of the lower middle classes; and under its banner are numerous groups and tendencies. To the example of the English Labour Party might be added many other similar cases of parties of the left in France, Germany,

---

"El Frente Unico del Apra y Sus Aliados," from *El Antimperialism y el Apra,* Chapter V.

the Low Countries, and Scandinavia. If in the European industrial
countries, where the proletarians are old and numerous, it has been
necessary to have an alliance of the proletarian, peasant, and middle
classes—forming common fronts under a single party discipline—in
Indoamerica, because of the objective conditions of our historical
reality, it is even more necessary.

Apra must be, then, a political organization, a party. It represents and defends the various social classes that are menaced by the
same danger or are victims of the same oppression. In the face of such
a powerful enemy as imperialism, it is indispensable to bring together
all of the forces which can cooperate in resisting it. This resistance
has to be simultaneously economic and political, that is to say, the
organized resistance of a party. As such, Apra must have its own
discipline and tactics.

We have said in the previous chapter that the struggle against
imperialism is also a nationalist struggle. It is well worth recalling that
while there are social classes *permanently* attacked and exploited by
the imperialist advance, there are also those which are only temporary
victims. A large part of our bourgeoisie in formation is of this type.
As a result Apra can ally itself with them in a transitory front, so long
as their strength is necessary for the common defense. It is enough
to recall that the stage of nationalist struggle against imperialism is
present in all our countries, and it undoubtedly will be for many years.

Outlining this position of Apra, the review *Atuei* of Havana,
inspired by the doctrines of Aprismo, has just published an interesting
theoretical appraisal of our realistic conception of the united front
with relation to the national bourgeoisies menaced by imperialism.
Important paragraphs of the article are the following:

> It is false, absolutely false that Apra doesn't need the
> bourgeoisie in the struggle against imperialism. On the contrary,
> it proposes to use in favor of the cause which it supports all of
> the divisions which arise between national capitalism and North
> American capitalism. It is ready to take part in all conflicts
> occurring between Yankee imperialism and the criollo bour-
> geoisie, and to weaken the major enemy by depriving it of arms.
> Apra will seek by all licit means to have the national bourgeoi-
> sie serve the ends which it is seeking, but it doesn't believe it
> logical to form a united front with this bourgeoisie or to con-
> stitute an organization to direct the struggle in which this class
> is represented, so that this class can weaken our forces and
> acquire by means of subterfuge and intrigue the effective control

of those organizations. Above all, Apra considers it infantile, stupid, and disgraceful to announce to the four winds the intention of misleading the bourgeoisie, because, while this announcement would set straight the proletariat concerning the objective which is being sought, it puts on guard the ally that it desires to use and makes difficult any pact. In the face of this childish tactic, in the face of this puerile strategy, which warns the enemy of the trap which is being laid, Apra counsels a rational procedure. It creates homogeneous organizations of forces contrary to imperialism, gives as the basis of their efforts the recognition of the class struggle, brings together under its banners all of the exploited and reaches with the bourgeois forces—transitorily anti-imperialist—transitory agreements, without confusing itself with the bourgeoisie, stating precisely in each case the extent of the agreement, its duration, and its objective. Apra neither misleads the bourgeoisie nor makes available to them knowledge of its own secrets, of its own discipline, of its own agents. Such a tactic has an advantage in preventing the bourgeoisie from becoming accustomed to its own unity. In Cuba, when the tenant demands of the Yankee landlord seven arrobas of sugar cane in place of six, Apra will put all of its forces at the disposition of the tenant, but in no way will give him entry into its organization. The tenant is also an enemy of Apra and will turn against it when the Yankee satisfies his demands. Even more, at any moment of the struggle, and inevitably afterwards it will be the ally of imperialism.

Where Apra cannot act as a party, it will act as a group and will organize the anti-imperialist united front, and where it exists as a party it will always tend to organize a common front under its leadership, allying itself with the forces which are transitorily anti-imperialist. The Aprista thesis so well explained by *Atuei* in referring to the united front, in spite of referring to the case of Cuba in particular, can be generalized and extended to the conflict of imperialisms in the other countries of Indoamerica. Apra considers Yankee imperialism only as the most dangerous, because it is the youngest, the most potent, the most menacing, the nearest, and the one that uses the political weapons of force with more freedom. To express that better, it is the one which has monopolized these political weapons with the arbitrary interpretation of the Monroe Doctrine.

Apra proposes to use all dissidence between national capital and Yankee capital, or English, Japanese, German, Italian, Spanish, Chinese, or Syrian, against our greatest enemy. We know that conflict between foreign imperialisms exists in Indoamerica. The laws of com-

petition which preside over capitalist organizations do not permit anything but transitory alliances. The belligerency among the capitalists
continues and is increasing. Our countries are an immense economic
battlefield for the imperialisms of the world, particularly the English
and the American. Must we lose the opportunity to use in behalf of
the anti-imperialist cause this implacable conflict? Not to make transitory pacts would be to engage in an "infantilism of the left." To make
permanent pacts such as those which were developed by the Anti-
imperialist Leagues in the Congress of Brussels would be to fall into
a reactionary and suicidal policy. Apra supports the tactical utilization
of all means of anti-imperialist defense which can be found in the imperialist competitions, using them as means of advancing, but never
falling into compromising agreements. China teaches us, also, that
it is dangerous to permit all of the tentacles of imperialism to join
together and press at the same time.

Since the struggle of the wolves exists, we must place ourselves
behind those that attack the most ferocious. When they, with our aid,
have destroyed the greatest sanguinary beast, we shall have greater
probabilities of successfully doing away with those remaining. We
know that basically the vast problem which imperialism presents Indoamerica, as in all the problems of history, is the antagonism between
classes. We believe that it is necessary to battle to the end for the freedom of the producing classes, because we know that their liberation
will be the definitive liberation of our peoples. The question now is
to know how to struggle against ominipotent enemies, and how to fulfill the necessary stages of this struggle. For the first great task of
national defense, the effort to affirm sovereignty, and for the economic
and political unification of our countries—the precursor step to the
final struggle—we need allies who will join a great nationalist movement under the banners of Apra. The anti-imperialist cause needs
allies! Whether the allies are more or less temporary, it needs them.

Constantly one hears of the possibilities of an imperialist war
between the United States and England or between the United States
and Japan. Many people counsel our immediate and unconditional
alliance with the possible enemies of Yankee imperialism. Lozowsky,
erroneously interpreting my point of view on this question—undoubtedly known to him only through people ignorant in politics—writes
me in one of his letters the Peregrullesqe truth that we must not confide in Japan, because it is as imperialistic a power as is the United
States. Anyone would think it impossible that a man such as Lozowsky

would mention such an elemental fact. However, this indicates the erroneous and disdainful concept they have in Russia of our intelligence and perspicuity. I answered Lozowsky that he did not need to tell me that Japan was an imperialist power; that that would not prevent us from trying to use its rivalry with North American imperialism should an opportunity arise. Because Indoamerica must always keep in mind the possibility of an imperialist conflagration in which, without doubt, the United States will have to play a transcendant role. Leonard Wolf, in his book *Imperialism and Civilization,* writes: "The rivalry between Japan and the United States, and the problem of the Pacific, is only one among many examples of this imperialist struggle for power and pre-eminence among the larger states of the world." We, the Indoamericans, must not forget that in that Yankee-Japanese rivalry and in the so-called problem of the Pacific, our destinies are involved. Only a wise, realistic, foresighted, "continental" policy on our part can save us in such a situation.

In a debate on the Monroe Doctrine at Harvard University last autumn, between Professor Baxter, aided later by Professor Clarence Haring, some students and me, one of the young defenders of North American imperialist policy accused me thus: "you Latin Americans would join forces with Japan in case of a war against us. That is why we must maintain openly the unilateral nature of the Monroe Doctrine." The excessive statement and the corollary which my opponent attempted to derive from it was the logical consequence of his first simplistic statement. However, it is proof of a more or less popular belief, and therefore a more or less widely accepted belief, in the United States. The unreal, the absurd, is to state the question in such terms. War between the United States and some other imperialist power or between the United States and various powers, or between the United States and all of Europe—which not for simple prophetic disposition but for deductions of an economic nature, Edison* predicted a few months ago—should not be something which surprises us. Within the dialectic of the historical process of capitalism in its final imperialist stage, to predict a war is not to speak like the witches in the first act of *Macbeth.* Even more, within the system of the economic-political relations of the imperialist states, war is inevitable. The absurd thing is to take the means as the end. Those in our coun-

---

* Reference here is to Thomas A. Edison, the inventor, and amateur authority on world problems.

tries who, hoping that in the next imperialist war Japan or England will come to save us from the Yankee clutches, and fatally postpone until then the solution of the problem of our emancipation, are ingenuous. No one will save us but ourselves.

The essential solution for Indoamerica is to be able to count upon a politically organized and disciplined force capable of indicating, with authority and certainty, the most realistic direction for all to follow in the case of an imperialist war. It is to be hoped, then, that there will be parties of Aprista ideology in one or more of the states of Indoamerica. From a position of leadership in the government, it will be more possible to lay down a policy along continental lines in case of war. Power is also an eminent tribune from which to accuse and fight the governments and groups, those accomplices of imperialism, which in that case will try to divide us. We must not forget that when a war occurs between the United States and any other rival power, imperialist pressure on our governments will be very severe. The attempt will be made to involve us in the conflict, in order to use our blood and our resources. The logical imperialist plan would be to use us and sacrifice us wherever possible. There will be invoked also in this case the doctrine of the "defense of the interests of North American citizens" and in the name of this doctrine many excesses in the power of the strongest will be excused.

At the outset of the next imperialist war in which the United States will take part, we shall run grave risks if a foresighted policy does not guard the sovereignty of our peoples. All the North American sources and industries of raw materials based in our Indoamerican countries would be the target of their enemies who will try to attack the Yankee power in all of its positions. No one can guarantee that we would not be assaulted as being under North American control. Were not the German colonies in Africa attacked? So long as we do not adopt an energetic and realistic policy freeing us from our colonial or semi-colonial condition, there will hang over Indoamerica the danger of becoming a wide battlefield. If our countries are today the scene of an implacable economic struggle of imperialist competition, in the event of war—the violent culmination of all the competitions of capitalism—they will necessarily be the scene of tragedy.

As in the Great War of 1914–1918, the colossal adversaries will try to bring into the conflict all of the countries which are subject to them. Pretexts will not be lacking. In the hour in which the great interests of imperialism are in play, it would not be difficult to create myths and raise very high resonant and magical orders of the day. The literature of war always tends to make it sacred, which is not difficult when propaganda is organized and well paid. New principles, similar to those of Wilson would push our youths into the defense against some "enemy of Justice and Law" which would be Satanized as such because they were in conflict with the United States. They could invoke so many things! "Pan Americanism," and "young America against old despotic Europe," would appear in such a case as the moral aspiration on which would be hanged our neutrality and sovereignty.

Only a clear anti-imperialist consciousness in our peoples would free us from such an immense danger. Only an Indoamerican national political party could form and lead this consciousness. It is such a party that would keep us from falling into an imperialist conflict, without any prospect other than that of our being the serfs of the power that won. We must not forget that the investments of imperialist capital in our countries makes us the spoils of war. Economically, we form a part of the North American or English empire. If the empires dispute, the serfs pay. Until we understand this, we shall be nothing more than were the slaves of antiquity whom Aristotle defined as "the rich booty which produces wealth."

The formation of an anti-imperialist consciousness in our peoples is, then, the first step towards our integral defense. This consciousness is economic and political, or to express ourselves with more precision, is a consciousness of the *Indoamerican economic nationalism,* without which our peoples cannot conserve their liberty.

Against the Pan Americanist demagogy, which is the continental patriotism of the North American empire, we must impose upon ourselves the economic nationalism of Indoamerica. This nationalism will go beyond the limited and localist, false patriotism of the spokesmen of chauvinism, and will include the twenty countries which form our great nation. It is this nationalism which will teach us that in the face of the great imperialist interest of the United States, we must place first our great interest in the peoples who form the states of Indoamerica, united by the supreme necessity of defending themselves. This Indoamerican economic nationalism is what Apra advocates.

In dealing with this subject, it is worthwhile to analyze some of the principal aspects of it, to understand the affirmative statements of economic nationalism. Once before, from the illustrious platform of the National University of Mexico, I sketched some of the points

related to this exceedingly important topic. I shall summarize here
the central ideas then discussed; to arrive at the optimistic corollaries
which, without exaggeration or phantasy, allow us to believe in an
organized defense of Indoamerica, based on the moral force of our
economic nationalism. Taking as a possibility those words of Hegel,
in his *Philosophy of History,* that indicate a probable destiny of the
Americas as "perhaps the struggle between North America and South
America," we shall face the issue.

Imagining that one hundred years after the Hegelian statement
it will become a reality, I began by formulating and defending this
thesis: a war between two imperialist powers is not the same as a war
between an imperialist power and its economic colony. We shall see:
War between England and Germany, or between France and Germany
was not the same type of war as the recent struggle between China
and England. As I have said before, it was an English military man
of certain importance who, when I asked him at the moment of mobilization of the British army for China in 1926, if they were going to
do away with that country—which didn't seem to me particularly difficult given the technical military superiority of the English—answered
me very clearly: "We shall take good care to fire as little as possible.
Remember that our interests are there. Remember that the Chinese
are workers who increase our capital. If we exasperate them too much,
they will do away with our interests, they will go to their huts to eat
a handful of rice and live more or less tranquilly. Then English capital
will have suffered irreparable losses."

The struggle between two rival imperialist powers is logically
a war without mercy. The war of an imperialist power against a power
that is economically subordinate to it has other characteristics and
requires other tactics. The capital which is invested in colonial or
semi-colonial countries is going to be increased by foreign workers.
Imperialism exports capital; it doesn't export workers or peasants.
The real profit is in cheap labor. Capital which emigrates is going to
be augmented by the native workers who labor for a minimum return.
If those workers rebel by taking part in a national anti-imperialist
uprising and the armies of the dominant country pitiously exterminate
them, they would be rapidly destroying their own workers and their
own instruments of labor. Or they would be creating in them a spirit
of revenge and rebellion which would do away with the tranquil exploitation which imperialism needs in order to prosper. This explains
why the imperialist powers use a tactic of "stick and carrot" with the

imperialized countries under their economic control. This explains also why they prefer to corrupt rather than suppress. In which case, they are better off than by suppressing all interior resentments, employing the very able tactic of *divide et impero*. Thus they impede the formation and strengthening of a national spirit which would bring with it the unanimous impulse to rebellion.

In the struggle of a rebellious people against the imperialism enslaving them, imperialism is faced with the danger of killing the goose that lays the golden eggs. Either it must submit to the conditions that the goose imposes, or it must kill it and lose everything. This explains for us many peculiar aspects of the history of contemporary aggressions. For that reason, when one of our countries, or a part of it, the smallest, the most insignificant and the most backward, rises audaciously against imperialism, we must prove that in those wars, so clearly unequal, victory does not always come to the strongest. Simply considered, the question of which would win in a struggle between one of the countries of Indoamerica and the United States, evidently the latter would be victorious. But the dialectic of the facts doesn't give us such an easy answer. There is an immediate case: Nicaragua. The most powerful country on the earth must have some reason—some reason that is neither piety nor generosity nor the spirit of justice—for not having exterminated brutally a country of seven hundred thousand inhabitants. Looking closely at the tactics of imperialism in that country, as in any of the rest of ours in similar conditions, we will note that the greatest efforts are not directed towards creating unanimous resistance of the subjugated people against the subjugating empire. The greatest efforts are directed towards dividing the opposition, towards stimulating national or local jealousies, and towards turning one group against another. This policy is being carried out in each dominated country and is concentric in Indoamerica. It is also used to incite one country against another. . . .

How can we undermine the divisionist intrigues of imperialism and work for the formation of a widespread and clear Indoamerican anti-imperialist national consciousness? We can divide the answer into two parts: by political action which has as its immediate objective the unification of our countries for the formation of a great united front of anti-imperialist states . . . and by propaganda among the masses, especially among the working classes, so that the hand that labors will be the hand that defends, demonstrating that the boycott and passive or active resistance will be used against imperialism. This

nationalist consciousness which, not finding any other name, I have
called economic nationalism, must bring to our peoples that conviction
that the wealth which imperialism exploits is ours and that that same
wealth must be converted into our best defense. If imperialism uses
it today as an instrument of national slavery, we must transform it
into a weapon of liberation. It is not necessary to elaborate further
on such a suggestive point.

For this work of awakening, of forming a consciousness of economic nationalism, which is an anti-imperialist consciousness, Apra
must be an authentic party representing the working masses, unified
as a great front. It doesn't concern us that the workers belong to red
or yellow organizations, political or apolitical ones. What interests us
is that they are workers and that they aid us in giving strength to the
great anti-imperialist common front. The old quarrels of the Communists against the Socialists, and against the Anarchists, and against
the Syndicalists, their quarrels among camarillas and their in-fighting,
made Communism fail noisily when—through the Anti-imperialist
Leagues—they attempted to form a true united front. The leagues
brought with them the original sin of being criollo Communist organizations, sons of an anemic mother and heirs of paternal phobias. For
this reason we have seen that the powerful labor and peasant organizations remained outside this attempted front. It is infantilism and
absurdity, not just infantile leftism, to attempt, for example, to make
the vast labor organization, united under the banners of the CROM
or the CGT, submit through the Anti-imperialist Leagues to the Communist Party.* It would be equally so to insist in Argentina or Brazil
that any of the powerful, apolitical, trade union organizations enter
the official Communist camp through any league formed *ex profeso*.
No one who understands Indoamerica can deny that this is absurd.

Will our cause have allies in the United States? In Lozowsky's
letters, to which I have so many times referred, the Russian leader
discussed this question a great deal. "The logical allies in the United
States of the Latin American anti-imperialist forces are only the North
American workers. The intellectuals and other elements are false
allies, are enemies of the working classes." In replying to Lozowsky
on this point, I recalled an interesting incident between him and
Dunne,† the Yankee Communist trade union delegate, during the

---

* Haya refers to the two principal Mexican labor groups of the 1920s.
† William Dunne, longtime United States Communist leader.

Congress of the Red International of Labor Unions in Moscow, which I witnessed as an observer designated by the workers and peasants of Peru in 1924. The discussion centered on a certain question about the unions of Negro workers in the United States, and Lozowsky presented his point of view in strict accordance with Leninist theories. The Yankee opposed him for practical reasons. Lozowsky insisted. Dunne, an impulsive man, shouted at Lozowsky: "that would be possible in Russia, but it is impossible in my country; if you want an organization such as you propose, go ahead and try it." Lozowsky diverted the ire of the practical organizer Dunne with a disarming response: "I shall go when you are president of the United States." The memory of this dialogue was very much alive when I answered Lozowsky. Theoretically his point of view was beyond discussion. In terms of classes, imperialism exploits the colonial working classes, and it is the duty of the workers in the imperialist country to express solidarity with them, since they are exploited by the same class. Practically, however, the question has several interesting aspects.

The relations between the imperialist countries and the imperialized nations bring with them some complications worthy of note. It is not possible, for example, to think of the emancipation of India from the British Empire, without recognizing that the effects of this separation would be projected violently upon the English economy and would affect all social classes. The astute Lloyd George, "a man who has learned much from the Marxists," according to Lenin, has demonstrated in his famous Green Book on the English agrarian problem, that England imports more than sixty percent of the food it consumes and that the sudden loss of the British colonial empire or the end of communication with it for a long time would have disastrous effects. This would have occurred during the last European war if the German naval blockade had been successful.

The paradoxically pacifist doctrine of Gandhi, who leads his compatriots in noncooperation, would have had the most violent effects on England if we can imagine that all of the citizens of India, obeying the counsel of their great leader, had gone on strike and refused to work. The effects of Hindu passive resistance would have been disastrous in England, especially among the poorer classes. It is certain that this would have been a stimulus for the social revolution; but the English workers preferred not to cooperate insofar as the agitation in India was concerned.

The English coalminers have complained constantly against their comrades on the European continent for their lack of solidarity during the strike of coalminers in England, which was taken advantage of by the strong demand for the products of competing mines, whose workers did not go on strike (France, Germany, Czechoslovakia, and other countries). The same kind of complaint had been launched by the continental workers against those of the island on previous occasions. Class solidarity even among the imperialist countries is not shown to be so effective, then. This is further illustrated by the case of the English miners' strike of 1925 and 1926 which was aided effectively only by Russia and was faced with total indifference by millions of European and American workers.

These failures of labor solidarity are determined by economic reasons that are too obvious to require explanation. "Wages are based exclusively upon the competition among the workers," said Marx and Engels in their manifesto of 1848, studying a part of the evolution of the proletariat. As a result of the increase in production of armaments in England during the mobilization of troops for China in 1927, the workers in the war materiel factories in Newcastle refused to cooperate with the workingclass movement in favor of "hands off China," begun by the Laborites. The workers saw in that period of emergency the possibility of an increase in wages. It is evident that such failures of class solidarity are transitory. But they exist, they are produced and repeated, and in some cases they continue for a long time. They appear particularly in the countries where capitalism is incipient or is already in decline, and where unemployment makes even more distressing the conditions of the proletarians. In both cases, they appear as a kind of national collective egotism, or fear of losing cherished positions, either because of their abundance or because of their scarcity. This is very apparent in certain countries of Europe at the present time.

In the United States the capitalist "golden age" permits a certain well-being for the majority of the workers. This welfare constitutes "the work which is not paid for," the labor of the servants of the North American imperialism in all regions of the world. This benefit is indirect or direct. It is indirect because the easy and rapid multiplication of Yankee capital invested abroad brings to the United States a stream of wealth which is translated into national welfare, in a high standard of living capable of being extended eventually to the proletarian classes. It is direct when the Yankee workers who work for the same company, which also exploits the native workers of Indoamerica,

Asia, or Oceania, receive a higher wage than is paid to the native worker in any colonial or semi-colonial country. The wage scales of the great trusts—with activities inside and outside of the United States—in petroleum, mining, or industry, reveal to the North American worker his advantageous position. If we also keep in mind the almost total ignorance which exists about other countries in the working class of the United States, and the nationalist propaganda of capitalism about the superiority of race and the civilizing mission of the North American people, we shall understand that it is difficult to break these barriers and create links of solidarity between the North American workers and our workers. Class action in this sense is limited to those minor groups of "intellectual workers," but without any effect on the great masses. Some day it will come, but one must wait a long time. In my answer to Lozowsky's question on this point, I said that for now we have potentially valuable allies, even though they may be transitory, in the intellectuals and in some representatives of the North American middle classes. Sentimental or intellectual allies in the strict sense of the word, but allies nonetheless.

We must observe that in a country which becomes imperialist there occurs a phenomenon similar to that which is produced in the country to which imperialism comes: The middle classes suffer the rigor of displacement or of shock. They feel it in their economic effects; they are always the classes least favored by the transformation of capitalism. In periods of crisis large sectors of the middle classes sink. "From the doctor, from the lawyer, from the priest, from the poet, from the sage they have made wage workers," said Marx and Engels in the first part of their immortal Manifesto, eighty years ago. It is easy, then, to encounter in certain parts of the North American middle class allies for our cause. Not permanent allies, but allies who in a given moment offer cooperation: Writers, professors, students, and religious pacifists form for now the majority of the North Americans interested in our welfare. From their ranks have come some decided propagandists, sincere and capable of anti-imperialism. I believe that it is through these allies that our cause can come to interest the masses. The American Communist Party and its Anti-imperialist League of the Americas have revealed too much of their world political affiliation to be able to lead in the United States a vast movement of solidarity with the cause of our peoples. Within its ranks, not very numerous, they organize noisy protests which only serve the imperialist agents and their press as demonstration and proof of the idea that the Indoamerican protests against imperialism are managed from Moscow.

So long as the sharpening of the capitalist crisis doesn't have repercussions in the North American proletarian classes to the point of arousing in them solidarity with the workers of Indoamerica, our anti-imperialist cause needs its intellectual allies in the United States. So far the best books against North American imperialism—we say it frankly—have appeared in North America. It is worth remembering that even if we still have in our countries politicians and "patriots" who deny the existence of imperialism and its dangers, it is the North American intellectuals who have warned us of it. For those who doubt this, I repeat these energetic words of Mr. Samuel Guy Inman, Professor of Columbia University:

> In the smallest countries of Latin America, controlled by our soldiers, our bankers and our petroleum kings, we the North Americans are developing our Irelands, our Egypts and our Indias. The policy of the United States in Latin America, with its combination of bribes, of warships and of dollar diplomacy, is essentially imperialist and signifies the destructon of our own nation, exactly as Egypt, Rome, Spain, and Germany and all the other nations were destroyed which wished to measure their greatness by their material possessions rather than by their passion for justice and by the number of their friendly neighbors. (From *The Atlantic Monthly*, July, 1924.)

VIII

THE HISTORICAL TASK OF APRA

FOR THE CRIOLLO PATRIARCHS OF MARXIST ORTHODOXY, THE CONCLU-
sions of the previous chapters imply, without doubt, an audacious
profanation of all the sacrosanct concepts of a creed which they consider absolute, static, and inviolable. However, it is necessary to
remember that there exists a profound difference between Marxism
interpreted as dogma and Marxism in its authentic significance as a
philosophical doctrine. In the former everything is quietism and paraly-
sis; in the latter everything is dynamism and innovation. The immortal
maxim of Heraclitus the Obscure, picked up by Marx through Hegel,
must not be forgotten: "Everything moves, is negated, becomes; it
is in eternal return. . . ." On this is based the dialectic of life and
of history.

The normative line of Marxist philosophy is inseparable from
that of the development of its economic and social theories. Movement, contradiction, negation, and continuity, preside over universal
and human development and inspire the ingenious structure of the
complete system of Marx. "Marxism is a total concept of the world,"
Plekhanov has written, but "concept" is not dogma, and in the Marxist
concept, the principle of "the negation of negation" is primordial and
permanent.

The doctrine of Apra signifies within Marxism a new and
methodic confrontation of Indoamerican reality with the thesis which
Marx postulated for Europe and as a result of the European reality
in which he lived and studied in the middle of the last century. If we
accept the fact that Europe and America are very far from being identical because of their geography, their history, and their present eco-

---

"La Tarea Historica del Apra," from *El Antimperialism y el Apra*, Chapter VI.

nomic and social conditions, it is imperative to recognize that the global and simplistic application to our environment of European doctrines and norms of interpretation should be subject to profound modifications. Here is the sense, the direction, and the doctrinary content of Apra: Within the dialectical line of Marxism it interprets the Indoamerican reality. Insofar as the interpretation of a new reality, as characteristic and complicated as is ours, must negate or modify the precepts which are believed universal and eternal, it will fulfill the law of contradictions of development: continuity conditioned by negation.

This attitude of Apra establishes already a total separation of it from the Criollo Communists, prostrate before the *sancta sanctorum* of their cold orthodoxy, whose immutable curtain they do not dare to raise. He who is on his knees does not walk; and if he attempts it before first getting onto his feet, he will have to drag himself along. This is what happened in Indoamerica to the criollo Communists. The result of their functioning as unthinking repeaters of an imported creed, is shown in the stagnation of the movement of the Third International in our countries. For the tranquility and satisfaction of imperialism and of feudal exploitation, the Muscovite dogmas lack significance and content for our peoples. Realistic action, true and efficient, is not known to the agitated leaders of criollo Communism except through their reading of the episodes of the Russian revolution, which moves them to tears.

The line of divergence between Apra and Communism became definitively fixed in the Congress of Brussels of 1927. Until then, our ideology had passed through a necessary stage of definition and study. Once its postulates were proclaimed in 1924, the active work of confrontation and amplification became necessary, which in three years served to build solidly the general bases of our doctrine. After the Congress of Brussels, where our points of view were triumphant in its resolutions, in spite of Communist opposition, we dedicated ourselves eagerly to work under the inspiration of the principles of Apra. While criollo Communism continued to stumble under the reins of Moscow, we freely undertook the Indoamerican revolutionary task, opening our own way.

We examine now, in summary, our doctrinary position.

Without abandoning the class principle as the point of departure of the struggle against imperialism, we consider fundamental the question of understanding exactly the diverse historical stages of the class struggle, and the realistic appreciation of the stage through which it is passing in our peoples. We are not unaware, then, of the class antagonisms within the Indoamerican social environment, but we present in the first place the thesis of the greatest danger, which is elemental to all defensive strategy.

The greatest danger for our peoples is imperialism. It menaces not only as an exploiting force, but also as a conquering force. There is, then, the imperialist phenomenon, with the economic fact of exploitation, the political fact of an oppression of a national character. Furthermore, as we have seen, the penetration of imperialism—especially in its contemporary and typically North American form—creates a violent juxtaposition of economic systems. Imperialism does not study what stage of evolution, what grade of development, a people has before giving its penetration a systematic aspect of cooperation and of impulse without violence. Imperialism invades, injects itself into our poor organisms without fear of paralyzing great sectors of them. An economic law impells it towards the weaker peoples. The culminating form of the capitalistic system in which there reigns the "anarchy of production" is that sharpened anarchy, imperialism, with which it invades us and absorbs our incipient economic structures.

We maintain, then, that our present historical task is the struggle against imperialism. It is the task of our time, of our epoch, of our state of evolution. It imposes upon us the temporary subordination of all other struggles which result from the contradiction of our social reality—and which are not collaborating with imperialism—to the needs of the common struggle. It is worth saying that we accept in a Marxist way the division of society into classes and the class struggle as expression of the process of history; but we consider that the greatest oppressing class—that which really backs all the refined system of modern exploitation ruling our peoples—is that which imperialism represents. Imperialism fulfills in them the function that the grand bourgeoisie does in the more highly developed countries.

When one examines this proposition, he will find that it is unopposable. Large capitalism and big industry have not arisen in Indoamerica as a product of its economic evolution. They have arrived, have invaded in a conquering fashion, and have opened their way into our midst destroying all possible competition, detaining the process of the formation of a true national bourgeoisie, and using partially our primitive feudal and semi-feudal economic architecture, to convert it into an ally and subjugated servant.

Under the imperialist system, our grand bourgeoisie, as opposed to petty bourgeoisie, then, is an "invisible" class. It is the same grand bourgeoisie of the powerful, far away, and advanced countries that acts upon our peoples in a characteristic form. It invades us with its system and upon invading us, not only agitates and transforms our backward economies, but sweeps away and totally changes our social architecture. It uses part of our feudal and middle classes and some of the incipient bourgeoisie in its firms and in the juridical and political defense of its economic conquests, but it proletarianizes and impoverishes the rest, that is, the majority. From these and from the peasant masses it begins to form a new industrial proletarian class under a modern system of exploitation. As it penetrates more into our countries, its influence is extended and sharpened. From being economic, it becomes political.

Thus it is that the struggle against imperialism assumes its true character as a nationalist struggle. Because it is the national majorities of our countries, the productive and middle classes, that suffer the effects of imperialist invasion with the establishment of modern forms of industrial exploitation, it is the total population of each country that must pay the fiscal burdens necessary for the service of the large loans and concessions. Because of these, the sovereignty of various of our states has on many occasions been drastically menaced.

In the face of this reality, Apra places the imperialist problem in its true political terrain. It establishes the primacy of the struggle for the defense of our endangered national sovereignty. It gives to this postulate an integral and new content. It indicates as a first step towards our anti-imperialist defense, the political and economic unification of the twenty republics in which is divided our great Indoamerican nation.

It is in this initial stage of united front action that the working classes must cooperate decidedly in the fulfillment of the first two complementary points in the maximum program of Apra: joint action against imperialism and the economic and political unification of the Indoamerican peoples. Under the movement directed by Apra, the working classes that make up its ranks will be led to the seizure of the largest number of positions that they can realistically conquer and use. On coming to power under the Aprista banners and united with the middle classes, they will be able to participate in the great work which is stated in the third point of Apra: the progressive nationalization of the land and of industry, that is to say, the defeudalization of the countryside and the liberation of the peasant—peon, serf, Indian community member, sharecropper, and small proprietor—and the organization of the new state economic system on the cooperative basis to control industries, destroy imperialist monopolies, and assure the national control of wealth.

For this great task we need the collaboration of the united front as a party, as we have demonstrated. Combatting the demagogic phantasies of the prophets of criollo Communism, who offer in each speech red paradises, Apra maintains that before the socialist revolution can bring the proletariat to power—a class only in formation in Indoamerica—our peoples must pass through previous periods of economic and political transformation and perhaps through a social—not socialist—revolution which carries out the national emancipation from the imperialist yoke and Indoamerican economic and political unification.

The proletarian, socialist revolution will come later. It will come when our proletariat is a distinct and mature class, able to lead by itself the transformation of our peoples. But this will not occur until much later. For now, leaving the kingdoms of illusion and prophecy, we undertake the task that is indicated to us by our historical moment: the struggle for national sovereignty and conquest of power by our party, to procure from that position of power the political and economic union of our countries, forming a bloc and a federation of states against a common oppressor. We need "our French revolution," or to speak in our own idiom, our "Mexican revolution" combining the struggle against feudalism with the struggle against imperialism and establishing a precursor era to later transformations.

This is not pure socialism? This profanes the sacred doctrines inspired in the revolutionary books? This may be, but it is reality. Let the hairs rise on the necks of the theorisers of criollo Communism, bad interpreters of true Marxism! Let them accuse us of betrayal, of reformist opportunism, or of fascism! Apra for the last four years has been proclaiming a new realistic and firm political creed, negating the previous negations which had been converted into dogma. Apra rejects misleading demagogy and those who disfigure our cause. So that our opponents will not be too alarmed, it seems to be reassuring to cite the last paragraph of the editorial article of *L'Humanite* of Paris of February 28, 1928, official daily of the French Communist Party, which exactly translated said this:

The major part of the countries of Latin America are in reality feudal or semi-feudal monarchies. For that reason, the social context of the anti-imperialist struggle is, before all, the democratic revolution, the annihilation of the last feudal vestiges, the liberation of the peasants, the agrarian revolution. Only behind these events can one see the outlines of a bloc of independent worker and peasant republics in struggle against the dollar.

It is sad, but necessary, to break the old dreams of impossible revolutions in the European mode. It is cruel, but indispensable, that the impact of reality destroys the beautiful and intricate panoramas constructed hurriedly by tropical phantasy, borrowing from Europe, persons, doctrines, episodes, and circumstances, until a complete illusion of a stage is created adaptable to foreign tastes. But a few modern industrial factories founded by imperialism, a few cities built on European lines, and a few hundred people dressed in Paris and London fashions cannot make history skip over inescapable stages of development. It is absurd to envision in our present economic and social reality—colonial or semi-colonial, "feudal and semi-feudal"—an industrial, capitalist Indoamerica, master of all of the refinements of technology, where the period of bourgeois control has been fulfilled, and where the hour has come to sing the triumphal hymns of the advent of an exclusively proletarian government, well adjusted to the framework of the orthodox theories of pure socialism.

The social reality of our peoples is otherwise. Our present historical stage does not correspond to the language borrowed by improvisational social theorists. A practical program of struggle against imperialism in Indoamerica cannot be a Russian salad or mere promises. The struggle against imperialism is linked to the struggle against feudalism, to the preliminary process of economically and culturally emancipating the peasant. In this struggle the workers intervene, contribute, and take up the weapons to achieve positions of predominance imposing their rights of organization, of education, of meeting, of striking, and of progressive participation in the benefits of state controlled industries. They use for their benefit all the political conquests possible within a functional democracy and become by means of the party in power, one of the directing classes of the anti-imperialist state. The decided contribution of the proletariat to the extinction of feudalism and the struggle against imperialism and for national liberation, opens a new step of development, affirmation, and class progress. Cooperativism and the nationalization of the land and of all industry that it is possible to nationalize, and the organization of a new system of national economy which opposes the monstrous exploitation of imperialism—centralized as far as possible in the national economic government—these are the first tasks internally for the Apristas of each country.

The influence of the working class will be the greater as its importance as a defined and conscious class is more effective. In the more industrially developed countries, worker cooperation with the anti-imperialist movement of national defense must naturally be qualitatively greater than in the countries where industrialism is more incipient. Under the banners of a party with a well defined economic program such as Apra, the anti-imperialist movement will go further as the revolutionary impetus which accompanies it is greater. It should not have and cannot have more limitations than reality. Nothing can or should be sacrificed to it; and it is absurd to formulate programs or plans for progress along fixed lines, without knowing how strong the movement is and under what objective conditions it is to be generated. A party such as Apra does not ignore any realistic possibility for the present or the future.

Promoting the unification of the Indoamerican countries so that a great economic and political organization can be formed to confront imperialism—attempting to balance its gigantic power in order to control the production of our soil—is without doubt the necessary task of Apra, before and after its first political victory anywhere.

What, then, will be the type of state which we have referred to several times in this chapter as the Anti-imperialist State?

In the article "Que es el Apra?" we said: "Within the capitalist system, and in accord with the dialectics of its historical process, Latin America would infallibly become a North American colony." We have seen that the state in our countries is either feudal or semi-feudal; but it is always colonial. We have seen that the state in Indoamerica, within its present feudal or semi-feudal capitalistic economic architecture, depends inevitably on imperialist support, whereby that state becomes an instrument of domination over our peoples and cannot find an economic direction other than the slavery imposed by imperialism. We repeat: Within the dialectic of the world capitalistic system, our countries have no other possible liberation. Imperialism is a stage of capitalism—it is again repeated—the culminating stage. Our countries are in the first stages of capitalistic development or are

advancing towards them, seeking our liberation from feudalism or
attempting to do so. That is our path. Our countries and imperialism
are, then, within the same orbit, although on different historic planes,
chained to the same system, wheels of the same machine—although
wheels of different diameters—which connect within the mechanism
at a given movement. What, then, is our alternative?

For some there is the hope—good guardians we are of Pandora's
Box—that some day Indoamerica, or what is even more unlikely,
some one of its isolated countries, will be converted into a formidable
power, a rival of the United States as the latter has become the rival
of Europe, after having been its economic subject. For others the
answer is the fulmination of a social revolution resulting in the total
liberation from the capitalist system through the dictatorship of the
proletariat and triumphant Communism. Both hypotheses, generally
proposed in the camps of chauvinist nationalism or of simplistic and
borrowed revolutionism, represent the thesis and antithesis with their
irreconcilable opposition of opposites. It is worthwhile to analyze,
if only briefly, each of these hypotheses before giving the realistic
synthesis which Apra proposes.

The sudden transformation of our countries, with their remaining
feudal problems and complicated ethnic problems, into autonomous
capitalist powers rivaling the United States, could not compete with
the dizzying advance of Yankee imperialism over us. Our progress
towards autonomous capitalism is not equal to the formidable and
enveloping progress of the imperialist capitalism of the United States,
which is succeeding not only in controlling almost totally our economic life, but which attempts to impede our free development or
that being pursued by other imperialisms in some of our countries.
(An example is the issue of wheat and meat with Argentina which
led to bitter discussion in the Pan American Congress of Havana; a
conflict to which British imperialism is a party.) Before any of our
countries will succeed in developing an autonomous economy, the
United States will have succeeded in completely dominating its economy. The growing level of investments and loans in our countries does
not permit us to suppose that within the present economic system,
and even less in the case of isolated countries, there can be presented
to the United States a front of twenty rival powers. On the other
hand, the economic capacity of the United States does not permit us
the belief that its power will soon decline, at least soon enough for its
fall to signify our emancipation. Even if we could imagine this, would

the fall of the United States through military defeat by another imperialist power free Indoamerica? Or would it reduce us to submission
to another master?

After the imperialist war of 1914–1918, the German colonies
did not become independent, they became British, French, or Japanese colonies. A change of master, but not a removal of the chains.
In the same way, the British imperialism that has ceded primacy of
influence in Indoamerica to the United States might recover it. Or
Japan, or Germany, or some other power, would take the position
of preponderant domination.

We repeat again: Within the capitalist world system, Indoamerica is slated for colonial status. Even when we give full play to
make-believe and imagine that we shall come to form a group of
capitalist powers rivalling the present empires in Europe, North America, and Asia, such an ingenuous and complacent thesis would present
the tragic perspective of new competition and incessant and ruinous
struggle.

In the face of this thesis, usually repeated among the ingenuous
theoreticians of our ruling classes, is raised the antithesis, which like
the thesis, is borrowed from the European mentality. It announces
that the only remedy against the imperialist virus is the socialist revolution, the dictatorship of the proletariat, and Bolshevik Communism,
when not Libertarian or Anarchist Communism.

We have already shown—even with the testimony of the true
Marxist Communists themselves—that neither Communism nor the
dictatorship of the proletariat is possible at the present moment, given
the systems which now control Indoamerica. Communism supposes
the abolition of classes: "In the Communist society there will not exist
classes. Saying that there will not be classes means that there will also
not be a state." (Bukharin, *Historical Materialism,* New York: International Publishers, 1925, and *A.B.C. of Communism* by the same
author.) But "to be able to realize the Communist social order, the
proletariat must be master of all power and all state force. It cannot
destroy the old world when it doesn't have power in its hands and has
not been for some time *the dominant class,*" Bukharin adds. We do
not need to insist, then, on showing that historically, Indoamerica has
not come to the hour of the proletarian dicatatorship, much less to
Communism without classes and without the state. This has been
objectively shown in previous chapters. It is useless, also, to spend
more time in proving that Anarchist or Libertarian Communism is

even farther away, or that it is not possible to jump from the feudal or semi-feudal era in which we live to that of perfect Communism without passing through industrialism, as the Russian Populists once insisted.

One objection remains: Is it possible, without breaking the rhythm of history, that the Indoamerican countries can achieve their emancipation from imperialism and leave open the road to the complete realization of social justice?

According to the partisans of quietist Marxism, it will be necessary to await the fulfillment of historic stages: that our feudal countries become capitalist under imperialism; and that they separate capitalistically from the economic colonialism which imperialism imposes upon them. And then—once this first negation is produced within our countries and they become independent powers—there will be produced the second negation: the socialist revolution, with its dictatorship of the proletariat and its march to integral Communism. A process of centuries which would imply no struggle against imperialism, but merely resistance to it without giving social and political content to this struggle as Apra proclaims. Our road is more realistic, more precise, more revolutionary, and more constructive.

PART THREE

The Anti-Imperialist State

IN THE SELECTIONS CHOSEN FOR THIS SECTION, HAYA DE LA TORRE discusses the reorganization of the Peruvian state after the victory of the Aprista Party, so as to make it an efficacious instrument for struggling against imperialism and asserting the country's full economic independence. His theory of the role of foreign investment in the Latin American nations and a number of miscellaneous issues upon which Haya and the Apristas generally took pioneering positions are also dealt with.

Haya labels the kind of state which would be organized after the Apristas come to power the "Anti-imperialist State." As he pictures it, particularly during the 1920s and 1930s, this state will be a transitory form of political organization, to continue in existence for an undefined length of time. Its purpose is to bring about the modernization of the Peruvian economy and to establish fully the country's economic independence.

By implication at least, Haya indicates in these earlier passages that the time may come when Peru is ready for the establishment of a "proletarian" regime, more or less along the lines of the Soviet Union of the 1920s. However, such a system is utterly inappropriate for Latin America at its stage of economic and social development. Haya argues that because of the backwardness and weakness of the proletariat, Peru and the other Latin American countries will in the foreseeable future need to be ruled by the multi-class anti-imperialist state. The immediate problem, he insists, is national emancipation, not a proletarian revolution.

Haya emphasizes two characteristics of the anti-imperialist state. The first of these is that it will put great emphasis on raising the technical and general qualitative level of the economy as a whole and governmental service in particular. To this end, he stresses the need for a career civil service, putting an end to the system whereby people get government jobs by means of letters of accreditation from influential politicians. He undoubtedly goes to somewhat romantic lengths, in discussing the completeness with which patronage will be eliminated.

The second aspect of the anti-imperialist state discussed by Haya, and the one on which he places most emphasis, is the establishment of a national economic congress. It is to consist of representatives of every economic interest group of any importance in the country. Its role will be to study the economy in detail, assessing its resources, its needs, and the possibilities of fulfilling these needs and, on the basis of this continuing study, to make recommendations concerning issues of economic policy and programs to the regular congress, elected, as in the past, on a geographical basis. He is perhaps too sanguine about the possibility of eliminating partisan politics from the deliberations of this national economic congress.

One might argue that this idea has similarities to the "corporativist" notions widely current in the 1920s and 1930s, particularly in the fascist regimes. However, it differs fundamentally from these, in making the economic congress only an advisory body to the democratically chosen political congress. The conept is perhaps most strikingly like suggestions put forth in Sydney and Beatrice Webb's *Constitution for a Socialist Commonwealth of Great Britain,* published right after World War I. However, Haya gives no indication that he drew directly from either of these sources.

In any case, the national economic congress, or "fourth power of government," as Haya refers to it in the last of these selections, was never actually established. During the 1945–1948 period, when Apra controlled the Senate and had a plurality in the Chamber of Deputies, a bill for its establishment was introduced and debated in Congress. The Apristas, however, were never able to get the bill enacted.

In these selections, too, is found Haya's fundamental position with regard to foreign investment, one of his most important contributions to Latin American politics. Haya argues that both those who claim that foreign capital should be allowed to come into the Latin American countries wherever and however it wishes, and those who maintain that it should not be allowed to come at all, are wrong. He asserts that it is both true that Latin America needs the resources and the techniques brought in by foreign investors, and that the foreign investors need to come to Latin America for larger profits than they can earn in their own countries. As a result of this latter fact, he concludes that the Latin American governments can and should admit foreign capital under the conditions which these governments themselves establish, conditions that fully preserve national sovereignty and contribute to national economic development.

Haya goes even further than this statement, however. He argues that there should be representation of foreign investors in the national economic congress that will be established after the victory of the Apristas. Since their cooperation will be needed for the economic transformation of the country, he says, they must be represented in the body that is to establish the lines along which this transformation will take place.

One of the tasks of the anti-imperialist state will be to "nationalize" the basic elements of the Peruvian economy. In his earlier writings, Haya does not go into detail concerning the nature of this nationalization and its implementation. In the selection from *Treinta Años del Aprismo,* however, he goes to some lengths to explain that nationalization does not mean socialization, but rather Peruvianization, bringing the basic elements of the economy under the control of the Peruvians.

This passage from Haya's 1954 book raises the question of whether he had changed fundamentally his position from that of two or three decades before. It is true that in the 1920s and early 1930s, Haya and the Apristas generally did not define what they meant by nationalization of the economy, but one might well draw the inference that Haya did not do so because he took for granted that everyone knew that nationalization meant that the government would take over the sectors of the economy involved. Particularly is this the case in view of his argument that the land which was nationalized should be turned over to peasants' cooperatives organized for that purpose.

On the other hand, the clear implication of the *Treinta Años del Aprismo* is that he had made no such change. He presents his argument there as an elaboration of a point formerly left obscure. However, it seems more likely that Haya's position in 1954 in fact represents a substantial modification of his earlier point of view. It would seem to reflect the doubts about the advisability of virtually complete government control of the economy that were general in the noncommunist left throughout the world after World War II, as a result of the Soviet and Nazi experiences, and that found expression, for instance, in the statement of the Congress in 1951 which re-established the Socialist International, *Aims and Tasks of Democratic Socialism.*

Several other aspects of these selections are worthy of comment. One of these is the emphasis that Haya places on the need for strong municipal governments. This position was in contrast to the actual situation in Peru, where no municipal elections had been held since 1919. Subsequently, during the administration of President Fernando Belaúnde Terry (1953–1958), the Aprista congressional delegation sponsored legislation reinstituting municipal autonomy, under which two municipal elections were held before the military coup of October 1968.

Another item of significance is Haya's insistence at various points on the need to retrieve and rehabilitate the Indians, a concern of his since his youthful days in Trujillo. During all of the periods in which the Aprista Party has been legal, it has laid special stress on appealing to the Indians, and at various times has developed considerable support among them, although this backing did not find political expression, since only those Indians who could read and write Spanish were eligible to vote.

Finally, it should be noted that in the selection from 1945, Haya de la Torre was considerably ahead of his time in the emphasis which he placed on "human capital" in the development of the Peruvian economy. This phrase did not enter generally into the vocabulary of the economists until a decade and a half later. Haya early understood the importance of a country's people as a resource for the diversification and development of its economy.

I

THE NATURE OF THE
ANTI-IMPERIALIST STATE

POLITICAL DOCTRINE IN INDOAMERICA IS ALMOST ALL EUROPEAN
based. With the exception of one or two examples of independence
and realism, the philosophy and science of government, jurisprudence,
and doctrinary theorizing are nothing in our countries but plagiarisms
and copies. On the right and the left, we find the same lack of creative
spirit and very similar vices of utopian foreignism and lack of adaptation. Our surroundings and our imported modern cultures have not
yet emerged from the sterile stage of transplant. With fanatical ardor
we accept without criticism the European maxims and rules. Thus,
we raised fervently, a century ago, the slogans of the French revolution. Thus we agitate today under the banner of the Russian revolution
or the inflamed slogans of fascism. We live seeking an intelligent
master who will free us from thinking for ourselves. Even though our
historical process has its own rhythm, its typical characteristics, its
intransferable content, the paradoxical thing is that we don't see it
and do not wish to see it. We use borrowed descriptions or we look
from alien viewpoints. We have the same false security of those who
for centuries believed that the earth was the center of the universe
and the sun revolved around it. For our ideologues and theoreticians
of right and left, our Indoamerican world doesn't move. For them,
our life, our history, and our social development are only reflections
or shadows of the history and development of Europe. For this reason
they don't think for themselves, but assess, measure, name, and follow
these factors in accord with the historical classification and political
norms dictated by the Old World.

"El Estado Antimperialista," from *El Antimperialismo y el Apra,* Chapter VII.

This mental colonialism has established a double dogmatic extremism: that of the representatives of the dominant classes— imperialist, reactionary, and fascist—and that of those who call themselves representatives of the subjugated classes and speak a Russian revolutionary language which no one here understands. On this opposition of opposites, thesis and antithesis of a borrowed antagonistic theorization, Apra erects as a realistic synthesis its doctrine and its program. An essential part of them is the theory of "the anti-imperialist state. . . ."

Once again the Mexican Revolution offers us interesting points of reference. One frequently hears students of politics and European or Europeanized Marxists ask the grave question: What type of state is the present, post-revolutionary Mexican government, without the class concept of its origin and formation? The orthodox Marxists have looked at the evolution of the state which Engels studies in his suggestive book *The Origin of the Family, of Private Property and of the State* for the present status of the Mexican state, after the revolution, without encountering it. Some of the most authoritative spokesmen for the Mexican Revolution have attempted a definition when they say: "The Mexican state accepts the division of society into oppressed and oppressors, but does not wish to be considered in either group. It considers it necessary to raise and protect the present conditions of the proletariat, until they are on an equal level with those of capital in the class struggle; but wishes to maintain intact its freedom of action and its power, without submitting to any of the contending classes, to continue being the balance, the mediator and the judge of social life." (Vincente Lombardo Toledano, *La Libertad Sindical en Mexico, op. cit.,* Chapter II, pp. 84–85). However, if this opinion confirms that the post-revolutionary Mexican State does not fall within the known classifications, it does not explain in class terms its real and characteristic significance.

The feudal state, representative of the great landowners and ally of imperialism, being defeated with the Porfirian dictatorship,* gave birth to the new Mexican State which is neither a patriarchal peasant state, nor a bourgeois state, nor a proletarian state, exclusively. The Mexican Revolution—a social, not a socialist revolution—does not represent definitively the victory of a single class. The social triumph

---

* The dictatorship of Porfirio Diaz (1876–1911), the overthrow of which constituted the first phase of the Mexican Revolution.

would correspond historically to the peasant class; but in the Mexican Revolution other classes are also favored: the working class and the middle class. The victorious party—party of a spontaneous united front against feudal tyranny and against Imperialism—exercises control in the name of the classes which it represents and which in historical order, in terms of the fulfillment of its objectives, are: the peasant class, the working class, and the middle class.

It is worthwhile to keep distinct the active and representative elements of the revolutionary party victorious in Mexico—as in the revolutionary struggle of Indoamerica against Spain—who have been almost exclusively men of arms, confirming the liberating action and temporarily taking for themselves the advantages of victorious force. This merely episodic and necessarily transitory aspect, which is called "the revolutionary militarism," apparently complicates the historical picture of the Mexican Revolution. It is not strange that some biased or obtuse commentators have judged that great social movement as a mere change in oligarchic positions or a primitive and bloody dispute of caudillos and factions. Contrarily, many too simple analysts of the other extreme have believed that they also saw in the Mexican Revolution the definitive appearance of an authentic workers' socialist movement. But it is necessary to remember . . . that the Mexican Revolution, without a previous scientific program, without a defined doctrinary orientation—as a biological, instinctive, and insurrectional movement of the masses—does not offer at first glance a clear delineation which precisely classifies its social content.

In the Mexican Revolution, there is the initial period of struggle for electoral rights, suppressed brutally by the long Porfirian dictatorship. But the period of democratic romanticism—choked in the blood of its apostles—was succeeded by the violent social push of the peasant masses, taking advantage of the objective conditions favorable to a movement of frank economic demands. The laboring masses seconded the movement and contributed to give the revolution its truly social character. Separating what is purely military—rivalries, caudillosmo, barbarism—or what is exclusively political in terms of individuals or groups, which are purely subsidiary elements, the Mexican Revolution appears and remains in the history of social struggles as the first victorious effort of an Indoamerican people against both feudal and imperialist oppression. Confused, apparently by the tremendous fascination of its great tragic episodes, the Mexican social movement is, in essence: First, a citizens' upheaval against a feudal dictatorship, that despotic suppressor of democratic rights; then, a peasant uprising against the class which that government represented; and finally, a joint action of the masses of city and country—peasant, worker, and middle class—which crystallized juridically in the Constitution of Querétaro of 1917. The socio-economic content of that fundamental law of the Mexican Revolution is anti-feudal and anti-imperialist, in Article 27, and pro-worker and semi-classist, in Article 123, and semi-bourgeois or liberal in its total inspiration.*

A state constituted by this victorious movement of a united front to maintain and to complete the revolutionary conquests, which are summarized in the Mexican constitution, encounters—as the first and most powerful barrier—the problem of national sovereignty against imperialist opposition. Post-revolutionary Mexico finds that no social conquest against feudalism can go very far without running into the imperialist barrier operating in the name of "the interests of its citizens," a right bequeathed by the feudal state which was the instrument of imperialism. Again we confront the argument formulated in Chapter III: The Mexican Revolution cannot advance more in its social conquests because imperialism, master of all the instruments of violence, objects. Consequently, the revolutionary programs have been backed by only one great factor: anti-imperialist opposition. The struggle of ten years, following the promulgation of the revolutionary constitution presents us clearly with this conflict; on the one side the post-revolutionary Mexican state trying to apply with good sense or without it, the conquests translated into constitutional precepts, and on the other, imperialism, sometimes openly, sometimes playing on reactionary sentiments, always opposing the total application of the principles that had been won. Exercising in large part the economic control resulting from its penetration in the pre-revolutionary period, imperialism uses all its forms of pressure, provoking and aiding reactionary factionalists in efforts to recapture the government and to divert it from its revolutionary mission. Mexico, isolated, has a disadvantageous position in this overwhelming, immoral struggle.

What then in principle is the primordial role of the post-revolu-

---

* Haya refers to the Constitution written by the Mexican Revolutionaries that was adopted early in 1917 and remains the Constitution of the United States of Mexico. Article 27 of the Constitution contains a long list of labor legislation; Article 123 outlines a program of agrarian reform, which subsequent governments have continued to implement. These two articles contain the essential social elements of the program of the Mexican Revolution.

tionary state in Mexico? What is its true class nature? Constituted as a result of the triumph of three classes, which have won benefits in differing degrees, the historical adversary is not only the almost defeated feudal power. It is imperialism, which is reincarnated in the dying enemy, impeding the fulfillment of victory. The state thus becomes the instrument of struggle, effectively or poorly used, of these three classes against the imperialist enemy which fights to impede the consummation of the defense of the peasant, worker, and middle classes, united against the menacing imperialism. Every possible conflict among those classes is subordinated to the great conflict with imperialism, which is the gravest danger. The state, consequently, has been converted into an anti-imperialist state.

It does not matter that this historic mission of the state is not absolutely fulfilled in Mexico. It doesn't matter that the instinctive and nonprogrammatic character of the Mexican Revolution doesn't permit a clear permanent manifestation of this role of the state, making it appear sometimes as being diverted or as serving, alternatively, opposed interests. It is well not to confuse the state with the government. Institutionally and juridically, the Mexican state has its normative principles in the Constitution of Querétaro, which is anti-feudal, anti-imperialist, and democratic.

What are the results of historical experience?

Those who study the Indoamerican anti-imperialist movement of emancipation—especially the great Mexican lesson—must distinguish and separate two important elements for a correct analysis: on the one hand, the juridical principles of the state, embodied in the Constitution, that characterize it as an anti-imperialist state, and as an instrument of the defense of the three classes which are simultaneously menaced and which must fight to maintain their conquests; and on the other hand, the method of political fulfillment. The juridical principles proclaimed by the Mexican Revolution are undoubtedly anti-imperialist. Their practical application supposes the installation of an economic and political system in accordance with the new type of state. It is impossible to coordinate the theory of an anti-imperialist state with the old application of an economic, political, and social concept that does not correspond.

The most transcendental aspect that the historical experience of Mexico offers in presenting the new type of state, is the contradiction between theoretical anti-imperialist proclamations and their systems of practical application, which are partially unconnected with the former. It is from this contradiction that there can be most clearly inferred the true characteristics of the whole great post-revolutionary Mexican problem. For some, the great question may be rooted in the conflict of interests, more or less antagonistic, among the three classes which are represented in the state and which fight one another for pre-dominance, or in the struggle of these classes against feudal reaction which, while having lost political power, still conserves other elements of strength.

However, in examining in more detail the historical Mexican reality, we soon find that such antagonisms are absolutely subordinate to the common pressure on the state from imperialism, which, it is true, is allied with feudal reaction. The conflict is rooted fundamentally then, in the difference between the political texture of the state and the economic structure. In the second part of the brief preface to the German edition of their *Manifesto,* Marx and Engels, referring to the historical lesson of Paris in 1848, insist that this has demonstrated that the working classes cannot easily seize the government as it exists and make it serve their own interests. The Mexican Revolution has likewise shown that the triumphant anti-feudal and anti-imperialist revolution also cannot use the old apparatus of the state to serve the revolution's ends. When the anti-imperialist movement captures the state from the dominant classes—an instrument of the oppression of imperialism—it must transform the state. The new structuring of the state—of which we see an unfulfilled effort in Mexico, but whose experience is incomparably valuable for our people—suggests to us the bases of a true Indoamerican anti-imperialist state.

An anti-imperialist state cannot be a capitalist or bourgeois state of the type of France, England, or the United States. It is necessary to deny that if we anti-imperialists don't accept as the post-revolutionary objective the characteristic bourgeois type of state, we will fall inexorably under the wheel of imperialism. The quality of the anti-imperialist state must be essentially that of a defensive struggle against the greatest enemy. Once the defeat of imperialism is achieved in a given country, the state will become the bulwark sustaining the victory, which presumes a political and economic structure. Imperialism will not cease its aggression, and its attacks will have to seek a weak-point in the new state mechanism erected by the triumphant movement. The anti-imperialist state must be, then, above all a state of defense, which counterposes to the capitalist system determined by imperialism, a new system, distinct from the old, which will tend to proscribe the old oppressor regime.

Thus, while the imperialist offensive is apparently pacific during the period of "economic penetration"—and the struggle is not seen clearly until the noose is tightened, when force comes in defense of interests already conquered—the defensive struggle after the defeat of the old feudal state, the instrument of imperialism in our countries, will have to be an apparently peaceful struggle, perhaps, but an implacable one nonetheless in the economic field. For this reason, after the defeat of the feudal state, the triumphant anti-imperialist movement will organize its defense by establishing a new system of economy, scientifically planned, and a new state mechanism which will not be a "free" democratic state, but a war-disciplined state, that limits the exercise of economic rights in order to protect all from the incursions of imperialism.

The new state organization must evidently be something called state capitalism which was widely utilized in the period of the imperialist war of 1914–1918 and which in Germany reached a truly extraordinary level of organization. But it is necessary to point out the differences. State capitalism of the type mentioned is a defense against capitalism itself concentrated in moments of danger in its instrument of oppression and of defense. During the European war, the belligerent imperialist powers established so-called state monopolies. Production and commerce were placed totally or almost totally under governmental control. The bourgeois class in support of the state surrendered its own economic sovereignty. But once the conflict was passed, private capitalism recovered the control of production and the circulation of wealth, and state capitalism, an emergency measure, had only served to reaffirm the power of this system.

In the anti-imperialist state, engaged in a defensive economic war, it is indispensable also to limit private initiative and the progressive control of the production and the circulation of wealth. The anti-imperialist state, which will have to direct the national economy, will have to deny individual or collective rights of an economic nature when their use implies an imperialist danger. It is impossible to conciliate—and here is the normative function of the anti-imperialist state—absolute individual liberty in the economic sphere with the struggle against imperialism. The national proprietor of a mine or a hacienda, who sells his property or business to a Yankee entrepreneur, doesn't carry out a merely private contract because that buyer not only invests money in an operation, but one can say that he invests sovereignty. Behind the new interest created by this apparently simple economic operation, is political support, the force of the imperialist power backing that investor, with a point of view which is different from and opposed to that of the country which receives the investment—the interests of the foreigner. Will that be a private operation? Certainly not. The anti-imperialist state will therefore have to limit the individual use and abuse—*jus utendi, jus abutendi*—and will have to reduce the economic freedom of the exploiting and middle classes and will have to assume, as in state capitalism, the control of production and commerce progressively.

The difference between the anti-imperialist state and European state capitalism will be based fundamentally on the fact that while the latter is an emergency measure in the life of the capitalist class, a means of security and an affirmation of the system, the anti-imperialist state will develop *state capitalism as a system of transition towards a new social organization,* not for the benefit of imperialism—which supposes the return of the capitalist system of which it is a form—but for the benefit of the productive classes, which will be gradually trained for their own self-government and the use of the riches which they produce.

If the anti-imperialist state doesn't separate itself from the classical system of capitalism and instead stimulates the formation of a national bourgeois class, stimulating individualist and insatiable exploitation—supported by the classical statement of democratic-liberalism—it would fall quickly into the imperialist chains from which no bourgeois national organism can escape. For this reason, a vast and scientific organization of a nationalized cooperative system and the adoption of a political structure of *functional democracy based on the categories of labor* will be indispensable in the new state. Thus, by both means the anti-imperialist state will carry out the work of economic and political education needed to consolidate its defensive position. Thus, also, it will efficiently and in a coordinated way channel the effort of the three classes represented in it. The anti-imperialist state will direct its historic path towards another economic system which negates and defends itself from the present one for the progressive control of the production and wealth—through the nationalization of the land and of industry says the program of Apra. This must be the keystone of Indoamerican unity and of the effective economic emancipation of our people.

II

THE ORGANIZATION
OF THE NEW STATE

LIKE THE FRENCH REVOLUTION, "THAT OF '48," AND THE COMMUNE of Paris for the pre-revolutionary Europe of the last century, the Mexican Revolution has been the first contemporary social movement offering our peoples an invaluable experience. Its successes and its errors—principally its errors—offer a fecund source of transcendent teachings which it is worthwhile to gather and carefully analyze with a firm sense of our reality.

The thesis of the anti-imperialist state, suggested by the great historical experience of the Mexican Revolution, will undoubtedly engender numerous debates. At the risk of being too repetitive, and while recognizing that the question must be dealt with more extensively, it is necessary to stop to examine and answer some of the possible polemical points which will certainly be formulated by our obsessed Europeanizers. The first objection will undoubtedly be to the collaboration of the middle classes in the new state structure. In the collaboration with the middle classes, such as Apra advocates, is based one of the fundamental differences between the state capitalism adopted in Russia, upon the establishment of the reforms which gave rise to the New Economic Policy or NEP, and the capitalism of the anti-imperialist or Aprista state. Lenin defines this new policy as "a contract, a bloc, an alliance between the Soviet state, that is to say the proletariat, and state capitalism against the small proprietor (patriarchal and petty bourgeoisie)." State capitalism in Russia is exercised, then, under the dictatorship of the proletariat and against the petty bourgeoisie and middle classes, as a transition towards integral social-

---

"Organizacion del Nuevo Estado," from *El Antimperialism y el Apra*, Chapter VIII.

ism. But we have demonstrated already that the dictatorship of the proletariat is historically impossible in our countries until defeudalization takes place, or until—in the great majority of them—there really exists a defined proletarian class conscious of its own existence.

We do not forget, upon coming to this point, an essential question which must be dealt with more fully on another occasion. The proletariat, the Indoamerican industrial working class, is not, for the most part, a factory working class of the well-known, predominant European type. The labor conditions and surroundings of a factory worker in large-scale industry contribute to the preparation and to a better and more rapid definition of class consciousness. Our proletariat, due to the peculiar nature of the greater part of our typical industries— petroleum, nitrates, mines, sugar, lumbering, tobacco, and others— don't have the conditions of the great European industrial proletarians—in factories, shipyards, shops, etc. The objective conditions that determine the formation of a working class consciousness must be remembered in talking generically of the Indoamerican working class.

It is necessary to specify what type of industry is meant and what is its age and degree of development, as determinants of the formation of class consciousness. The workers of a textile factory, a South American experience, are much more organized, capable, and revolutionary than the petroleum workers—who are half workers from the countryside and half factory workers or are perhaps migrant farm workers— or than sugar workers and certain kinds of miners—whose work is more variable—although these latter groups are more numerous. Not only must we think of the quantity of workers that there are in our countries, but also of their nature; the latter being determined by the type of industry in which they work.

We have shown, then, that our social reality imposes—in this implacable anti-imperialist struggle of the Indoamerican peoples—the collaboration of the middle classes of the city and the countryside, because our capitalism is colonial and most of our dominant classes are feudal. The starting points of the movement of Russian emancipation and ours are different. We proclaim as the primary question our struggle against imperialism; Russia proclaimed as a principle the dictatorship of the proletariat. We are going to obtain our national emancipation as the first step of our social transformation that must commence and base itself on the defeudalization of our countries. Russia has succeeded in emancipating itself from imperialism by means of its proletarian class, European, organized, strong, and capable of assuming the governmental function through a class party. We have not yet reached the bourgeois maturity of an industrial system which permits our nascent proletarian class to assume exclusively the dictation of our destinies. Russia, before the Revolution of 1917, was already a great European power. It had achieved, centuries before, its national unification and a high level of culture in its upper classes. The statistics of its finances and the level of development of its science and its art give us an index of a civilization relatively higher than ours, in spite of its autocratic system of government and its social divisions.

Indoamerica, which in large part still lives under the despotic and barbarous system of czars, without pedigree, and sensual and semi-barbarian pseudo-republicans, has before it the initial task of its unification and the disadvantage of its vulnerable geographical position. Furthermore, the Russian dominant and middle classes formed part of the characteristic European bourgeoisie and "petit-bourgeoisie" with their prejudices, their culture, and their complexes. They could, therefore, be submitted in whole or in part to a proletarian party—even if it was not very numerous in proportion to the peasantry—that was very defined, compact, and well directed by intellectuals of advanced occidental mentality. Once in power, that capable proletariat has formed "a contract, a bloc, an alliance" with capitalism "against the little patriarchal proprietor and petty bourgeoisie."

We, lacking a strong proletariat trained to govern, or even any modern industrial proletariat—as is the case in the great majority of our countries—need the alliance with the middle classes for the struggle against imperialism, which in our countries is the struggle for an immediate national emancipation. A party which includes in its ranks all the classes menaced by imperialism and which organizes them scientifically, not on the basis of the postulates of bourgeois democracy but on the basis of a classic form of functional or social democracy, will be the only effective instrument of struggle against imperialism. In this party of united front, the classes menaced by imperialism will be represented in accordance with their role in production. Our feudal countries, upon being emancipated, must give pre-eminence to the peasant class, the productive class of the land—pushing first its demands, then those of the industrial working class and the middle class. It is clear that if we invert this order, we shall fall again into the bourgeois state, under the wheels of the imperialist machinery. But, establishing the organization of the anti-imperialist party on strictly scientific bases, and recognizing that the struggle against imperialism is an economic struggle, we cannot invert the order of representation of classes in the party first and then in the state. It is indisputable that in our countries there is no other form of struggling against imperialism than by political movements, a united front, which assures that the national sovereignty will install a new economic system. The organization of production on new cooperative bases is the defense against imperialism.

How should it be organized? In accordance with the economic reality in each Indoamerican state or region. In the predominantly agrarian countries, in those ruled by feudalism, which is the principal ally of imperialism, the defeat of that ally will be the principal task. If thereafter, there appears a more or less powerful colonial bourgeoisie—also an ally of imperialism—it will also have to be defeated; but a movement of economic emancipation, such as the struggle against imperialism, has to start at the beginning. What would be artificial—and here is the senility of the veteran criollo vulganizers of European Socialism—would be to attack the colonial or semi-colonial bourgeoisie before defeating the feudalism which is the basis of the Indoamerican economy.

It is likely that with European phrases we will be told: "But if you give a position in the new state to the middle class, you will come to power with that class which is the embryo of the bourgeoisie of the future; it will betray you when it feels strong, surrendering itself and surrendering you once again to imperialism." The objection is unilateral. To accept it, one would have to accept a state in which the middle classes predominate. It is necessary therefore to establish the fundamental difference existing between the historical role of the middle classes—petty bourgeoisie of city and countryside—of Europe and the middle classes of Indoamerica. In Europe the dominant class is the high bourgeoisie. In Indoamerica it is the large landowners.

In Europe the middle classes, once the struggle against feudalism had been won, have themselves undergone bourgeois domination of which they are subjects. The European middle class is a definitively subjugated class, the remains of a victorious class. Its capacity for belligerence is domesticated, and its attitude has become egotistical and inferior. It is the class which "carefully guards its banknotes because it cannot liberate itself."

It is easy to observe in the history of medieval Europe a similar period before the anti-feudal revolutions, when the young bourgeoisies tended to become the dominant classes. The historic adversary of the middle classes—the feudal ruling class—is the target of their aggression here as in Europe. But behind the feudal class—characteristic of Indoamerica—is imperialism, the major enemy of the middle class. Then, the middle class uses its capacity, its *elan* of belligerency, and struggles necessarily against both. We know why the middle classes struggle against the large landowners and against imperialism. They will wish to overthrow the first, occupy the dominant position, and ally themselves with the latter to save themselves. But the most rapid advances of imperialism will destroy quickly the middle classes, before they can take advantage of imperialism.

The belligerent capacity of the middle classes, therefore, must be used to the benefit of national liberation. They must join in the defense of the anti-imperialist state. The mechanism of this state—it must be repeated—supposes a new economic structure, based on partial or progressive state control over the production and the circulation of wealth. All of the classes affected by imperialism will logically contribute to the defense of this state.

The middle classes, as the first victims of the imperialist economic offensive, in the face of this situation, consequently, either will have to fall ruined by imperialist monopoly or be controlled by the anti-imperialist state. Economically and politically the second alternative offers greater advantages. In the feudal state, that colonial instrument of imperialism, the middle classes have only one place: They are subjected and gradually enslaved. But as collaborators with the anti-imperialist state, they become temporarily cooperating classes and therefore favored. Until the evolution towards full state capitalism—the anti-imperialist state is a state of transition always in evolution—the middle classes, even under state control will have a more effective security and freedom than under the imperialist pressure that will sacrifice them inexorably as a condition for its own incessant and monopolistic growth.

The Indoamerican social reality—especially that of the majority of nations with elemental economic development—presents us this obvious case of middle classes trapped in a dead end street by the imperialistic machine that advances upon the basis of their destruction. The small proprietor, the small merchant, the small farmer are defeated and enslaved, by irresistible competition, by the action of the monopoly which annihilates them. The famous North American monopolies of small commerce—the so-called "five and ten cent" stores of which the famous Woolworth is a formidable representative

—implies the destruction of all small competitors. The sale of soft drinks, of milk, of short-order meals, candy, fruits, has fallen into the monopolistic tentacles of this new trustified form of commerce. In the face of a branch of Woolworths, there is no small shop or store able to compete. This class of commerce is one of the most rapid forms of the economic propagation of imperialism. North American imperialism, gigantic monopolist, the most perfect, complicated, and dangerous of the world imperialisms, brings to Indoamerica typical problems that can be resolved only in terms of our own reality.

To the role of economic collaboration of our middle classes in the struggle against imperialism first, and for the organization of the anti-imperialist state later, we must add realistically the value of its undoubted intellectual contribution. The dominant feudal class does not generally provide us with intellectuals. The intellectual comes in greatest numbers from the middle classes; from the nascent bourgeoisie, the petty bourgeoisie, and the urban middle class. The intellectual, who in many cases may incline towards imperialism, must be won over, and be oriented within a program of cooperation. The engineer, the school master, the doctor, the white collar worker, the professional in general, are indispensable elements of the middle class who can contribute much to the anti-imperialist state.

Within the ideological discipline of the party, strictly controlled by the clear economic character of its program, the middle classes will offer us their technical collaboration. This collaboration is necessary, and we must seek it in order to defend the economic characteristics of the anti-imperialist movement, not limiting it to the negative and ephemeral phase of defeating the enemy, since our fundamental objective must be the efficient and integral reorganization of production. The ignorance predominant in our working classes, determined by the feudal character of our social groups, and the imminence of the imperialist danger, demand immediate defense and impose upon us the use of all the elements of struggle and with them "the weapons of thought," of which [Anatole] France spoke. The science and experience accumulated by the middle classes of our countries, must aid in our emancipating movement.

Thus, the role of the middle classes within the anti-imperialist state becomes indispensable as a role of cooperation. While state capitalism is being consolidated—a more or less long period after the taking of power by the anti-imperialist party—the contribution of the middle classes will be invaluable. It will contribute to a well understood and energetic state program of economic orientation and the organized spread of cooperatives as the bases of a better contribution of the progressively educated middle classes within the economic structure of the new system.

Again the Mexican Revolution offers us a valuable lesson. The lack of scientific and economic organization of the state, the lack of an integral structure of revolutionary political apparatus—consequence of the instinctive and unprogrammed character of the movement—has produced the preponderance of the middle class in post-revolutionary Mexico. Ideologically, politically, and economically, the Mexican Revolution, in practice, has not used the middle classes but they have to a large degree used the revolution. Speaking with European terminology we would say—so that the Marxists with a foreign dictionary will understand us—that the Mexican Revolution is infected with a petty bourgeois tendency. But this infection is not an organic ill and, to a large degree, is a bureaucratic infection. We must establish a clear distinction: The semi-class or petty bourgeoisie illness of the Mexican Revolution is due to the fact that preventative measures were not taken in time. The question was to build a new state, as a scientific apparatus constructed on the economic principle of affirming the predominance of the productive classes. But we have already seen that the Mexican Revolution is an admirable attempt, the errors of which, while obvious, grave, and undeniable, are our best lesson. The easier an evil is recognized, the more easily is it cured. The experience of Mexico in this case shows us the negation that arises in the strict organization of the anti-imperialist state with any possible deviation from limiting the middle classes to circumscribed role.

There is undoubtedly another polemical question which will be made by simplistic souls: Will the anti-imperialist state make deals with imperialism?

Yes.

An anti-imperialist movement does not presume a regressive action in the economic field or a merely lyrical impetus for a soap-bubble ideal of national freedom. Rather it is a historical step forward towards social emancipation and towards bettering the economic welfare of the subjugated. Anti-imperialism does not run up the absurd banner of "freedom for freedom's sake" when this is at the price of progress and culture in exchange for retrogression. Precisely the opposite: The anti-imperialist struggle implies the use of freedom as the jumping-off-place for progress. We don't attempt to return to idyllic

primitive forms of life for the sake of their being the pristine and
natural expression of freedom; nor is Rousseau's social contract the
new gospel of this struggle. Anti-imperialism as Apra expounds it
must obtain the economic liberation of the peoples subjugated by
imperialism, because the yoke which today weighs upon them is a
hindrance to their development. Consequently, liberation must be
always conditioned on the realistic proposition of achieving the greater
development and more rapid progress of the liberated peoples. If this
were not the outstanding objective of the anti-imperialist struggle in
its true modern and revolutionary significance, we would fall into a
blind and negative nationalism, both racist and reactionary. Anti-
imperialism is, above all, a great constructive impulse.

The defenders of imperialism have an argument which we must
not ignore: "Our countries need capital—they say—and this must
be allowed to enter, from wherever it comes and however it comes."
Who has not heard in Indoamerica such expressions in the stupid
oratory of our cheap politicians and tyrants, in the conventional language of our shopkeepers and even in the ingenuous thinking of many
ignorant sectors of our popular masses?

The claim is apparently undeniable. The Indoamerican countries
offer a wide field for the exploitation of riches, and everything in these
countries truly representing technical progress and industrialism is
due to foreign capital. No one could deny, then, that the immigration
of capital is absolutely indispensable and that if that is imperialism,
we should feel happy with it.

However, it is important to insist on a more detailed analysis of
such interesting questions and to deal with the claim as it is generally formulated. However, let us divide it in two parts, and answer
each of them separately.

Our countries need capital? The answer is affirmative: Yes.

If they need it, must it be allowed to enter where it wants and
how it wants? The answer is negative: No.

This last answer must be explained further.

So long as the capitalist system dominates the world, the peoples
of Indoamerica, like all the economically backward ones, must receive
capital from abroad and deal with it. It has already been clarified in
these pages that Apra stands on the realistic basis of our epoch and
our geographical location and the economic history of humanity. Our
economic time and our space indicate a position and a path: While
capitalism continues as the dominant economic system in the most

advanced countries, we must deal with capitalism. How should we deal with it? This is the great question.

It is evident that because of the belief that "our countries need capital from wherever it comes and however it comes," Indoamerica has received it without conditions. Without conditions on its part, but submitting to any by and in benefit of the immigrant capital! This submission and this one-sided unconditional attitude is due without doubt to the ignorance of the economic laws which direct the export of capital, totally unknown to our "statesmen" and "generals-presidents." For this reason, imperialism has created the fetish of foreign capital, messianic, redemptor, and infinitely generous.

Fetishism and ignorance replies with fear when someone indicates the dangers of imperialism: "If you oppose the conditions of foreign capital, it will never come and then our country will be submitted to barbarism and degradation. . . ." Is this not the usual argument given by our public figures, those agents of imperialism and spokesmen for its providential mission? With different words, with different objectives, there is not a conscious citizen of Indoamerica who doesn't remember reading or hearing this Pan American language. It is the vacuous and oft-repeated song of the devotees of imperialism, prostrated, convinced—and let us not forget it—well paid. . . .

It is not difficult to understand that the modern capital which seeks, outside of its country of origin, fields of profitable investment and means of increasing it, does not emigrate in order to do good, to contribute to world progress, for the attraction of adventure, or because of the patriotic dream of carrying abroad its flag, its culture, its language. *The emigration of capital obeys an economic law as imperious as that which impells the economically undeveloped countries to receive it.* It is this economic fact which determines the whole political system, thus complementing the general characteristics of what we have called imperialism. "Economic necessity indicates," write Nearing and Freeman in their well-known book on Yankee imperialism, "that all modern and industrial society *must* develop foreign markets for its excess products; *must* control the sources of food, fuel, minerals, wood, and other raw materials; *must* look for business opportunities for the investment of excess capital." (Scott Nearing and Joseph Freeman, *Dollar Diplomacy*.) Or to cite a spokesman for imperialism, let us see what Harry T. Collings, Professor of Economics at the University of Pennsylvania, writes:

In the first place, it must be made very clear that we do not invest our money in Latin America because we wish to control its political and economic life. Money is not so magnanimous that it can first serve political ends. The capitalists demand interest before interventions. *We have invested money in Latin America since 1900, because it is a better market than the United States for investments.* . . . Since 1900 the United States has produced more capital than it can invest here at a high rate of return. Consequently, some of this money, the most audacious part, sought lucrative investments abroad. (*Current History,* New York, September 1927).

One of the secrets of the "lucrative investments" which Professor Collings mentions is found in the unconditional way in which our countries have received this capital. In our America there is a competition among the governments to offer this unconditional welcome. Unconditional competition of demand, we would say in more precise terms. The lack of a common political-economic line among the Indo-american nations—we have already dealt with the importance of division among our nations in favoring the advances of imperialism—has put the United States in an advantageous position for investing, without difficulty, its immense excessive capital, taking advantage of this competition. If a country imposes conditions, there are nineteen others which give free passage. Examining a recent table of investments of North American capital, the reader will see that Mexico—the only country which so far has carried out an anti-imperialist movement in America—is the one which has received the smallest proportional increase of Yankee capital of all of the Latin American countries since 1912.

From 1912 to 1928

Percent of increase of investments of North American Capital in Latin America

Cuba	536%	Costa Rica	557%
Mexico	61	Honduras	1,233
Chile	2,906	Guatemala	85
Argentina	1,025	El Salvador	1,066
Brazil	676	Panama	520
Peru	328	Ecuador	200
Venezuela	5,300	Haiti	600
Colombia	6,150	Ste. Domingo	600
Bolivia	750	Nicaragua	566
Uruguay	1,440	Paraguay	350

This table is a clear expression of the already mentioned competition of "unconditional demand." The capital which has immigrated to our countries thus has not become a force for progress, a means of liberation, but rather chains of slavery. Behind each investment is a contract, a concession, when not a diplomatic treaty. The clauses of those agreements are based on the tacit premise of unconditionality. The combination of those agreements constitutes the interests of the North American citizens which the United States cannot cease to defend, according to the emphatic declaration of Mr. Hughes,* which he has repeated various times. The defense of those interests consists of military expeditions, bombardments, and violations. Or in the language of Mr. Hughes: "Temporary interposition," two magic words which left stupefied and convinced† the Latin American delegates present at the Sixth Pan American Conference in Havana.

To the candid thesis of the feudal governments subject to imperialism, which proclaims that "all capital is good," is opposed the antithesis of the extremist radicals: "We do not need foreign capital." The Aprista synthesis announces that while the present economic order continues in the world, there is good and necessary capital and unnecessary and dangerous capital. It is the state and only it—the anti-imperialist state—which must control the investment of capital under strict conditions, based on the need obliging excess capital to emigrate from the great industrial centers. The capitalist stage in our countries must be fulfilled under the aegis of the anti-imperialist state. We do not forget that many Latin American countries lack a proletarian class, properly speaking, or one exists only in a primitive, elemental, and nascent form. For these peoples to fulfill the capitalist stage, it is necessary to organize this state, as Apra proposes.

Another objection to this extraordinary and exclusive faculty of the state to control investments of foreign capital and the concessions which are made to it, will come from the partisans of individual freedom, those favoring the exercise of property rights, and those heroic and practical devotees of the freedom and hereditary rights of Rome to the benefit of the dominant class and, in the last analysis,

---

* Charles Evans Hughes, Secretary of State under Presidents Harding and Coolidge.
† Apparently Haya means that Hughes convinced the Latin American delegates of the inability of their countries to block the intention of the United States to interfere in their internal affairs. No effective opposition to Hughes's frank assertion of interventionism was offered at this conference.

of imperialism. This idea has been outlined before, but we insist upon it. Individual rights must be limited by the needs of the majority. A free contract of concession or of sale between an Indoamerican citizen and a Yankee capitalist is not a matter of private business. We repeat it a thousand times: In that freedom of contract, in that alliance between the capitalist, or large landholder, or mining or agrarian proprietor—who are small capitalists in relation to imperial capitalism—and foreign capitalism is based in large part the problem of the sovereignty of our countries. The interests of the "co-nationals" of Mr. Hughes—which the United States will not fail to defend—are in large part, created by the exercise of this freedom. Assuming exclusive private control over the investment of capital in the name of supreme collective needs, the anti-imperialist struggle cannot be carried on victoriously by our peoples, as has been clearly proven in Mexico. The authors of the Civil Code of the Federal District and Territories must have understood this in establishing limitations on the classical rights of property, in the name of the primary need of public security. The anti-imperialist state demands a new and complete juridical structure in accordance with the new economic structure.

Applying to public law this limitation of freedom which is imposed by our struggle against imperialism, we get to the interesting question concerning the limitation of national sovereignty. If we begin with the Pan American principles and affirm that the sovereignty of each of the Indoamerican countries must be limited by the communal interests of all of them, we would fall into the absurd thesis of Mr. Hughes, supported with boldness by the representative of Peru before the Sixth Pan American Conference of Havana, advocate of the interventionist theory. From a "Pan American" point of view, the limitation of the sovereignty of one of our countries, in the name of the interests of the rest, is as absurd a thesis as that of universal suffrage as it is practiced in the majority of our countries. But from the anti-imperialist Indoamerican point of view—separating America into the America which exploits and the America which is exploited, between imperialist America and the America subject to imperialism, and automatically rejecting the imperialistic Pan American concept—we find that among the Indoamerican peoples, the limitation of sovereignty in the name of the common interest of peoples menaced by a common danger is necessary. In the same way that a contract between a large or small Latin American proprietor or capitalist and a Yankee capitalist *is not a private matter,* a public contract between any of our countries and the United States is also not a contract involving only the contracting parties.

I shall explain myself, taking at random an historical example. The Panama Canal, or the Canal of Nicaragua. Panama, turned into a republic *ad hoc,* in the use of its new *sovereignty* contracted with the United States and ceded the Canal Zone. Theoretically, that business is something absolutely exclusive between the two contracting countries. If we analyze the principles of national sovereignty and the contractual capacity of free states, there is no cause for objection. But if we go deeper into the question, we see historically that the cession of the Canal Zone compromises all Indoamerica economically— because Panama thereby became an economic and military bulwark of imperialism. We must see that the limitation of the absolute sovereignty of Panama to contract the cession of the Canal Zone implies a right—a right of the interests of the community of Indoamerican nations—the exercise of which would have kept them from danger. In the case of Nicaragua, the issue is similar; Nicaragua, in the name of its *sovereignty* cedes, sells, or mortgages. But any of its acts will have repercussions and consequences not only for the neighboring countries of Central America, but for all of the Indoamerican countries equally menaced by imperialist conquest.

Following further this line of reasoning, we find that not only large contracts, the danger of which might diminish with simple argument concerning the so-called public or international utility, but even small contracts, concessions of minor importance, imply for our countries uncertainty about real dangers.

The private contracts to which we have previously alluded, between Indoamerican private citizens and Yankee capitalism, become public interests and, in the concept of the spokesmen for North American imperialism, "interests which the United States cannot refuse to defend." I have already referred to the arbitrary nature of the concept of "danger" to these interests, and to the form of "defense" of them. When are those interests in danger? What form or means of defense must be adopted to save them from this danger? The answers to these questions pertain absolutely to those who execute the drastic measures of imperialism. It is human to believe that our interests are always in danger and that they are never sufficiently defended. This is the law of the usurers and the money-lenders from which Uncle Sam never escapes. If we understand the danger and the unilateral way in which imperialism operates, we will see it a thousand times repeated, each time greater than the other, in the history of Haiti, Santo Domingo, Honduras, Cuba, and palpitatingly and sadly in Nicaragua, in which the implacable perfidity and brutality of imperialism is fully proven.

The problem is not, then, the "danger" of the interests of imperialism nor the "defense" of them. The issue is the interests themselves. When these interests are created by the free action of an individual as such, or of the state operating as a sovereign entity, there is being created at the same time a right of seeing "danger" and of "defending" those interests, and these things have an impact not only on the individual or state concerned, but upon all of the countries whose community of interest is compromised with each advance of the common enemy, whatever its direction.

We must recall, further, that imperialism is establishing its juridical literature, its codes, decrees, etc., and the precedent for this is its immense strength. Thus, an act of violence today justifies a greater one tomorrow. All of them together result in a juridical thesis which the representative of Peru in Havana called solemnly "the right of intervention" and which in the Protestant language of Mr. Hughes is defined as "temporary interposition."

The question of the limitation of individual freedom and of the sovereignty of each state in the name of the interests of the rest is fundamental. The theory of Apra resolves it with clarity and with realism, giving the total power of control to the state and establishing the principle of the federation of the Indoamerican states. Until this is achieved, the tendency towards coordination of a common political direction—the basis of economic unity and a step towards integral unity—appears as the immediate task of Aprismo. Openly to expose in time the democratic and liberalizing prejudices—not the principles—which imperialism uses in its service.

The anti-imperialist state establishes, then, the new lines of our juridical system of defense. We remember certain interesting words of Trotsky: "A State which has in its hands a nationalized industry, a monopoly of foreign commerce and a monopoly of the acceptance of foreign capital, for one part of the economy or another, for this sole reason already controls a rich source of resources the combination of which may make its economic evolution more rapid."

III

THE SCIENTIFIC, TECHNICAL, AND MORAL
ASPECTS OF THE ANTI-IMPERIALIST STATE

WE APRISTAS ADVOCATE A NEW TYPE OF STATE, BASED NOT ON THE citizen as quantity but on the citizen as quality. For this, it will have to be a state in which all those who contribute, in one form or another, their labor to the formation of the national wealth participate.

We desire a state in which each man participates, without abandoning his vital function as a worker. We desire a state in which the technician and the expert direct state activities so as to put us efficiently on the road which will best resolve our great national problems. We attempt to organize a technological state; we attempt to approach a functional democracy. This is the fundamental principle of Aprismo insofar as the organization of the state is concerned.

From this it develops that one of the points unique to our program is what we call the economic congress. If we do not know our economic reality, if we do not even know how many inhabitants Peru has, if we have not scientifically studied our vital problems, it is necessary to start first with an investigation of these problems. As we lack the administrative techniques of investigation, which we have never had, we must bring together an assembly of an economic type representing all those who participate in some form in the production of wealth: national and foreign capital and labor (since they form part of our economy), commerce and industry, transport, agriculture, and so on. With the worker and the peasant facing the entrepreneur and the proprietor to discuss together our reality, to investigate what we are economically and, once we know what we are, what we possess, what

Part of a speech of August 23, 1931, in the Plaza de Toros in Lima.

we need, and what we can have—not in arbitrary or empirical terms, but in terms of indisputable facts and figures—we can then commence the reorganization of the state. We will know where we are going and know what must be the economic backing for our political promises.

For that reason, Aprismo has not begun with a list of promises which might turn out to be impossible to fulfill in a country such as ours where everything remains to be done. Because it is necessary to renovate the political concept and, giving it an economic context, to investigate our reality, discover our resources, and see if, with the bases of our economy, we can construct our future policy. If we know what our true economic organization is, if we discover what is needed economically, and understand what are our sources of true wealth, and if we can come to know the minimum bases of our economy, we will then have the foundations for a new program of reconstruction on the basis of production: Production which can be guaranteed and financed by the state since it will be able to count on the will to work as its cornerstone.

This plan of economic progress is a national plan and not just a party one. It is the plan necessary for the reorganization of the state; it is the plan of a new assembly in which eloquent discourses on pure democracy and beautiful promises of reconstruction are not proclaimed, but rather one in which statistics will be the guarantee of all that is attempted in politics and in administration. This plan doesn't exclude some reforms of an immediate nature to the structure of the state. We must tend fundamentally to organize a state with capable servants, with specialized and technically trained employees. To this end it is necessary to exclude, insofar as possible, the petty politics of administration, and to abolish patronage, establishing an orderly hierarchy, with civil service examinations for all potential state employees, doing away with the letters of recommendation, and ending the begging at the door of ministries and using government jobs as payment for elective favors.

The government employee must be guaranteed security in his position, but he must obtain his post by merit. The letter of recommendation is a degrading institution, as is political patronage, and has established a dangerous form of corruption impeding the legitimate service of the public employee because of his insecurity and in addition, because of the obligation to serve the cacique or influential politician responsible for his employment so as to have the support of that politican's politics or his aspirations. The state, served by politically and morally independent employees, will give us a state which really responds to the aspirations of the country. We shall no longer see a public employee begging for favors, we shall see a functionary of the state, worthy of respect and from whom we shall demand the maximum energy and cooperation, since his job is guaranteed and only a failure to fulfill his duties will cause his dismissal.

For this reason, Aprismo proposes functional democracy, as the basis of the organization of the state. The citizen-worker, laborer or intellectual, must be the basis of the technical orientation of the republic in accordance with Aprista principles.

This principle of merit, which is a moralizing and useful one, must be extended also to the army and navy. The armed forces must dedicate themselves completely to the tasks which are assigned to them by constitution: to defend the honor and integrity of the nation and guarantee the rule of law. The army as an institution must be divorced from politics and converted into a technical and moral body. Its organization must respond to the amply democratic criterion of general obligatory military service, with a length of service varying with the degree of preparation or with the military preparation of the individual before he is recruited. The promotion of officers must be based on their technical capacity and their honor, so it is not converted into favoritism or payment for political services.

The preparation and orientation of national defense should be carried out in conformity with a plan worked out by a defense council or board, qualified to serve as adviser to the executive in everything related to military policy and technique. As the army is a means of incorporating the Indian into the nation and into civilization in general, its rank and file will be largely Indian. For this purpose the barracks must be adequate and hygienic. The army must serve as the basis, too, for the organization of military camps formed in the jungle to begin the exploitation of this large portion of our national wealth. These colonies, however, will not be exclusively military, but will include teachers, engineers, agriculturalists, and industrialists.

The army must contribute, furthermore, to the material and moral progress of the country. For this purpose there will be formed battalions of engineers and railroad workers who will have the job of constructing highways and railroads. In this way, costs will be reduced, civic consciousness will be raised, and individuals will learn to work with modern tools and up-to-date methods.

General and military instruction must be perfected, probably by people who have been trained in Europe. The officers of the army must be carefully selected, not with an eye to a policy of domination and expansion, but so as to form a guarantee of the free development of our economic possibilities. The army, the civil guard and police, the navy, and the air force constitute democratic institutions that guarantee the national existence and must have as their basis an absolute separation from political activity. Otherwise, those elements which should safeguard the nation and defend its legal forms would be converted into factors of dissolution. We, on this opportunity, must ratify our feelings of solidarity with the members of the Army, the Police, the Civil Guard, and the Air Force.

I must repeat today what I have said many times. The majority of the Army, of the Navy, of the National Police, is formed by men belonging to the middle classes, to the working classes, and to the peasantry, which are classes supporting our party. Consequently, we cannot be against the Army. We would be against it if we were oligarchs and aristocrats. We know that the forces of national defense are constituted in their majority by members of the great Indian race which we wish to bring into the national life. We know that from a class point of view those who give their blood for the National Army are workers, peasants, and members of the middle class, who are generally oppressed by the aristocracy and the oligarchy.

We do not attempt to make use of the Army politically. We wish the armed forces of the country to keep their independence, and we are absolutely partisans of having the state guarantee them not only independence and progress but also dignity and honor. The arguments of those who are trying to promote differences between the Army and the Aprista Party lack all basis. Our support of the armed forces is not mere oratory of the moment, it is based on our economic and political concept of the state, is the logical result of our ideology, and a logical result of our program of reorganization.

To add to our concept of the army, I only need say that our party supports a reduction of the period of obligatory military service to one year, more or less.

Our plan of economic organization based on an agrarian economy presumes a program of government which tends to make a reality of the collaboration necessary to give impetus to the agricultural production of the country. The creation of an agricultural bank has been supported by the party since its establishment in 1924; an Agricultural Bank not in the limited sense of the term, but as an organizer of agrarian cooperatives, as a guarantor of the indigenous communities, as a planning and technical instrument of the activities of the agrarian workers. This is a vital point in our plan of agrarian reform, since it is beyond comprehension that in a principally agricultural country, there does not exist any protection for our major activity of production.

A fundamental point in our program refers to the collaboration of the state with national production and the development of small industry which must be based on economic democracy. We need to obtain also the consumption of what is produced, particularly those non-manufactured products which make up a large proportion of our economy. For this reason we propose a national economic congress. We suggest a plan of protection and backing by the state for small industry and small commerce, so as to organize effectively the national economy.

I must now insist on our point of view with regard to foreign capital, and I wish to give a more detailed explanation of our position in this regard. I have said that we consider foreign capital necessary to countries of elemental economic development such as ours. But it is also necessary to remember that the lack of native economic expertise has permitted the establishment here, as an article of faith, of the idea that we need foreign capital and that since we need it, we must accept it wherever and however it cares to come. The error lies in the second part, because those who argue that to control foreign capital is to drive it away, are ignorant of economic law: the economic law of the expansion of capital which pushes it to come to us with as much force as we are pushed to receive it. If we discover the possibility of a balance of forces, we can then live in good relations with foreign capital, without falling into dependence upon it, defending the equilibrium of our own economy and making foreign capital a cooperator in national economic development.

With the reorganization of our economy, we shall have to face the reorganization of our finances. This point is of extraordinary importance in moments, such as this one, of truly upsetting world crisis. Nothing has been done in this direction in Peru. Professor Kemmerer was called, but the country soon lamented the results of his mission. No financial policy is more dangerous than that of the "gold exchange standard" for countries of reduced radius of eco-

nomic action such as ours. Looking with a little attention at our present situation, confronting it with the reality of the world, we must
agree that the abandonment not only of the "gold exchange standard" will be imperative but also that of the "gold standard." It is
necessary to see things clearly. Peru is a producer of silver and the
remonitorization of silver must bring us great benefits. If in the great
countries one notes already the tendency to temporarily abandon the
gold standard, why must we wait until the last minute to adopt the
measure that will save our economy and free the backing of our
paper money from a useless standard? We propose as an emergency
measure the abandonment of the gold standard and the minting of
silver money in the greatest proportion possible. There should circu-
late in the country a money which inspires confidence and satisfies,
so far as possible, the factors which determine its exchange value.

Another fundamental consequence of our economic concept of
politics is what we call economic regionalism. We consider that before
a full investigation of national reality is undertaken, there must be
an understanding of the economic geography of the regions. The
political region must be built upon the basis of the economic region.
This economic regionalism involves, therefore, so-called decentralization, that is to say it implies and supposes decentralization, but it goes
much further because it does not regard it as an end in itself but
rather as a means. Thus the economic region is our method of
decentralization, and we might say in passing that Aprismo has been
decentralist since its foundation.

Economic regionalism will bring the political delimitation of the
regions in accord with their zones of production of wealth. Upon
economic regionalism will be established political regionalism without
losing national unity and without losing the harmonic cohesion of the
regions with the central government. We maintain that in all levels
of the administration, the economic concept of the region must be
primary so as to give economic independence insofar as possible to
each region, and upon that base we must erect our educational policy
and administration. A new political demarcation of the country must
be made. On the basis of economic regionalism we must raise our
educational system.

The education and culture of the people constitute important
parts of the program of the Aprista Party. We have to retrieve culturally millions of men who are separated from all possibility of a truly
civilized life. We must raise to the level of human beings the millions
of Indians who live forgotten, although they are the heirs of the

former owners of this country. But we must orient our education in accordance with our economy. We must prepare men to work and for work. We must establish forms of a practical education of a technical nature and of a modern character in an integral manner. We shall have a public education molded in a unitary school system which does away with the differences which today exist between the private primary schools and the state operated primary schools. The unitary school of the state is, without a doubt, a means leading to the formation of a national consciousness and the formation of a good concept of politics and of labor in the country. . . .

To deal with all of the concrete proposals of our immediate program would take too much time, but I have dealt already with the principal ones and those that are strictly associated with our plan for a preliminary investigation of our economic reality. I should have to refer to many others, and I might merely repeat a list which is obvious: problems of hygiene; problems of communication; problems of general culture; problems of linking and bringing closer the various elements which make up the nation; problems of protection and guarantees for the workers; of education for the workers, of respect for their rights and the improvement of their material and moral conditions; problems of guarantees for the middle class, of guarantees to the small proprietor, to the small capitalist, to the small merchant; problems which are completely encompassed within our economic conception of the state, which presumes the total reorganization of our social system of economics and politics. . . .

We understand that our minimum program and our maximum program are limited by the exigencies of our present reality; that is to say that in addition to our economic, political, and social crises which demand immediate solutions, we have before us a total crisis which also demands immediately a solution of a national character.

The best foundation for our party is, consequently, our desire to embody the moral force of the country and to show the road to a new dignified and humanistic policy. The moment has come to demonstrate also that in Peru the national masses can construct democratic bases without resorting to bribery or to the old-style politics. We wish to demonstrate also that if Aprismo is an economic concept, it is also a political thesis and an ideology. But Aprismo is above all a moral force of intelligence and of culture in the country. In this truly sacred effort, in this struggle doubtlessly without precedent in the nation, we must rise as a true group which, without forgetting the problems which are fundamental for the country, shows the way not only for the government of the state but for the forms of struggle to capture that government.

I understand perfectly that our effort is difficult, that our task is burdensome. It not only is necessary to point out the national ills, with all the clarity that our program contains, but it is also necessary to have faith, optimism, and strength in the face of a gigantic plan to solve them. I understand perfectly that our task is difficult among a people where political passions lead to the greatest extremes; where all constructive energies appear dead; difficult in a people in which violence and hatred respect nothing, and set truly debasing examples for the younger generations; difficult in a people where it is necessary to commence by establishing the very basis of a state organization. But Aprismo enters as a new moral force and, with a high feeling of responsibility to the country, attempts to assume the direction of public affairs.

Aprismo has its perfectly determined principles, and Aprismo does not exclude the cooperation of any honorable citizen who wishes to contribute to our ideas and the proposition of making Peru rise.

What Aprismo demands of its members is honesty, sincerity, and the firm resolve to sacrifice if necessary. We are not a political party for the purpose of dividing public posts. We are not a political force making false promises; we are far from demagoguery. We wish to demand of the people the fulfillment of their duties at this moment. We say to the people that it is necessary to reprieve the Nation, morally and materially; and that it is the forces which have until today remained apart from the political life of the republic, which are the purest, the strongest, and the majority in national life, who must fulfill this task. But we are and will be the forces of the left: The right has failed.

We are going to demonstrate that the left can govern the country. We are also going to demonstrate that our force will not be wasted in useless extremism. Those who call us a dissolving force are mistaken because Aprismo is itself a perfectly systematized and disciplined organization which marches with its feet on the ground looking very closely at our reality. We, then, are fulfilling a truly great task. I speak to all those who do not share the ideals of Aprismo, who fight ideas with ideas; who do not resort to the detestable methods of political passion; who contribute to elevating and dignifying the national consciousness. Aprismo is a creed of justice, a creed which presumes nobility and learning, which could not fall into vengeance or rancor. We open our arms to all those who wish to discuss our ideas. We are disposed to respond to all those who wish to debate principles. We are not exclusivists or opportunists. Our force justly takes a place in the public consciousness. It must demonstrate generosity and must demonstrate that the hour has come to give an example to the country and to America and prove that it is possible in Peru to conduct politics in a more worthy fashion.

Our attitude does not presume pessimism or weakness. We have a clear consciousness of our political position. We know very well that each Aprista can respond as I do to the question of whether we pay something to augment the ranks of our Party. For that reason I may ask, not only of the Apristas, but of the country as a whole, if they have known any of our party to give a single centavo to corrupt a conscience or to buy a vote. Only those who cannot comprehend the great manifestations of the awakening of the civic consciousness of a people can put a price on it. But it is not possible in Peru for a policy of corruption to win, such a policy would divert the conscience of the people and impede the march to great accomplishments.

For that reason we must present ourselves always before the country telling what Aprismo really signifies; proclaiming that it may be that we are mistaken—we don't believe so—but that it can never be said of us that we proceed insincerely and, even less, that we proceed from self-interest.

It is very difficult to raise the spirit of a people, it is very difficult to lead the great masses of men on new paths and to new political theories. But we are carrying out this task. We, the Apristas, without exception are demonstrating to Peru that it is possible, finally, for the people to understand and, if they don't fully understand, to feel this new idea of an integral program; that it is not necessary to lose ourselves in useless extremisms; that we do not need European recipes to define our movement; that our movement arises from our reality and that if it arises from our reality, it is Peruvian, and absolutely Peruvian.

For this reason, Aprismo on the one hand raises the banner of scientific government, of a government based on the economy, of a government based on research, of a government based on capacity. On the other hand it raises the banner of a political movement confirmed in action. We are those who, while proclaiming the need for an efficient government, a government of method, a government of discipline, invoke emotion, enthusiasm, faith, and decision in those who are called upon to institute that type of government.

We must feel ever stronger. Our movement is going forward, singing victorious songs. I have just seen here the salute which you have made to me, waving your election certificates; that is, without doubt, a hopeful sign in a country where moral value has been unknown until now, not value which is bought, but the value of the ballot box.

That attitude indicates then that Aprismo is sustained by the good people, those who really practice democracy. For this reason we defend and will defend the secret ballot, which is less corruptible than voting in public. For that reason we will maintain the principle of free and legal elections, because free and legal elections will give us victory. For that reason we demand the independence of the elector and guarantees for the elector. For that reason we try to get everyone to understand what it means to vote.

We are contributing to the establishment of real democracy. For that reason convinced of the justice of our democratic principles, we prefer to be defeated to sacrificing what is moral and pure in our movement. We wish, whether victorious or vanquished, to leave the country an example of a party which sought power without any force other than the enthusiasm of the people. We wish that our mark in national history be that great effort which can never be erased from our memory. We are the heirs of the magnificent ideas of Manuel González Prada.* We who know that Prada could not become President of Peru and that another important politician who was also a rarity in our political milieu, don Nicolas de Piérola, was defeated in 1904, wish that this case not be repeated. We seek the voice and the vote of public opinion and that national aspirations not be betrayed. For that reason we have organized a well defined and disciplined force in order to demonstrate that in Peru there is sufficient backing to require respect for the opinion of the majority.

With full consciousness of our historic mission, we wish to leave an example for the future: We wish that the young generations of Peruvians who come after us respect the law and our example. We wish that the bright trail of the Aprista Party not be lost. Its ideals may be heresy for many today, but they will, according to the Master, [Gonzalez Prada] be orthodoxy tomorrow.

---

* Gonzalez Prada (D. 1918) was a Peruvian philosopher and writer, whose disciple Haya de la Torre has considered himself to be. Haya and his student associates named the night schools for workers, which they established after 1918, Universidades González Prada.

IV

THE MUNICIPALITY IN THE
ANTI-IMPERIALIST STATE

THE PROGRAM OF THE PERUVIAN APRISTA PARTY CONSIDERS THE reorganization of our municipal and parliamentary system of government as an essential complement to the efficient organization of the state and as the experimental basis for functional democracy. The extension of the radius of action of the municipalities and an increase in their level of authority is an essential condition for the effective political and administrative decentralization which national progress demands. With the municipalities organized functionally, maintaining the legal rights which foreigners still have to participate in these local governments, they would be technically entities of local administration, with a close understanding of the local region and with sufficient autonomy to act with efficacy.

Giving more power—political, economic, and administrative—to the municipalities, and including in them trade union and technical representatives, the present excessive governmental centralism would be reduced. The municipality would be the true basis of the state organization and the best practical school of government.

As the functional municipality would be the immediate local government of an economic region or part of it, the functional parliament would represent all of the economic regions, or the nation. Thus economic regionalism is the point of departure for functional representation in the parliament, from the moment that territorial division would be in accordance with the reality of the real or potential productive labor of each region. But in the functional parliament

---

An excerpt from a manifesto published clandestinely in Peru, February, 1932.

proposed by the Aprista Party not only will all sectors of the production and circulation of national wealth be represented, but the professional and technical groups, dependent or not on the state, and the great cultural centers will also be represented. Legislation, in all its aspects, would be the political-juridical work of a functional body basing everything on technical criteria. The exclusively political direction of all legislative work will be subordinated to the needs of reality technically interpreted. Novice empiricism, confusionist opportunism, phantasy, and the desire to apply to the country that which is not applicable to it—characteristics of our present system of legislation—will be progressively corrected, disappearing from our parliamentary practices.

On the basis of the functional municipality and parliament, the new organization of the state will be implemented, without violent interruptions of continuity, and its application will be introduced scientifically, without fear of alterations or postponements whenever regional or national reality requires this.

V

THE ECONOMIC CONGRESS

IT WAS IN 1931 THAT WE SUGGESTED THE INITIATION OF A NATIONAL Economic Congress. Another congress? Another assembly? Then we tried to explain it. The National Economic Congress must bring to light the best method of coordinating dissimilar and antagonistic movements. . . . It must give the state the formula of relationships so that the economy's automobile runs in a straight line and doesn't deviate. The economic formula must resolve the fundamental problem of not destroying, under a directed economy or under a state planned organization, that which is indispensable for the healthy economic life of the country; that is liberty. A dictatorial formula was easy; a statement of totalitarian planning was easy; but it was difficult, much more difficult, as Harold Lasky* says, "to assemble the train while it is moving."

To give our economic life a new direction, a new coordination, and a new sense, maintaining at the same time that which is fundamental and essential to it, is the basic form of an orderly and cultured democracy.

That was the great proposal which brought us in 1931 to suggest the economic congress. Our point of view was very clear. Our economic reality, or more precisely, our geo-economic reality, is absolutely different and distinct from the reality of other peoples. We cannot, we must not, think that we will find a solution for us which is not tailored to our problem. Therefore, we must face and focus upon the reality of our country, in order to attempt a solution

---

Excerpts from Haya's lecture on October 9, 1945, in the Municipal Theater of Lima, the last of three speeches on Aprismo.
* Harold Lasky was a British political scientist and socialist. He served as president of the British Labour Party in 1945–1946.

which will be peculiar to it. Our problem of a nation with two economic velocities is not the problem of the United States; nor is it the problem of France, nor of England. Nor is the fact that there exist in our geo-economy capital of clearly foreign origin on the one hand, and capital of clearly national affiliation on the other, a problem of homogeneous development. Such are our singular characteristics which do not correspond to any country of Europe.

The most frequent mistake in judging the problems of Peru is to see them from Lima, as if they were only the problems of Lima. To harmonize this diversity and to coordinate the multiplicity and heterogeneity in the economic sphere, was the proposal of the formula of the National Economic Congress.

However, I don't want to go on and continue this analysis without recalling that there is also a double velocity in the political sphere. On a certain occasion, a North American journalist asked me: "How do you propose to establish democracy in a country with a majority of Indians?" I answered him: "Just as in Peru there are two ethnographic dimensions, there are two democratic velocities; two forms in which democracy exists and acts. . . . Do you know what is the essence of modern democracy? The representative function emanating from a free, authentic vote, is it not? Well, this representative function emanating from free elections has been eclipsed in civilized Peru for twenty-five years. However, it continued to exist and with the feminine vote and full freedom of expression in the greater part of the indigenous communities of the country." I said to him: "A Mayor of an indigenous community in our highlands is elected by the vote of men and women, in the majority of cases, with greater authenticity and exercise of sovereignty—or, so as not to offend you, with equal authenticity and sovereignty—than the President of the United States."

The novelist Ciro Alegría has written in *El Mundo as Ancho y Ajeno* an eighth chapter which is excellent for its politico-social expression and symbolism. He relates a difficult and crucial moment in a community, the heroic community of Rumi. He offers us in those pages the democratic concept of Rosendo Maqui, the Mayor of bronze who someday will be immortalized in stone as was the Mayor of Zalamea of Spain, exalting thus all of the force of communitarian democratic organization. . . . The *Ayllu** is in danger. The commu-

---

* *Ayllu* was the name of the local Indian community of Inca times. Haya here extends the use of the word to mean the typical Indian community still surviving in highland Peru.

nity of Rumi is in danger, and Rosendo Maqui calls it together. The men go and the women go. He outlines the situation in serene and firm words. He asks a vote of confidence. The community parliament discusses it in a lively way. Finally, he must be reelected, and he is. But in all of that description, in all that dramatic episode of this very Peruvian novel, there lives what has become immortal in the Peruvian indigenous community when it has functioned freely: the democratic spirit, the responsible sovereignty of the members of the community who confer on the Varalloc or Mayor the sovereign authority of the collectivity. We have then, a democracy of slow and primitive progress, like our economy, alongside that other, coastal democracy which has stumbled so often and which sometimes has remained ominously behind the other, supposedly slower, one.

This digression was necessary to bring some perspective to the central theme of this lecture. Our idea of the National Economic Congress has been strengthened during these fifteen years when the program of the Aprista Party was proscribed, and all the while, it has been strengthening itself in contrast to the frustration of the other politicians who could not solve the issues which we were raising.

During these fifteen years many solutions have been suggested for the economic problems of our country. First we have heard about "highways," kilometers and kilometers of highways. The public, always ironic, made pointed jokes about the highways, saying that some were kilometers of going and others, kilometers of coming. Highways were for a while the individualist panacea for a unilateral focus on our economic problems. Is a highway a good idea? Is a highway bad? These questions must be answered, although this may seem like heresy, in accordance with the economic conditions of a particular zone. The highway is a dynamic factor in the circulation of wealth; but only if there is wealth produced. If wealth is not produced and if production doesn't increase, may not its benefit be illusory from the moment in which accelerated circulation reduces production? Here are two arguments: There are those who argue that highways and the resulting circulation of wealth accelerated production. There are those who maintain that production determines the mechanism of circulation. In certain areas the highway arrives and civilizes; in others the highway acts as a drain and makes things more dear. The highway is like a system of magnificently installed pipes and tubes which connect empty tanks. But if the tanks have not first accumulated a great deal of water, what happens? They are quickly emptied and the tanks remain empty.

It is not, therefore, just a problem of circulation, because that is to presume that production already exists. Has our capacity for production been assessed and measured? Has there been a calculation of the significance that a highway has as a means of circulation when it connects a newly formed center of production with others? There are highways which are very good because they are a kind of bridgehead to the future—Tingo María, for example. But there are highways that perhaps it would have been better to have studied at length in a National Economic Congress.

With regard to this I don't take a position pro or con. In the light of experience I merely present the situation from the point of view of Lima for whose needs any highway is convenient. If we place ourselves at another angle, perhaps we should listen to the voice of certain provincials.

However, I refer to this aspect because highways were considered the solution of all our economic problems. Their importance was overestimated. True, we have the Inca tradition of great longitudinal roads and of penetration roads: These are the roads of which the chronicles of Pedro Pizarro, Cieza, and Garcilaso tell us. It is true that Peru was a country of great roads, although some people argue that they carried little commerce.

Really, it is painful to see magnificent centers of economic production or of great scenic beauty which are cut off from all communication with the rest of the country. It is evident that it was indispensable to link the region of the jungle with the highlands and with the coast. The jungle is like a colony of Peru. . . . It is necessary to reach out towards it. But I am underlining only one aspect of this problem, that there was empiricism, mistaken estimates, and perhaps a political objective. It is enough to say that technically we must not commence with this. It is clear that it is not bad that a beginning was made somewhere. But in any case, more importance should have been given to regional considerations in dealing with the basic problems of each zone of the country, insofar as communications are concerned. Every highway is good, because it is progress at least in principle. But it is good at the same time—and this is our position—to develop every center of production linked by the highways, so that we don't generate a conflict between a well organized, modernized sector and a disorganized, backward one.

There have been other aspects of the economic debate. Peru needs foreign exchange; consequently Peru must export. This is one formula. Another formula is that Peru must eat before it exports, and consequently should not export before having resolved its own food problem. I am simply repeating propositions, and I'm happy that some of them are applauded, although you may well applaud others which are quite contradictory. We are an "immature" country, as Hegel would say. Production today cannot evolve nor be intensified without mechanical means. If you wish to develop food production, housing, and clothing manufacture on a grand scale, mechanization is indispensable. If you wish to intensify any aspect of production in the country, you will need foreign implements. How can you pay for these? It is necessary to have foreign exchange to pay for them. That is another aspect and another formulation.

Then comes the point of greatest importance: What are we going to do with the economic potential of Peru? The easiest thing, the European thing, what Moscow and Berlin dictate, is: "Divide what there is and then worry about it." But our answer is the answer of the Peruvian historical space-time: There is something more than this simplistic and Europeanizing answer. We are not countries of excess population; we are not Belgium, we are not France, we are not Germany, we are not England. If only 3.2 to 3.3 percent of our coast is cultivated, and our coast is a small part, a very small part of our national territory—one thousandth—Peru is still to be built. Our economic infancy is increasingly evident, in terms of our geographic space and our economic possibilities. Don't we have, then, a chance to resolve our problems in another way?

To this suggestion there is the counter argument: But it is very difficult! The problems of Peru are gigantic. How can we overcome the tremendous obstacles of nature? This argument has much in its favor. But a voyage to Machu Picchu, a pilgrimage to Ollantaytambo, a vision of the four tambos equally distant twelve leagues from Cuzco, would give an answer arising from our past. It is difficult to erect on the top of a mountain a city, which because of its grandness appears fantastic, but it was built when there was a noble, strong race capable of building it. It is difficult to construct in the wilderness of hard rocks, geometric monoliths such as the galleries of Pisac, which appear to be an audacious attempt at colossal pyramids, but it was done. It is difficult to transport gigantic rocks across a river, chisel them, assemble them, and present them in all of the beauty of a portentious edifice, not only taking into account the military nature of the work but also the harmonic integrity of the landscape. In the Inca architecture there is that: Not only the effort, which demonstrates the astonishing power and discipline of a race, but the delicate and fine sense of those *amautas,* architects or wisemen, directing the imperial culture, who took into account the plasticity of the landscape, the profoundly esthetic sense of integrity, locating on each mountain a great edifice, a palace, tower, sanctuary, or fortress, melding them with the sky, the vegetation, the rivers, the canyons, the roads, with all aspects of nature, in such a way that the architecture appears integral and continuous with its surroundings.

The problems of Peru can be resolved only by those who still live in these altitudes and who have the task of resolving them. We must look to ourselves, after seeing a little of the still existing subterranean irrigation systems of Nazca; after seeing the ruins of Chan Chan, those dikes of earth which are forerunners of those gigantic dams being erected today in the State of Washington; the terraces that make possible agriculture in the high places and avoid erosion; the canals; the experiments in reforestation; all these things indicating that this Peruvian scene was always bitter, always hard, always difficult. It has never been an easy problem to dominate nature here in order to establish a civilization; but this was done because with faith mankind can conquer mountains and because here in Peru there was the necessary faith and strength. Those who are capable accomplish the feats of history, and those who are incapable are forgotten.

In face of the present problems, democracy inseparable from economics will establish an economic system. We must face the great question of creating for democracy—that democracy which Roosevelt called dynamic democracy—a legal apparatus, a technical apparatus which gives democracy a voice in the economic field. We must say—and Lasky also makes this comment—that in the English or North American democracy, the juridical architecture of the state and its forms of organization are adjusted to their precepts, so refined, so adjusted, so rigorous that they have undoubtedly avoided the possibility of giving today's democracy this new and elastic economic dimension. Roosevelt with his "New Deal" encountered at every step the limitations of a democratic organization, whose venerable juridical structure already had the prestige and experience of a hundred years' success. In England the same thing occurred. There were created agencies alongside of the government, and the Parliament itself functions sometimes as an economic committee. The unwritten constitution of England permits many paradoxes, including the creation of the post of Prime Minister which does not exist in the constitution. But being realists, adapting themselves to the vital problems of today, they attempt to resolve them by applying means which give democracy the new characteristics of a dynamic economic democracy.

It has been said, and perhaps this is not wrong, that it is easier to govern England than to govern our small countries, which is like having to manufacture and run a locomotive at the same time. Be this as it may, the truth is that history offered us, and still offers us, a great opportunity here in our space-time. In the same way that we are presented economically with the great possibility of making productive 94 percent of our great coastal desert if we irrigate it, we are also offered the great chance to make here in the Americas and here in Peru, the experiment of an economic democracy, without hurting established interests and while solving great problems for ourselves and for the continent. To give this economic dimension to democracy it would be necessary and urgent to create a true organization which would be adapted exactly to our possibilities and to our needs. We have—I am going to repeat it—the necessary factors for our production: national capital and foreign capital. We have beyond this, and in another velocity, our production of small industry, of small agriculture, of small mining, of small handicrafts. We have seen that this difference, this contrast between those two economic velocities, presents the country a truly harmonic solution. When someone mentions the national economy, it is necessary always to ask: To which economy do you refer? To that which is beyond the Andes or to that which is in Lima? To the economy which belongs in the mechanism of a foreign economy or to that which still has the symbolism of the woman who uses her spinning wheel, of the llama that walks through the canyons, or of the Indian who plows with his ox, when he has one and when not with a wooden plow which he himself has made— who before plowed with a song on his lips, according to Carcilaso,* and today has only grievances and complaints.

To coordinate, assemble, and readjust all that belongs to Peru, all that forms a part of Peru, all that is within the gravitational field of Peru, is our task. How to coordinate it? Our legal mechanisms are perfectly known and defined. We are carrying on a battle to give democracy its traditional excellence, its normative laws, its guarantees of solvency, its prestige, and its institutional authority. This is as nec-

---

* Carcilaso de la Vega, one of the early post-conquest chroniclers of Peru, himself of half-Inca descent.

essary as the bread of the spirit. We cannot, then, complicate too much our democracy, an organism which has only recently been re-established and purified. We cannot complicate it and confuse it, with a new political paradox, which might be taken to be falacious propaganda, demagogy. It is important then, to create an integral agency which relates the economic function and the political function of democracy. That agency must have the same democratic mechanisms of the juridical and legal organizations—representation, vote, freedom of expression—to give it the powers of initiative and direction, prestige and authority, for the active participation of all the factors of the economy which meet or coincide there.

The National Economic Congress is, then, a great proposal for the coordination of the two economies, of the two velocities, of the two directions within the state, and for the participation of all the factors determining those two velocities, those two economies, those two directions. Our first formulation of the economic congress refers to the ABC's of the whole economy: Separate and distinguish what are economics and what are finances, delimit the fields, and then within the field of economics, formulate these perennial questions, as valid today as they were fifteen years ago: How many are we? What do we need? What do we produce? What do we consume? What proportion do we consume of what we produce? What do we import for consumption? What must we export? What must we not export? In what must we invest?

The economic congress must deal with the new universal categories of contemporary economics. The first category is the factors of production. They are no longer capital and labor, but capital, state, and labor. The second, capital is not only expressed in money and kept in banks, sometimes idly, nor even that which is invested in business for circulation and exchange. Capital is also the man who works, who produces. In Peru the man who produces is irreplacable capital, because of the biological conditions of our elevated altitude. As a result, in calculating investments in money, it is also necessary to calculate them in units of men; because badly invested human capital is lost. It is human capital that for being lost becomes a charge upon the state. Thus, the sick man, the man suffering from malnutrition, the man with vices, the uneducated man, is part of the debit of the state. Social security pays it, the hospital pays it, the welfare home pays it, the community pays it.

Human capital is not "human capitalism." Someone has said

that it is better to use the phrase "human factor." I insist on human capital, making the same distinction between capital and capitalism. Capitalism may cease to exist; but capital will always represent an expression of accumulated labor. How the product of that labor is exchanged or is not exchanged, determines if we have or don't have capitalism; but capital exists before capitalism. Therefore, human capital is what represents the responsibility of man within this new concept of the economy.

Hence, financial capital and human capital are two factors of production, which are related. There is human capital which can have its expression in numbers within financial capital. For that reason our economic congress will deal with these three fundamental factors: capital, state and labor. And within capital there will be included human capital. Then comes the Aprista premise: "It is not a matter of taking wealth from those who have it, but of creating wealth for those who do not have it." The other formula, to take it, is European. It is easy. It is the easiest. But it is more, it is an attack on liberty. We have a wide stage on which to test our own capacity to create wealth for those who do not have it, because here is the land, the sky, the geography, the territory, and here is the man capable of fulfilling the task.

We return, it is clear, to the Aristotelian postulate: First, to feed, to clothe, to house, and to educate, that has formed the essentials, for the last 2,500 years, of any form of good government. We have said this. But do not forget that we belong to a country with a double economy, a double velocity, and that because we live thus in duplicate, we have to do many things twice and at the same time. This involves resolving problems which provide solutions internal to our economy, without separating these solutions from our obligations and our links with the other side of the motive force of our economy. We cannot proudly declare ourselves to be insular and close the frontiers, and say that nothing interests us in the outside world in an epoch of growing interdependence. That is really the center of this great problem, that we cannot avoid forming economically a part of the continental whole, of the Indoamerican whole of the inter-American and world whole. At the same time that we have the obligation to resolve our internal problems, many aspects of these can be solved easily if we proclaim ourselves Robinson Crusoes on a new island, which neither imports, nor exports, nor pays. It is easy to say, don't sell it abroad, eat it yourself; but it is difficult to resolve this problem in a moment of interdependence, as is shown by the international solidarity of UNRRA,* and when we are buying from abroad and must pay our debts.

For this reason, what is important as a fundamental idea of the economic congress is that it have the status of a deliberative body of the greatest efficiency, so that it will not err because of the human fallibility of a single focus, but will see all, in an organized and coordinated fashion. It is thus that we have planned this congress which, because it represents the diverse regions of the country, cannot from the start be composed only of voices in accord or harmony; because there will be clearly opposed interests; because it is exactly the task of the congress to coordinate these opposing positions; because with a unilateral criterion we cannot resolve our problems.

The difficult thing in Peru, as we know, is that the problem is multi-dimensional and must be mediated in the economic congress. It will be constituted on this basis: Representation of capital—both national and foreign—and of labor. In the same way that foreign capital is represented in our banking institutions of greatest importance; in the same way that municipal legislation allows foreigners with a certain period of residence to take a post in our councils, why not, if within our juridical apparatus they have this right, should they not have a seat in an economic congress, since this congress will have to see to what degree the foreign economic interests are cooperating in the optimum functioning of our national economy.

An economic congress, then, has to face this problem of capital; the problem of industry. It will have to face the problem of agriculture, of large and small agriculture; of the agriculture which varies from the vast technically equipped plantation of the coast to the modest community lands of the highlands. An agriculture that includes the large and small renter; includes the *yanacona*†; the sharecropper; all the various forms and variations of labor on land. It includes the agriculture of the great idle landholdings of the highlands and the vast, intensively farmed holdings of the coast, and presents all possible paradoxes so that a single law cannot be applied to it, nor a single standard.

That agriculture is loaded with taxes, from the legislation of

---

* The United Nations Relief and Rehabilitation Agency, which provided relief for devastated Europe and some other areas after World War II.
† An Indian agriculturalist, working under semi-servile conditions.

1915. In that agriculture we have placed our hopes because from it comes the bread of life, the rice and the beans, the potatoes and the corn of daily use, the food of the people.

But that agriculture, in another aspect, is also to a certain degree guaranteeing us progress and new techniques. It gives us foreign exchange, and the question is whether that foreign exchange should be used to bring in machinery which could produce more industrial products, which would not only improve the food of the people, but their housing and education as well. Today even houses are built with machines. Today all of the things that man needs are produced with the aid of mechanization and the technology of our epoch. Peru needs that type of machinery, machines which will improve the conditions of life, machines which will permit us to increase the food production and to improve the housing of our people, their education and their training. These machines must be paid for with money. This money must be in foreign exchange. Up to what point must the rule of necessary payment dominate? It is up to the economic congress to decide.

The modernization of our highland agriculture and the intensification of our industrialism—a great remedy for the large landholding system and the servitude of the mountain region—represent positive and efficient investment in productive works and the creation of energy. All this imposes upon us a new organization and an economic direction perfectly coordinated by an assembly representing all of the living forces of production.

We need iron and coal. True. We need machines. True. We need to extend our productive agricultural areas, on the coast and in the highlands. Exactly. We need to intensify and improve our highland agriculture; we need fertilizers. We need the reorganization and readjustment of the production of our artisans, which has declined since colonial days. We also need to mobilize a cooperative system and prevent its being discredited in the hands of political demagogy. We need to give our whole economy a new vitality by stimulating production and consumption, and indicating to each zone and each sector a radius of productivity and market.

This is the fundamental task of the economic congress which must have its agricultural division, its industrial division, its basic economy division and its financial division. It must create a permanent structure, and there must be represented therein all the elements and aspects of the national economy, an economic congress bringing together the efforts of all the productive elements of the country: labor, technical, intellectual, and especially professional.

An economic congress that not only doesn't exclude, but one that incorporates the armed forces of the republic. It must include the illustrious Navy, which will aid us valuably in the organization of the merchant marine, in fishing, and in meteorological observation. The Navy could give us not only a single large training school for both naval and merchant seamen, maritime, and river workers, but also perhaps—our great ideal—an efficient school of customs experts, so that our ports are not centers of contraband but rather agencies, professionalized by the Navy, carrying on expertly such important activity.

It will be an economic congress in which the Air Force will tell us all that it is doing and all that it can do to cooperate in the air and commercial traffic of the country. Today it is our military aviators who carry out the daily job of communicating with the other side of the Andes, with the isolated departments and provinces of the Amazon region which need the things flown in so that the cost of living can be kept at least reasonable. When we know that those small planes which I have seen, are the same small planes which for twenty years have dusted the cotton fields, when we know that those small planes, fragile and dangerous, rise above the green inferno of our jungle in the direction of San Martín and other departments and lose themselves in the blue of the sky, even when a violent storm menaces, then we see that it is true that the aviator defies death every day, in peace and in war. Those aviation companies which are sustaining and maintaining our commerce have brought the country 600,000 soles a year; and never until today has Peru imported a commercial plane.

We need the Army's cooperation in these efforts. Its military engineers, its sappers, its sanitary corps, and its other professional and technical elements can bring much to the economic congress. The armed forces are fundamentally interested in the problem of nutrition, which will be a question before the congress, because the studies of the medical corps show constantly that the ill-fed men— in Peru this alarming phenomenon is growing ever greater—are incapable of serving their fatherland.

All will have their place in this congress. All creative men; all men with technical capacity; all men who have an interest to represent and an idea to offer will be called together. The technician or the artist, the worker or the peasant, the doctor or the teacher, the economist, the lawyer, the engineer, the artisan, the foreman, all men who engage in labor or intellectual work will have representation in this functional assembly.

We wish furthermore that this congress not permit the professional critic his sterile speech.

We wish that in the economic congress all voices will be heard; all initiatives. Together with the dilettante there will no doubt be the man who brings the profound voice of experience. Together with the amateur there will be the man who brings us the teaching of the soil; the man who brings in his voice the fifteen, twenty, or thirty silent years of dealing with the immediate problems of our highlands, of our provinces, of the jungle. All will have there a place, all will have there a tribune.

We wish thus that the fundamental questions of Peru will be dealt with with different eyes, with different words, without everyone feeling that he has the final solution to our problems. No. With humility, with the humility which is imposed by the magnitude of our urgent problems, everyone must go in order to cooperate. Knowing that we can be wrong, and hoping that some other opinion can increase our knowledge, illuminate, and teach us.

But this economic congress will be an extra-party and apolitical congress. Aprismo submits it to the nation, so that it can be converted into a permanent national agency. The economic congress will have a plenary body and an organ of permanent consultation. But one or the other will always be the representative and the expression of all the life forces of Peru. Three regional assemblies will be created: one in the north, one in the center, and another in the south, with a subcommission for the jungle area. The economic congress will establish its philosophy upon the basis of a geo-economic formulation related to the three factors of production, capital, state, and labor, and which can more or less be presented as three great circles of production: One which commences on the Rio Tumbes and terminates on the Rio Santa, including it. Another which commences in the Santa and terminates on the Rio Acarí, inclusive, having for its center Lima. The other which commences on the Rio Arcarí and includes everything up to Lake Titicaca and all of the zone of the South. Three great circles of production to which must be joined two subsidiary circles of potential production, the focii of which are Iquitos and Madre de Díos.

In the first circle of production we have predominantly petroleum, the highly technical agriculture of sugar and rice, and mineral extraction. In the departments of San Martín, Cajamàrca, and Amazonas is the zone of the human capital which is the social base of its productive efforts. This great circle includes the Santa and its Corporation, because from there must originate the irrigation of Viru and Chao, which will make productive a hundred thousand fecund acres in the rich departmental zone of La Libertad. Furthermore, the Corporación del Santa,* magnificent achievement and the pride of our Peruvian engineers, is the hope and base of expansion for our future industrialization. The Corporación del Santa is a pride of Peru; and the work that is being carried out there, and which must be organized with a better direction, guarantees Peru a true hope for its electrified industrialization in steel, coal, zinc, and so forth.

The second circle of production is the zone in which there predominates a coastal agriculture dedicated to cotton, an advanced industrialization in Lima, and the production of minerals in the region of Junin, which is typically a mining region. This is the central zone of production, with its subsidiary zones and its contribution of human capital from the departments of the interior.

The third circle of production is the zone of Arequipa, Cuzco, Puno, Tacna: a grazing zone, a typical agricultural zone, a zone of less developed industrialism, a zone above all where the human capital is of the indigenous race, communal and traditional.

These three circles of production are cut by two axes of distribution and consumption: The axis of the coast and the axis of the highlands, where the problems of distribution and of consumption are, respectively, similar, where the ethnic problems are homogeneous; as are those of malnutrition, the problems of education, the problems of health. The malaria of the coast also marks a yellow longitudinal zone from Tumbes to Tacna. On the coast tuberculosis is also prevalent making Callao and Lima the first and third cities, respectively, in mortality from this cause. In the highlands also we have similar problems of distribution and of consumption. Thus are formed the two axes which cut the three circles of production.

There is the vast geo-economic geometry of our congress. Each

---

* The Santa Corporation is a Government Organization for developing the Santa River Valley, and among other projects undertook sizable irrigation projects and the establishment of the country's first steel plant.

one of the circles of production will have a permanent council in that congress. In that congress will be heard the voices of all, the suggestions of all, the initiatives of all the elements of production. From that congress will come each year a great plenary body which will form the permanent assembly of the National Economic Congress.

With these fundamental characteristics, the National Economic Congress will have the voice of numbers in Peru. Pythagorically, it will give numbers a symbolic, almost mystical function in our new democracy. We wish that figures be what guides politics. Parliament has the voice; has the last word. But the National Economic Congress will have the figures. We should say with Galileo that the science of politics is going "to speak in mathematical language."

It has been said that the economic congress may debase a bit the august functions of the legislative power. I am sure that each legislator will feel happy that alongside the legislative power exists another expression of initiative, suggestion, foresight, and counsel. We would say that democracy has been criticized because representation has been based solely on quantitative factors. The man who lives to be twenty-one years old is a citizen and, if he knows how to read and write, votes. But the new democracy introduces qualitative values. For this reason, in the economic congress the man who works or who exercises a function will have a voice and a vote. Here is the answer to the most frequent criticism of democracy. The quantitative factor cannot be excluded; nor can one exclude qualitative reality. From the synthesis of the two comes functional democracy. It considers man according to the function that he represents and carries out in the collectivity. Purely political democracy only considers man as a responsible and conscientious citizen, capable of casting a vote representative of national sovereignty. Now these two factors of democracy coincide, converge, and harmonize to coordinate and resolve the great problem of establishing an economic, political, and social democracy in our epoch.

Thus the economic congress represents the systematization, expressed institutionally, of the economic norms of modern democracy. Thanks to our instability and our institutional infancy, thanks to the fact that we are not countries as consolidated and strong as the United States, we can go ahead and, with this example, demonstrate the possibility of resolving the question of economic democracy by creating a permanent agency which represents the expression of this new aspect of contemporary democracy: the National Economic Congress.

Immediately the question is raised: How will the economic forces be represented in the congress? This point I cannot answer yet. The legislators will answer it. Here is the philosophical basis of the economic congress. It is not just an additional congress. It is not a new assembly which may meet periodically with specific and circumscribed purposes. It is a fundamental institution needed by the country in order to ascertain its productive potentialities, to investigate its economic reality, to discover what is its potential as a creator, consumer, and distributor of wealth, in a concert of American nations in which we do not yet know precisely what we are nor what we represent.

For that reason the economic congress will carry out the task of giving us a technically competent budget which we do not have; a treasury accountancy system, which we don't have; and good laws of tax assessment and collection, which we don't have. For this the eight thousand decrees, laws, and legal instruments which make up our present tax legislation must be changed into an organized tax code by legislation, and for this it is necessary that we adopt a modern tax policy. It is necessary that we not be fearful of a budget deficit—after all, the United States has one—so long as we effectively create wealth for Peru, which can serve in the future to balance the budget.

This economic congress must organize our tax system. We, the Apristas, are in principle against new taxes. We believe that if the levying and collection of the present taxes is readjusted, we would have a more than adequate return permitting us to revise and eliminate a whole series of useless taxes. I refer to the indirect taxes. Gasoline is produced in the North and costs 80 centavos in Lima, 75 centavos in Callao, and one sol, fifty centavos in Puno. Why? There are provincial and district taxes. Often a tax is created—for example, to recover the tower of the Church—but the bureaucratic agency created to collect the tax, makes the tax illusory—the recovering of the tower (which finally collapses) becomes illusory.

We have a feudal tax criterion, one which, to a certain degree and in certain aspects, corresponds to some zones of our economic organization. We have the feudal criterion of income and of the collection of taxes. In the Middle Ages, the collectors of taxes sometimes descended in the middle of the night, particularly in the ghettos.

Here we are little short of this situation. But there is a difference: the difference that we have not resolved the great problem of making those whose income is equal pay equally. The paradox of our taxation is that not all those who earn a thousand soles pay equal taxes. . . .

Thus we see that the job of the economic congress is going to be to give us good tax laws, which don't increase the rate but which systematize the payment of that rate. We shall have a good budget law that is not afraid of a deficit—in fact we have never had well balanced budgets. It will organize investments so that we know when, how, and where we are going to use the money we need to create productive works. The economic congress, finally, can give us a good organization for the Ministry of Finance, because it's no use to have good Ministers of Finance so long as the Ministry is badly organized.

In the same way it will pay attention to the great problem of the human economy. It will pay attention—and much attention—to the great problem of our infant mortality rate. In Lima 150 children die of every 1000 children born. The calculations of the pediatricians indicate that the number approaches 250 or 300 per thousand, as a national average. But in the United States, for every 1000 children born, 48 die. It is necessary to attack these problems, which are economic and social problems as well as moral ones. I asked a medical specialist: "What is the reason for this death rate which is so terrifyingly high?" The doctor responded: "The reason is illegitimacy." I said: "In other words, it is an irresponsibility which is a problem of education. It is the lack of morality which exists in Peru, because there is no freedom to teach the people their social duties and to compensate them with their civic rights."

Thus the economic congress will be able to deal with the basic questions of our social life. It will confront and coordinate the needs of capital and labor. It will indicate their problems scientifically and not simply at random. It will not deal with a single problem because that problem is not unilateral, since its roots affect the whole economy. What should the living minimum wage be? There will be no recourse to demagogy in a speech in the chamber to answer the question, but its answer will be based on the investigation of the reality and will be ratified by experience. In these times of economic crisis, the most facile demagogue is the economic demagogue. Consequently, speculators who gain at the expense of the need and hunger of our people must be stopped; they must understand that the great problem of food, clothing, shelter, education, and work at a just wage are problems that affect the integrity of our economy, that are going to be resolved, but that must be resolved logically and intelligently. These are problems that cannot be resolved with an announcement, with an offer, with a speech. No. Behind all of this there must be erected a system; there must be a clear and scientific method of investigating reality. Once we know what are our needs, we shall resolve the great problem of giving our producer what justice, the high prestige, and good quality of our production requires. Let us hope that it can never be said of us what Max Weber wrote on studying the fall of the Roman Empire: "It fell because of a crisis of labor. It fell because in a sea of slavery—comments Ortega y Gasset—the imperial fish, lacking water, was choked."

The economic congress is going to teach our rich to think in terms of the twentieth century; and is going to teach our people to think in terms of this century also. It is going to teach our rich that they cannot continue thinking that the world does not go around, that the world does not progress, because Ptolemy has for some time been disproven. They must learn that in terms of Copernicus and Einstein the world moves and that the world moves incontrollably towards improvement. Millions of men have not died in the fields of Europe and Asia so that things should continue as they were. This revolution which humanity confronts can be a revolution without barricades; but it is very profound, because it is a revolution which is definitively and thoughtfully transforming the bases of the economic organization and social structure. It is necessary to think well and to study hard. We need to avoid in this epoch, by means of a wise social policy, what Weber said of the fall of the Roman Empire.

The crisis of labor brings to mind the pneumocomiosis of the mine worker at 4,000 meters altitude. Dark predictions indicate that if the conditions of the miner, whose lungs are irreplacable for this job, remain as they are, in twenty-five years we will not have any more Peruvian miners. The labor crisis brings grave work-connected diseases which also must be prevented: malaria and tuberculosis. In addition, Peru must be saved from the sad prestige of having a city which is the first and another the third in the world in mortality from tuberculosis. We must make the total effort so that our workers do not die of malnutrition in the highlands because we don't give them enough to eat.

To this end, with this purpose, with this desire, the congress will go ahead, without stridencies and without violence, discussing all the problems around the table of its diversified deliberations. Studying them in all their amplitude and utilizing the incontestable capacity of expression offered by the facts. We hope that they will know how to use these, and that the hands placing those problems on the table will be the gentlemanly and patriotic hands of other Peruvians, who being conscious of the problems to be resolved and sure of the magnitude of the question, will say: We are going to undertake the task, because we are all competent to do so. We are going to attempt to alert our intelligence and our wish to resolve the great national problems. That is, to give to Peru economic dynamism, economic coordination, economic health, exactly in this moment when a new and healthy stage of its political life is initiated, and when we have the renovating guarantee of an ethical affirmation of the rights of citizens.*

There is no democracy without political freedom, without the guarantees of the rights of citizenship. But there is also none without social justice and its counterpart of a just economic organization. We are seven and a half million inhabitants, in a country of immense dimensions and vast possibilities. We are a people with all the power to realize our great destiny. We must overthrow, after the political tyrants, the moral tyrants: egoism, indifference, and arrogance.

Furthermore, the economic congress is a guarantee of the improvement of production, and of the acceleration and increasing of wealth. It is also a guarantee for getting out of the circumscribed and rather anachronistic framework of our method of developing production in Peru. It is a new road—we must do a great job for a great Peru. We must look at the destiny of Peru not only within its oasis surrounded by deserts. We must defeat, as did the Hollanders, only in reverse, our great obstacle of Nature: Where they took the water off the land, we must put water on the land.

This all is our task, and this is the economic task of our great congress. I repeat that its voice should not be confused with the voice of a party. It should not be said that in it, all those who today represent the life forces in the country did not have a part. No one will be missing! So that no one can be excused, we will make it

---

* Haya is referring to the fact that only a few months before he gave this speech, democracy had been restored to Peru with the election of President José Bustamante y Rivero. The Aprista party had been legalized for the first time in eleven years, and Haya could come out of hiding.

obligatory by law that the life forces of the nation must participate in that Assembly. Industrialists, agriculturalists, merchants, grazers, yanaconas, workers, artisans, members of Indian communities, renters of land, according to their category, intermediaries, financiers, professional bankers, technicians, military men, sailors, aviators, artists, priests, and teachers, all of Peru, all the forces of the fatherland are going to take a new role in the task of affirming and exalting our democracy. A new assembly will open for all of you; for all the country; for all those who have something to say, some word to contribute to the orientation, to the good economic direction of Peru. No one should withhold his cooperation, then.

The bill is ready and will soon pass our chambers.* We make of it a banner of the rectification of the erroneous economic paths which until now the country has followed. This new destiny of Peru will be opened with the participation of all the Peruvians. Thus we shall establish democracy with guarantees for all, democracy which is not going to diminish the riches of anyone, but which will increase the riches of all. Democracy which seeks, with the unanimous participation and cooperation of the Peruvians, the solution of the thousand problems which today obstruct and menace our march forward as a democratic country. We will give America an example to follow in the economic sphere, as we have given them one in the political field.

We will make a social revolution without bullets, as we have made our bloodless "95."† We will make Peru the new empire of social harmony on the basis of justice and the rights of everyone. Here we shall create a place for each of us in labor, in the home, in hope, and a place for each of us in the new life of Peru. There is land enough for every home, for every cradle and even for every tomb. There is land enough for home and for school, for work and for recreation. There is land enough for planting and for pasture. There is land for the people who suffer and for the people who laugh. There is more than enough land for all, wide and fecund land, black and Peruvian land. Consequently, all that is lacking is energy and coordination, faith and decision, the desire for triumph which is the will of the strong.

---

* Haya was overly optimistic here. A National Economic Congress along the lines outlined by him never was established.
† Haya is referring to the Revolution of 1895 which made reformist Nicolás de Piérola President of the Republic.

Thus democracy will not be in Peru the unfulfilled stage of transition lacking the final step towards another promised form of justice. No. Democracy in a country like ours can carry, contain, and realize social justice. That is the proposal of our great Aprista Plan of a National Economic Congress, to demonstrate that integral justice is also possible in our fatherland. And that social justice is going to be realized, so that democracy is really completed along with an integral program of social morality, justice, and the affirmation of national unity. That is the voice of the people. . . .

VI

A RETROSPECTIVE VIEW

THE STATE PROPOSED BY APRA MUST BE "FIRST OF ALL A STATE OF economic defense opposing the capitalist state determined by imperialism, a new system, distinct, unique, which must proscribe the old oppressive regime." But the new state, which cannot be the "capitalist or bourgeois of the type of France, England, or the United States"— countries where capitalism has its origins and its base—it also cannot be a "feudal" state. I called it generically the "anti-imperialist state," because it must organize "a new system of economy, scientifically planned" under a form of state capitalism, but different from that experimented with in Europe during the war; although directing the national economy and controlling or nationalizing progressively the production and circulation of wealth. In my book of 1928— written more than four years before the election of Franklin D. Roosevelt as President of the United States—I could not cite, as an example of this state control, the North American economy of the New Deal, but did refer as "cases of partial statization of the economy" to Argentina's handling of petroleum and to that Uruguay, with the reforms, too little studied in other Indoamerican countries, which were introduced by the Partido Colorado and its "distinguished man of government José Batlle y Ordoñez."* The new state, which

---

An excerpt from "El Aprismo en Un Mundo Cabiante," from *Treinta Años del Aprismo.*

* Haya refers here to the establishment by Argentine President Hipolito Irigoven of a government oil firm, Yacimientos Petroliferos Fiscales in 1922; and to Uruguayan President Batlle's establishment of government firms in insurance, oil refining, electricity, telephones, banking, and several other fields in the first two decades of the twentieth century. Batlle was twice president of Uruguay, in 1903–1907 and 1911–1915, and enacted the labor legislation and policies of economic nationalism which made Uruguay a pioneer in Latin America for several decades.

would not be one "of class," but one of the democratic representatives of the three major classes of our countries, the peasant, the worker, and the middle class, "would channel efficiently and in an organized fashion the efforts of the three classes represented in it," and would be the "cornerstone of Indoamerican unity and of the effective economic emancipation of our peoples."

* * * * *

In that "logical scale" of development the subsequent step is "the great work indicated by the third point of Apra: the progressive nationalization of land and of industry. . . ."

This proposal of "the progressive nationalization of land and of industry" has been used by the various and diverse critics of Aprismo for the purpose of discrediting and misrepresenting it. However, by sticking with the germinal ideas of my book of 1928, recapitulated here, I think that it is possible for an unprejudiced reader to understand it.

First of all *nationalize*—a word which undoubtedly lends itself to more than one interpretation—is not always a synonym for *socialize*. There are socialist nationalizations, or merely socializations, but there are others not effecting the institution of private property, but only the foreign or non-national character of property. This type of nationalization one finds in certain legislation of the capitalist countries which do not permit foreign ownership of certain industries, or limit proportionately the percentage of foreign holdings. This is justified when those sources or means of agricultural, mineral, or industrial production or transport or communication might represent, or actually do represent, economic-political interests exceeding mere property rights.

When one talks of "nationalization" of the basic British industries—coal mines, the iron and steel industry, internal transport, electricity, civil aviation, cable and radio, or the Bank of England—the word has another connotation. It does not involve the rescue of those firms from foreign hands, but their *socialization,* that is to say, their expropriation and transfer to the *nation,* represented by the state. Nationalization of the railroads of Mexico virtually turned over to the workers in 1937 the collective property of that firm. But the "nationalization" of Argentinian, Mexican, Bolivian, or Brazilian petroleum, or the so-called "autonomous firms" of Uruguay, are as we have already noted, a total or partial statization; as is, within Aprista cooperative planning, the law approved by the Congress

of Peru on December 11, 1946, and February 28, 1947, creating
the Peruvian Petroleum Corporation. Similar are the industries of
tobacco, guano, salt, and phosphorous in Peru; or of tin in Bolivia.
However, the most complete and organic form is that carried out in
Uruguay in 1911, 1912, and 1914, with the monopoly and state
administration of the insurance companies, the Mortgage Bank, the
Bank of the Republic—with a section of rural credit—the production of electricity in the whole country, of the railroads, and so forth.
These measures were carried out upon the initiative of the Partido
Colorado and especially of its chief, the distinguished statesman, José
Batlle y Ordoñez—one of the greatest, or perhaps *the* greatest creator of the modern democracy of Indoamerica, whose extraordinary
accomplishments are little known, due to the ignorance which our
countries have of one another. The martyr ex-President of the Uruguayan Republic, Baltazar Brum, leader of the same Batllista Party,
called this the intervening state—and this I noted in my book of
1928—"Industrial-State" or administrator-state "which doesn't seek
dividends, which is interested in improving the public service, which
pays wages and salaries permitting the workers who serve it to live."
A state as an "altruistic and human employer aiming for the happiness of its servants and attempting to do everything for them which
is within its power." But the Partido Colorado has never been socialist.

The Aprista program only sets forth in a general way that
"cooperativism and the progressive nationalization" of the agricultural and industrial wealth are the defensive means of the state for
effective de-feudalization and for resisting imperialist excesses and
compensating for the "economic imbalance thus created." The general Aprista doctrine does not go into detail—to do so would be
prolix—concerning the type of nationalization. It is only necessary
to point out that it not be socialist or communist, because socialism
and communism—as well as fascism, as has often been said and
repeated—"are specifically European phenomena, ideologies and
movements determined by a social reality with an economic evolution
very different from ours." Thus the "progressive nationalization of
wealth" can be understood as ownership, co-ownership, or state control and vigilance, depending upon the case, of certain sources of
wealth; especially those which, because they are the property of
foreign firms, are, as a result, in the hands of the governments of the
nationalities to which those firms belong. Aprista nationalization
inclines to nationalization by means of development corporations—in

accord with the mechanism of the democratic State of Four Powers*
—and to the stimulation of agricultural and industrial *cooperativism,* but it respects and guarantees private property, as is the case
in Mexico.

Nationalization is not advocated for its own sake, because much
emphasis is placed on the magnitude of the problem, on the necessity of studying it intensively so as to avoid imposing a hurried nomi-
nal nationalization which might result in a bankrupt firm because of
the failure of the reform itself. On the other hand—and this must
be unequivocally stated—a wide field must be left for private initiative, national and foreign, in its constructive action in promoting the
de-feudalization and the industrialization so indispensable to the
progress of our peoples. A companion and simultaneous task is that
of stimulating and accelerating the evolution of the more backward
zones of our economy. . . .

To carry out this task is a work of social creation, *not necessarily socialist.* Although for the spokesmen of North American capitalist extremism—the faction which attempts to take capitalism back
to nineteenth century laissez faire—anything which involves intervention by the state, through control or planning, is *socialism;* just
as they denounce as communism any democratic movement which
tends to resist the advances and excesses of those capitalists when
they attempt to impose themselves on our countries as new conquerors with the support of their governments and marine corps. It
is true that some official spokesmen for the Mexican Revolution and
some others, lowering themselves to copying even the names of
European political parties, speak with the greatest sincerity, but little reason, of criollo "socialism." They believe still that a "socialist
order"—for example, on the model of British Labour Party—is
possible in our countries of rudimentary industrialism, the economic
colonists of foreign capitalist empires. But it is also true that in the
last twenty-five years—and above all after Hitler led a National
Socialist Party of German Workers—the criollo "national socialisms,"
those believing in a mimicking, Europeanizing socialism, isolationist
in each country, and foreign to the principal problem of uniting the
Indoamerican people as the only means of resisting the imperialists,
have lost influence. . . .

---

* Haya refers here to the traditional three branches of government—executive,
legislative, and judicial—plus the proposed economic congress, which Apristas
regard as a fourth branch or power of government.

Our frank words about these parties did not win Aprismo many friends, as might be imagined, although our relations with all the Indoamerican democratic and socialist parties have been friendly. It was very hard for us to struggle against the "mental colonialism" imposed by Europe and especially when that colonialism also came under the banner of "anti-imperalism" and "revolutionary." We insisted on pointing out two Indoamerican historical events as indications of the new road for our peoples to full independence in a world of change: the *University Reform,* the starting point of our release from that "mental colonialism," and the *Mexican Revolution,* the starting point of our economic emancipation through de-feudalization and anti-imperalism. Both historical antecedents must be taken advantage of to refine their teachings and go beyond their limitations; and both mark, above all, an obligatory change in our terms of reference. In place of taking as certain anything from Europe, we must turn our eyes to our own Indoamerican stage. . . .

* * * * *

The situation is—taking the example of Indoamerica and the United States—*that our countries need North American capital as much as it needs to seek investments in our countries.* For this reason, our countries can stipulate the prerequisites of the immigration of the aforementioned capital. . . .

These conditions will be effective if the Indoamerican states unite, so as not to repeat the cases which we have already seen, where one state attempts to condition the entry of capital, but another obsequiously opens its doors to imperialism and surrenders to it. This is another demonstrable example of why Aprismo maintains that without the political and economic unity of Indoamerica, constructive anti-imperialism will only prove to be temporary, incomplete, and in the end, inoperative.

In conclusion, this principle of Aprismo should be mentioned: to the "necessary and good" foreign capital—coming to our countries to contribute to the demise of the feudal regime and to stimulate the methods of capitalist industrialism, insofar as that signifies civilization—must be given ample governmental security. Not only should this be through recognized, regular guarantees to all kinds of foreign capital, but in accordance with those to be provided for by the democratic state of four powers—within the economic power—which is described elsewhere.

PART FOUR

Democracy and Dictatorship

HAYA DE LA TORRE HAS BEEN THE PRINCIPAL LEADER OF ONE OF THE major democratic parties of Latin America for more than four decades. As such, he has suffered extensively at the hands of successive dictatorships in his native country, undergoing several long periods of exile, incarceration, and underground activity.

In previous parts of this volume the reader will have encountered some of Haya's ideas concerning possible improvements of the traditional concepts of democracy. He has particularly stressed the need for a National Economic Congress representing all of the key interest groups in each nation as an advisory body to the legislature and administration chosen by universal suffrage. Never, however, has Haya challenged the necessity of a democratically chosen government, guaranteeing the civil liberties of speech, press, assembly, and organization to all of its citizens.

In this section, Haya de la Torre's ideas on the conflict between the aspirations for democracy and the reality of dictatorship, which has so long characterized most of the Latin American countries, are set forth. He makes a strong assertion of his belief that Latin America is "ready" for democracy and cites as proof the existence of various democratic regimes in the area. He counters the arguments of those who act as apologists—both in Latin America and the United States—for the Latin American dictatorial regimes and rationalize their positions on the grounds of the inappropriateness of democracy for an area as economically backward and so highly illiterate as Latin America.

Haya's innovating importance in the discussion of democracy and dictatorship in Latin America is probably his insistence on the interdependence of democratic attitudes and behavior in the two segments of the western hemisphere. As early as World War II, he was insisting on the importance, for the United States as well as for Latin America, of democracy becoming the pattern in the countries south of the Rio Grande. Then and later he was insistent on the need for cooperation between elements of the democratic left in the United States and Latin America, and for the United States Government's support of democratic regimes and forces in the Latin American countries.

I

IS LATIN AMERICA READY
FOR DEMOCRACY?

WHAT WE FREQUENTLY HEAR AND READ IN DISCUSSIONS OF THE POLITical problems of our America in the United States is: "You Latino or Indoamericans are not yet ready for Democracy." They prove or attempt to prove their claim by saying: "in the countries of Latin America the people frequently support long dictatorships, scandalous electoral frauds, vile oppression. If such things would occur for a single week in the United States, the people would rise in a new civil war."

This is said and written even today. When one comments, with a discussion group or in a public assembly, on the case of our dictatorships, the drama of our usurpations, the dolorous paradox of criollo rulers who adhere orally to democratic ideals while denying and mocking them in practice, one then hears or feels the objection present in the eyes or murmurs of the audience: "Still backward people, not prepared for democracy, a function of cultured people; if it is possible to impose on them a dictatorship, they deserve it!"

Then there is the problem of explaining and knowing how to explain. I remember that in England this theme was discussed extensively in the Bryce Club in Oxford. Each time that the theme of Latin or Indoamerican history became the subject of debate, one had to be ready to hear from the student who was astonished by the willingness of our peoples to bend their heads to such despots: "Here," he says, "our Democracy has been won through struggle. When a king

"No Estamos Listos Aun Para la Democracia?" Incahuasi: April 1943, published in *Y Despues de la Guerra Que?* pp. 101–108.

pushed his nose into Parliament, he lost his head. The Revolution in England would start today or tomorrow if an absolute monarch or autocratic dictator were to appear."

If one suggested that in Russia, Germany, or Italy it had also been possible to have dictatorships, the reply came immediately: "Three nations of monarchical and aristocratic tradition. Their dictatorships are rooted in a collective ambition for control of the world. Communists or Nazi-fascists have risked their citizens' liberty to gain the dreamed-for universal power. There, dictatorship has a historical explanation. But in the underpopulated and new Latin American republics that gained their sovereignty under the democratic banner, how can one explain despotism except as cultural and political inferiority?"

These arguments are revived now that the problems of a democratic peace are being discussed with progressive vehemence in the United States and even in England. When democracy is discussed in our America, smiles and these well-known objections flourish. Here and there one reads in newspapers and magazines notes and opinions about our incapacity for the authentic and complete exercise of democracy. Duncan Aikman, the celebrated author of *The All American Front,* alludes to our taste for dictators and frauds in a penetrating article in *The Atlantic Monthly* of October. Mr. Laurence Martin, professor of the University of Chicago, writes in *Harper's* of September that nothing justifies the hope of a democracy in the grand style—the North American type—in the four little Central American republics of Honduras, Nicaragua, El Salvador, and Guatemala, whose peoples, culturally backward, undernourished, and individualistic, are spiritually and materially semi-colonial. And he forgets that Costa Rica, their Central American neighbor, while very small, poor, and a fifth sister of the other four, is a model of democracy and a miracle of culture!

Because of this case, and those of Mexico and Colombia, another argument is frequently made in the United States concerning the curious relationship said to exist between the exploitable riches of our countries and the prevalence of dictatorships. It is claimed that where there is much to extract from the soil and subsoil, the large entrepreneur needs a strong government. Economic colonialism works against democracy.

Thus, the Mexican insurrection is a double movement: for the democratic organization of the state and for the economic emancipation of the country. Colombia, after Panama, put aside its rebelliousness and its impotence and affirmed a solid freedom, as vigorous, or more so, than that of the United States. Costa Rica, less rich than its sisters of Central America, and without Nicaragua's problem of the canal,* lives more for its people and for its culture by selling its bananas and its coffee without mortgaging itself. These cases, like the recent ones of Chile and Uruguay, disprove the popularized conclusion that the peoples of our America are spiritually and politically incapable of exercising democracy.

If we were to go a bit deeper into this difficult subject—particularly into this matter of the democratic paradoxes of our oligarchic regimes—we might come to some stimulating conclusions. The first of these would perhaps place primary importance on the system of economic relations between the great industrial democracies and our countries. And we might come to attempt a brief and relative statement of the relationship between the great foreign financial enterprises and the criollo anti-democratic oligarchies. Theodore Roosevelt, in his presidential message of 1905, said in reference to the Monroe Doctrine: "It is always possible that mistaken actions towards this country or towards its citizens in some state unable to maintain order among its own inhabitants, incapable of assuring justice on the part of other peoples and with lack of will to do justice to its respectable neighbors, obliges us to go into action to protect our rights. . . . " From this we might deduce that a solid Latin or Indoamerican Democracy depends in large part on a new system of economic relations between the large capitalist countries and our own. This is because the business of supporting oligarchies, dictatorships, and frauds to earn money ends in being a bad deal.

For an improvement in the North American public image of the political reality of Indoamerica, the journey of Vice President Wallace† has been an efficacious step. No declaration has been more interesting for us, because of its repercussion on the popular masses of the United States, than that of the Vice President mentioning that democracy in Chile is an effective, vital, and working reality.

When Mr. Wallace says that he "has seen democracy functioning in Chile," he helps to destroy a very generalized idea in the

---

* Haya refers here to frequent suggestions that a second canal between the Caribbean Sea and Pacific Ocean be built through Nicaragua. For many decades this possibility was a disturbing factor in internal Nicaraguan politics and an excuse for U.S. intervention in the little nation's affairs.
† Vice President Henry Wallace visited several South American countries on a goodwill tour in 1941.

northern country about our psychological incapacity to live and act within a regime of liberty. This is important in getting our neighbors to respect us, since there is nothing more degrading in their eyes than a people or a man incapable of carrying out against despotism what Locke calls "the right of resistance," one of the essential principles of the United States' concept of republicanism. This is because every North American who has read the Declaration of Independence knows that the democratic purpose of his country is to assure their inalienable rights to "Life, Liberty and the Pursuit of Happiness"; that for this are organized governments emanating from the consent of the governed, and that "whenever any form of Government becomes destructive of those ends, it is the right of the People to alter or to abolish it, and to institute new Government laying its foundation on such principles and organizing its powers in such form, as to them shall seem most likely to effect their Safety and Happiness."

For that reason, most North American citizens don't understand the existence of a despotism which doesn't have the tolerance of the oppressed. Alien to our feudal background and the ferocity of our autocracies, they consider that when these exist they are the result of the public will, or are a malediction merited by the moral inferiority of the people. Such opinions about our incapacity for democracy are common in the United States. Since there are not many cases demonstrating the contrary, since it is our despots and their claques who defend the fallacious necessity for a "strong man," and as the great merchants and investors of the imperialisms earn more under the protection of tyrannies than with alert democracies in Indoamerica, it is very difficult to convince the man in the street in the United States that we are not a race of slaves.

But the opinion of Vice President Wallace is of great importance in favor of our thesis. He has seen in Chile a magnificent democratic coordination and has justly eulogized it. He has not forgotten the "leaders" of the old country, of the conservative Chile of a century of good government, since they cannot be forgotten particularly by a man of the left. . . . Perhaps it is time to say in merited homage to Chilean democracy that it owes its exemplary process to the historical gift of a responsible conservatism—the most responsible of the continent—capable of making of Chile what Wallace has said: an asylum against oppression for the great exiles of the past and a tribune for all ideas. Also, for what the Vice President didn't come to say: an exemplary school for rightists who know how to lose, even in recent times, as in 1920, 1938, 1942.

This is democracy, even though those who live it and enjoy it at close hand see its defects, which is always the way to see it. Government and legislative opposition—and in Indoamerica, the feudal-colonial heir of so many miserable oligarchies—tolerance and respect for new ideas, without being fearful of them, this is Democracy! Chile has achieved it, in spite of having been so often called militarist and Prussian, and until recently, a refuge of Nazis. Its case is an example for us, and for the North Americans, incredulous of our capacity for democracy, a fact.

It is important, very important, for us that the great electoral masses of North America come to understand that the peoples of Indoamerica really are ready for democracy. And that the despotisms which still humiliate us are as ominous for us as the Nazi-Fascist-Falangisms are for the European peoples. And it is important, very important, that the North American voter know that we hate despotism, even though we are sometimes impotent against it. Thus, votes in favor of the imperialist political groups of that country seeking fruitful alliances with our tyrants, crowding around and eulogizing them, will cease. This is important because we must not forget that in the elections of last November there entered the House of Representatives of Washington a goodly number of supporters of the isolationsist and imperalist thesis.

For that reason, we are extraordinarily interested in the North American voter, that is to say, the people of the United States. If they know nothing of us and having no other sources of information than that provided by criollo despots and their Goebbels-like "intellectuals," or the capitalist investment firms allied to the tyrannies, or that of the reactionaries and imperialists of their own country, then they will think that we still need tutelage and controls. . . . But if the authoritative voice of Vice President Wallace is joined to that of the good neighbors, those North American supporters of our capacity for democracy, the desired day may come when the people of the United States comprehend that it is necessary to struggle against the despotisms south of the Rio Bravo as against those on the other side of the Atlantic.

To this we must be inclined, not only for the strengthening and support from outside of the position of the anti-imperialists within the United States—such as the Vice President—but also to make vigorous our democratic and anti-imperialist conscience, such as that possessed by Mr. Wallace.

There are two—among many—principal political currents in the United States with regard to the problems of the peace. Let us not forget: that of the conservatives, reactionaries, and Imperialists—of whom a good number were elected to the House of Representatives last November—and that of the liberals and progressives of whom the Vice President is an authoritative spokesman. The latter so far have the majority. However, as Wilson also had the majority until the end of the previous war and lost it at the last moment because of the confusion of the voters, it behooves us to cooperate energetically so that the forces of our side remain in power in North America.

Also, the people of the United States need, very much, education concerning Indoamerican problems. They also want to hear our voice. Chile not only has made it heard, but has given living testimony of its democracy. Chile, for this reason, has rendered a great service to the continent, because it demonstrates to a great leader of anti-imperialism and of democratic ideals that not everything is obsequiousness, dictatorship, and conformity in our America.

For the good of all, for the future of our continent, for the United States to respect us, we need to consolidate democracy in each Indoamerican country and combat the despotisms where they exist, in Asia or in Europe, but principally here in Indoamerica. Let the North American people know that we certainly are ready for democracy and that the tyrannies which still subjugate our peoples do so by force, as France and Spain support their Gauleiters.* Let them know that we are not afraid of intervention in the political life of other countries, because this revolutionary war is just that: a liberating intervention by the Democracies to end the tyranny subjugating the people oppressed by totalitarianism.

We also are "intervening" in the North American political life to support democratic and anti-imperialist leaders in the United States. Our moral action of sympathy and support must weigh much in the future electoral decisions. Let us strengthen then this consciousness of good intervention, because thus will be reborn in our peoples the historic Indoamerican interventionist tradition which moved San Martín and Bolívar to cross frontiers to defeat tyrannies and make liberty possible.

---

* *Gauleiter* was the title of regional leaders of the Nazi party in Germany. By extension of its meaning, Haya uses it here to mean Petain and Franco in World War II in France and Spain.

II

CIVIL DEMOCRACY AND
MILITARY DICTATORSHIP

THE FALL OF PERONISMO, BLOODILY INITIATED WITH THE IMPRESSIVE events of last June in Buenos Aires, was foreseeable. Perón had already worn out all the demagogic resources during recent years, and after his "anti-imperialism" against the United States suddenly ended, and the failure of his boasting about "the third position," he had nothing left to do but to launch himself against the Catholic Church. Here, the exhausted patience of his own supporters in the armed forces, the basis of his dictatorship, struck against the demagogy with a desperate insurrection. The naval uprising of Buenos Aires had the dimensions of a premeditated tyrannicide, the frustration of which did not reduce either its tremendous gravity or its unforeseen consequences in the direction of restoring civil government and returning the human rights to the oppressed Argentinian people.

The militarism of Perón is typical of criollo militarism throughout Indoamerica. It is clear that Perón surpassed all of the excesses of demagogy and succeeded in hiding his policy with a camouflage of "socialism" and with a great flourish of personal style, misleading appreciable sectors of public opinion in and out of Indoamerica by the brilliance of his gestures of *justicialista** boasting. For a while, he succeeded in attracting many sincere, credulous ones, when he

---

"Democracia Civil y Dictadura Militar," July, 1955, published in *Pensamiento Politico de Haya de la Torre,* Volume V.
* *Justicialismo* was the word most widely used by Perón to describe his type of regime. *Justicialista* is the adjective form of the word which can be liberally translated as "social justice."

announced that he was working on secrets of atomic energy—with prodigous cunning—or when he presented himself as the paladin of the federative union of the Indoamerican States. This ideal having been sustained in the Rio de la Plata in the days of Independence by [Manuel] Belgrano and by [Bernardo] Monteagudo. Belgrano had proposed in the Congress of Tucuman of 1816 the formation of "The United Provinces of South America," with its capital in Cuzco and with an Inca-Emperor as sovereign; and Monteagudo, in spite of his enmity towards Bolívar, had been a fervent supporter of the ideas of continental unionism of the Liberator.

I have maintained and maintain now that political militarism— that of the generals assaulting civic power, with a mask of redeeming providentialism hiding low ambitions and odious liberticidal intentions—is the political cancer of our peoples. The falacious claims of the generals-politicians, or *politiqueros,** about the incapacity of the citizens of Indoamerica to live within a civilized democracy, have no more basis than the sick militarist obsession for usurping legal government and satisfying their personal desire for dictatorial command. That democratic life is possible in our continent is demonstrated by history: Always when the armed forces of a country have respected the constitutional and civil order and have fulfilled their basic duty of being its servants and not its destroyers, we have had democracy. We have it in exemplary fashion in Uruguay and in Costa Rica, in Chile and in the British and Dutch Antillean and tropical dominions. Unstable Ecuador is demonstrating the benefits of civil government and has succeeded in recent years in submitting the military politicans to control. Brazil is saving itself from the risk of conspiring generals; Bolivia is opening the path towards free government, having dominated the barracks agitators; and Mexico, which Blasco Ibáñez described in his damaging, violent, and pejorative book, distributed all over the world in three languages—*El Militarismo Mexicano*—is today an advanced republic of democratic social progress governed by civilians.

In the First World War, Clemenceau, leader of the victorious French against German militarism, made famous a phrase which Churchill repeated as the theme of his leadership in the Second: "La guerre, est un affaire trop serieuse pour etre confiée aux militaires."

---

* A depreciating word for political manipulators, dedicated principally to using political activity for their own advancement and enrichment.

In the politics of the state, which is since Aristotle a science and a technology more serious than that of war, the statement is valid. Bolívar—cited by Germán Arciniegas in his magnificent book *Entre la Libertad y el Miedo*—left, as a civil testament, forgotten and betrayed, these immortal words: *"A happy soldier doesn't ever acquire any right to rule his country. He is not the arbiter of laws and government; he is the defender of its liberty."* Also there is this memorable Bolivarian quote, *"The military spirit is insupportable in the civil government."*

We are now in the Atomic Age. War has now become a colossal crime against culture and against the human species. The "science" and the "art" of war are no more sublime expressions of heroic patriotism, or epic means of universal progress. Genocide is a despicable crime, and "universal death" its fearful result. However, the catastrophic innovations of scientific war have caused a strong division among the men who study and practice it. Now there are two types of military men: the "pre-atomic" and the "atomic."

Those in the first category have nothing to do in a mechanized contemporary war, whose arms they neither possess nor understand. Their "science" belongs to the armies and navies of an epoch which appeared very advanced until fifteen years ago and presently are primitive and distant. Their geometry is that of Euclid, their physics is that of Newton and Dalton; their strategy and their tactics belong to that which had as its basis gunpowder canons, cavalry movements, and the rules of attack and defense of Napoleonic origin, with a few posterior improvements.

All of this today is as innocuous and obsolete as would be the brilliant armor, the swordplay, and the medieval aggressive lances and catapults after the discovery of the first artillery or of platform muskets, precursors of the rifle and great grandfathers of machine guns and light automatic weapons. But nuclear energy and the total war, which the atom engenders and which calculates today the geometrical curves in land, sea, and air, push to one side the military man (with his brilliant uniform, soaring plumes, and decorative sword), who doesn't know the new science whose secrets are like the mysterious and still inscrutable beat of the electromagnetic fields. Of the transformations of energy into matter and vice versa; of electrons, protons, and neutrons and of the extremely complex calculations of their velocities and of their reactions and thermal disintegrations, the "pre-atomic" military man knows nothing. It is thus explainable that as people useless for the new war, they devote themselves to making it—as in the past—against their helpless people. They opt for the politics of adventure and apply their reactionary concepts of control over a barracks to the government of a state. Thus, the "pre-atomic" criollo general pretending to be a statesman is nothing more than an individual displaced from his own profession invading another, and supplanting by force the civilized right of peoples to freely govern themselves.

From there the militarist regimes in our countries become totalitarian, imitating the Nazi-fascists, and add to their terrorism a misleading demagoguery of "socialization" and support of the lower classes. Invoking "order" and "justice" they strangle liberty. Mouthing "patriotism," they are provokers of hostile jingoism and chauvinist nationalism, to mislead their peoples, in this epoch when the world is preparing to organize great continental communities and advance towards the installation of ecumenical super-states.

America, ours, if it is not to be left forgotten on the path of history, must free itself from the anachronistic forms of anti-democratic domination. The "pre-atomic" military men who infest as transgressors the civil field of politics—which belongs only to the parties educated in civic discipline—must either return to their barracks, or place themselves alongside their peoples. Continental union and the formation of a Bolivarian army at the service of the power that emanates only from popular sovereignty and the common security of America, will save us from the militarist danger. The case of Perón demonstrates the disastrous results of armed dictatorships, but at the same time announces the end of an epoch of barbarism beyond which the resolute will of our peoples, united, must go.

III

ARE THE PEOPLE INCAPABLE OF A DEMOCRATIC CIVILIZATION?

THE MILITARY RULER OF VENEZUELA, COLONEL PÉREZ JIMÉNEZ, declared recently to *Time* magazine of New York that the Venezuelan people were still incapable of living, with full rights and duties, a civilized democratic life. He said that such incapacity justifies the existence of a military government, or in other words, a dictatorship.

This assertion is not original. It has been repeated in America every time a general has taken control of the government. In Spain it forms part of the three or four set replies which General Franco has developed for the journalists of the Free World when they ask him some indiscreet question about his despotism. The people turn out to be poor because of their backwardness or barbarism and are thus officially declared worthy of government from the barracks. For the purpose of preparing them for the meritorious life of democratic liberty, they are administered with the utmost possible demagogy, corruption, and tyranny.

Our Indoamerican incapacity for democracy is the handy argument used here and there to justify the endemic malady of our militarism, proneness to conspiracy and coup d'etat, and unlimited usufruct of the benefits of government by means of tyranny. It is said that for our democratic life, we are hampered by climate and race. They have coined easy commonplaces to repeat such as that which maintains that democracy is incompatible with the high indices of illiteracy which, without doubt, are a dishonor to our republics.

"Pueblos Incapaces Para Civilización Democrática?" May, 1955, published in *Pensamiento Politico de Haya de la Torre,* Volume V.

What is certain is that when militarism has been controlled or liquidated, democracy has been possible in Indoamerica, in spite of racial and climatic variations: Costa Rica is a country of the tropical zone and its democratic spirit and system are exemplary. In the same Caribbean, where there are the ferocious militarisms, in the republics called "independent," stable democracies of mestizo "colonial" peoples are appearing that quickly become models to be followed in the rest of our America: The West Indies—destined sooner or later to form part of our community—are showing the way. Jamaica is a case, Puerto Rico is another, and the Dutch Antilles are closely behind them.

Uruguay and Mexico are the two poles of our Democracy. Uruguay, a temperate country, with a Latin-European racial predominance, is without doubt among those republics on the line of the great social systems of Switzerland and Scandinavia. With those, they are ahead of the North American democracy. Mexico with its 30 millions of inhabitants, in majority mestizo, has other problems; but without doubt, it advances with sureness towards an integral democracy. It is important to point out that the first step in the Mexican democratic development has been the elimination of militarism—even revolutionary militarism—and the sure establishment of civil government as the unequivocal mark of the institutional progress of the country.

In spite of its partisan agitations—perhaps a little French mimicry—Chile is a stable democracy, one of the most stable of America. The fact that a veteran general* now presides over the country is not a basis for doubting Chilean civil democracy. His mandate comes from an unfraudulant election, and he is the only Chilean general who in a period of several decades was tempted by bad policy—let's say a temptation or contagion of Central American origin—and the only one who thirty years ago, overthrew a civil government and established an ominous dictatorship. Its end was a beautiful victory of Chilean civic opinion when public consensus threw militarism out of power. Now the general, without ornaments or arrests, has

---

* The reference here is to General Carlos Ibañez, who was elected President of Chile in 1952. He had presided over the only dictatorship Chile has had in the twentieth century, between 1927 and 1931. However, he returned to office in 1952 by popular election and in 1958, turned his post over to his duly elected successor, President Jorge Alessandri.

returned to power backed by the legitimacy of election, to amend old and misguided steps and to behave as a president respectful of the rights of the people.

It is good to remember that Chile has given America relevant lessons which make us believe in the civil decency of democracy: General [Manuel] Baquedano was the victor of the war of 1879–1884 between Chile on the one hand and Peru and Bolivia on the other. The triumph of Chilean arms made them masters of the entire Bolivian coast and of the huge nitrate zone of Peru, and Baquedano returned to his country after having occupied Lima, over whose viceroyal palace floated, for two long years, the victorious banner. In spite of this, when Baquedano was proposed as a candidate for the presidency of Chile—and the elections took place during the last part of the war, in the heat of repeated Chilean victories—the general was not elected. The victor was an honest and poor civilian: Don Domingo Santa María, the victorious president, who at the end of his mandate did not have a house in which to live and whose friends gave him one. Baquedano never became president of his country.

In addition to the almost legendary self-sacrifice of President Balmaceda—whom Getulio Vargas imitated perhaps with equal benefit for Brazilian civil government—to save Chile from internal struggle and certainly from a military dictatorship, one must remember two other more recent and eloquent examples.* The election of Alessandri in 1920, was made possible because the Conservative party, on account of the decisive intervention of Archbishop Crescente Errázuriz, voluntarily made way for the candidate of the Liberal Party who supported a program of the separation of Church and State and had the reputation of being a terrible revolutionary. The triumph of the Popular Front in 1938 was a similar occasion. Aguirre Cerda came to power by election that year with only a majority of about 4,000 votes. This marked the fall of the right, and the Casandras of the coups d'etat predicted one in Chile. The chief of the Chilean Army—a conservative general—stepped forward to

---

* J. M. Balmaceda was president of Chile from 1886 to 1891. An advocate of extensive social reforms, he was overthrown by conservative elements in a short civil war and committed suicide upon his defeat. Getulio Vargas, the Brazilian ex-dictator who was reelected freely to the presidency in 1950 also committed suicide when the military sought to oust him in 1954.

deny publicly the subversive rumors and to counsel the defeated candidate [Gustaro] Ross to accept the electoral decision.†

I have visited Venezuela—and not only Caracas—during its democratic period in 1946, just before the elections. I was in the Andean region which is traditionally conservative and the breeding ground of tyrants. I ascertained for certain that the Venezuelan people were not barbarians, that is to say, incapable of democracy. I attended demonstrations of citizens which did not differ from those of democratically civilized countries. I learned after my departure that the elections for members of the Constitutional Assembly were carried out in as orderly and honest a fashion as in any cultured country.

I think that Bolivia demonstrates clearly how the elimination of militarism opens the way for the advent of a democratic order of profound social significance. The case of Bolivia is singularly stimulating for all of the Andean Zone of Peru, Ecuador, and Northeastern Argentina, populated by millions of descendents of the subjects of the Empire of the Incas, whose race, whose language, and whose demands are the same. Bolivia is teaching our states with native populations that they—a fact confirmed by Mexico and Guatemala—are proper places for democracy. Even more, Bolivia shows that in their native organizations and habits democracy is practiced—the systems of elections are an example in the communities of Inca tradition—but always with a high degree of social sense. This is something which the Bolivian experiment is discovering. When the negative, anti-democratic factor represented by imperialism is pushed aside, the indigenous institutional life encounters its traditional path of freedom and discipline, spontaneous characteristic of its natural way.*

To my mind, nothing is more forced and violent than the

---

† Arturo Alessandri, leftist candidate in the election of 1920, won a narrow victory and was only allowed to take office after considerable political maneuvering. Pedro Aguirre Cerda, candidate of the Popular Front of Radical, Socialist, and Communist parties in 1938, won an equally narrow victory. Rumors that he might not be allowed to take office proved fallacious, as Haya indicates.

* Haya is referring here to the revolutionary regime of the Nationalist Revolutionary Movement (MNR) which seized power in 1952. It carried out a thorough agrarian reform and took many other measures to incorporate the Indian majority into the economic, social, and civic life of the nation. Unfortunately, the MNR regime made the mistake of building up the armed forces, which finally overthrew the MNR in November 1964. Most of the program launched by the MNR government, nevertheless, remains intact.

implantation of regimes of military dictatorship in Argentina and in Peru. Psychologically, both peoples are pacific—perhaps too much so—but unadaptable to regimentation and the regime of the barracks. It is clear that in Peronista militarism, demagogy and terror are ingredients which are much better combined than in Peru, where the experience of collective intimidation is much longer and more cruel. But to both peoples there is attributed excessive subservience because of their apparent submission in the face of brutality. Profoundly within each, however, there is a type of passive resistance, which is sometimes active, unavoidable. I don't believe that I am mistaken when I argue that at any moment—this happened in Peru in 1945—in Peru or in Argentina civil liberties might be restored and militarism would fall. The peoples will enter immediately into democratic paths as people who take a familiar road.

In Brazil I understood well that it is, among our peoples, the one least apt to tolerate a dictator, especially of the somber military type which we know in the other states of the continent. Getulio [Vargas] was a civil boss during his long tenure as president. Last August, a few weeks before the tragic events, the president was exposed to many gibes from platforms and cafes which were as entertaining and biting as those of the theaters of the Mexican neighborhoods . . . or those of Paris.

Soon the hour of the drama arrived. When in the mind of the Brazilian people the conviction matured that Getulio sooner or later would pay for his defiant "0 petroleo e nosso," there came the improvised suicide. Thus Getulio closed the way to a possible military coup, and he showed himself dauntless but sincere.

All of which supports my premise: perhaps another measure must be applied to the case of Spain. The history of Spain is the history of the struggle of the people for freedom; we might point out many phases in its development that offer proof of their indomitable desire for freedom, from which originate the names applied to those indomitable and fierce people, independent and individualistic. We note in passing the rising of the communities against Charles V, the war of independence against Napoleon, the establishment of the first republic in 1873, as a reaction against the chaotic situation of the country and military uprisings. The most recent and exemplary phase is represented by those elections of April 12, 1931, which brought the second republic. This was the first time that the Spaniards could show their civil aspirations, and they decided to attempt to overthrow a wornout institution and to take pacifically the path of liberty. This conquest closed the road to military dictatorships for the time being. Thus the generals of totalitarian spirit who had to submit to this pacific and overwhelming impulse, worked to suppress it, using foreign arms; and the civic and cultural development of Spain was stopped. But Spain doesn't sleep, and it will emerge from this nightmare of totalitarian horror, disposed to take the wide road, natural and proper for the peoples: the road of freedom.

With respect to our America, political militarism, the professional general-conspirator who converts his army into an armed political party, and the armed forces into forces of occupation in their own country, represents in America anti-democratic totalitarianism. All our people might live without armies, but they do not accept to live without freedom.

The remedy? It is the union of all our armed forces into a single continental army—from the moment in which, after the Rio Pact of 1947, there cannot be war among us—for defense against any extra-American aggression. An Interamerican command arsenal would mean fewer pre-atomic generals and more soldier-citizens of an America united for liberty.

PART FIVE

Latin American Unity

THE THEME OF LATIN AMERICAN (OR INDOAMERICAN AS HE FRE-
quently calls it) unity runs through all of the writings of Víctor
Raúl Haya de la Torre and is discussed in connection with virtually
all of the other subjects with which he has dealt. There are, however, principal essays on this issue.

The first selection is taken from one of the early collections of
his essays and journalistic articles, *¿A Donde Va Indoamérica?* Written in the late 1920s, when Haya was living in Europe, it reflects his
conviction that Latin American unity must serve as a basis from which
Indoamerica can deal on a par with the United States. He is obviously quite suspicious of any move in this direction which may be
taken with the support and stimulus of the United States, although
he does not deny completely the value of unification of the area
even if it is carried out under those circumstances.

The other selections are taken from Haya's writings during and
after World War II. During the war he was much concerned with
two issues: Whether the Good Neighbor Policy would persist, and
if not, what would happen to a divided Latin America; and what
might happen to the area if the United States were to lose to the
Axis powers and its military protection be removed from Latin
America. In the wartime passages he also insisted that only democratic regimes can adequately defend the area.

The last selections reflect the growing pressures towards Latin
American economic unity arising from the establishment of the European Common Market. Haya is strongly in favor of the establishment
of a counterpart Latin American Common Market, as a first step
towards his old ideal of a united Indoamerica.

I

DIFFERENT KINDS OF
LATIN AMERICAN UNITY

Señor [Enrique] Villegas, head of the Chilean delegation in Geneva, has received extensive commentary in the European press, from his declaration that in case there is constituted a federation, total or partial, of the states of Europe, those of Latin America will be obliged to form also a federal bloc of self defense. Señor Villegas, with a modern mind, although with a capitalistic point of view, has based his interesting declaration on economic grounds. He has referred especially to the possibility of an arrangement among the countries producing coal in Europe for the purpose of limiting production or raising prices. Only Chile appreciably exploits its coal, and the greater part of the Latin American countries, especially those of South America, depend on imports of that fuel. The economic consequence of European accords on the limitation of production and price of coal, would be—in the judgment of the Chilean delegate—the formation of a united front of the Latin American states in self defense.

Coming from a powerful country of Latin America, such as Chile, and being apparently seconded by another even more powerful one, Brazil, the suggestion of Señor Villegas has produced alarm in Europe. Authoritative journals, attentive to international politics, such as the *Manchester Guardian,* declare that a movement towards the economic federation of Latin America must be seriously considered in Europe.

With evident realism, European opinion feels that isolated, sin-

1929, published in *A Donde Va Indoamerica?* pp. 239–243.

gle Latin American countries signify very little, as yet, in the world economic and political situation. United, they would be a factor of immense importance. If the union were total, Europe would see arise a nation of more than nine million square kilometres, with more than one hundred million inhabitants, master of immense wealth, and with the ability to support a population equal to that of the entire world at present. Even if Latin American economic and political unity only included the four or five major South American states, the infiuence of this new "bloc" of young peoples would be viewed with respect and doubtlessly even with suspicion.

For those of us who belong in the ranks of the defenders of the ideas of Latin American Federation, the declaration of the Chilean delegate invites analysis. Perhaps to many Latin Americans, especially the skeptical or unconcerned, this idea will come as a great surprise. The project of unifying our peoples is considered by those who believe that history is a dramatic succession of episodes and not the social expression of a deep economic rhythm, as "pretty idealism." Especially in the smaller countries of Latin America, or in those which are most isolated, localism is very prevalent, and the hostile and egoistic kind of patriotism is most primitively expressed. The few who, "with eyes to see," understand the possibility and great future of a united Latin America, are ridiculed. When they are not called babblers and Bolsheviks, they are piously applauded as supporters of impossible causes. However, in the more economically developed peoples, the idea of a Latin American union comes as the result of the lessons of that development. National limits appear artificial and negative when the homogeneity of the economic problems shows that political frontiers—which had their historic reasons in the feudal epoch before Independence—constitute obstacles to the productivity and the profitability of labor in its modern forms.

It is worthwhile to remember, however, that within this political concept of Latin American unity, there are two currents that should not be confused. Using modern technical terms which are strictly applicable to our economic reality, we must accept the words *impe-rialist* and *anti-imperialist*. The projected federation of Latin America can be imperialist, that is to say, a product of the economic policy of the United States—as is the project of European federation—or it can be "anti-imperialist" if the federation intends an economic defense of the national productive masses from imperialism.

In the United States the policy of the economic domination of

Latin America has two tendencies. The older, and easier, is summed up in the statement *divide et impero*. But the progress of the modern economy tends to free it of all classical formulas. The contemporary form of trust in the capitalist economy, teaches that by uniting, one can also reign. This is as true in economics as in politics. Modifying the rigors of competition that underlie capitalism, but that also contain the seeds of its destruction, as Marx discovered in his Hegelian application of the theory of the "negation of the negation," modern capitalism which covers nations and continents develops better in the form of international organization.

This is understood by the rulers of the economic empire of the United States. The Federation of Europe projected by M. Briand* is only a corollary to the Young Plan† which would practically convert this part of the world into a colonial federation governed by the International Bank. The suggestion of Señor Villegas for a Latin American federation, seems to be a project for the economic defense of Latin America against the threat of the economic unity of Europe, but is actually one under the control and direction of the United States which, dialectically, needs the European federation from the economic point of view, but at the same time understands the danger from the political viewpoint, a danger which must be balanced by establishing an equilibrium between the continents.

Thus the federative idea of Señor Villegas is not an anti-imperialist idea, although it arouses resistance in certain North American sectors. The European economic danger is secondary for Latin America compared with the North American danger. The federation of our countries from the anti-imperialist point of view would also be an economic federation, but not on the basis of governments submitting directly or indirectly to North American control.

Hence the young Latin American generation, supporting the union of our peoples, would have expected from Mexico a policy directed to the formation of a bloc of economic defense for Latin America, a union which by the unity of leadership could fix uniform conditions for the necessary invasion of North American capital in our countries. The international policy of Mexico has in some

---

* Aristide Briand, French foreign minister in the late 1920s and author of a project for a United States of Europe.

† The Young Plan was a program for scheduling German reparations payments to the victors of World War I, in which the Bank of International Settlements played a major role.

moments marched in the direction of assuming the historic rôle of making it the leader of this Latin Americanist policy. The most efficacious initiative from Mexico in this regard was that of continental citizenship. But then, for unknown reasons, the Mexican Senatorial commission, which was to leave for the south seeking continental approbation for that admirable project, did not come about, and with that failure, the hopes of those of us who were sure of the magnificent reception which the nineteen peoples would have given to this mission were dashed. It would have placed Mexico in a unique position before America and before the world.

Those of us who know and love Mexico realize very well that that country has given America as much as it can in the midst of its revolutionary situation, its grave international problems, and its necessary improvisation of leadership; not everyone has the capacity to see the historic future of a united Latin America. We know also that a new stage must come in Mexico and that men of wide political thought must direct again their international action towards the objective of Latin American union which—not for sentimental motives but for pressing economic ones—signifies the only salvation of our peoples.

In spite of the dangers which it involves, because of its imperialist origins, the declaration of Chile has for the unionists and anti-imperialists of America a useful side. It destroys in one blow all the objections of those too short-sighted to see the possibility of a Latin American union. When an idea is launched thus, as it was launched by Señor Villegas, in a European assembly, it is very clear that the question has been previously studied. The Chileans are among the Latin Americans who least frequently use vain words, since they live farthest from the tropical climate that produces excesses. The declaration of Señor Villegas is an admonition: *Latin America can unite and is going to unite.* Either it does so through the will of the more powerful, in agreement with the United States, or it unites through the omnipotent volition of its peoples with or without, the approval of the United States.

With the settlement of the Tacna-Arica question,* the most important cause of hostilities in South America, the southern states of our continent see clearly that they cannot advance any further

---

* Haya refers here to the settlement of the border issue between Peru and Chile, originating in the War of the Pacific (1879–1883) between Chile on the one hand and Bolivia on the other. In the settlement, Tacna went to Peru and Arica to Chile.

under the limitations of political separatism. A South American bloc must be the immediate corollary of the settlement of the Tacna-Arica question. It is necessary now that the governments freest from North American influence and most advanced in political ideology assume a realistic attitude. The federation is not good or bad in itself. It is a political instrument that can be, like all instruments, the means of progress or retrogression. Using the lexicon apt for this problem, we shall say that the Latin American federation can be the weapon of either the liberation or the oppression for our peoples.

As the great majority of the [present] Latin American governments have very strong bonds tying them to the United States, only governments emanating from the people, or new governments, can undertake this great enterprise. If it doesn't come about thus, the Latin American United States will be, as the dominions of the British Empire, component entities of a colonial commonwealth.

II

THE GOOD NEIGHBOR POLICY AND LATIN AMERICAN UNITY

YES, THERE IS AN ALTERNATIVE FOR INDOAMERICA TO THAT OF LIVING always under the defensive tutelage of its great and Good Neighbor.

Here, I wish to underscore succinctly an interesting aspect of this subject. As a result of the reduction of the imperialist tension in Indoamerica, due to the Good Neighbor Policy, it is said that "now there is no imperialism." A United States university missionary, who has just passed through Lima, proclaimed from a classroom of the oldest university of America that "there is no Yankee imperialism" and that there is only Japanese imperialism. The ingenuous propagandist was amiably and intelligently received by the Peruvian youth, who applauded him, in a hospitable fashion, as a good man. We must say once and for all, however, that no one is convinced in this way. Good Neighborliness does not imply the denial of historical facts because they are bad and cause twinges of conscience. It is better to change them—recognizing them—amend them, correct them. It is not a matter of converting into idyllic memories the brutalities perpetrated by North American imperialism in these countries, of which our glorious Sandino* is the latest victim. It is a matter of pointing them out exactly as damning facts, as events which have caused great damage to good relations between the Americas, and especially, as facts the negative consequences of which are still felt, because Fascism takes advantage of them, capitalizing on those resentments.

February, 1938, published in *La Defensa Continental,* pp. 41–43.

* Augusto Sandino, a Nicaraguan Guerrila leader against the United States Marines occupation of his country in the 1920s and 1930s, was assassinated in 1934, when after the withdrawal of U.S. troops, he came to Managua, under a safe conduct, to discuss the laying down of the arms of his guerrilla forces.

What is involved also is preventing illusions that might be prejudicial. It is necessary to work for a good and stable Inter American accord, but it is well to bear in mind that so long as the United States of the North is "potent and large" and the Disunited States of the South continue weak and divided, our destiny will always be to rely on the protection of the stronger. I return then to a familiar theme: What would Indoamerica be like if the United States were defeated in a war? Or, what would Indoamerica be like if there arose in the United States an imperialist fascism advocating the absorption "in the Austrian manner" of our divided countries, dominated by castes of chauvinistic frauds?

Although these are not immediate risks, they are possible. After a recent voyage to Europe, former President Hoover declared to the North American press that his country ran the danger of turning fascist. Furthermore, history teaches us that many powerful empires perished by defeat or by disintegration. Thinking about the future of our countries obliges us, therefore, to recognize that our security and sovereignty depend excessively on the United States.

The true road to salvation appears clear: Abolish all imperialism in Indoamerica and unite Indoamerica economically and politically. To nationalize progressively all the wealth and constitute a great federal republic that secures solidly the security and sovereignty of our peoples on the consistent bases of democracy and social justice.

The politics of the Good Neighbor, the anti-fascist front, the democratic alliance of North and Indoamerica to defend ourselves against International Fascism, are guarantees of immediate security, laudable, necessary, and worthy of support. But we must not forget that they are fragile. The permanent, durable guarantees for these Indoamerican countries are those that they can give themselves, based upon their union.

To work for it is the duty of all Indoamericans capable of understanding that the dream of Bolívar is today an imperative necessity. Part of the task is to convince the people and government of North America that it is to their advantage to have a united and strong neighbor and ally—a help and not a burden—rather than twenty small ones, divided and antagonized by jingoisms of fascist inspiration.

We must be convinced that so long as we are not united, we live under the tutelage of the strong neighbor today and under the chains of some colonialism later.

THE AXIS MENACE AND
LATIN AMERICAN UNITY

IN THIS UNIVERSALLY TRAGIC HOUR, RECRIMINATIONS ARE FRE-
quently heard. In the face of the formidable victory of force, the
world which believed in law accuses itself of not having been more
foresighted. The reactionary conservative pacifism of Chamberlain or
Daladier,* the confidence in the respect for their "neutrality" by the
rulers of Holland and Belgium, the fact that no action was taken in
time during the totalitarian "maneuvers" in Spain,† all these things
and many others, which they now understand with reproach and self-
indictment, are heard in the vehement language of the desperate.

We are not going to use it ourselves, but we are going to permit
ourselves some reflections. The Saxons of Europe and of America
say a bit disdainfully of the Indoamericans that we always leave things
for *mañana*. If the crucial stage in which humanity lives were not so
grave, we might tell both of them, with admonitions and smiles, that
they waited too confidently to take care of things *mañana*.

This is proven not only by the difficult situation of England, but
also by the belated North American action in taking steps to prepare
to fulfill a double responsibility: to their own nation—for which they
may be more or less ready—and to the Indoamerican continent, for

---

June, 1940, published in *La Defensa Continental,* pp. 26–33.

* Neville Chamberlain and Édouard Daladier, the prime ministers of Britain
and France respectively, were leading protagonists of the "appeasement" of
Hitler, and in September 1938, had signed with Hitler and Mussolini the
infamous Munich Pact whereby Czechoslovakia was partitioned.

† Haya refers here to the participation of German and Italian armed forces on
the Franco side in the Spanish Civil War, 1936–1939.

which they don't seem to be completely ready. Both things they left for *mañana*.

Pan American lethargy, the wavering policy of more or less innocuous conferences and declarations in which the men of Washington and our short-sighted rulers of recent times have wasted valuable time, has been awakened from its sweet pacifist and almost tropical sleep by a brutal, implacable, and enslaving blitzkrieg.

Although our time has not come yet for irreparable recriminations, it is necessary to make up for lost time. If we have consciousness of our destiny, we shall attempt to do what has been left undone. Above all, it is important to renovate the aged Pan Americanism, which has been formal and dignified, of which the image and symbol is the clean, flashing, and cold "Pan American Union" in Washington, a sanctuary of bureaucracy under an administration which is kindly but myopic in terms of seeing fundamentally, with wise eyes what these times require and of recognizing the multiple problems of the Americas.

So long as we continue embraced in such a "Pan Americanism," the future of our peoples will be in the hands of the same type of appeasing, "gentlemanly" leadership—the Chamberlains of this hemisphere—who confide in peace, in good will, and in everything which makes money. (This in spite of the fact that it is a paradox of these violent times that the present war demonstrates clearly that not only money provides armed might, that there are attributes of will and emotion, of courage and audacity which, in the service of fanaticism, are worth at times as much or more than proud gold.)

It is time that the men of Indoamerica confront the task of thinking for ourselves and by ourselves. We must not continue being confident that the Pan American Union is going to defend us by itself. We remember that we live in a period of such unforeseen occurrences, that nothing is fantastic or impossible, and it is not a pessimistic conjecture to say loudly that our rich, undefended, divided continent, isolated by politicians without vision, can be conquered more easily than Holland and Belgium, than Norway, Poland, Finland, Lithuania, and France.

It is clear that we need the aid of the United States. It is most clear. But the mistake, a dangerously blind one, would be to depend for everything on the powerful neighbor that will also have to defend itself from Europe and from Asia. This which is perhaps not something of tomorrow—and perhaps it is—gives us time to think that the days, months, or years of waiting are a brief time. However, we must not make calculations like those of Chamberlain who expected the war in 1945, or like Henry Ford—and many other Yankee leaders—who wagered that the war would never come.

The experience of some Saxons who lost their fear of *mañana* and acted in a most tropical fashion is a valuable experience for us. We do not forget that this war is for control over the world and that totalitarian imperialism pardons nothing. It pardons least the weak and those of us who are not of the white-Aryan race and who, therefore, are ethnically inferior in their eyes.

Nor do we forget that there are two dominant maxims in this hour of naked realism: "the chain breaks at its weakest line"— and Indoamerica is that in this hemisphere—and "strength through union," a teaching of Peregrulle, a frequent North American inscription on their porticos, but one that those on this side, arrogant apostates of Bolivar, consider to be extremely common.

In these days, everyone is hanging on the words coming from Washington. So far, however, there are more words than deeds, while from the other side come more bold moves than words.

"Continental solidarity" is talked about, as has been "mutual consultation," and all of the innocuous things emitted by the Pan American Union in the pompous and meaningless conferences of Lima and Panama. However, the world has changed in a few weeks all of the significance of these words. The fancy speeches of the conferences and subsequent emphatic declarations are worth little or nothing in the face of the danger.

The truth, the hard truth, is that the rapid blows of war have changed the course of history and have confounded in a new Babel of strange lexicon the old value of words. Now it is necessary to speak a new language.

To cooperate is not to allow oneself to be trapped. Until now our rulers, more or less timidly, have gotten onto the bandwagon of Washington, and there have felt secure. Little have they thought that if Africa becomes a German colonial empire, it is a mere jump to Brazil and that nation shares a frontier with the Guianas, which Germany will claim if victorious. The Guianas border Venezuelan petroleum and are on the road to Panama.

Little do they think that the fifth columns of the Rome-Berlin-Tokyo Axis are not bad dreams but realities and that the protectors of totalitarianism in our countries are the criollo dictatorships—all potentially fascist—who, while gritting their teeth, cheer Roosevelt, but who in their hearts imitate Hitler even in the accomplishments of the Gestapo.

Little do they think, even in the face of the certain risk, that our hundred-year-old independence will be ended one day with the same disconcerting rapidity with which so many stronger countries lost theirs in a few weeks. The only answer is *strength through union.* But, we must warn against fusion or incorporation within the North American empire and the theme of Pan Americanism, but rather encourage the alliance of the forty-eight United States of the North with a federation of the twenty united states of the South.

It is imperative to think of all these things. To cooperate in the solidarity of the Americas, pointing out the danger where it exists without imitating the ostrich tactics of those Saxons and French who left things for *mañana.* To cooperate, not committing suicide in a new empire, but forming early a solid Indoamerican union, bloc, or federation, to agree in conditions of equilibrium and efficient coordination with the North American Federation, which must be our *ally*—not our master—in this effort for common liberty.

To form this Indoamerican bloc or federation, it is necessary to begin now to arouse the consciousness, or to reawaken it, and direct it—because it does exist deep down in our popular instinct—indicating the dangers within the continent which we have in the criollo dictatorships, in the fifth columns, in the anti-constitutional practices and lack of liberties, in tyrannical totalitarianism, and in the betrayal of democracy. This must be done either with the governments, if they march in tune with their peoples, or in spite of them, to channel and awaken them to the reality that may be the price of our destiny.

But it is necessary to make it clear that in order to defend a great and common continental sovereignty, it is necessary to correct that deformed conception of the sovereignty of each country which has made the Indoamerican rulers imagine that each one of the twenty states is an island. It is important to teach them that they make up a great continental whole, inseparable, and vigorously linked. It is an essential priority that they learn, in the new language which the war teaches, that to have a free country, it is necessary first to have a free continent. Liberty without strength is difficult to maintain—as the war also teaches—and strength without union is inconceivable.

Thus, it is necessary to undertake the most urgent task of

making Indoamerica strong in order to cooperate efficaciously in the defense of the Americas. In commencing to unite and defend ourselves, it would be well to think of these points:

An Indoamerican pact with the United States of the North, promising assurance of the maximum affirmation of democracy in both groups of states, abandoning and combatting all dictatorial or totalitarian practice and guaranteeing the essential liberties of man and the citizen, under a constitution that must be strictly fulfilled.

An Indoamerican pact with the United States not permitting in the territory of both groups any form of imperialism, establishing severe conditions for economic and political relations between the United States and Indoamerica, among which will be the Inter Americanization of the Panama Canal; that if we must defend it, all of us must possess it: like the Suez Canal.

An Indoamerican Pact with the United States constituting an Inter American Tribunal with authority for enforcing the previous clauses. Before this tribunal could come any citizen or group of citizens of North or Indoamerica.

An Indoamerican Pact with the United States, whereby the latter would recognize the unification of the states of Indoamerica in a federation that would establish an immediate alliance with North America and thus establish the common front of both Americas.

It is evident that the Pan American Union, the fusion of the twenty Indoamerican republics in a great federation with the United States of the North, is unpopular with us. However, this is not the case with a loyal alliance with the United States, nor is it true with a Bolivarian union of Indoamerica, which would be realized gradually and progressively. It is evident also that a defense of Indoamerica is not a matter of national knowledge or of interest to the majority in the United States, because the North American people hardly know us. They do not know us because we are twenty small states, dispersed and weak, contributing little to the world economy, culture, and politics.

But if the government of the United States aids us in uniting and our continent appears converted into a great nation of more than one hundred million inhabitants, immensely rich, and based on a united race with two sister languages, with a profoundly linked tradition and history, we would be a worthy ally of the great and good neighbor of the North.

We must stimulate a profound and vast change in the public opinion within Indoamerica and directed towards the United States: so that we understand the urgency of union and they understand the importance and convenience of aiding us in this great enterprise which is the only road, constructive and without jealousies, towards building a solid continental defense.

The dictators, the criollo politicians, enemies of the spirit of Bolívar, the jingoists of localism may be opposed. But before it is too late, and in order to aid the common defense, those of us who understand the language of history in our decisive times, must act. Aprismo has advocated all of this for the last fifteen years. But it is still not too late for us to be heard.

IV

OUR IGNORANCE OF INDOAMERICA

NOW THAT WE UNDERSTAND THE BOLIVIARIAN IMPERATIVE OF RE-
alizing the unity of the peoples of Indoamerica, a grave fact, which is
due to our governments, our politicians, our educators, and our journalists principally, becomes of singular importance: the little knowledge we Indoamericans have of one another.

It was only a few weeks ago that in a great daily of Buenos
Aires, a certain, well-known Central American writer lamented the
deplorable ignorance of his country, on the part of the uneducated
and more or less educated people of the Plata region. Upon reading his comments, I thought how my wanderings through the small
republics of Central America had shown me what little knowledge
people of certainly not very low social levels in those states had of
other sister peoples.

This is a universal evil, a result of our mental colonization by,
and fascination for, Europe and our disdain for everything which is
ours. It is much easier, for example, for a young Indoamerican to
know where Dieppe and Lake Balaton in Europe are, than where the
city of Quetzaltenango or Lake Chapala are in our continent; and
surely he will be better informed of the ruins of Egypt and Pompey
than of those of Chichen-Itza, Machu-Picchu, or Chan-Chan, and he
will not know how many cities with the name of Trujillo, of Córdoba, of Santiago, or of San Pedro there are in the vast Indoamerican nation in which we have been born and live.

In our schools and colleges the history of Indoamerica is seldom taught. An absurd petty nationalism stimulates disdain for other
peoples who, being neighbors and brothers, have much to teach and

July 1940, published in *La Defensa Continental,* pp. 23–25.

to offer to even the more advanced countries. Nor has there been so far, on a systematic and continuing basis, an effort at juvenile and popular exchanges through travel by students and workers in large groups and with a sense of learning and understanding. Even in our greatest newspapers, the information about the sister countries of this continent is always relegated to summary, isolated items that seldom relate anything important.

We have become accustomed to considering each of our countries as an island—and as a primitive and faraway island. Actually being islanders, the British have more continental understanding than any of our fellow-citizens. And a British politician—with what pain they are proving this now—knows that the frontiers of his country are much further than the surrounding sea.

In Indoamerica, however, except when we come to the garrulous literature of our post-banquet Americanist speeches, or to the occasional summary news printed or broadcast on the radio, the feeling of continental union is not strengthened nor encouraged. This happens for a simple and clear reason: lack of knowledge. Not our students, nor our intellectuals, nor our politicians seek to know the peoples who make up this great continent. The lifelong ideal of everyone is a voyage to Europe, to return to Europe. Anything else is without importance. In politics—that wide field for a vast labor of continental understanding—narrowness and arrogant nationalism have been maintained, stubborn and damaging. Both left and right have lived long years without knowing the other countries of the great continental group. Some have done so from ignorance and because they imitate Europe, to whose fluctuations and struggles they pay principal attention. Others have done so because of jealousy, repeating the jingoisms and hostilities of the old world which are so helpful to mediocre politicians here. However, our leaders, particularly those of the generation before ours, were renegades to Bolivarism. They were vassals of Monsieur Chauvin; obsequious imitators of everything that the European scene taught them.

The first step towards an effective continental solidarity must be made in the press, in the schools, in the parties. Each daily and magazine, large or small, should carry informative propaganda about the Indoamerican countries. There are many photographs, many brief and well informed articles on the countries of our continent. It is necessary to teach our youth, profoundly, the history of the twenty sister states which form our great nation. It is necessary to carry to the parties a profound and tenacious Indoamerican spirit. A national policy without a continental spirit will never be an Indoamerican policy nor truly patriotic. And we need urgently such a spirit for the defense and security of all, in this hour when divided continents such as ours must unite or perish.

V

LATIN AMERICAN UNITY AND
THE YANKEES

FOR YEARS, FOR MANY YEARS, WE APRISTAS HAVE RAISED AS OUR supreme ideal of all political activity in our Indoamerican continent, that of the unity of our peoples. In the process of propagating this ideal, I have been to almost all the countries of our great continental fatherland. Everywhere I found support among the young, and in all the lands through which I passed, I heard voices of comprehension.

When Aprismo had to act in Peru, it raised the Bolivarian banner with renewed faith. An entire people saluted the ideal of Indoamerican unity with the same enthusiasm with which its forebears had saluted the triumphal passage of the liberating armies of the continent upon their return from Ayachucho. We the Apristas have never deviated in our path. Not Russia, nor Spain, nor Berlin, nor Rome modified our clear and clean line of action, destined to the foresighted work of affirming more and more the solidarity of Indoamerica.

We believed that this glorious work of fulfilling the dream of Bolívar was sufficient for a generation. We had not time to waste in dispersing our energies and our eagerness for Russia, nor for Spain, nor for Germany, nor for Italy. For that reason, we many times appeared indifferent to the European fascination. We believed that it was necessary to free ourselves here of all mental servitude, either of the left or of the right. We believed that our social justice could be achieved without asking counsel of any European master, be he called Stalin or Hitler, Franco or Mussolini. We believed that it was necessary to seek the destiny of a rich and undefended continent,

October, 1940, published in *La Defensa Continental*, pp. 15–22.

little populated in relation to its vastness and dangerously divided by myopic politicians, apostates to the ideas of Bolívar and vassals of Europe.

Today the march of history places us in double jeopardy. On two sides our common sovereignty is being risked if we Indoamericans do not unite. If totalitarianism wins, because we are only one step from Africa, which will be dominated by the victor, we shall become expanded Belgiums or Hollands. Even if it is stopped, there is the grave risk that in the face of the danger, there may be a hurried surrender to the control of North America, whose good neighborliness may be changed when the politicians of imperialist tendency return to power. Between these two dangers there is only one solution that insures our security: *previous Indoamerican union.* This will make us stronger in the event of aggression and will make more secure the alliance with the United States if we join forces for common defense.

We must not forget that it is necessary to unite in Indoamerica against all imperialism, whether European, Asiatic, or Inter American, black or red, no matter how it is masked, even if it is this dangerous Francoite "Hispanoamericanism," which is undermining us so much in the name of colonial love for the past, waving the banner of a culture which we must renovate and *recreate* here.*

We must not forget that the first step for social justice is the progressive nationalization of our wealth and that the Aprista idea of Inter Americanizing the Panama Canal is not a utopia. (Certain leaders of the Partido Revolucionario Cubano thought it was, but now believe that the Inter Americanization of the Panama Canal is the most urgent and worthwhile part of the Aprista program.) With Panama Inter Americanized and having united all which we are being obliged to defend, we will have a "live" guarantee against any possible imperialism from the North. We shall have a "pawn," and finally, the unused and anachronic Pan Americanism of Mr. Rowe† and company will no longer be a bureaucratic colonization of Indoamerica, but a policy of equilibrated and egalitarian alliance—bilateral in rank and dignity—between the states of Indoamerica and the United States of the North.

---

* Haya is referring here to the campaign carried on in Latin America by the Franco regime during and just after the Spanish Civil War.

† Leo Rowe was the long-time Secretary-General of the Pan American Union.

I return again to say with that optimistic sadness which should be in us—we remember Keyserling on the sad theme—a constructive motive and of good faith; I return to say it as in years past: We work for the union of Indoamerica—thus, with this anti-colonial name, truly ours—we work for the realization of Bolivarian thought. It is the youngest and the most uncorrupted who are the depositories of this idea which demands enthusiasm and above all tenacity.

We thus free ourselves of European romanticisms, whether Russophile, Anglophile, Germanophile, Hispanophile, or Italophile. "Let the dead bury their dead," and let us think of ourselves. We shall not suffer more for the misfortunes abroad, because we have plenty ourselves; and foreswearing all unconditional Europeanism, as sons of the great Indoamerican fatherland, we shall undertake the stupendous task of uniting it and making it strong.

United States Senator Wiley has suggested, in a declaration made to United Press, the usefulness of the formation by states of Indoamerica of a great economic and political unity. Perhaps now that a prominent man of the Yankee state proclaims it, our criollo politicians will begin to think of the transcendency and urgency of an initiative which, if it' had been attempted twelve to fifteen years ago—when Aprismo suggested it bravely and tenaciously—would have given us greater security for these crucial unsettled hours when our common destiny is being determined.

In the United States they have come finally to a level of comprehension which we Apristas have always held with respect to relations between both Americas. They now understand that it is not Pan Americanism—imperialist and absorbing, even though seen through the silk of the most appeasing rhetoric—that will resolve the problems of living together of the two great economic, political, and ethnic groups of this hemisphere. It will be Inter Americanism, which is something else, because it presupposes what Senator Wiley has just formulated, the coexistence of the "countryside and raw material" America and the "industry and capital" America, each structured in separate state groups, capable of equilibrating relations in an effective and durable good neighborliness. . . .

When twelve or fifteen years ago we began this unionist and admonitory campaign, we were called romantics, and many of the old epithets, which had been used disdainfully in the last century by our myopic politicians against the prophetic call of Simón Bolívar, were dragged up from the dust. Parties of the left and parties of the right—obsequious imitators of whatever their European tutors sent them to think and do—considered it absurd and unrealistic to accept as a first ideological postulate of any Indoamerican political action, the procuring of the union of our twenty states. Some lost themselves in the vacuous internationalism dictated by Moscow or Amsterdam,* and others circumscribed themselves in a noxious chauvinism, a sure way to catastrophe as Europe is today showing us, and they forgot that the dialectical process of the world, which passed from feudal dispersion to the formation of great nations, advances in its present stage to the establishment of powerful continental units.

In this process, those continents without the capacity to govern or defend themselves will be vassals of the more powerful. If the Indoamerican peoples do not make themselves stronger by unity, they will be like Africa and like Oceania, colonies either of the totalitarian imperialisms or of the non-totalitarian imperialisms which more or less benignly will have to continue being our tutors or bosses until we have reached the historic consciousness of our own emancipation.

There exists today, when the world is settling accounts, a new possibility which appears extremely interesting in the declarations of Senator Wiley: That North American public opinion understands what a heavy burden it is for the United States to have to look after twenty somewhat arrogant states that proclaim themselves "free and independent" with great pomp and circumstance, and that nonetheless remain so only because the cannons of the great imperialisms have not yet received orders to direct their sights towards these coasts. The United States must understand that it would be much easier to work out common defense, in an equilibrated alliance, with a power of 130 million inhabitants, formed by the twenty united states of Indoamerica, than to continue this heavy and costly game of being the guardians of dispersed and disarmed states.

On the other hand, the totalitarian powers, which have just divided the world in the secret provisions of the Tripartite Pact, do everything possible to prevent the formation of the Indoamerican Union, which would be an impossible barrier for the aggression against our peoples planned by Berlin, Rome, and Tokyo with the crafty and cunning prostitution of that decadent and bleeding Spain

---

* Amsterdam was, between the two World Wars, the seat of the Socialist-controlled International Federation of Trade Unions. Haya uses the word here to refer to the Second International Socialists.

which seeks the reconquest of its "Empire." That opposition of International Fascism to every proposal of Indoamerican union has helped to make the leaders of Washington understand that nothing would be more dangerous to the totalitarian imperialist plans than the formation of a great political power in Indoamerica.

Now, upon hearing for the first time in the United States, authoritative voices—and an even greater victory because they come from the Republican Party—proposing the formation of a powerful Indoamerican unity, it is to be supposed that the statesmen and political leaders of this side of the Rio Bravo are going to consider the idea a good one. It is of great importance that an initiative come from there. When it is launched among us, it is of little value.

The words of Senator Wiley, and the warm commentary which the North American dailies have made on it, are not new in our latitudes. For fifteen years they have been proposed in something more than the vague terms of the after-dinner speakers' praise of continental solidarity. As the action-oriented program of a movement in the support of which thousands have undergone persecution and death, Apra has raised Indoamerican unity as its standard. But now it is no longer merely Peruvian opinion backing this ideal, but the potent voice of a sector of Yankee opinion. And this will generate much thought.

It doesn't matter, it is clear, whether the unity of Indoamerica is a Peruvian or a United States triumph. What is important is that it be realized for the welfare and security of all. We the Apristas with great pleasure give the honors of the initiative to whoever wants to enjoy them, including Senator Wiley. What interests us is that for the common defense, we follow the only sure road. If this happens, the jealousies and emulations, the chauvinisms and national arrogances are superfluous.

We must think of the fact that our countries have lived their beautiful and gratifying illusion of independence for a century—being the only peoples of a disarmed continent that have not followed the way of Africa, Oceania, and the greater part of Asia—and that this situation cannot endure in a world which is going to decide its new directions on the battlefield. Even if the totalitarianisms are defeated, it will be necessary for us to be strong, so that they do not revive, and even stronger so that the victors of this side do not abuse their victory.

If Senator Wiley's words are the announcement that North

American public opinion is going to initiate the only action possibly effective for the defense of the Americas, stimulating the union of our twenty divided countries, the United States of Indoamerica appears now as a possibility. It is up to the criollo politicians to rectify their ways and cooperate together for the realization of this great ideal. It will be up to our responsible parties, which heretofore have followed the European dictators of the left and the right, to change their mistaken directions and to recognize as the first point in their political programs the postulate of the joint action of the Indoamerican peoples for the political and economic unity of the states of Indoamerica.

VI

LATIN AMERICA NEEDS
A COMMON MARKET

THE LATIN OR INDO AMERICAN COMMON MARKET IS THE NECESSARY step towards the economic union of the great continent, which to the south of the United States extends over a territory of more than 20 million square kilometres and has a population of more than 185 million, who, according to the estimates of the Demographic Institute of Washington, will exceed 500 million within forty-two years, whereas the United States and Canada will only reach 300 million.

The Aprista program, which since 1924 has advocated an economic union—as a prologue to the political—of the Latin or Indo American continent, is reinforced now that the Common Market of Western Europe and the recent accords of eleven European states on a free trade zone among them, establish European unity as the next goal of a real united states of the West.

On the other hand, the Russian plan of forming with the satellite states another common market, and those of the Asiatic economic union, and that of the economic-political union of the Arab states, sketches a world of great regional groupings, foreseen in the Aprista plan as a world newly aligned into continental peoples or states. The United States and the Soviet Union are already of this type, as are the British Commonwealth China, and India which with their vast areas and immense populations advance rapidly towards the same characteristics.

The organizers of the European Common Market have expressed, over and over again, their proposal to negotiate jointly with Latin America. It is true that the European Common Market includes

---

"Hacia la Unidad Económica," August, 1958, published in *Pensamiento Político de Haya de la Torre,* Volume I.

Africa, colonies of the Caribbean, and Polynesia in its plan for transforming them into "associated territories" and fostering their economic development for the purpose of overcoming their situation as
"underdeveloped" zones. However, if one takes into account the
prodigious economic size which the united European states of the
Common Market represents, they will have sufficient capacity to extend the radius of their program of economic aid and trade beyond
the areas of those associated territories. The leaders of the plan
for European economic unity have categorically indicated this. The
recent speech of the president of the Economic Commission for
Europe, Professor Walter Hallstein, given in the Hotel Atlantic of
Hamburg, last July 28, fully confirms a policy oriented toward establishing a system of West European-Latin or Indo American economic
relations.

However, this new system of relations of Europe, economically
coordinated with our continent, imposes logically the previous economic coordination of the latter. The efficiency of the new system of
relations of economies, organized in groups of states, makes necessary
a change in the concept and structure of forms of production and
exchange from limited national fields to regional ones. Once the
unrealizable aspiration of "isolated self-sufficient states"—which produce all they consume—is abandoned, all the countries of the world
become oriented towards the integration of homogeneous groups of
countries in wider zones of interdependent economies that establish
on a broader basis the relations with other regional groups of associated countries. Only within this new economic arrangement of inte-
grated zones in common markets can there be agreement without
risks of disequilibrium. But it is obvious that the new and large economic conglomerations cannot maintain relations with the small and
weak economies of isolated countries—especially the underdeveloped
ones—without weighing heavily on these smaller nations. Therefore,
Latin or Indo America, in a world organized in great economic
combinations or common markets, must organize itself regionally
also in order to accomplish its own industrial development.

The meeting of the Economic Commission for Latin America,*
in Santiago de Chile this year, has established the basis for a Latin
or Indo American Common Market. In spite of that, the realization

---

* The Economic Commission for Latin America (ECLA), an organ of the
United Nations, has since 1948 taken the lead in stimulating Latin American
economic development and, particularly, in drawing up plans for the economic
unity of the area.

of this program demands the most decided cooperation of each of our states. This must be not only on the part of each government, and of the technical bodies specialized in the study of our national economies and of their regional or continental interdependence, but also of the industrial organizations, of the workers' trade union organizations, and of the political parties.

The Latin or Indo American common market requires, it must be noted, agreement on a vast and complex technical program that must be seriously undertaken by means of organized efforts of research and planning. However, at the same time—as has occurred in Europe and is obvious in the Asian and Arabian countries—it requires an extensive public relations campaign. We live generally dominated by simplistic economic notions and prejudices, which are often anachronistic. A little behind the advances of the world, they remain easily at hand, apparently logical commonplaces about self-sufficiency and autarchy, which in modern economics are no longer accepted. To re-educate our backward economic consciousness, it is necessary to have a common effort to explore the world reality and our own. We must ascertain the basic possibilities of coordination and make a new estimate of our inherent capacity for development beyond our limited horizons and hopefully on a continental dimension. On the other hand, we, the governed and the governors in our countries, must not forget that this is the indelible "economic mark of our time." Yes, it is incontrovertible and inescapable.

There is no doubt about the viability of the profound change of economic concept and practice in Indoamerica, such as has been produced in Europe and is gaining ground in other continents. The project of a Latin or Indo American common market excites the interest and the sympathy of various sectors of the economy in each country of our continent, not only that of the working and middle classes, who aspire to greater progress through growing industrialization, but also that of the progressive sectors of the national industrialists themselves, who confront the problems of limited markets, of customs difficulties, or of the unfair competition of large and coordinated extracontinental commerce. On a small scale, and less obviously than in Europe—a zone of high industrial civilization—we are experiencing a healthy change of economic criteria, determined in large part by the insoluble problems which our national isolation and our limited markets produce, but also by the incontestable fact that the rest of the economic world is organized regionally and we remain a conglomeration of isolated countries which leaves us in an insular position affecting all of us. The project of a Latin or Indo American common market, therefore, will have to become a major public aspiration, influencing the opinion of all social sectors aspiring to the economic emancipation of our peoples, because only through economic coordination and unity can they cease being vassals of the more powerful economic groups that imperially dominate the countries which are weak and backward because of their separateness.

It is necessary to have a series of Latin or Indo American conferences for the purpose of studying urgent problems. The study of dislocated or competing production, the coordinated expansion of markets, the compensated exchange of products, the intercontinental organization of transportation, the revision of customs barriers, the creation of a Latin or Indo American Bank of Reserve and Finance, and the study of a continental currency which would end the unequal struggle of seventeen or eighteen different monetary systems with the dollar and the pound, would be among the tasks confronting these conferences. The planning of coordinated industrial exchange—the community of iron and coal of the formerly rival European countries, now the basis of the European Common Market, is a patent example for various branches of our industry—would be another of their objectives.

The Latin or Indo American economic conferences which might be preceded and complemented by meetings between neighboring states, constitute an unpostponable necessity. On the other hand, those meetings of our states would have for their objective the presentation of a program of possible relations with the great economic units of other continents, and to start with the United States, with which we must establish a system of relations without hegemony, based on a true "democratic Inter Americanism without empire," starting from the delineation of our respective economic orbits— of a super-developed zone together with another that is underdeveloped—would maintain and reassure our autonomy and permit a coordination of frameworks, exempt of subordinations, so that Indoamerica can develop freely and in unrestricted dealings with the rest of the world. This program, which does not involve implicit hostilities towards anyone, contains a proposal for progress, an objective of liberation, and the best form of incorporating our peoples as a body and in an organized fashion into the economic world of today. Thus democracy, which we prefer to live under while strengthening it constantly, will fulfill its socio-economic purpose of insuring the welfare, prosperity, and security of each of our peoples.

VII

THE UNITED STATES FACES THE LATIN AMERICAN COMMON MARKET

THE VISIT OF PRESIDENT EISENHOWER TO FOUR LATIN AMERICAN capitals coincided with the second meeting of the representatives of Argentina, Brazil, Chile, Paraguay, Peru, and Uruguay—to which Mexico has also adhered—to establish the bases of the economic union of our America on the basis of a free trade zone, or common market. The European press, which rarely takes us seriously as individual countries, has commented unanimously, on the great importance of those two events, and above all, on the declarations of the North American leader, in Santiago de Chile, favorable to the growing Latin American movement towards the coordination of our continent.

When the European press calls the unionist tendency of the peoples of Latin America "a state of consciousness," it infers that that great continental nation, until now impotent because divided, might in unity signify a power of unforeseeable influence in world politics. Because, if as isolated states we have lacked and presently lack importance in the universal political scene, which is dominated by great regional groups, it is evident that united in a vast continental zone of production and exchange, the Latin American community represents a geographic area of 20 million square kilometres with about 200 million inhabitants, whose actual and potential riches are equal to those of other parts of the planet.

The zealous commentators on the speech of President Eisenhower in Santiago de Chile have recognized, in their measured words

"Estados Unidos Frente el Mercade Commún Latinoamericano," April, 1959, published in *Pensamiento Político de Haya de la Torre,* Volume I.

of approval for the projects of the Latin American common market, an opportune effort not to upset an environment frankly favorable to the unity of its twenty republics. There are not lacking those reticent individuals who, more right than wrong, note the jealousies of certain North American sectors over the rise of a great economically cohesive continental nation south of the great northern federation. Without any circumlocutions, they point out that, perhaps with a criterion limited by narrow interests, the imperialist sectors of the United States have been and are adversaries, hidden or open, of any proposal for the union of Latin America.

Their allies have been and are still, those among the Latin Americans who have dreamed of an autarchy in "each republic," isolated and all-powerful. Its supporters are the people themselves, whose instinct has brought them to discover a historical reality which is now undeniable: that in a world in which not only "space is power"—as the United States itself demonstrates—but in which interdependence is the norm and nationalist isolationism and limitations are the sure way to inferiority and subjugation.

A revealing similarity in the points of view of the great empires has been, until now, the jealousy which Russia as well as the United States has had towards the movement towards the organization of common markets. Those of Europe—that of the "six" which will be eight with the adhesion of Greece and Turkey, and that of the "seven" of the EFTA*—have been coordinated only in spite of and against the unconcealable resistance of North America and Russia. The Communist parties and the conservative spokesmen have gone out of their way to discredit the new economic unities established in Europe and proposed in Asia, Africa, and Latin America. It has, therefore, been a truly remarkable victory that President Eisenhower, obliged by the circumstances, has made remarks favorable to the plan for a Latin American common market. In spite of his reservations, the words of the chief of the government of the United States carry with them a full recognition of the importance that economic coherence has for our peoples.

It can be said, thus, that opposition to common markets is a characteristic imperialist posture. Therefore, it is a reactionary attitude inspired by the well-known principle of the strong dividing the weak in order to rule. It is, in consequence, an authentic anti-

---

* European Free Trade Association.

imperialist objective to support the formation of great defensive economic groups, based on the equally well-known slogan that in unity there is power. For Latin America, the badly understood, isolating nationalisms of "each republic" have proven to be disastrous failures after more than a century. The return to the great original watchwords of our independence, expressed by its leaders, is today an inescapable imperative for common security. Only if united can the Latin American states regulate and control efficaciously the foreign investments that are still needed to push forward our industrialization and to obtain, truly, our second independence. Only united can we guarantee and assure our autonomy in the face of the strongest interventionist risks. Only united, too, can we increase our economic power, fully exploit our natural resources, and realize our aspirations for a just and stable social democracy, such as is stressed by the postulate "freedom with bread."

The common markets of the super-developed states require the counterpart in the common markets of the under-developed countries. A new world economic equilibrium will not be possible until the association of the large is matched with the association of the small. Only thus will the latter cease living in the subordinate position of offering themselves to the highest bidder. For if it is an apparent gesture of freedom to defy one purchaser by giving oneself to another, the change of masters is not emancipation. So long as we confront our weakness with their strength, such a system of relations will be unjust and dangerous.

Fortunately there is appearing in our peoples what the European press calls a Latin American "state of consciousness." Its elemental and simple definition is the revolutionary awakening in "each republic" to the reality of our interdependence and to the evidence of our unbreakable association as integral parts of an indivisible whole, the dynamic coherence of which can convert twenty entities, which separately signify little, into a creative power of untold magnitude for the future of humanity.

VIII

PERU AND THE LATIN AMERICAN
COMMON MARKET

THIS MONTH THERE WILL MEET IN CARACAS—THE BIRTHPLACE OF
the Liberator Bolívar, who dreamed of the unity of his America—the
directors of Foreign Commerce of the three republics of Gran Colombia, to study the creation of an area of free trade among them.
On their side, Brazil, Argentina, Chile, and Uruguay are studying
resolutely an accord of the same kind. These are the initial steps on
the promising path towards the Latin American common market
which is a forerunner of the economic unity of our continent.

Peru must not remain apart from the planning of continental
economic coordination, but rather must join in, since it did not assume in time the initiative for which so many factors qualified it.
From Lima was issued the initiative for the Congress of Panama
of 1826, when Bolívar was governing from Peru, and the most
advanced suggestions for the economic and political unity of our
America in this century come from a socio-political movement which
is in its origin, thought, and action, the work of Peruvians.

When, in 1924, the Apra was founded with the demand for
the economic and political unity of the twenty states of our continent as one of the five basic points of its Americanist program, there
abounded skeptical objectors, who with excessive criollo simplicity,
would offer a verdict which then appeared incontestable: "That utopia of continental unity neither you nor your grandsons will see."

In our book of 1927 *Por la Emancipación de América Latina,*

"El Perú y el Mercado Commún Latino-americano," April, 1959, published in
Pensamiento Político de Haya de la Torre, Volume I.

and in *El Antimperialismo y el Apra* of 1928, we answered these pessimistic replies with an alternative of faith and logic which had the repercussions of an invocation among the young intellectuals and workers, and thus arose Aprismo. However, when inspired by its five great slogans of continental vision there was founded in 1931 the Aprista party, or the Peruvian Peoples party, reaction, deep and backward, took occasion to condemn the new socio-political movement as "foreign" and "internationalist." On such pretexts, all members of the party were deprived of their citizenship rights for almost two decades. Thus, the only party in Latin America inscribing as the first point of its program the economic and political unity of the continent, heroically suffered much persecution. However, in spite of this, it remained united and unswerving in the sure hope of victory for its farsightedness. Today, not our grandsons, but those who initiated this idea, are seeing its fulfillment.

Thirty years have passed. We have seen the rise and defeat of Nazi-fascism, which also had fifth-column agents in Peru. After that terrible war, we watched Europe initiate its unification and form its first community, with more than 200 million inhabitants. With this passage of time and chain of events, it becomes apparent that Aprismo had been thirty years ahead of its time in pointing out the unitary destiny of our peoples. Rodó was correct, as I repeated, in speaking of this same theme of continental unity, in the University of Montevideo in 1954: "The heresy of yesterday is the creed of today."

By greater coincidence, the initial movements towards these ends have risen in two sectors, that of Gran Colombia and that of Argentina, Brazil, Chile, and Uruguay, which was the prediction in the aforementioned book, *Por la Emancipación de América Latina,* from the speech we gave in Paris before the Cell of Exiled Apristas in January 1927. The central text of this speech was incorporated in February of the same year in the resolution on Latin America of the World Anti-imperialist Congress of Brussels.

Heavy with history, nourished with farsighted predictions, the Aprista program of continental unity appears now incontrovertible and peremptory. When Europe unites, when the Arab peoples unite, and when those who are thought of as the backward African peoples proclaim their desire to federate, Latin or Indo America cannot but incorporate itself in the world which is defined in terms of regions, which is organized in "continent states" or peoples, a world which has before it two unrivalled powers directing the economic-political universe, that are continental unions of territories and of peoples, whose power is due fundamentally to their dynamic vastness and compact coherence: the United States and the Soviet Union.

All of Peru must not forget that the salvation of its almost endemic economic crisis, of its predominant poverty and social backwardness, is in large part to be found in the expansion of its markets, in the independence of its economy, in the coordination of its production and exchange with the other states of Indoamerica. In the same way, each of these countries is in a reciprocal situation. It is because of that that seven of the most important and advanced of our republics are taking the first steps towards the regional market.

Corollary of the strengthening of its democratic systems, through the elimination of the barbaric backwardness of our states under the ominous brutality of dictatorships, must be Latin American economic unity, systematized in a common market and with a single currency. Only thus, can we achieve our economic emancipation and insure our security and social welfare.

PART SIX

Imperialism

IMPERIALISM HAS ALWAYS BEEN A PREOCCUPATION OF VÍCTOR RAÚL
Haya de la Torre and anti-imperialism an essential part of his doctrine. It runs through virtually all of his writings, regardless of their
formal subject matter. He has consistently defined imperialism as
being basically economic in nature. The political, social, and cultural
domination of one country by another flows from economic influence. The first selection here provides a good example of the kind of
foreign economic penetration to which he is opposed, and which was
so common when Haya began his political activities right after World
War I.

Haya accepts Lenin's reasons for economic imperialism—as the
reader will already have noted. These are the need for markets
abroad, the need for cheap labor, and the need for new fields for
profitable capital investment. Haya has laid particular emphasis on
the last of these; however, he has consistently argued that Lenin's
definition of imperialism as inevitably being the "highest stage" of
capitalism is not the situation in Latin America and other underdeveloped areas, where it is rather the beginning stage of capitalism,
the stage first bringing in capitalism and modern industrialism. Nor
does Haya accept the Marxist-Leninist corollary to Lenin's definition
of imperialism that the underdeveloped areas should not accept foreign capital, for fear of the political and other implications which the
admission of such investments may involve. He has argued that Latin
America needs foreign capital, but that it should set the conditions
under which such capital would be permitted entry. The second
selection deals briefly with these questions, which also appeared in
earlier sections.

The third, fourth, and fifth selections deal with Haya's attitude

towards the question of imperialism during World War II. That strug-
gle made him an ally of the Yankee imperialism which he had been
fighting for two decades. However, it is clear in these passages that
Haya insisted that Latin America should not succumb to United
States imperialism while joining with the United States to fight the
Axis brand. He insisted that Latin America take an active part on the
Allied side in World War II so that it would have a place at the peace
table, and there be able to defend its interests effectively.

He also insisted that the Latin American countries should not
submit unilaterally and unconditionally to all of the desires of the
United States, as is made clear in selection four. Finally, as selection
five illustrates, Haya had an inkling that as a result of arrangements
between the United States and Latin America beginning to emerge
during World War II, it might be possible in the post-war period to
work out forms of United States help to Latin American development other than those represented by the unrestricted private foreign investment in the Latin American countries so indicative of
unrestrained imperialism.

I

IMPERIALISM IN CENTRAL AMERICA

THE FOUR OFFENSIVES OF IMPERIALISM ARE ACTIVE IN CENTRAL America: the economic, the political, the military, and the cultural. As in the Antilles and as in Panama, imperialism in Central America is obvious and four-sided. Economically, the imperialist offensive is carried out by the great companies. Of them, the brilliant North American writer Carleton Beals has said, in his lectures at the University of Mexico, that they would not be tolerated by the North American people "for five minutes" if they carried out their exploitation there as they do in Central America. The American companies in the Central American isthmus represent the most violent, most unconditional, and piratical form of monopoly. They have succeeded in making themselves all powerful, and their force is today so great that they determine changes in the national and international political life of those countries, intervene in elections, designate diplomats, dominate a part of the press, and even could involve the peoples in war, inciting among them a misleading, petty, local patriotism, which only favors imperialism. Recently this was obvious in the dispute between Honduras and Guatemala, which was actually a conflict between the United Fruit Company and the Cuyamel Fruit Company, two of the gigantic sentinels of Yankee imperialism in Central America.

Each one of these four offensives has its special tactic and corresponds ably to each of the countries where it functions. Whereas in Costa Rica imperialism is cautious and astute; in Nicaragua it is brutal and pitiless. In Guatemala, as in Honduras, and in El Salvador, the North American legations are the government of proconsuls.

Berlin: April 1929, published in *¿A Donde Va Indoamérica?* pp. 45–52.

They issue orders. To exert pressure, they threaten fomenting a revolution if their desires are not met. Imperialism has at its call caudillos ready to seize power. The caudillos, the heads of parties are in most cases in Central America, except in Costa Rica, unconscious puppets under the total control of the great master who, from the North American Legation in each country, pulls the strings. For this purpose, it has in its hands the economy of each republic and some groups of opposition politicians in reserve. The political corruption of the great majority of the leaders of those countries is despicable. Ambition, ignorance, and fear turn them into the professional class of the satrapy; humble before the foreign power which demands everything, despotic and terrible with their inferiors and those they govern. They can do nothing worthwhile.

Subjugated by those politicians—devotees of success by whatever means—are the national masses, sometimes desperate and skeptical, sometimes rebellious and optimistic. Deep within each conscientious Central American, who is free of spirit, there perhaps exists an internal conflict, between the feeling of defeat that declares everything lost and the secret whispers of hope that everything is to be won. However, in those noble, generous, and virile peoples, they stand forth like islands of faith. There are many who respond sadly that all is corruption and chains, that it is better to adapt to the circumstances and live. But there are also many who refuse to submit, who in each rebellion offer total sacrifice as if impelled by some holy and deep desperation. To each spark of liberty they respond warmly, to each brave action they answer with joy, as if they were rejecting completely the heavy atmosphere of pessimism and the inferiority complex with which the progressive loss of national liberty is invading all, generating in certain areas what we can call a colonial consciousness.

"The four offensives" of imperialism adopt in Central America, then, characteristic forms which are worthy of a kind of detailed study which journalistic articles, necessarily short, can only outline. In accordance with the differences of each of the Central American republics, the imperialist offensive tactics change, adapting themselves marvelously to the reality. This tactical realism is perhaps the most extraordinary feature of their complicated maneuvers.

The economic offensive is, then, principally in the hands of the great companies exploiting the natural riches of Central America, especially those dealing with the two most important products of that whole zone: fruit (bananas) and, on a lesser scale, coffee. The control of bananas is disputed principally by two great companies: United and Cuyamel. The first is far more powerful than the second and has under its control the economy of Guatemala and of Costa Rica, and has strong indirect influence also in El Salvador. Cuyamel has its headquarters principally in Honduras.* There exist other companies exploiting other products of less importance.

It is not only the *production* of wealth which is in the hands of imperialism, so is its *distribution*. The great companies own, directly or indirectly, the railroads in Central America. Costa Rica, which owns its own coffee and which makes serious and increasingly effective efforts to free itself from imperialist slavery, has under government control one line: that which links the capital with Punta Arenas, its port on the Pacific. But in Central America the means of transportation belong to the foreign companies. They dominate the distribution lines, thus controlling national and foreign production, assuring themselves a monopoly. Steamship companies belonging to the fruit companies complete this total domination of vital Central American wealth. The economic empire controls lands and seas and—as we shall see further—their profits are fabulous. The economic exploitation of Central America by imperialism is one of the most monstrous cases of "legal" piracy by the imperialist offensive.

I think that I have said this before. The viceroys of the old colonial imperialism were sent from the metropolis. The viceroys of this imperialism "without pain," according to Mr. Carter, and "without territorial ambitions," according to the Puritan reiterations of Mr. Coolidge, are bought within these territories. The state is, then, the instrument of the national oppression of modern imperialism, especially in Latin America. For that reason, the flags, the constitutions, the national anthems, all the superficialities of the fatherland and of patriotism are left floating on the surface. They are the cork-like symbols which float over the flood. But, imperialism captures the economic roots, securing the people with its claws, although leaving their arms free—they must be free so that they can work well and so that they can bring the hand to the heart in a salute of emotional patriotism—giving the impression that the whole organism is capable of free movement.

---

* Shortly after Haya wrote this, the Cuyamel Fruit Company was bought out by United Fruit.

Imperialism pays attention to form, to contracts, to treaties, to written documents, signed and sealed. They say that Pancho Villa never raped a woman without formally wedding her. He married as many times as he raped, but the next day he had the matrimonial register destroyed. It is the same with imperialism. There is no violation or assault lacking its document, a well-written contractual instrument. It doesn't matter who signs it or how it is made. The case of Bunau Varilla* signing the contract for the cession of the Panama Canal Zone is characteristic. What is important is that everything be "legalized" in this way. Thus it has always been. In the case of Central America, there are numerous weddings. The most recent in Guatemala is without doubt typical.

On April 30, 1923, Señor Adalberto Aguilar Fuentes, Secretary of State for Development, "with authorization and instructions of the President of the Republic (General Don Lázaro Chacón, old and loyal servant of Estrada Cabrera and no less than the legal successor of General Orellana, ex-aide of the famous dictator) signed a contract with Mr. Norman Eric Anderson, "as representative of the Compañía Agrícola de Guatemala" (the United Fruit Company), a contract which is a *model* of the imperialist juridical instrument.

By virtue of that contract, which I have before me, and "considering that the Government desires to stimulate the agricultural, industrial, and commercial development of the Pacific Coast of the Republic," the Government authorizes the Company—that is, the United Fruit Company—"to make explorations and carry into effect the technical labors that it deems necessary on the maritime and land coast of the Pacific Ocean of the Republic of Guatemala, between the port of Champerico and the River of Slaves for the purpose of determining the most appropriate site to construct a port."

Article 1 of this model contract specifies that, among other things, "Within the zone three miles on each side of the port which the company constructs, there will not be permitted the construction or establishment of another dock, or embarkations or disembarka-

---

* Bunau Varilla was an official of the bankrupt French company which had unsuccessfully tried to build a canal across Panama. With the rebellion of Panama against Colombia and the almost simultaneous recognition of the new republic by the United States, Bunau Varilla turned up in Washington as the first Panamanian minister and soon afterwards signed the famous Canal Treaty, a source of controversy between the United States and Panama virtually since the day in 1903 when it was signed.

tions of any kind." Article 2 adds that "the Company will have the right to carry out the agricultural and industrial development of the properties which it now possesses . . . to export and import, whether from other parts of the country or from abroad, through the port and docks which it constructs." It specifies, furthermore, that "all cargoes which enter the aforementioned port will not need to enter or touch any other port or customs house of the Republic."

Article 5 ends with the interesting provision: "The Company will be permitted to import, warehouse, and re-export for the use of its own ships or those used by it or consigned to it, all kinds of fuel, without paying import, export, or any other kind of duties or taxes, whether these are national, departmental, or municipal, whether these are now in effect or may in the future be established."

According to Article 6, "the government exempts all ships belonging to the Company, and those which under any arrangements it has at its service, as well as the fuel, provisions of the ships, and the cargo which they may receive or discharge, of all taxes or port payments, on tonnage, lighthouse service, or pilotage and of all port taxes which exist or which in the future will be established, whether by the Government, municipalities, or any other natural or juridical person or any territorial division or entity."

In Article 11 it is agreed that the Company will establish a hospital—indispensable in those regions because the terrible working conditions, climate, and malaria, as well as alcohol and other diseases, devour the lives of workers, and imperialism requires that they not all die. In Article 12 the Company "is obliged to pay the Government one centavo for each stem of bananas which it exports." The stems of nine or more hands sell in the United States for three dollars and sixty cents and the Companies do not spend even 25 cents in transportation costs. Thus, its *civilizing* mission pays imperialism.

Article 14 is of great interest. And I quote: "The Company will have the unique and exclusive right to regulate, organize, and administer the port, railroad, and agricultural enterprises and other works and private enterprises that are established in virtue of the present contract. The Company will have the freedom of contracting with its employees and workers *in the form and under the conditions which will be agreed to and established between them.* Taking into account the nature of the business of the Company, it will have this right continually during the life of this contract, to work all of the enterprises authorized by this document on Sundays and holidays, so that they will not interrupt their labors."

For three miles around the Government concedes the "free use of government lands," with the right to "cross national rivers with their roads and aquaducts without other permission: according to Article 15, and in accordance with Article 16 the Company has gratis all the construction materials that it needs from lands and waters.

Article 17 is the agreement of the Government "to expropriate private lands which it [the Company] thinks indispensable for its authorized labors." The Company will pay taxes on real estate, but not on lands used for railroads or trolleycars, nor will it pay other taxes or imposts on its properties, as specified in Article 18.

Article 19 says that "in compensation for the extensive capital which the Company invests, exports will be carried out only with previous consent and arrangement with the Company," and it will have the right "to cover docking fees, port fees, and all other charges established or which will be established in the future."

The contract is for fifty years and the Company will enjoy all of the privileges and tax exemptions with regard to the cultivation of bananas, say the final articles.

II

IMPERIALISM:
THE FIRST STAGE OF CAPITALISM

. . . APRISMO—SUMMARIZING ITS THEORETICAL PRINCIPLES—CON-
siders that imperialism, "last stage of capitalism" in the industrial
peoples, represents in ours the first stage. Our capitalism is born with
the advent of modern imperialism. It is born, then, dependent and
as a result of the culmination of the capitalism of Europe—England
especially. Because of the natural conditions of the United States, the
development of capitalism in that country was accomplished rapidly,
until it reached the imperialist stage. Latin America as a result is a
field of struggle between European and North American imperialism, and our economic dependence becomes increasingly grave with
the victory of the powerful neighbor over the European competitor.
The methods of North American capitalism exhibit more fully the
phenomenon of capitalist concentration. Our incipient capitalism is
absorbed by the great imperialist capitalism. The economic life of
Latin America thus remains increasingly more subordinate to North
American imperialism, to European—particularly the English—when
that has been successful.

Imperialism has in our countries zones for the investment of
capital and the exploitation of raw materials and markets for the
sale of industrial products. The investment of capital in the exploitation of our raw materials gives the imperialists control of our production, and investments in governmental loans complete its economic
domination on the level of finances and permit the total or partial

Excerpt from "Independencia Economica de America Latina," undated [1930],
published in *A Donde Va Indoamérica?* pp. 255–257.

subordination of the state. The markets for industrial products are thus increasingly monopolized. . . .

Socialism cannot be imposed until industrialism has fulfilled its great historic stage, and for the industrialization of our peoples, it will be necessary, so long as capitalism exists, to have capital. Thus the state—tending towards the socialist nationalization of production —will have to establish the conditions under which it may come. As capital in its turn expands by the workings of an economic law, capital will always be invested, whatever the conditions. Hence, the anti-imperialist state will receive from imperialism all the manufactured products it needs and will sell all of the raw materials that large-scale industry always needs in increasing amounts.

This economic law forcing large-scale capitalism to accept whatever conditions are imposed, in return for the chance of investment, was never recognized by the classes today representing the Latin American state, classes of a feudal type, interested in whole or in part in using imperialist expansion for the time being. Only a type of state representing the classes oppressed by imperialism and oriented towards the nationalization of production can control imperialist capitalism and properly channel its imperative of expansion.

III

INDOAMERICA IN THE "IMPERIALIST" WAR

THE ERROR OF THOSE WHO ARE ONLY ABLE TO SEE IN THE GREAT conflict between the Democracies and the Axis a formidable imperial dispute between two gigantic blocs of nations, and who are not aware of the other internal conflict within those blocs, is a grave one in the integral appreciation of this struggle. If one looks at the question from the social and economic plane, he discovers in the present war all of the other "internal wars" within each of the two alliances. These are aggravated by the prolongation of the struggle and make increasingly obvious the revolutionary content of the phenomenon itself.

Since this is not a mere imperialist war, but rather a revolutionary war—in that the national interests in the struggle are increasingly subordinated to the other struggle of economic, social, and ideological interests—we, the peoples subject to the risks of imperialism, also have a place in this war. And our place is not—as some opportunist criollo governments and their spokesmen maintain—that of an obliging and obsequious attitude of a chorus on the side of the United States and in the service of its interests. Our place in this war, which is as national for us as it is economic and social for all, is a post for the defense of our interests. By defending them, we help to defend, through a solidarity in the democratic cause, those of the others that are in common with ours. Between them and us there exist both bonds of community and contradictions of separation. . . .

Thus it is explained why it is imperative that there be a greater and more active participation of the Indoamerican peoples in this

---

Excerpt from "Intervengamos Mas en la Guerra Para Tener Derecho A exigir Mas en la Paz," Incahausi: 1943, published in *Y Despues de la Guerra Que?* pp. 24–25.

war. Not to create another supplicating chorus in the great tragedy, but to live it and struggle in it, so as to have the right to think like defenders of a cause that for us is democracy and is anti-imperialism. Only thus can we be seated at the tables where the Treaties of Peace are signed. . . .

IV

COOPERATION DOESN'T MEAN SUBORDINATION

THE GRAVE INCIDENT—OF MUCH GREATER SIGNIFICANCE THAN MAY appear at first glance—provoked by the recent speech of Sumner Welles,* with regard to the Chilean declaration postponing the break with the Axis, imposes on all citizens of Indoamerica the right to judge and discuss it. The repercussions of that speech are not limited, since they affect all of us—if we admit continental solidarity as something more than mere words to be used and abused on various occasions.

Let us analyze the case as objectively as possible: In the first place, our advocacy of the cause of democracy does not imply an obligation to accept the infallibility of Mr. Sumner Welles. The North American Undersecretary of State can be mistaken. Furthermore, since the acts of public men must be judged publicly, it is evident that Mr. Welles has already made two serious mistakes in his relations with Indoamerica: He was mistaken in Cuba†—a somewhat distant memory—and he was mistaken in Rio de Janeiro** recently

---

"Con La Cause de la Democracia, Si . . . Pero El Presidente de Chile Tiene Razon!" Incahausi: October 14, 1942, published in *Y Depues de la Guerra Que?* pp. 52–55.

* Welles was Undersecretary of State and the principal figure in charge of U.S. relations with Latin America.

† Haya refers here to Welles's strong opposition to U. S. recognition of the revolutionary government of President Ramon Grau Jan Martin (September 1933–January 1934), which opposition was largely responsible for Grau's overthrow and the beginning of Colonel Fulgencio Batista's domination of Cuban affairs.

** Haya refers to the early 1942 conference at which it was agreed, over Argentinian and Chilean objections, that all American countries would break relations with Axis nations.

in his inaugural speech with his imperious method of address, demonstrative of a certain lack of tact which has been much censured in the North American Press and by prominent North Americans.

We accept then, that Mr. Sumner Welles *can* be wrong, that he is not infallible, even when his words are backed by the prestige of the collossal power which he represents.

I suppose that the fundamental error in the speech of Mr. Welles consists in confusing and equating the position of the Government of Chile with that of Argentina in respect to the cause of democracy, which we are all ready to defend. In fact, Chile has a popular government, truly democratic, freely elected by a true majority. While Argentina has a Government of marked fascist tendency, a product of a dubious election challenged by the most powerful democratic party of the Plata—the Unión Cívica Radical—and its policies are restrictive of democracy: state of siege, electoral frauds, etc.

It can be inferred, therefore, that Mr. Welles demonstrated, at the very least, an ignorance of the political reality of both countries. And not to be informed on such notable facts and to confuse, in the same accusations, two governments which, democratically considered, are very different, is a mistake—and a grave one—for a man who exercises the ministry of foreign relations of such a powerful nation. Then, it is worthwhile to underscore a fact: Chile has not broken relations with the countries opposed to democracy, but is today, with Colombia, Costa Rica, and Mexico, the model country of demoliberal organization, the republic where liberties are strictly respected. That is to say, that it is an Indoamerican nation in which is lived and is practiced the anti-totalitarian constitutional system for which the peoples of the United States, England, Russia, China, and their allies are struggling. . . .

The peoples of our continent must give all for the defeat of imperialist Nazi-fascism, and we must never forget that we are against Nazi-fascism because it is imperialist, that is a suppressor of liberty. For this same reason we must oppose all imperialism, so that Indoamerica does not become the new India of this hemisphere after the war.

V

INTERVENTION VERSUS IMPERIALISM

WE MUST REMEMBER THAT IT WOULD NOT BE FAIR TO AFFIRM THAT all economic or financial interventions by a rich state in another, less-developed one implies imperialist intervention. Unilateral economic extension, uncontrolled and anarchic—that is directed only by the interests of the investing capitalism—is imperialism. But a coordinated financial intervention consisting of systematic aid controlled by the state, needing capital for the development of its country is not a menace to sovereignty, nor is it a sword of Damocles. In this case also there is good and bad economic intervention. The good puts capital and the capitalists at the service of the interest of the developing people and is a factor in the just relations and true neighborliness between the wealthy state and the poor. The reverse is the form of dictatorial and exploiting economic intervention with "financial advisers invested with dictatorial powers," a "dollar diplomacy" at its orders.

In order to organize, also a good economic intervention, it is advisable to organize an Inter American Financial Committee which studies the needs of each country and organizes efficiently its aid in serving the best economic relations between the two Americas. This structure, based on the principles of good democracy, which are those of good neighborliness, supposes the maintenance of an economic equilibrium, which imperialism tends to destroy, and the coordination of a state system of Inter American cooperation.

It can be affirmed, therefore, that the new organization of our

Excerpt from "Intervención e Imperialism," Incahausi: 1943, published in *Y Despues de la Guerra Que?* pp. 69–70.

hemisphere and of the world will have to be based precisely on the organization of the interdependence of states, that is, on the principle of just intervention. Because it is the old and absolute concepts of sovereignty which caused the war. . . .

PART SEVEN

Democratic Inter Americanism
without Imperialism

DURING THE LATE 1930S AND EARLY 1940S, HAYA DE LA TORRE'S attitude changed substantially towards the United States and its relations with Latin America. The series of articles collected in his book *La Defensa Continental*, set forth the nature and implications of this change. These selections from that book make clear the reasons for the change in Haya's position with regard to hemispheric relations. He was much impressed by Franklin D. Roosevelt's Good Neighbor Policy. And, in the second place, Haya came to the conclusion in the late 1930s that Latin America was faced with a much greater and more pressing threat than that presented by the United States: the danger of Nazi-fascism.

Haya did not forswear his opposition to imperialism, nor did he change his long-held opinion that imperialism was basically economic. He did, however, come to the conclusion that the Nazi-fascist imperialism embodied a danger to the Latin Americans well beyond the economic domination that the area had experienced at the hands of the Yankees. It involved an ideology of racism that consigned the Latin Americans to the role of inferior beings, because they were not "Aryans." Furthermore, in case of a Nazi-fascist victory in the western hemisphere, that stigma of racial inferiority could never be overcome, unlike the one of economic inferiority to the imperialists which Haya remained convinced that Latin America would sooner or later surmount.

In the face of the racist imperialism of Nazi-fascism, Haya felt that it was necessary for Latin America and the United States to work together against this menace. This conviction, however, reinforced his arguments in favor of certain aspects of the Aprista program. He felt that the world crisis presented by Nazi-fascism made the unification of Latin America essential. Only then could it deal on a basis of equality with the United States and be an effective partner in the struggle against the Axis Powers. He also found in the new situation further confirmation of his ideas on the Aprista or anti-imperialist state, the establishment of which became much more urgent.

Haya has been accused frequently of turning his back in this period—and subsequently—on the anti-imperialism so prominent in his earlier writings. The reader will have to judge for himself whether or not such is the case. But, to me such an interpretation of Haya's point of view is erroneous.

Haya had always argued that the principal characteristic of imperialism was its representation of an economic penetration by the industrial countries into the underdeveloped ones. The political and military aggressions against the latter were aimed at protecting the industrial powers' investment and trade interests. He also had always stressed that the Latin American countries should be willing to accept foreign investment, but only under certain conditions.

Haya did not turn his back on these ideas. Rather, as the first selection indicates, the policies of the Roosevelt administration led him to believe that such a setting of conditions by the Latin Americans would meet with a more friendly attitude from the United States Government than in the past. The Good Neighbor Policy also indicated to Haya that the United States Government was no longer going to use strong political and military pressure to support economic imperialism as it had previously. Haya therefore felt that, in the face of the Nazi-fascist menace, which he believed would reduce the Latin Americans in general to slavery, it was possible for the two parts of the hemisphere to join in common defense.

One particular aspect of Haya de la Torre's arguments in this section is worthy of special note. This is the advocacy in the Plan Haya de la Torre, the last selection, of collective intervention for the purpose of defending democracy in the Latin American countries. Haya put forward this idea in 1941, long before it had adherents in other Latin American countries. A few years later the Uruguayan Government officially made a similar proposal. More recently a number of democratic leftist leaders in Latin America, most notably ex-President Romulo Betancourt of Venezuela, have urged the establishment of an Inter American Tribunal to protect the civil liberties of the citizens of the American republics and to take other measures on a hemispheric basis to defend democracy.

I

THE INTRODUCTION TO
CONTINENTAL DEFENSE

WE MUST REMEMBER THAT APRISMO, AS A CONTINENTAL ANTI-IM-
perialist postulate, formulated its program when dollar diplomacy,
incomprehending and arrogant, still ruled in the United States. From
1924 to 1933, the initial period of the Aprista movement, Indoamerica suffered many aggressive manifestations of the expansionist
policy imposed by the leaders of the Republican Party from Washington. Aprismo was the answer and the opposition to that policy.
It was the first coherent and concrete movement to confront, with
a truly Indoamerican ideology, the interventionist tendency of the
United States, defended and articulated by the Secretary of State,
Mr. Charles Hughes, in his well-known declaration before the sixth
Pan American Conference in Cuba in 1928.

Starting in 1933, with the election of President Roosevelt, there
came about a healthy and unexpected change in the attitude of Washington towards our peoples. The Good Neighbor Policy, announced
vaguely in the first years of the administration of the Democratic
president, was later defined and strengthened. The desire to establish
a more just system of relations between both Americas seems clear.
President Hoover's initiative in pulling out from Nicaragua the invading Marines, who fought the heroic Sandino, was completed by
President Roosevelt along with the more concrete acts of returning
political sovereignty to Santo Domingo and Haiti, of abolishing the
Platt Amendment, weighing like a chain on the Constitution of Cuba,
and of assuring greater guarantees to Panama in 1938.

In the face of this promising "turnabout" of Pan Americanism—

The Introduction from *La Defensa Continental*, July, 1941.

which to a large degree represents a victory of the Indoamerican
anti-imperialist crusade—Aprismo faced the new reality without false
hopes but free of intolerant prejudices. We Apristas have always
maintained that our movement is not one of aggressive jingoism
against the people of the United States. We have pointed out in
every movement in Pan American policy the financial interests determining the imperialist expansionism and moving the will and opinion
of the people of the United States, who are ignorant of the problems
of Indoamerica and who are badly led by leaders subject to the
influence of Wall Street. We know and we cannot forget that North
America and Indoamerica are and will be neighbors so long as they
exist as populated continents. Our attitude of alertness and of protest against the tendency towards the hegemony of the strongest has
had as its constructive inspiration the search for new and more just
forms of intercontinental harmony.

The Aprista ideas never denied the indisputable value of the
United States' contribution to world civilization. Nor has it been
unaware of the significance of efficient cooperation between industrial, highly technical America and agrarian America, the producer
of raw materials with an incipient economy. But we maintained, and
we still maintain—this is the reason for existence of Aprismo—that
the price of that cooperation could not be and cannot be our vassalage and that new formulas must be found based on the principles
of equality and equilibrium, in conformity with the reality which
each day is more evident. This I maintained and defined in my book
El Antimperialismo y el Apra, basing my argument on an assumption
which can be summed up as: "We need the United States as much
as it needs us." Economically, politically, and militarily the march of
world events demonstrates the truth of this statement.

Happily the Good Neighbor Policy marks the first step towards
a new era of relations between the two Americas. The Good Neighbor Policy is, however, only a conciliatory formula which establishes
a favorable climate for attempting more advanced and secure norms
of coexistence. So far, it is only an attitude of good will not yet
implying the definitive guarantee that our peoples need to live in
assurance of a democratic Interamericanism without empire.

In truth, and it is worth underscoring this, the fault is to a large
degree ours that the Good Neighbor Policy has not been consolidated, surpassed, and assured in a healthy and permanent program
of just relations between the two continents. Dispersed, disoriented,

and circumscribed, our governments have attempted to take advantage of the new attitude of the North American leaders for the limited ends of a utilitarianism without permanence and without grandness. In the Inter American conferences of recent years, the attitude of the representatives of Indoamerica has only been expressed in flowery praise to the Good Neighbor, or in minor propositions almost always motivated by strictly national interests, or the achievement of easy successes destined for internal consumption. There has not been on our side, so far, a full answer, on a continental scale and with unitary vision, to the Good Neighbor. It is not possible to hope that once the new line of Inter American policy by the President of the United States has been established, he will also indicate to us the path to follow, to complete it, and to give it efficacious content in benefit to Indoamerica.

There remain grave problems which the Good Neighbor Policy cannot resolve without the coordinated cooperation of our governments and of our peoples. The continuation of those problems causes the uncertainty and uneasiness which still dominate us in confronting the unexpected reality of the war in Europe and its possible worldwide repercussions.

The duty of all the citizens of both Americas is to cooperate in the clarification of our true attitude towards the situation presented now by the European chaos. But the greater duty is ours, the Indoamericans, because so far we have not known how to define our position in the face of these problems, nor in our relations with the United States, nor in the face of the formidable questions with which European situation forces us to deal in terms of our very existence as a sovereign community of peoples, scattered though we are in jealous, divided, and, therefore, weak countries.

II

THE NORTH AMERICAN-
INDOAMERICAN FRONT

THE RELATIONS BETWEEN THE TWO AMERICAS HAVE IMPROVED EX-
traordinarily during the administration of Franklin Roosevelt. It is
true that with regard to Puerto Rico "good neighborliness" leaves
much to be desired, and it is also certain that the suspicious indul-
gence by Washington of some criollo tyrants indicates that the imperialist interests of Wall Street still have more influence than principles.
But a fact of important consideration is the attitude of the North
American government towards the nationalization of petroleum in
Mexico. In this case, and for the first time in America in a matter of
such magnitude, the strong allowed the application of the law of the
weak, which is almost always the one closest to true justice. President
Roosevelt, who in various Indoamerican cases has shown excessive
tolerance for our criollo stranglers of democracy, has known this time
how to be a Good Neighbor.

It is worth noting in passing, that he had only the choice of
repeating the dualism of Wilson—apostle of democracy and liberty
north of the Tropic of Cancer, bombarder of defenseless peoples and
imperialist invader of weak countries south of the Tropic of Cancer—or to be loyal to the announced Good Neighbor principles. He
decided to be loyal, and this is a fact the present and future transcendency of which it is just to underline.

Published in *La Defensa Continental,* pp. 35–41. There is an obvious contradiction between the date given in *La Defensa Continental* for this piece, February, 1938, and the fact that it has references to events which occurred subsequent to that date. The mistake would seem to be that of Haya himself in
dating the dispersed material assembled for that volume. Internal evidence
suggest February, 1939, as a more likely date for this article.

It is important, however, to make a simple reflection: this policy initiated by Roosevelt towards the peoples of Indoamerica is no more than a government program adopted by the President, as lasting as the New Deal, or as the presence of Mr. Hull as Secretary of State. That is to say, that it is a temporary policy, without any guarantee of continuance. Thus, although the Yankee Democratic party may be considered less imperialist than the Republican, we know well that Wilson was also a Democrat, prophet of the *New Freedom,* and in spite of all this, it was Wilson himself who ordered invasions, bombardments, subjugations, and other atrocities in various Indoamerican countries. On the other hand, the democratic concept of the United States is very elastic and does not exclude acts of tyranny and brutality, especially in weak countries, when it is a matter of defending the interests of its large capitalists.

It could happen that President Roosevelt and his partisans would lose the majority in the next elections and that there would come to power a Republican of the type of the other Roosevelt, great anti-monopolist within his country and archetypical jingo imperialist outside of it, who according to the recent judgment of a North American journalist, took Panama in a manner "which suggests the methods of Mussolini." Or it could happen that there would be elected another Democrat—Mr. MacNutt* or whoever it might be—who would not consider it convenient to include the Good Neighbor policy in his program, and who would resort to the wavering demo-liberalism of Mr. Wilson to fill the theoretical vacuum, which might result in practice as Big Stickish as Roosevelt I.

Do not forget that the President of the United States, according to an insightful definition by the Coles,† "is, a constitutional monarch elected for four years," and that Winston Churchill writes the truth in his book *The World Crisis* when he affirms that the President of the North American union "is invested with direct function of such practical importance that he has no parallel on the earth." This deepens doubts about the permanence of any attitude inspiring the men of Washington. In relying exclusively on the presidential good will to

---

* Paul MacNutt was Governor of Indiana in the 1930s, gaining a bad reputation among liberals for his handling of various strike situations. He was subsequently named by President Roosevelt as High Commissioner to the Philippines.

† G. D. H. and Margaret Cole, British Political Scientists and Leaders of the Fabian Society.

treat us as neighbors and not as barbarians, much depends upon the degree of knowledge future presidents have of our peoples and their concept of the Indians and mestizos. We remember that Mr. Hoover came to visit in 1928 and his policy was hardly distinguishable from that of his cold imperialist predecessor.

Thus, because of what historical experience shows, I believe that President Roosevelt's policy of "good will" towards the Indoamerican peoples is a guarantee of security, but not a permanent guarantee. It is only a policy which could be changed with a change in the executive of the United States.

The common front of Indoamerica and North America removes the danger of the Fascist International in the New World so long as it is effective and efficient. It is not enough to have an alliance of mere words or bureaucratic formulas such as the unfortunate Pan American Union. Nor is it enough to have a complicity of tolerance in which, in the name of democracy, the government of the United States supports tyrants and thus loses the sympathy of the oppressed peoples of this part of the continent. Such a front against the Axis Powers must be a unity of peoples. Democracy must be its banner, but a Democracy that does not tolerate tyrants in any of the countries included in the Anti-fascist Front. Each usurper or despot, even if he pretends to be only a temporary one like Dr. Getulio Vargas,* is a potential fascist, is an enemy of democracy, is a kidnapper of freedom. Its discrepancies with International Fascism are only because they consider it inconvenient to surrender to the authoritarian tutelage of their European masters, or that—and this is decisive—they cede to the pressure of Washington in order to "keep up appearances."

From this we conclude that the front of North America and Indoamerica against the plans of conquest of the Axis Powers must be a popular one. It must be rooted in the great national masses of both Americas; it must be rooted in the confidence and the unity of international action. This supposes the exclusion of tyrants and tyrannical methods from any country that participates in this great democratic alliance. Because fascism is a tyrannical system—a system of oppression and of penetration—and invades in many different ways; as illustrated by the examples of Abyssinia, of China, of Austria, and now that of Peru.

---

* In 1938–1939 Getulio Vargas was governing Brazil as a dictator, and was organizing a so-called "New State" regime which had strong similarities to Portuguese and Italian Fascism.

I think, then, that an alliance of this kind can stop the advances of the Axis Powers, but I put conditions on its efficacy. If the peoples and the governments that are truly democratic by their origin and their conduct don't constitute this alliance, fascism will continue invading our America, using the petty Central and South American tyrants whom it has at its orders.

It is evident that Nazi-fascist imperialism plans to conquer the Indoamerican peoples. This is shown in the incontestable cases of the Brazilian Integralistas,* General Cedillo† in Mexico and General Benavides** in Peru, not to mention other minor puppets of the Axis Powers. It is certain also that this campaign of domination exploits the racial and language links between Indoamerica and Spain as a means of penetration, using General Franco for this purpose. The campaigns in favor of the "Spanish Empire" and of "Hispanismo" are being stepped up. Spanish propagandists of the Fascist International, visit Indoamerica, speaking of the necessity of returning to the Spanish yoke, and it is clear, by means of it, the imperial chains of the Germans, Italians, or Japanese. Fascism has taken Franco as its jailor in Spain and as an instrument for "Hispanizing" us, a word which today is a synonym for making us fascist. Today the Hispano-fascists come to speak to us of the glories of their race, of the greatness and the Franciscan charity of the Corteses, Almagros, and Pizarros, "Falangistas before God." They talk of the panacea of the monarchy of Ferdinand VII and Isabel II and of the Spanish America, which is what they wish us to become again, under the Fascists. All of this they say to an America, which is Indian, *mestizo, chola,* "hairless," *gaucho, roto,* an America which is ours: Indoamerica.

All this—tied to the more direct propaganda of International Fascism, which is buying many dailies known as those "of law and order" in our countries—obliges us to be alert and imposes upon us the formation of the Democratic North-Indoamerican Front. However, such unity must be conditional. The Front of the New World

---

* The Integralistas were the fascist party organized by Plinio Salgado, which was a major political force in Brazil in the late 1930s.

† Saturnino Cedillo was the last of the revolutionary military caudillos who dominated various Mexican states. After serving for a while in President Lázaro Cárdenas's cabinet, he resigned in 1938, returned to the state of San Luis Postosí, where he launched an unsuccessful rebellion in which he lost his life.

** General Oscar Benavídes was president and dictator of Peru at the time Haya was writing.

against the Fascist International must not signify our submissive and unrestricted union with the powerful Good Neighbor. We do not forget—ah, we cannot forget!—that the "good neighbor" can return to being bad and what it has been before, as we have said above. We do not forget that imperialist interests, even when in the case of the petroleum of Mexico they have suffered a defeat under the protection of the Good Neighbor, are the capitalist interests of exploitation, of dominion, of subjection, and of absorption. We do not forget either that peoples which are rich and weak, like ours, are envied as much by fascist imperialism as by North American imperialism. Now, if in this period there is a "good neighbor" that does not wish to serve the interests of the imperialists of his great country, we do not forget that that "good neighbor" is a man and that Good Neighborliness is a precarious, temporary policy, the continuance of which depends upon the victory of a platform in a party convention and the acceptance by a still unpredictable electorate.

Consequently, it is necessary to form the Front: it is necessary to demand that it be efficacious, amply and sincerely democratic, but that it be only a transitory recourse.

IS THERE A DEMOCRATIC IMPERIALISM?

THOSE INTERESTED IN HAVING OUR INDOAMERICAN PEOPLES ADOPT A passive and risky position of neutrality in the face of the tremendous armed conflict between totalitarianism and democracy, use an argument that is worth examining. They say: "This war is a struggle of two imperialisms, the totalitarian against the democratic; Germany and its vassal countries against the tacit and each day more complete alliance of the Anglo Saxon empires of Europe and America." They add: "In the face of this imperialist contest, our peoples, a disarmed Indoamerica, rich and coveted by both forces in the struggle, must adopt a neutral attitude, since both imperialisms are for us equally dangerous."

It is clear—and one must attempt a reply—that from the purely economic point of view, the imperialism of one or another of the peoples at war implies equal risks. But it is also true—and this is a very simple aspect of the discussion of this transcendental theme—that economics is not the only motive of this struggle. Its determining stimulus is economic, that is clear. The character of this gigantic contest of vast technical cruelty is imperialist, no one doubts it. But there is something more than this. The war also has its "superstructure," and the war today moves and brings into conflict two political philosophies that do involve our weak peoples.

When an imperialism adopts as its ideal racial differences—proclaims that men are superior or inferior according to the blood which they have in their veins and the color of their skin—then the peoples who do not belong to the chosen race must fear doubly the

---

"Is There a Democratic Imperialism?" April, 1940, published in *La Defensa Continental*, pp. 69–74.

victory of that imperialism. It will not only bring economic hegemony, the exploitation, and subjugation of peoples because of their poverty and weakness, but enslavement because they are "inferior" and not Aryans. This is the essence of the Nazi-fascist philosophy which teaches the war of the races.

An economic imperialism is more tolerable. People who dominate or exploit because they are rich can lose their dominant economic position if they become impoverished. In the same way, a capitalist of today can be a beggar later, and a fortunate worker has the possibility of achieving the class situation of a bourgeoise if chance permits him upward mobility. But he who is born a Negro or an Indian, quadroon or mestizo, cannot modify the color of his skin or the contours of his face. As he is born, he will remain, Aryan white, Negro, yellow, red, or mixed.

That is, in my opinion, the fundamental difference between an imperialism which in addition to being economic is racist—Nazi-fascism—and the Saxon imperialisms which do not divide men or peoples according to their colors or blood, but according to their purely economic situations. Against the former, the struggle is more difficult for the peoples who in addition to being poor are not purely Aryan, such as ours. . . . Against imperialism, which is merely capitalist and exclusively economic, the proletarian countries have the possibility of defending themselves when the system of exploitation that controls them is abolished.

We recall that in the confusionist propaganda of the Nazi-fascists they use the theme of anti-capitalism. However, there continues to exist its racial mysticism, that is to say the inexorable division of humanity according to ethnic groups. According to this, if Nazi-fascism triumphs, it may abolish the capitalist system, which today divides men and peoples into poor and rich, but there would remain a much more dangerous gradation for the non-Aryan peoples, a form of caste system from which only death can redeem a man.

Going deeper into these reflections, we discover the demagogic and misleading nature of Nazi-fascist anti-capitalism. If capitalism is imperfect and inhuman because of its exploitation and subjugation of great social masses, due to economic differences, racism will not suppress this subjugation—even if the exploitation is remedied—because societies and peoples will be classified and dominated due to irremediable differences of race.

Hitler in *Mein Kampf* alludes to the peoples of both Americas and says that while those of the North maintained the purity of their Germanic race, those of the South, or Indoamerica, degraded and mixed theirs, producing an inferior mestizo. Rereading this paragraph of the Nazi-fascist bible, we are classified in the category of inferior peoples. If the European Jews—so many of whom are so blonde and so white—have been persecuted because their race is not pure, what can be expected by the Indoamerican Indians and mestizos who constitute eighty-five percent of the population of our vast continent.

There is, therefore, another argument which it is important to discuss. The neutralists, the criollo philo-fascists and philo-communists, capriciously link imperialism and democracy. They speak, it is clear, of "Democratic Imperialism." However, they forget that democracy, as a principle, as a norm, is anterior to capitalism. It is a purely political conception, and its imperfection consists exactly of the fact that it has not been capable of resolving and overcoming the economic differences among men. Proof of this affirmation are the noncapitalist countries, poor peoples, where democracy has been and is possible. Colombia is one example; Costa Rica is another. Chile has the characteristics of a firm democratic structure; and, if things go well, Argentina and Uruguay, will make their way down the same road. It is clear that in Great Britain and in the United States, capitalism and democracy *coincide*. Before the economic system of financial industrialism there was the Magna Carta, the Revolution of Cromwell, and the North American Declaration of Rights, even though it is true that in the States that Washington liberated Negro slavery existed for many years.

The essential element of democracy is liberty. Liberty to oppose even the system under which one lives. In democratic countries it is possible to use liberty to attack capitalism, imperialism, and even democracy itself. In the totalitarian countries—and in this Russia is totalitarian—no one can dare invoke liberty to oppose Nazi-fascism or communism. This is to say that democratic organization even in the capitalist and imperialist countries leaves the road open to improvement, progress, and perfection. Democracy is so ample in its essence of liberty that it is possible under it to deny it, end it, or renovate it. Thus it is possible—in the case of the poor countries where it exists— to apply it with success to poor, mestizo, and disarmed peoples.

This is the difference between a pro-Nazi attitude and a position in favor of democracy. This is the basis of opposition to the simplistic position of those who affirm that in the face of a struggle between totalitarianisms and democracy our peoples must remain neutral, indifferent, and passive.

We are always anti-imperialists, but we also are always democrats. We struggle for the abolition of all imperialism, whether it comes from the totalitarian countries or from those where Democracy exists. But we reject and fight the totalitarianism that wishes to replace the impartial differences of the economic imperialisms with the other differences of race. Our position in this struggle is to maintain with democracy its essence of liberty. We wish to use it to abolish imperialism and by means of what has been called "dynamic democracy"—I as an Aprista say functional democracy—to surpass and perfect political equality, opening the way to economic justice among men and among nations.

IV

THE ECONOMIC ASPECT OF
CONTINENTAL DEFENSE

IN SPITE OF THE FACT THAT THE SAXONS HAVE GREAT FAME AS
"practical" men, it is not possible to recognize them as being such
insofar as Pan Americanism is concerned. As it has been conceived
and worked for by the leaders of the United States, it has only given
minimum results.

An excessive and formal adherence to what the Indoamerican
governments think and do and a frequent ignoring of the opinion of
the peoples, who in many cases are opposed to their governments,
has characterized the modus operandi of Pan Americanism. Guided
by such lines of procedure, the leaders of Washington have many
times made unpopular and even odious everything connected with
the Pan Americanist tendency.

It is certain that the unpopularity of Pan Americanism culminated with the conference of Lima in 1938, which had as its objective the exultation of democracy in a country submitted to the most
extreme ciollo totalitarianism. Then not only Indoamerican public
opinion, but also some notable representatives of public opinion in
the United States, understood that the Pan American proposals had
lost so much prestige, that they ran the risk of no one ever believing
in them again.

The Conference of Panama indicated that Washington doubled
its efforts to have "the jeers of Lima" forgotten, attempting to regain
the influence which had been lost. Perhaps because of time pressures,

---

"Aspecto Económico de la Defensa Continental," August, 1940, published in
La Defensa Continental, pp. 114–121.

that meeting accomplished little, and Pan Americanism continued accumulating digressions and lyric votive offerings.

It is curious, however, that in spite of the fact that Pan Americanism lost sympathies in continental opinion for lack of an efficient and realistic direction, there exists in our people an increasingly deep desire to arrive at some method of systematic relations between Indoamerica and the United States of North America. This explains the good will with which the latest calls to an Inter American assembly has been received, and perhaps this is the reason why in the recent one, there was introduced a new way of action for Pan Americanism.*

We are not going to believe, it is clear, that the conference of Havana has yet marked a total change in the deficiencies and vacillating methods of Pan American orientation. Far from this, the Inter American assembly of July has proved that in the difficult circumstances through which the world is passing, there exists the intention of coordinating the policy of both Americas. However, it has demonstrated, once again, that there are missing the solid bases for the adoption of efficacious methods.

The most outstanding defects of the present organization of Pan Americanism come from its very structure. The Pan American Union is subject to antiquated norms and is today an old apparatus ill-adapted to the contemporary requirements of cooperation by the peoples of this Hemisphere. In epochs of tutelage and "dollar diplomacy," the Pan American Union was a useful mitigator of the imperialist "big stick." Today, the new democratic and constructively dynamic relations between both Americas demand a more elastic and more modern structure for the facilitation of those relations.

There has been lacking until now a practical spirit of Pan Americanism, and the best proof of that is that both in the political and economic spheres—more in the latter than in the former—we find ourselves still far from efficacious coordination.

In the first place, it has not been possible so far to create a moral force with sufficient power to guard the stability of democracy

---

* Haya refers here to the Lima Conference which was the first one where a major attempt was made by the United States to develop a common attitude of all Pan American Union member states in face of the danger of a new European war; to the Panama conference of September 1939, which agreed that all member states would remain neutral in the new war, and warned all belligerents to stay out of the western hemisphere; and to the Havana Conference of June 1940 which agreed on joint occupation of any Dutch or French colonies in America that the Germans might try to seize.

in the twenty countries of Indoamerica. Most of our peoples live under tyrannies, despotisms, and the anti-juridical rule of regimes of force. While they exist and can exist, democracy will be undermined, and totalitarianism will have a propitious field. An excellent regularization of Inter American relations presupposes Inter American relations for democratic purposes and presupposes, first of all, a firm basis for anti-dictatorial constitutional norms in all of our countries and an effective action on the part of the other states each time a despotism installs a totalitarian bulwark in any one of them. For this moral force to exercise all its constructive power, Pan Americanism must not listen only to what the governments do and say, but that they give jurisdiction and law to what their peoples wish and demand.

In the second place, Pan Americanism has not yet been able to create a solid and clear economic organization that would create a positive basis for relations between the Americas. This great vacuum is, without doubt, the consequence of the lack of defined Inter American policy, and the result of the absence of a new democratic spirit in the functioning of the system of relations which it must create. Again we encounter the fact that it is the governments—often not representing the opinion of their peoples—which alone have a voice and vote in Pan American action. Thus the interests of those governments prevail, exclusively, in the systematization of relations between both Americas.

We contemplate, for example, the recommendation of the Foreign Policy Association of Washington for the adoption of a complementary program for a Pan American economic cartel. It consists of the following:

1. Investigation of the economic resources and productive capacity of the whole hemisphere.

2. Development of the sources of strategic materials in Indoamerica.

3. A program of acceleration of development of agricultural products in Indoamerica which do not compete with North American ones.

4. Development of industry in Indoamerica.

5. Ratification of the agreement on the Inter American Bank.

6. Completion of the Pan American Highway and other strategic means of communication.

Examining these propositions, we find immediately that the difficulty is not in outlining a program of what "should be done," but in indicating the best way of realizing it. The Foreign Policy Association of Washington seems to imagine that in all our countries there are institutes of investigation or official statistical services as perfect as those in the United States. It is unaware of the difficulties of fulfilling such a vast plan. These proposals provide lyrical and vague aims appealing to our principal desires, but offering very few practical results.

We Apristas have suggested—coinciding in many points with the proposals of the Foreign Policy Association of Washington—a program which suggests viable procedures:

1. To call in each country a meeting of an economic congress or "round table" of all of the vital forces of its economy—capital and labor, commerce and industry, agriculture and transport—without excepting the foreigners who form a part of the national economic dynamism. That economic congress would investigate the economic resources and productive capacity of each country and would make concrete suggestions concerning its development. It would not only be a congress of a governmental type, but would be functional-democratic, and in it must participate capitalists and workers, as we have said; and they must take into account all points of view to bring about the coordination of a plan for the national economy, with a view to its forming part of the continental economic organization.

2. As a result of these national economic congresses, there must meet a great economic congress or conference of all of the American states—also with a functional representation of the vital forces of their economies—to which would be brought the conclusions of each national congress, and in it would be studied the possibility of an exchange of products among the countries of Indoamerica, and between these and the United States, providing for the coordinated development of industry in the various Indoamerican countries in accordance with a program of cooperation instead of competition.

3. With the conclusion of this Inter American economic congress, there would convene a conference of experts from both Americas who would study the following fundamental points: unification of exchange rates, at least among the twenty Indoamerican States, and the stabilization of the exchange between this money of the agro-mineral countries and the dollar which is the money of a great industrial country. On this basis, and always taking into account the fact that the economy of the agricultural nation and that of the industrial country must not be confused or mingled, there must be established an Inter American banking system that guarantees the stability of

the common money and systematizes the relations with the Federal Bank System—of the industrial capitalist type—of the United States. The structure of an Indoamerican bank in coordination with the latter—for the development of the agricultural and raw material countries—must be different from that of the present great banks. In our countries, the credit of labor is necessary for the service of agriculture, of mining, of new industry, and of large and small commerce.

On these bases, the industrial development of Indoamerica will be accelerated, the production of an agriculture not competing insofar as possible with that of the United States will be intensified, many of its products will be absorbed reciprocally between the Indoamerican countries, and commerce with the United States will be systematized, the excess of production being sent to other continents. The Pan American Highway and the coordinated defense of the hemisphere will be correlated with a new system of economic relations between both Americas.

If we consider that in case of German victory . . . there will be produced in our continent a price war, it must be kept in mind that a low money, of a barter type—an aski mark or an aski franc or an aski lira—will be the competitor of a gold dollar with a strong backing and excessively dear in relation to our type of depreciated money. If with the price war there come totalitarian offensive and political subjugation, the defensive front of both Americas will have to build a totally new economic machinery based on the differentiation between the two types of production existing in our hemisphere: the economy of the under-developed Indoamerican countries, and the highly developed economy of the United States.

Political defense is, then, fundamentally linked to economic defense. However, as a Pan Americanism attempting to link the twenty states of Indoamerica with the forty-eight of North America in an empire is inadmissible, so is any possible order of economic relations of the two Americas attempting to fuse systems and equalize conditions. They must be allied and not merged.

Applying the democratic principle to the Inter American economy, it must be recognized as imperative that in structuring a new system of financial and commercial relations between the industrial America and the agricultural America, the living forces of production must be heard, not only the voice of the governments. This is the objective of the national economic congresses that would be the forerunner of the continental or Inter American economic congress.

Thus, there would be no fear that the commerce of Indoamerica would be easily absorbed and dominated by the totalitarian countries. Well developed, an Inter American economy has nothing to fear in selling its surpluses of production to the rest of the world. A large part of them will be absorbed in this hemisphere, and the rest will leave, without risks to our stability and sovereignty, for Europe and Asia.

In this realistic situation, a resort to forced and more or less fantastic "cartels" would not be necessary. We would not improvise weakly but would carry out a creative and constructive work, lasting and strong.

V

PAN AMERICANISM OR
INTER AMERICANISM?

IN DEALING ONCE AGAIN WITH THIS SUGGESTIVE AND CURRENT SUB-
ject of the "new political language" of Indoamerica, it is necessary to
assess certain words which represent important concepts. A "New
Inter American political language" signifies a new and renovated terminology, words freed from whatever subterfuge hides prejudices
and disagreeable reminiscences.

In order to rejuvenate our political idiom, it is important to
remember once again Don Quijote when he affirmed that "in this
matter of enriching the language, the vulgar and the commonplace
have their power." Even more in dealing with the political idiom—it
must be popular and *democratic* in order to better symbolize the
living lexicon with the contemporary wave of history.

Democratic or popular—this must be noted—in the sense of
translating loyally the aspirations and understanding of our peoples.
Without this there is no politics, and even less a unifying and constructive language capable of interpreting them. We are going to create and are in the process of creating a new form of expression, and
we need it to be—as languages are when they first appear—a simple
and vital manifestation of the aspirations of a New World.

As the political dictionary has a literal order that is not always
alphabetic—although America commences with an A—it is worthwhile to consider certain key words which a new idiom of relations
among the peoples of this side of the planet will have to determine.
Perhaps none is more important, after establishing and spreading the

"Panamericanismo Interamericanismo," September, 1940, published in *La
Defensa Continental,* pp. 65–68.

word *Indoamerica* as the denomination of our part of this hemisphere, than excising, so as to replace it with another, the phrase
"Pan America" and its derivatives "Pan Americanism" etc.

"Pan Americanism" has been in its origin and essence the more
or less covert and more or less pharisaical policy of "dollar diplomacy" of the North American "businessman" and Secretary of State
in his relations with the peoples of Indoamerica. But with the policy
of the Good Neighbor, dollar diplomacy has been buried—and it is
"deader than a mummy of the pharoahs" according to the sharp
expression of the understanding diplomat Mr. [Claude] Bowers,
North American Ambassador in Santiago de Chile—Pan Americanism, as it was conducted and interpreted since the foundation of the
Pan American Union, has no reason to exist.

Pan Americanism is a phrase which suggests and is associated
with the idea of Pan Germanism, "big stick," or "Ministry of Colonies," as Manuel Ugarte called it. I remember what a little Panamanian Negro once told me when he heard a speech of mine in the
National Institute of his country criticizing the Pan American Union:
"I think that Pan Americanism is a *pan* which is going to be eaten by
the Americans."* Here is the power of the vulgar language and the
use of which Don Quijote spoke, in giving value to the political
idiom. Pan Americanism always has sounded bad to us, and although
it had its epoch and its apogee, it is a phrase, it is a method, and it is
an organization which must be replaced by something more modern,
more democratic, more precise, and more efficient.

Furthermore, Pan Americanism is confusionist. It is the continued expression of the gravest and most visible political error of not a
few men on both sides, insofar as the relations of both Americas are
concerned: the error of imagining that to give them unity is to merge
or amalgamate them in a single and undefined mixture. On that level
Pan Americanism has failed and will fail because the problem is not
one of merger, but of coordination. Agrarian America and industrial
America, Indoamerica and Saxon-America cannot make an indigesti-
ble *pudding* in the oven of Pan American effects, no matter how hot
it is. Exactly what is involved is to delimit and agree, to establish
the elements and calibrate them. To estimate the value of each of the
economic, political, and social forces which constitute this and the
other America and to make each feel that it must live together with

---

* "Pan" is the Spanish word for bread.

the other coherently, that they will be neighbors so long as the planet exists and this wide hemisphere is habitable, and that they must be "good neighbors" through mutual respect and mutual aid.

But good neighborliness does not mean to make the Americas a "boarding house," but rather it means that each must live in its own area, united by a sure and ample path of reciprocal aid and permanent alliance against any common enemy. This is not the "Pan Americanism," which infers tutelage and patronage, that is to say, disequilibrium, the disdain of the strong and the resentment of the weak. It will be "Inter Americanism," which is something different.

Inter Americanism expresses a relation of equality of conditions, coordination, equity, that delimits "the relations between" the two Americas, not their confusion in a single "pan"—whole—and they should never be confused. Thus, the first constructive step to make "good neighborliness" function with a new dynamism of cooperation and justice, must be to renew its basis of relationship and to abandon the superannuated Pan Americanist machinery, establishing instead a modern system of equal and open relations.

If we abandon the enveloping and absorbing tendency of the old Pan Americanism—under the auspices of which have flourished the imperialist and dictatorial tendencies of so many governments—we shall enter into a new Inter Americanist stage without empire, which will begin by defining the two great economic camps into which the Americas are divided; that one, in which industrialism predominates, and this one, in which agriculture and raw materials prevail.

That delimitation is essential. It determines the two rhythms, two ways of being and working, of producing and consuming. Two economic levels and two commercial, financial, and in the end political attitudes. There is no room for confusion between the two, there is no room for *Pan,* but rather for *Inter,* bi-lateral cooperation, which is to say, the two Americas equally respected and equally respectable.

Popular usage has given the phrase *Pan Americanism* and its derivatives a bad reputation and a worse connotation. In the "new political language" of Indoamerica, the organization and methods of the "Pan American Union" must change. Our peoples desire now an "Inter American Coordination" which puts in a museum the Pan Americanist words and concepts—together with the dead dollar diplomacy—and which gives life to new modes of understanding and of mutual respect, as the basis of an authentic and democratic fraternity between the United States of the North and the states of Indoamerica.

"Good neighborliness," a bilateral concept of the Monroe Doctrine, and Inter Americanism, are three vigorous and modern concepts, expressive of a new democratic mode of looking at American political relations. They affirm an anti-imperialist conception of "equal to equal" between the two continents. They announce also that the old Pan Americanism must sleep the eternal and well-merited sleep of the pharoahs.

VI

DEMOCRACY AND
IMPERIALIST TOTALITARIANISM

IF WE CONSIDER THE POLICY FOLLOWED BY OUR GOVERNMENTS AND
our parties in the face of the grave situation created by the menace
of totalitarian imperialism, we must agree that it is characterized by
weakness and disorientation, when not actual confusion, and therefore, by danger. Whereas the totalitarians know where they are going
and what they want, we do not find the way to assurance and security. We are in a situation similar to that of the European democracies
five years ago, defenseless in the face of the sure steps of international fascism, who did not have any other recourse than to accept
the desperate Moscow intervention of the Popular Front, an institution admissible for only a precarious and anguished instant of
defense, but with little value for a creative move of pugnacious
affirmation.

Here in Indoamerica, something similar is happening to us. As
in 1933, 1934, 1935, and 1936 in Europe, we are losing precious
days, invaluable minutes on the watch of history which cannot be
repeated. We have lived hung to the European skirt tails. We have
not dared—we recall it—to think for ourselves in politics. If a party
was founded, it must have a name and slogans from the Old World,
cite, idolize, and pay court to the tutors and high priests from the
other side of the sea. If they came to power, they had to proceed
according to European models, imitating their words. Everything not
European seemed to us to be depreciated. All that Europe had done

"Democracia y Totalitarismo Imperialists," October, 1940, published in *La Defensa Continental,* pp. 75–82.

was traced exactly by our paid criollos with blind, submissive, tropical fervor which did not discriminate or even elaborate.

Now that Europe has nothing to teach but the lack of foresight, the mistakes of appeasement, and ominous failures in the face of imperialist terror and barbarism, the confusion here has been so profound that many of our political groups have been left disconcerted and shocked. One who has always walked with crutches or a cane can only take steps by himself with great effort. This explains why so many of the parties and governments of Indoamerica, vow that the European connection is broken, deliver themselves submissively and confidently, patiently and fatalistically, to the North American tutelage.

From colonial and obsequious Europeanism, we are passing to passive and unreserved Pan Americanism. Or, in the case of the torrid devotees of criollo Communism, from slavish and vainglorious love for Mr. Roosevelt to regimented, European, and pro-Nazi neutrality, preparing the atmosphere of demoralization and conquest. . . .

The submission to Europe is as useless and noxious—whether from left or right—as is the quietism and fearful rushing to the protection of the United States. There is no time in these tense hours for either demoralizing whispers or less than perfect cooperation. No one wishes allies without imagination, comrades without any initiative of their own, peoples who ask for defense and lack spontaneous combativeness. The position of the United States—which from its own national interest has the responsibility for our defense—is not so powerful that it does not require efficacious aid and initiative, nor so Don Quijote-like that it does not impose conditions.

There is also another consideration that we must take into account: the United States has before it such a complex and gigantic task that it is not going to fulfill it without our help. We must not wait for them to defend us, but we must join in that defense and prepare ourselves actively and resolutely.

In a very recent and suggestive article by Robert Sherwood, the author of *Abe Lincoln in Illinois,* there appear certain well-chosen data that we Indoamericans must take into account. For example, this: if the British navy were defeated or destroyed, Hitler would have at his command a naval power constituted by the squadrons of Germany and Italy and part of the French, all of which, without counting that of Japan, is six times greater than the naval capacity of the United States. In addition to this, he cites the report of the Naval

Affairs Committee of the Senate of Washington which, last May 15, noted these facts:

> It is clearly evident that the United States can be defeated without military conquest of its territory. An effective blockade against our foreign commerce could be carried out from points situated thousands of miles from our coasts, and certainly far from the radius of air action. Our distant positions will be captured and used against us as advanced bases. It will be impossible to prevent the establishment of bases, by force if necessary, in this hemisphere, from which there could be organized naval raids and air routes for the bombardment of our most industrialized areas. . . . Under the conditions previously enunciated enemy ships, except in the form of raiders, do not need to approach our coasts. With the loss of our outlying possessions and our foreign commerce, and subject to constant attacks on our coasts, our final defeat is inevitable. It will be only a question of time, depending upon our national will to resist. Without the power to carry forward the struggle against the enemy, there is no other alternative than subjugation to his desires.

The report which we cite was written before the *tripartite pact,* and when it was possible to have some hope that Japan would not intervene; nothing has happened since May to assure us that, even without it, the fundamental risks which the report announces could be avoided. Those who are confident that the United States can defend us under any circumstances and from an advantageous position, would do well to read the impressive revelations of this report by the Naval Affairs Committee of Washington, in addition to the Military Affairs Committee and everything that the Yankee Senate knows of the activities of the fifth columns in the United States and in the countries of Indoamerica.

We must make better use of the lessons of recent history and draw from them irrefutable conclusions. The first is that we weak peoples must not confide in totalitarian promises with respect to our integrity and independence. Abyssinia and Austria, Czechoslovakia, Norway, Poland, the Baltic countries, Denmark, Holland, and Belgium, are living and sufficient proofs of this. The second and very clear lesson is that the Indoamerican continent is an object of conquest by the Axis and that the attack on the Americas will follow the offensive against England. In addition, that attack may take place even without waiting for an end to the German-British struggle, in order to weaken the United States. Another irrefutable lesson is that of the Nazi strategic norm, always utilized so far: Take strategic points in weak countries from which to attack the strong ones.

The tactic employed by totalitarian policy which prepares—by demoralization—the climate for conquest is also a transcendental lesson of this war. It has been used everywhere except in England, where because it was inapplicable, its terrible influence failed. In effect, the fifth columns—which are of diverse types and various categories of collaborators—have as their purpose the preparation of the demoralization of the people whom they wish to conquer. They incite corruption, stimulate divisionism, disorientation, and confusion. They develop the action of defeatest cowardice, proclaiming the advisability of neutrality, and attempt thus to isolate from all protection those countries chosen to receive the next aggressive blow.

The lessons of this war have been most evident, and only by the shock of rapid blows and by the confusionist work of the agents of totalitarianism in our midst, can it be explained why immediate measures have not been taken against this obvious threat. We continue divided, and we continue confused. We hope that the United States will indicate the way for us, protect us and give us money—for not having defended ourselves. Our governments, in almost all of the continent, have so much egoism and such a lack of vision that in some cases it could be deliberate complicity, but in others is irresponsible shortsightedness. Each one is looking at itself. Each country thinks only of its own problems in strict localist terms; and when they go beyond these, they limit themselves to hoping for North American protection.

There could be no better climate for the concrete and tenacious plans of the totalitarian imperialist Axis powers to be fulfilled among us. We are repeating the history of the suicidal tactics of all the European countries which, because each was solely concerned with its own narrow interests, did not form in time a defensive barrier which could have been invincible, if it had been well prepared. None of our governments wants to know if beyond its frontiers, whether in the neighboring country or further away—but within the continent— there exists the seed or the breeding ground of totalitarian expansionism. With the example of Europe before them, they think and act "patriotically," in very limited national terms, while the enemy calculates and acts in a continental sense. The rulers and most criollo parties imagine that their frontiers of defense coincide with their arbitrary political geography. They deduce that all that occurs beyond is foreign to them.

An illustrious Mexican with an Indoamerican sensibility, speaking of our present situation and its dangers, about the obvious totalitarian plans, and the need for concrete and realistic action, told us the following a little while ago:

> We are giving such proofs of incapacity of assuming the responsibilities which are imposed upon us by our position as cooperators with the United States in the defense of common liberty, that it would not be strange if the North Americans, seeing us so dangerously irresponsible, would have to impose upon us by force the fulfillment of our duties and the adoption of practical methods to save ourselves.

This leads us to consider whether or not we are going to continue hearing admonitions such as that of Senator Wiley, who reminds the governments of Indoamerica that the only way to safeguard our freedom is to emerge from our dangerous indecision, to unite, to confederate, to foresee the danger, and to eliminate now all neutralist and confusionist enemies who work from inside in order to have us surrender, demoralized, to the conqueror.

VII

ON THE INTER AMERICAN
DEMOCRATIC FRONT

FROM HIS EXILE, MY PARTY COMRADE MANUEL SEOANE HAS WRITTEN an interesting and suggestive commentary on the Inter American democratic front. Those who have read Seoane's brilliant book *Nuestra América y la Guerra* (Santiago de Chile: 1940) must know well his ideas with respect to the position of the peoples of this continent in the face of the present European conflagration and in the face of its possible repercussions in this hemisphere.

Seoane interprets with loyalty and in depth the true Aprista attitude in this decisive hour of Indoamerican life. In support, I am going to cite here some of the best paragraphs of his recent book:

> In the pressing hour in which democratic regimes are living, it is necessary to go beyond the stage of egoism and incomprehension which was characteristic until yesterday. The United States can gain the support of our peoples if, for its part, it offers its own in a just way. Because we desire to be a help and not a burden, we wish to present and resolve pending problems. To be useful allies and not a drawback, it is indispensable that we strengthen our national economies. This implies reforming the systems of property or taxes that presently favor some great foreign interests, to the detriment of legitimate national expectations. It is obvious that we do not have a fundamental interest in defending a system which we consider unjust. The only honest price which we ask for our support is the equitable satisfaction of our legitimate aspirations in favor of an improvement in our economies.

"Sobre El Frente Democratico Interamericano," April, 1941, published in *La Defensa Continental,* pp. 122–126.

As a result, we do not clearly understand the unilateral criterion which seems to inspire the management of North American economic interests. The United States, if it lends the support of its banking resources cannot have the disagreeable role of zealous tutor of these investments, limiting their function only to what is convenient for that country. In this period, the need for defense is mutual, and therefore, the advantages to be obtained must be mutual also. The process of exchange of our respective products must be based on a cooperation favoring the general development of the continent and not merely the special desires of one party.

Dealing with the political aspect of Inter Americanism and of the so-called "aid to the democracies," Seoane says:

There is something more subtle, less understandable, and not for that less grave. If this alliance has as its objective the defense of the democratic system, those who coordinate their efforts to that end must scrupulously study whether those who join this effort are really democrats or not. It is a flagrant contradiction to unite democrats and dictators to defend democracy, to bring together free movements which are nourished by the conscious participation of the citizenry and despotic regimes resulting from fraud and disposed to perpetuate their power with the same methods as European Nazi-fascism. In that sense, the equal support given all Indoamerican governments, whatever their origin, not only causes surprise and confusion, but reveals a strategic weakness by leaving open a crevice for the lovers of dictatorship, through which today or tomorrow might creep totalitarian infiltration.

The reader has here the realistic presentation of our double objection to this indiscriminate front of the democracies, which hurriedly, and with an eye only to their quantitative value, is being formed. On the one hand is the plan for North American economic aid to the countries of Indoamerica, without consulting the needs of these countries. On the other is the rallying en masse of all the governments of this continent in a democratic alliance that is false because those who form it—in their majority—are not democrats.

Urgencies of war, the understandable desires of the men in Washington to present Europe with a single Inter American front, give to this new Pan Americanism of the "Good Neighbor" a characteristic of unanimity that is unreal and, consequently, dangerous.

To apply the old methods of Pan Americanism to this new reality in which we live is merely to put aside fundamental unresolved

problems. The Pan American Union and its policy of cautious proto-
col have been bypassed by an international dynamism determined by
the European convulsion which demands other norms of judgment
and solutions for the tremendous problems of this hour. Care must
be taken that the institution in Washington, good enough for the
placid epochs of governmental and oratorical Pan Americanism,
doesn't become like that of Geneva, which served to keep drowsy
those who dreamed of a pacific world, but which fell, shattered and
useless, at the sound of the first shots of war.

The danger of Pan Americanism telescoped with good neighborliness is its inconsistency in this moment of great definitions. It cannot
continue to be maintained at the price of loans, or with the precarious warmth of a solidarity lacking popular support. The money that
the United States invests in our countries as the monetary symbol of
good will remains useless, if it doesn't strengthen an Inter American
system of just and bilaterally advantageous economic relations. The
political front of common defense will be incomplete and fragile if
distinction is not first made between the Indoamerican countries truly
governed by democratic regimes and those pretending to be so only
to strengthen under the protection of the United States totalitarian
systems covered with a rhetorical disguise of freedom.

It is evident that the new Inter Americanism and true Good
Neighborliness must be directed more to the peoples than to the governments of Indoamerica. Unless the democratic principle of popular
sovereignty is consulted, any Inter American policy will be artificial
and slippery. Until today the United States has given credit as popular governments to all those in our continent that proclaim themselves
to be so. Only in Europe have the men of Washington had a discrim-
inating eye and ear. Only for the peoples oppressed by dictatorships
in the Old World have there been pronounced, directly and clearly,
words of anti-totalitarian condemnation. When Indoamerica is involved, the brutal tyrannies of Guatemala and Peru have been, for
the North American government, equal to the effective democracies
of Colombia, Costa Rica, and Chile, to name only a few cases. . . .

With just alarm, we Indoamericans must ask ourselves if the
Inter American Democratic Front is not a new name for the old Pan
Americanism which was marked by dollar diplomacy and which recognized as constitutional governments so many brutal tyrannies that,
before and after fascism, violated the civic and human liberties of our
peoples, enslaved them by armed force, and subjugated them for the
economic benefit of Wall Street.

VIII

PLAN HAYA DE LA TORRE

THE STRENGTHENING OF DEMOCRACY IN THE TWENTY-ONE STATES OF the Americas—especially in those of the Latin or Indo American continent—is a unanimous aspiration of our peoples. For this to be possible, however, it is necessary to give to democracy a realistic meaning, a positive and dynamic one, abandoning the vague phraseology which has served so well certain dictatorships of this continent in covering up their practically totalitarian systems.

The program that Aprismo suggests consists of the following twelve points dealing with strengthening the political, juridical, and economic aspects of Inter American democracy.

1. *Political Alternative of the World: Democracy or Totalitarianism*

The political organization of the world presents today two possibilities: democracy or totalitarianism. The first is based on popular sovereignty as the basis of the national sovereignty of the state. The second is based on the absolutism of dictatorship as the sovereign and despotic norm of national life.

Democracy established a relationship between the freedom of the citizen, limited by the freedom of other citizens, and the freedom of the state, limited in turn, by the freedom of other states. Totalitarianism suppresses and submerges the freedom of the citizen in the supreme freedom of the state. This tends to carry over into international relations with the end result of a vast organization of total vassalage.

In democracy, force is at the service of law. In totalitarianism, law succumbs to force, which thus becomes the only law. Totalitari-

---

"Plan Haya de la Torre or Plan Para la Afirmación de la Democracia en América," 1941, published in *La Defensa Continental*, pp. 144–157.

anism takes the concept of the state back to the primitive forms of autocracy, giving it new theoretical bases. Democracy tries to maintain and carry further the ideals of individual liberty which inspired the English, North American, French, and Indoamerican revolutions.

2. Position of the Americas: Fatherland and Democracy

The origin of the modern American fatherlands is linked, fundamentally, to democracy. The founders and liberators of the nations of both Americas combined the concepts of fatherland and democracy. When, after the French Revolution, the Napoleonic wars presented Europe with the struggle between political imperialisms, the peoples of Indoamerica "took no part" in that struggle: They took advantage of it to become independent. They sought the aid of England and used it to their benefit. They adopted the principles of the French Revolution and, following the example of the United States, took the republican-constitutional form of government, based on the notion of fatherland and the democratic ideal.

3. The Americas Face-to-Face with Totalitarianism

Faced with the struggle between totalitarianism and democracy, both Americas maintain their republican position. The United States, in defense of its economic and political institutions, as a powerful nation. And the Indoamerican States reaffirm their belief in the republican form of government, not only because their existence as free countries is essential to the exercise of democracy, but also because totalitarianism signifies the right of the conquest of defenseless peoples and—according to Nazi philosophy—the racist postulate of the ethnic Aryan-German supremacy over all other peoples of "impure" race, or color, or mixed, like ours.

In spite of the intercontinental problems that the predominance of the United States has created in this hemisphere in its relations with the disunited states of Indoamerica, before the common menace and in the face of an imperialism which, in addition to being economic, is political, anti-democratic, and racist, the twenty-one countries of the New World are in agreement on the necessity of a united defense.

4. Problems of Inter American Democracy

However, the problems that democracy confronts in the Americas are obvious. In the United States, where democratic liberties have achieved a high degree of acceptance and continuity, excessive capitalist influence presents a grave problem of internal economic and social inequalities and presents to Indoamerica another problem, which is the consequence of the colossal industrial and financial development of the United States, in the form of imperialist expansion over our newly developing economies.

In the peoples of Indoamerica, with their agrarian and mining economies, democracy has progressed with difficulty, having succeeded in establishing itself in some states, but having as an obstacle for its full realization, the dictatorships or despotic oligarchies that often have been underwritten and strengthened by North American capitalist expansion.

Both Americas, from different angles, are faced with the reality that the affirmation and defense of democracy, and the road to achieving these, is national and Inter American, political and economic.

5. Necessity of Democratic Affirmation in Face of Totalitarian Danger

In the face of the reality of the totalitarian danger and the imminent menace of the disappearance of the American nations, in general, as free entities and the subjugation of the Indoamerican peoples, in particular, as inferior races, the states of this hemisphere are confronted with the peremptory and primary necessity of constituting a defensive democratic front. The defense of democracy, however, is not only a question of force. It is, fundamentally, a problem of the real existence of a democratic organization, of its efficacy and authority. To give prestige to and morally to underwrite the democratic system, it is necessary to revitalize it with popular faith. This is only possible when a peoples can see that its liberties are unconditionally guaranteed in the permanent juridical norms of the state.

Democracy cannot be vigorously affirmed in the Americas without the unanimous cooperation of all the peoples and all the governments in making it respected. Only when each people and each government have an exact consciousness of the sanctity of democratic principles will these be strong and lasting.

6. Unity and Inviolability of Democracy

Democracy as the organic foundation of the American states is singular and unconditional. There is not a different category of democracy for each country. Its basis is liberty. President Roosevelt has well stated the general and Inter American postulates that define and apply it juridically: freedom of expression, freedom of religion, economic freedom, and freedom to live without fear. The constitutions of the twenty-one American states consecrate these freedoms, the democratic corollary of which is the existence of governments freely elected by their peoples and subject with them to duties and law, legally fixed and fairly enforced.

Thus, in Inter American democracy there is no room for distinctions and separations with respect to its applicability. Its affirmation and support are not isolated tasks or exclusive to any one state. When democracy is endangered in any one of them, the risk is to all. When it must be defended in one country, this is not an exclusively national duty, but is an American imperative. Associated by the effort of independence, democracy, and fatherland, their indestructible connection indicates also the inseparable link between country and continent, the teaching and civic heritage of the Liberators.

7. *Sovereignty and Democracy*

This concept of democracy as a principle of Inter American unity clarifies and corrects the warped sense of national sovereignty and the sovereignty of the state, giving them their authentic meaning. True *national sovereignty* cannot exist in the Americas without the basis of popular sovereignty, which is its democratic essence. The totalitarian states are characterized by the lack of this relationship of sovereignty, which is inseparable from democracy. The democratic concept of national sovereignty is based on the same general principle that rejects totalitarianism: the freedom of each nation and of each individual, limited only by the freedom of other nations and individuals. National and individual freedom cannot be absolute. Their relativity and limits are found in the freedom of others. This principle of sovereignty is totally inseparable from democracy. The freedom of the people cannot be suppressed by the sovereign state without destroying the juridical equilibrium of the democratic state. In the same way that the freedom of the individual is confined by the law when its excessive exercise would limit the freedom of others, the state cannot be so sovereign as to impinge upon the freedom of the existence of its citizens or that of other states. The violation of this principle, implying an attempt against democracy, makes defense necessary. For that reason, if all the American states must unite to defend their democratic existence from the foreign totalitarian menace, they must unite also to defend it from the domestic totalitarian menace.

8. Inter American Procedure of Democratic Defense

The previous postulates lead to the proposal of a procedure for the Inter American affirmation and defense of democracy:

a) With the democratic freedoms that guarantee the exercise of popular sovereignty as the norm of the national sovereignty established in all the constitutions of the republics of both Americas, an Inter American congress of the twenty-one states must consecrate those constitutional postulates as the juridical expression of the democracy of the New World, declaring their one and indivisible existence to be the basis of continental democratic sovereignty.

b) With all of the articles of the constitutions of the twenty-one states* of both Americas establishing the normative freedoms of democracy brought together, this Inter American congress will raise these constitutional principles to the category of "American international obligations." Thus, when they are not respected in any state, the others will have the right to demand their fulfillment in defense of the existence of democracy in the whole hemisphere.

c) With the interdependent principles of popular sovereignty and national sovereignty linked by these international American obligations, and these linked to continental sovereignty, the existence of which depends on respect for the democratic system, the pact of liberties of the twenty-one states of both Americas, based on the community of democratic postulates in their constitutions, would signify the true Magna Carta of democracy of the New World; and

d) Amplifying the resolution of the Inter American Conference of Havana, proposed by Brazil, which establishes the right of any American state to ask for the aid of the others in case its democratic stability is endangered by the political penetration of non-American ideas—or, in other words, by the work of the totalitarian fifth columns—the states of both Americas, maintaining that fundamental accord, will also establish the right of any state of the Americas to demand the aid of the rest when governments are proven to exist which, violating democratic freedoms, use their powers to impose non-American totalitarian procedures.

---

* Haya obviously leaves Canada out of consideration. It was not in the Pan American Union and played virtually no role in Inter American affairs, except for its relations with the United States.

9. *Creation of a Permanent Institution to Safeguard Democracy*

A corollary of these American international obligations for the maintenance and defense of the democratic principles will be the creation of a permanent intercontinental institution to enforce them. This institution can take the form of an American committee, with subcommittees, also permanent, in each state, constituted by representatives of the executive, legislative, judicial powers and of the great democratic political parties and universities if possible. Finally there will be delegates of the American committee, who could be diplomats and internationalists, especially designated.

This Inter American institution, the functions of which will be fixed by the congress of states establishing it, will have the character of an arbitrating tribunal for cases of differences in interpretation or of constitutional conflicts involving the fundamental, unalienable democratic freedoms of expression, religion, economy, and life without fear—the norms of popular American sovereignty. It would not affect or intervene in applied legislation, in accordance with the great principles of democracy, thus maintaining in this aspect, the complete autonomy of each state.

10. *Parallel Action for Solution of Inter American*
    Economic Problems

The affirmation of the postulate "democratic Inter Americanism without empire" implies the solution of the problem of economic relations between both Americas and that of the Indo or Latin American peoples amongst themselves. The Good Neighbor Policy has not resolved these problems, nor has it even suggested permanent formulas for possible solution, but it signifies the most important step which the United States has made in a century towards creating a favorable climate for ending all the differences between the two Americas.

In the economic order, the Good Neighbor Policy—based on a strict principle of non-intervention—has had as a healthy, immediate effect the total respect for the autonomy of the weaker American states on the part of the stronger. The application of this anti-interventionist policy has had its most expressive precedent in connection with the nationalization of the oil industry in Mexico and in Bolivia.

However, the Good Neighbor Policy with respect to non-intervention as it has been applied so far, presents the need of giving to its postulate of respect for the sovereignty and national freedom of each a sense of permanence and of equity avoiding all conflict in the future. In order to obtain this, keeping in mind the principle of "freedom only limited by justice," and the necessary bilateral nature of the resolution of any Inter American controversy, it is appropriate to seek formulas of democratic procedure which establish a system of living together and economic cooperation parallel to the political procedure of the affirmation and defense of democracy suggested above.

11. *Inter American Procedure for Economic Problem Solving*

The procedure for the solution of economic problems among the nations of this hemisphere must be inspired, as in those of a political order, in the coordination of two fundamental concepts: *sovereignty and interdependence*. The basis of a solid and harmonious Inter American association must be a clear delineation of the major economic zones of the New World: that of the United States, preponderantly industrial and financial, and that of the Indoamerican states, preponderantly agricultural and productive of raw materials. Both zones complement and need one another. To give their relations a system of cooperation without hegemony or imperialism is to apply to economic life the same democratic sense of freedom and justice that forms the basis of political life. For this proposition to be practicable, the great modifications which the end of the war will bring must be borne in mind and must be anticipated constructively. To this end, within the present objective conditions of both Americas, it is necessary to attempt a process of democratic action that tends to outline and resolve the essential questions of economic Inter Americanism, on the following bases:

a) The institution of an economic congress in each country of the Americas, made up of representatives of all of the living forces of its production, circulation, and consumption: capital and labor, industry, agriculture and commerce—national and *foreign* in the case of the Indoamerican countries—for the purpose of studying the economic reality and formulating a state plan of domestic action, with a view towards a cooperative Inter American program. These congresses, which would become councils or permanent consultative bodies, would propose to the governments of each country, the means convenient for fostering its economic-social organization and would amplify its activities through regional conferences.

b) An immediate corollary of the national economic congress and regional conferences would be the meeting of an Inter American grand economic congress, on the basis of the resolutions adopted in each country, with the function of coordinating Inter American activities and drawing up a general plan which would take into account the following reforms:

Delineation of the economic camps of the Americas and their functions of exchange and cooperation. Creation of an Indoamerican money which would not be valued like the dollar—the monetary symbol of a standard of living and labor not corresponding to our reality—but a currency stable in respect to the dollar, backed and guaranteed by gold, silver, and raw materials.

Organization of an Inter American Export-Import Bank in each state of the Americas with functions not limited only to granting isolated loans and credits. It would also be involved in the direction and guaranteeing of productive investment, establishing a system of guarantees and securities to maintain the stability of the currency, the effective extension of credits, and the encouragement of commerce between the United States and the Indoamerican states, and among the Indoamericans themselves. It would foster the establishment and organization of an Inter American customs union, stimulate the development of inexpensive means of communication and transportation, and seek the equalization of the duties on transit through the Panama Canal for all states of both Americas. Study of cooperativism, of protection and economic improvement for workers, of the technical improvement of agriculture and the maximum intercontinental consumption capacity of its products, should also be stressed. Complementary resolutions to avoid all the excesses of the economic hegemony of the most powerful, making the capital invested in each country a factor of cooperation with the state, and an instrument of progress, and not one of oppression or exploitation.

12. *Going Beyond Tutelar Pan Americanism to Democratic Inter Americanism*

The affirmation and defense of democracy in this hemisphere, through political and economic action organized in a parallel fashion, make it necessary to go beyond the present Pan Americanist philosophy, the historic mission of which as a tutelary organization has already been fulfilled. New methods must be found embodying a new American conception of cooperation and justice. We must learn to equate the importance of the national sovereignty of the states with the popular sovereignty of the citizens. From this equation arises the continental sovereignty of the Americas, whose *raison d'etre* is political and economic democracy.

Only when key democratic freedoms are exercised and harmonically guaranteed on all levels of the spiritual and material life of our peoples, both in the internal order of each country and in intercontinental relations, will it be possible for the individuals and the states of this hemisphere "to live without fear," and thus *democratic Inter Americanism without empire* will be the juridical standard of the New World, an open road, in turn, to the great future innovations.

PART EIGHT

Internationalization of the Panama Canal

FROM THE INCEPTION OF THE APRISTA MOVEMENT IN 1924, HAYA de la Torre has advocated the "internationalization" of the Panama Canal. It figured as one of the original five points of the Aprista program, and he wrote about it subsequently. To many, Haya's placing of this issue on a par with such questions as the nationalization of Latin American industries and opposition to imperialism may seem disproportionate. References to this issue in the foregoing sections, as well as these two selections, however, indicate why Haya has considered control of the canal to be a major issue in the relations between the two Americas.

Three aspects of the selections which follow are worthy of some comment. The first is that Haya addresses his arguments as much to the North Americans as to the Latin Americans. He advances the idea that the internationalization of the Panama Canal would be as much to the advantage of the United States as it would be to that of the Latin Americans. It would give the Latin Americans, he argues, a feeling that they have a stake in the defense of the canal, the key to the defense of the whole hemisphere; and that their cooperation in this endeavor is essential.

A second aspect is Haya's interpretation of the "internationalization" of the canal to mean "Inter Americanization" of it. In his earlier references to the question, it was by no means clear that he thought that the transfer of sovereignty over the canal should be from United States to the American republics as a whole. Rather, he seemed to favor a broader concept of internationalization.

And finally, Haya is at least as vehement in his opposition to unilateral Panamanian control of the canal as he is to the United States proprietorship of it. This position, of course, fits into Haya's general view that Latin America must ultimately unite in order to negotiate a modus vivendi on equal terms with the United States. It is obvious that Haya thinks that the internationalization of the canal can be a useful instrument for bringing about both of these eventualities.

I

SHOULD THE PANAMA CANAL
BE INTERNATIONALIZED?

IT IS KNOWN THAT ONE OF THE FIVE CONTINENTAL PRINCIPLES OF Aprismo is the internationalization of the Panama Canal as a necessary guarantee of independence and security for Indoamerica. What significance and implications are involved in the Aprista Plan to internationalize the Panama Canal? This is a question frequently asked in these times in which the defense of the canal is most important in the face of the threats of the totalitarian Axis brand of imperialism.

Some have opined that the Aprista postulate analyzed here is a remote ideal and is, therefore, a political principle that might as well be placed in the category of unlikely to be realized, romantic aspirations. Others, especially certain North American writers and diplomats who have expressed their opinions to me, feel the Aprista proposal concerning Panama is disquieting and dangerous from the point of view of harmony between the United States and Indoamerica. I think, however, that the internationalization of the Panama Canal, as Aprismo advocates it, has great importance for the future of the continent. Contrary to what those who lack the perspicacity and sense of historical dimension to appreciate our great problems may imagine— and in opposition to the North Americans who fear it is an obstacle to good neighborliness between our country and theirs—I maintain that the Aprista proposal on the canal is a very urgent matter and represents the most secure basis for a better Inter American relationship.

The Ramparts We Watch is the title of an interesting book written by an eminent miltary authority of the United States, Mr.

"Debe Internacionalizarse el Canal de Panama?" February, 1939, published in *La Defensa Continental*, pp. 100–109.

George Fielding Elliot (New York: Reynald & Hitchcock, 1938). A book designed to demonstrate the grave dangers to American security involved in the Axis plans for conquest, it judges with notable precision the great defensive problems of the continent. Mr. Elliot established that insofar as protection against any risk of "potential aggression" on the part of Germany, Italy, or Japan is concerned, the twenty states of Indoamerica "depend on the naval force of the United States."

In a study with much insight on the organization and power of the Yankee fleet ("Big Navy"), the New York magazine *Fortune* (March 1938, p. 55) has underscored that one of the determining factors, the principal and most imperious of them, for the build-up of the naval resources of the United States is the need to defend the Indoamerican countries—especially Argentina and Brazil—from a possible attack by Italy and Germany. Mr. Elliot's book sums up the reality of this danger and contends that "nor could the Argentine fleet, comparatively modern, reinforced by all of the naval power of Brazil and Chile, control the South American seas in the face of an attack either by Germany or Italy."

Elliot considers that "the key" to North American security is the Panama Canal. Although he says that it is "extremely improbable that secure transit through it could be interrupted by the action of the enemy," he believes that, given the "calamitous consequences" of a successful attack against Panama, it is necessary to adopt measures to deal with it. The most practical that the author suggests is the immediate opening of the Nicaragua Canal, which would cost approximately a billion dollars—"a considerable sum, certainly, but it is only a fraction of what would have to be spent . . . to build a new fleet."

One infers from reading the authoritative opinions of Mr. Elliot that, in spite of the security of the Panama Canal, it is not absolutely invulnerable. All near and distant defenses must be reinforced—the Azores and Bermuda are mentioned but Guantánamo Bay in Cuba is the principal advanced base. As a precaution the Nicaraguan way must be opened: an old project.

For their part, the spokesmen of the ambitious Axis powers have loudly and clearly proclaimed that the Panama Canal is an object of their designs. On the other hand, the United States is adopting very detailed and costly means to defend Panama.

Within this context, the diplomacy of Washington acts in some Indoamerican states. Cuba has already agreed to help the United

States in the defense of Panama, and it is expected that the United States will be able to count on the cooperation of Mexico, perhaps of Santo Domingo and Haiti, and certainly on the neighboring countries of Central and South America in a greater or lesser degree.

All this indicates that the military defense of the Panama Canal must be international, that is to say, "Inter American." In it must cooperate all the states of Indoamerica, for their own security, in proportion either to their nearness to the canal or to their power. Consequently—and this we must not forget—the United States needs Indoamerican material and moral help for the defense of the Panama Canal, and does not hide its desire that each one of our peoples be disposed to cooperate, in accordance with its abilities, for the success of this defense.

If this is true, there arises a question: If the military defense of Panama must have an international or Inter American character, why not reinforce it by giving the canal from now on also an international or Inter American character? It is an elemental maxim that one defends better what is one's own than what belongs to someone else. It is an elemental observation that no matter how much enthusiasm our peoples might have in the defense of democratic ideals, ideals championed by the great neighbor of the North, this enthusiasm would be more assured—an indispensable moral factor in case of war—if Indoamerica could defend in the Panama Canal something also materially belonging to it.

How to carry out that internationalization?

We shall clarify this: First the internationalization of the Panama Canal supposes—in Aprista terms—*Inter Americanization,* since Aprismo is an exclusively American political doctrine. It is worth saying that it signifies the participation of the states of the north and Indoamerica in the possession and control of the canal.

A book well worth reading, *L'Effort Democratique du Mexique,* by the brilliant French publicist René Marchand (Paris: 1938) has had a just impact in Europe. Chapter 18 in that book is dedicated to a summary and penetrating study of Aprismo. Monsieur Marchand sums up well the Aprista aspirations concerning the internationalization of the Panama Canal. He recalls the postulates of my book *El Antimperialismo y el Apra* (1928) in discussing this theme and its references to the administrative organization of the Suez Canal. He says, with reason, that the Aprista aspiration would obtain in Panama an internationalization similar to that of Suez, with the participation of the United States and of the states of Indoamerica.

Certainly, the aspiration is that the Panama Canal be international, or more exactly, Inter American, as the greatest guarantee for all our hemisphere against any foreign aggression and for the safeguarding of Indoamerica against any change of policy by the United States towards our peoples. Each state of this continent must form part of the administration of the Canal Zone and have the advantages and obligations of a co-proprietor. Insofar as the project of the construction of a Nicaraguan Canal is concerned, the North American government could form a vast company incorporated in all of the states of Indoamerica. Even if the North Americans were the largest stockholders, they would always give to their neighbors, with participation in the property, administration, and vigilance of the canal, as a concrete proof of security and of sincere and lasting "good neighborship."

Thus the internationalization or Inter Americanization of the canals of Panama and Nicaragua would be the best security of harmony between the forty-eight states of the North and the twenty of South America. The zones of each canal would cease to be foreign territories for Indoamericans and would be converted into real links of continental union. If some time, as a result of a democratic election, there should come to power in the United States the imperialist party of those who took Panama ("I took the Isthmus!"), and Yankee politics would retrogress to the ominous times of the occupations and bombardments of our undefended coasts, the Panama Canal—and that of Nicaragua later—would be the best outposts against any class of imperialism and a solid basis for insuring permanent good neighborliness.

It is not too much to repeat this: What is most important to the peoples of Indoamerica, insofar as the Good Neighbor Policy is concerned, is an assurance that that policy will continue, and to that end to take the possible precautions, taking into account the *not improbable* case that the new Rooseveltian policy will be substituted by the old Rooseveltian policy which is—as we cannot forget—its absolute negation.

It is worth noting in passing, once again, that those who think that we can abandon ourselves in an idyllic love of the good neighbor as if it were eternal, give the worst possible advice to our peoples. Even though it is true that we must cooperate today in the formation of a defensive democratic front in union with the great North American republic, it is also important to remember that imperialism is fundamentally economic, and that it is our prime duty to adopt all the precautions necessary for insuring our own independence. The best road to this is Indoamerican unity. One of the firmest points of support to achieve this objective would be the internationalization of the Panama Canal.

It is not the point of this article to insist on the demonstration of a thesis which I consider irrefutable: the convenience for the United States of an Indoamerican unity as the only way for a better continental economic and political organization. However, I shall present some arguments along those lines from the point of view of North American political interests.

First we must think that the internationalization of the Panama Canal could be used as a pretext and banner to be offered by the Axis Powers to the Indoamerican countries in return for a benevolent neutrality, in case of a war with the United States. It would not be surprising if, on the basis of a more ample plan of internationalization, the fascist aggressors would promise joint control of Panama to the states of Indoamerica. More than one German periodical has already announced clearly this possibility. Even if it were only a kind of "high demagogy"—in which the totalitarians are very skillful—the promise of such a great advantage without having to defend the canal would always carry more weight in our countries than would the obligation to defend something without gaining anything. The latter is, so far, what the United States asks of us.

On the other hand, if the canal were Inter Americanized, aggression against Panama would no longer constitute an attack only upon the United States, but an aggression against all the countries of this hemisphere, as co-proprietors of the canal. There would in that case be no basis for the "neutrality" of any Indoamerican state. Nor would there be any excuse for not participating in hostilities affecting "the key" to North American defense. . . . The internationalization of the Panama Canal would thus result in an excellent means of defending it. Each attack against it would be an offense against twenty-one countries, and the aggressors could not count on any ally on this side of the world.

Furthermore, what would the United States lose in having as partners in the sovereignty and control of the Panama Canal the united states of Indoamerica? Only a few million dollars distributed among new stockholders, compensated by a good administrative organization and protection in which all of the governments, all of the fleets, and all of the armies of the continent would participate in the Canal Zone. Thus this would become a true fortress of the security of the Americas and of the fraternity of all its peoples.

It is not too much to suppose that if Mr. Hull had brought to the Eighth Pan American Conference* a project for a continental military alliance based on something as concrete as the Inter Americanization of the Panama Canal, his proposals for a defensive alliance would not have failed. Because the Indoamerican States were suspicious of an unconditional and compromising link with the United States, they denied, not without some reason, an alliance implying links of dependence without practical compensations. In reality, Mr. Hull's project was based on a fear of European aggression that many of our diplomats—sincerely or not—look upon as an exaggerated alarm. The peoples of Indoamerica still hold the conviction that in spite of the good will which inspires the policy of President Roosevelt, there exists still, independent of that good will, the awesome expansive force of the North American economic system. If, however, as an effective barrier to all later imperialist risk, Mr. Hull had suggested, along with the need to defend continental security, that of securing the canal, by means of full collective intervention, in peace and in war, then Pan Americanism would have taken on a new more egalitarian and better guaranteed aspect.

Before announcing to us the imminence of an aggression of the totalitarian international—a real danger which some politicians of anti-democratic tendencies of our countries underestimate, believing that it involves only North America—he could have suggested the Inter Americanization of the Panama Canal as the securest means of defending it. While all of the technical difficulties involved were being worked out, the formal promise in the form of a resolution proposed by the delegation of the United States would have been sufficient. This would have constituted an evident proof that Pan American policy does not presume the imperial preponderance of the United States, demanding everything, offering nothing; but rather the loyal proposal of sharing with Indoamerica proportional sovereignty of that which we must all defend.

On the basis of the Inter Americanization of the Panama Canal,

---

* This conference met in Lima in 1938.

there could proceed the plan of renting or lending North American warships to our countries, which has been so many times suggested by Washington, or the project of President [Lazaro] Cárdenas [of Mexico], to constitute a continental fleet. But to ask military cooperation without the mutual understanding that mitigates the risks of an unconditional alliance of weak countries with the strongest nation on the planet, is very far-fetched.

In the great Bolivarian project of the unity of America, Panama must be its center. With the Inter Americanization of the canal, the ideal of the Liberator would be surpassed, because it would be carried out from that important geographical knot linking the United States of the North and the disunited states of the South. For that reason, Aprismo maintains the fourth point of its continental program as an American political imperative, so that good neighborliness and democracy will acquire a practical, constructive, and lasting anti-imperialist dynamism.

II

COMMON DEFENSE, COMMON CANAL

THE EUROPEAN PRESS HAS REVEALED THE NEWS OF THE JOINT maneuvers by the air forces of various Latin American states, in coordination with those of the United States, for the defense of the Panama Canal. Again there has appeared, full of logic, the argument of the internationalization—under the joint control of both Americas—of that important interoceanic route which if we have the obligation to defend, we all have the right to possess.

Almost simultaneously, however, with the information on these maneuvers, the daily newspapers of Europe have published the news of an unusual and ostentatious visit by the Minister of Foreign Affairs of Panama to the dictator Nasser, with the purpose of identifying the Egyptian problem of the Suez Canal with the proposal of the Panamanian ultrapatriots to "nationalize," under their exclusive dominion, the canal connecting the Atlantic and the Pacific in our hemisphere. All of this has brought forth the initiative of the North American senator from the State of Oregon, Mr. Wayne Morse, for the intercontinental "regionalization" of the Panama Canal under the control of the Organization of American States—OAS. This project is backed by another member of the Senate in Washington—Mr. Aiken—who advocates the internationalization of that route under the authority of the United Nations. At the same time President Eisenhower, in a hurried declaration, frankly expressed his opposition to such plans because the canal was already "nationalized" by the United States since the imperialist Mr. Theodore Roosevelt declared without any circumlocutions in 1903: "I took the Isthmus."

"Defensa Común, Canal Común," March, 1960, published in *Pensamiento Político de Haya de la Torre,* Volume I.

In reality, the extreme North American and Panamanian nationalists agree that the canal should belong exclusively to one American republic, and to not more than one: either to the United States, or to Panama. The latter on the basis of the fact that the canal exists in its territory—although alienated—and the former claiming full property rights because they were the builders and because, in being so, they created the Panamanian Republic.

The history of the Panama Canal is quite well known. The slogan of its republic, withdrawn from Colombia, is "Pro mundi beneficio." For the United States, with its extensive coasts, that passage between the two oceans is vital. The other passage, the natural one, which Magellan discovered, is distant and stormy, although Argentina and Chile internationalized and disarmed it by a treaty signed in and respected since 1898. But the Panama Canal is also comparatively vital for all of the other states of America, especially for Colombia, Mexico, and the Central American republics, which also have coasts on both the Atlantic and the Pacific. For the peoples of the west coast of South America, the most rapid maritime communication with Europe is the Panama Canal; and it is what unites all the Caribbean ports with the north and the Indoamericans of the western part of the hemisphere.

A ship leaving the Colombian port of Buenaventura with its destination the Colombian Amazonian port of Leticia, or another going from the Peruvian port of Callao en route to the Peruvian Amazonian port of Iquitos, needs to cross through the Panama Canal. However, this is also true of those leaving New York, Boston, or New Orleans, Havana, La Guaira, Veracruz, or Cartagena carrying cargos and people for Guayaquil, Callao, Arica, or Valparaíso. Panama is not a Suez, in spite of the enormous importance of the latter canal which links Europe with Asia and part of Africa. Panama is an internal route of American maritime relations, as well as being a more direct passage between other continents.

On the other hand, however, with the confederation of Arab republics,* Suez has ceased to be an exclusively Egyptian canal. Thus the purely national ownership of Suez, in addition to the fact that the juridical conception that interoceanic links must belong to a single

---

* Apparently a reference to the temporary joining of Egypt and Syria to form the United Arab Republic, which was established in 1958 but from which Syria withdrew in 1961.

and absolute owner, is already obsolete. The Treaty of Versailles internationalized the Kiel Canal, which is today open to all European traffic. Russia, from the days of Catherine the Great to those of Stalin has fought for the right of free transit through the straights of the Bosporus and Dardanelles. It would be inconceivable for the powerful Union of Soviets to accept a situation where its only exit to the Black Sea is governed by the will of the Turks.

Neither the large North American republic nor the small one of Panama has the right to declare itself master and owner of a canal which is the greatest artery for the economic life of all of the American peoples. Although no one is ignorant of the preferential rights of the Panamanians in this passage between two seas, the passageway cannot be subject to the changing, capricious decision of a single government. Expecially, when there are no guarantees against the rise to power of a criollo dictator, more violent and nationalistic than Nasser—let us call him a commander of police Remon*—who at his pleasure could open or shut its locks according to his personal sympathies or convenience.

The problem of Panama is a continental collective responsibility, and an important one. The intransigent posture of the United States, in not permitting Inter American co-participation in the administration and control of the canal, is as anti-American and as negative to an effective good neighborliness as would be turning over the complete dominion and destiny of that interoceanic route to absolute Panamanian dominion. Continental solidarity, advances in the planning of the Latin or Indoamerican common market, the possibility of a stable order without hegemony, of "democratic Inter Americanism without empire"—and thus without imperialism—makes it clear that the only just solution to the problem created by the appropriation of the Panama Canal by the U.S.A. is its internationalization under the joint authority of the twenty-one American republics.

Above all, we must keep in mind that the future of our America carries us towards realization of the Bolivarian dream of uniting it, so that unity assures true emancipation and greatness. Nor should we forget that in Bolívar's foresighted dream—hitherto betrayed— Panama was its center and its link.

---

* This reference is to Colonel Jose Antonio Remon, chief of National Police, elected President of Panama in 1952. He was assassinated in 1955.

PART NINE

The Word Indoamerica

FOR OVER FORTY YEARS HAYA DE LA TORRE HAS ARGUED IN FAVOR OF adopting the word *Indoamerica* to designate that part of the Western Hemisphere which is more commonly called *Latin America*. Although the Apristas loyally use this phrase, this is not one of Haya's theories and ideas that have had a notable impact on the political movements and peoples outside of Peru. Perhaps this is partially due to the fact that not all of the countries south of the United States are Indoamerican. Costa Rica, Chile, Colombia, Brazil, Argentina, Uruguay, Haiti, and Cuba (as Haya mentions) are almost devoid of an Indian population, and the same is true of the Dominican Republic and Venezuela. In these countries, the Indian population is either a small minority, confined largely to isolated areas or even reservations, or is almost non-existent.

Haya's preference for the term *Indoamerican* undoubtedly derives from his Peruvian citizenship and his own liberal intermixture of Indian ancestry, although his family is one of the most aristocratic "white" families in that nation. It is only in the Andean countries of Peru, Ecuador, and Bolivia, and in Guatemala in Central America, that the Indians constitute a majority of the population. In Mexico, Chile, and several Central American nations, there is a general intermixture of people of European and Indian ancestry, but even there the Indian cultural influence has been largely overcome by the European.

Even though Haya's attempt to popularize the use of the title Indoamerica for his part of the world has had relatively little success, there are two reasons for presenting here a few selections on this topic. Most importantly, the idea constitutes an integral part of his

political philosophy, but also, in his arguments on this subject, he
recapitulates many of his more general ideas on the need for the
non-Yankee parts of the Western Hemisphere to seek their own
solutions to their own problems.

I

WE ARE NOT ASHAMED TO
CALL OURSELVES INDOAMERICANS

FOR SEVERAL YEARS I HAVE BEEN CARRYING ON A BATTLE OVER "THE
Question of the Name." What, finally, should our continent—the
unity of which is clear to everyone, American or not, who travels
over it, who observes it, who explores its profound and disquieting
reality of varied aspects—be called? I return now to this subject,
which I consider important, because it is not only a dispute over
words, but a clarifying analysis of concepts.

In a series of lectures, about some of our continental problems,
which I offered eleven years ago at the University of Mexico, I took
as my initial theme for discussion the name which in justice—we say
historical-social justice—corresponds to this side of the New World
commencing on the Rio Bravo and going to the straits of Magellan.
Then, in examining the various names applied to our "Greater
Fatherland," I concluded that all of them not only had a significance,
but represented and defined a stage in our history. Therefore, they
must not be confused.

In effect, our divided "nation of twenty states" has been called
principally *Hispano* (or *Ibero*) *America, Latin America,* and *Indoamerica,* although other possibilities were *Eurindia, Indoiberia,* and
Indolatina. But the three best known names are not only mere continental denominations, *continental* not only in their *geographical*
sense but also in their *content.* Each one of these names has a historical, ethnic, spiritual, and political meaning. Consequently, those
who maintain that we must call ourselves *Hispano* or *Ibero Americans*

"No Nos Avergoncemos de Llamarnos Indoamericanos," 1938, published in
La Defensa Continental, pp. 50–64.

urge the prevalence of Spain and Portugal, of the Iberic as the tradition and as the norm, and imply that our true history began only with the European conquest of the sixteenth century. The partisans of the name *Latin America,* base themselves on the Latin trunk of the Iberic races and the Spanish and Portuguese languages. They recognize at the same time the fact of the powerful spiritual influence of the Renaissance and particularly the French culture—a vigorous influence on our peoples—and take into account the juridical and political value of the democratic theories, which inspired in the Encyclopedia and the great Revolution of 1789, gave ideological direction to the republican victory of the Independence.

On the other hand, those who wish us to lose ourselves in the great American empire of the North, propose the simple name *America,* or by its contemporary equivalent, *Pan America*—naturally, they are obsequious spokesmen for the elastic *Pan Americanism* which Washington rules and Wall Street often influences.

After a detailed inquiry, I reaffirm my conclusions of eleven years ago: The term *Hispano* or *Ibero America,* and its derivatives *Hispano* or *Ibero American* or *Hispano* or *Ibero Americanism* correspond to the colonial epoch. They refer to an exclusively Spanish America—or Portuguese when the word Iberian is involved—or they imply ignorance of the influences subsequent to the colonial period, which have determined new aspects of our continent.

The terms *Latin America* and its derivative *Latin Americanism* are more ample, more modern. They correspond, chronologically, to the nineteenth century. They include all of the Spanish and Portuguese of our history, without excluding the African contribution because they incorporate Haiti, which speaks French, in our great continental family.

But the term *Indoamerica* is the most inclusive, going much further, entering more deeply into the totality of our peoples. It includes the prehistoric, the Iberian, the Latin, and the Negro, the mestizo, and the "cosmic"—we say, remembering José Vasconcelos*—maintaining its validity as a term for the future. It is a term both "very ancient and very modern," corresponding exactly to the present revolutionary stage of our America, scarcely begun in Mexico.

---

* José Vasconcelos was the Mexican Minister of Education in the early 1920s. Discussing the uniqueness of the Latin American peoples, he referred to them as a "cosmic race."

Repeating my conclusions of 1928, I maintain that "Hispano or Americanism" equals imperialism; and "Indoamericanism" equals revolution, an affirmation or synthesis of the fecund and decisive period of history in which we live.

It is good to review some orignal references: Ricardo Palma, the celebrated Peruvian traditionalist, maintains that "the American voice is exclusively American, and not a derivative of the first name of the major pilot of the Indies, *Albericus Vespucio*. The argument is based on the verity that "America or Americ is the name of a place in Nicaragua and designates a chain of mountains of the province of Chontales," and the traditionalist deduces and presumes that although Columbus doesn't mention the new word in the *lettera rarissima* of his fourth voyage "it is more than probable that he verbally transmitted it to his comrades, interpreting it as indicating that gold came from the region called America by the Nicaraguans. (*Tradiciones Peruanas,* Vol. 1, "Una carta de Indias," Calpe.)

However, the theory most accepted today as we all know, is that which attributes to the German geographer Martin Waldseemuller, Professor of the Lorraine University of St. Die, the primacy in naming America, in his celebrated *Cosmographie Introductio* of 1507. Humboldt sustains this in his *Examen Critique de l'Histoire de la Geographie du Nouveau Continent (*1837), offering important details about the reasons of Hylaconylus, Latin name of the geographer, for believing mistakenly, that the New World should be called America "because Americanus discovered it."

It appears, thus, that America, discovered by mistake during the search for a new road to Asia, was also named by mistake. It appears that this pattern of mistakes insofar as rediscovering it and renaming it—particularly that part which is ours—prevails even today. Because "America" in the universal language of these days is the word applied to North America. *American* refers to the United States or to the Yankee for the rest of the world. The great republic of the North has for its official title the *United States of America.* Partly because of our shame and partly as a revealing indication of our colonial complex of inferiority, a good number of our people call the citizens and things of that country *American,* forgetting that we are also sons of America, and thus Americans, as much so as are our blonde and Negro "cousins" of the North.

Mistakenly also they have called "South America," the area which extends from Mexico to Patagonia. But this term, used by the delegates to the Congress of Tucumán in their declaration of 1816, and also by [Juan Bautista] Alberdi, [Domingo Fausto] Sarmiento* and other illustrious Argentines of the last century, is anti-geographical.

In a final note of his interesting book *Latin America, Its Place in the World Life* (1937), Professor Samuel Guy Inman of Columbia University correctly writes: "The dispute about what to call the people of South America when they are referred to as a group, is already old." Then after a detailed analysis of the "Question of the Name," in which he deals with the terms *Hispano America, Latin America,* and *Indoamerica,* words he uses in the text of his work almost indistinguishably, he recognizes that for his country the word combination *Latin America* is the most usual and logical, and without doubt, the most accessible to the English language.

Certainly, from the North American point of view, *Latin America* is a Saxonized and quite precise way to name it as a continental nation, while we do not adopt it definitively as ours. It would be forced and retrograde to call us *Spanish-America* or *Hispanic* or *Ibero America,* because the two first names exclude one republic of the importance of Brazil, which is not "Spanish," while the last excludes Haiti which is not Iberian, because it is Negro and speaks French; and yet it is—because it is Negro and a small, suffering, and heroic defender of the liberating enterprise of Bolívar—our sister people.

There is something more, however, in the debate of names: in these times of plans of conquest and penetration of the European internationals into our countries, political motivations predominate. Thus, as the spokesmen of the imperialism of the United States are all ardent Pan Americanists and dream perhaps of a vast American empire from pole to pole, also the Spanish imperialists and conservatives are all violent Hispano Americanists. Even many who are revolutionaries and leftists in Spain, don't hesitate to call us *Hispano America.* For its part, the fascist-racist Axis has found in Hispano Americanism a good historical reason to call us their "empire," and so our continent is designated in recent booklets and pamphlets of the "Falange" and other reactionary Spanish organizations at the service of the Fascists. Within each of our countries the subjects of Franco, his agents and propagandists, are attempting to "Hispano

---

* Alberdi and Sarmiento were leading figures among the group of Argentine intellectuals who fought against the dictatorship of Juan Manuel de Rosas (1829–1852). Sarmiento served as President of Argentina from 1868–1874.

Americanize" us in the same demeaning way in which the foreign invaders attempt the fascist brutalization of the indomitable Spanish people in the land of the mistaken "caudillo."

In Italy the Roman brand of fascism—in spite of its support of the imperial plans of Franco as instrument and vehicle for its dream of the "Ethiopization" of the New World—still continues because of Roman tradition to use the term *Latin America* as our label. It is also used, in hope of cultural expansion, in France, and because of the facility of expression, in England. In Germany, the Nazi faction of fascism—tactically using for its ambitions of expansion in America the useful vehicles of Spain and Portugal—calls us *Ibero Americans;* and this is the official name of its famous Institute of Berlin, formed around a library given by the Argentinian professor Don Ernesto Quesada.

Even though, curiously enough, there are also on the Spanish Republican side no lack of writers who "Hispano Americanize" us, it is important to note that this designation for us is not popular in the Peninsula. It must be said that it is not the populace, but the more or less intellectual elites and aristocracies who do this. The Spanish people name our "Great Fatherland" simply *America* as formerly they called it *Indias.* For that reason *Indoamerica* has a Spanish flavor, being a word constructed from two forms of distinguishing us, popular throughout the centuries: *Indians* and *Americans.* The creole who returns to Spain—it is not too much to remember this—is popularly called *Indian.*

The political reason doesn't elude those of us who advocate the name *Indoamerica.* On the contrary, we underscore and exalt it as being singularly significant. The name of our continent is not only limited to semantics. In a vital sense, it is a question of history. But it is worth repeating that this new word of the Aprista lexicon has also its undisputable defenses in what we may call, with elevated political interpretation, "historical semantics."

It is, as I indicate above, the best amalgamation of those who maintain the thesis of Hispano Americanism and the antithesis of Latin Americanism. The concept Indoamerica completes the trio, because in being a synthesis, it incorporates all the reasons for the other two—adduced in this polemic—and determines and points out to our continent, its social, ethnic, political, and unique linguistic content.

The simplest and most common objection to the word *Indo-*

america, and its derivatives *Indoamerican* and *Indoamericanism,* is the argument that in some of our countries the pure Indians are a minority, as is the case in Costa Rica, Cuba, Colombia, Chile, Brazil, Uruguay, and Argentina. The answer to this is not difficult. Considering Indoamerica as a whole—and the reason for the common name —the numerical value of the Indian is majoritarian. We are not dealing only with the pure Indian, but also with the mestizo. It cannot be denied that our continent, in spite of its cities and sporadic white islands is, in quantity and quality a mixture of Indian and white, and to a lesser degree, of Indian and Negro. . . .

But it is not the numbers, the census data, the statistical index, that supports Indoamericanism as a name and as an idea. It is something much deeper and more teluric, more concealed and living: It is in our spirit and our culture that there flourishes a reserve of strength emanating from the remote ancestry of the old races in these ancient lands. Germán Arciniegas, a brilliant Indoamerican writer— from Colombia where the pure-blooded Indians are a minority—has written in his beautiful book *America, Tierra Firma* (1938) these enduring words of truth:

> Our culture is not European. We are denying it in the soul every instant. The cities which perished under the empire of the conqueror are very dead. The idols are broken and the Mexican libraries are burned. But we carry within a haunting *negation.* We are displaying it each time we examine our conscience, and it not possible for us to suppress the American part of our spirit no matter how silent it seems. On the other hand, it is a matter of conscience not to practice a kind of surrender which would place us as servile imitators of a civilization which satisfies us in many ways, but which in others makes us disconsolate and discouraged.

These are the words of a young writer who does not yet use the word Indoamerica, but who does brilliantly and indirectly establish its defense. They say much about the cultural reasons for which our points of view coincide. The Indian is within us. André Sigfried has seen it well, although partially, in his *Amerique Latine* (1933), in noting that "the basis of the population is *red,* whether in Bolivia, in Peru, in Venezuela, or even in Chile, where the *roto,* a mestizo, cannot be considered in any way as belonging to the white race, because in spite of the claims to the contrary, the traveller who knows how to see can make no mistake, because he finds himself in the presence of an Indian." Although Siegfried talks of a "white America" in over estimated opposition to the red, he is quite correct in recognizing and proving the importance and influence of the Indian in our blood and in our mind.

With more penetration and greatness, Count Keyserling goes deeper in the much discussed and suggestive *Meditations* which are for their content and their thesis Indoamerican and not "South American," as he improperly entitled them. In Keyserling we, who feel below the lack of pigment the beating of an Indian heart, see many truths. They are painful sometimes, because they cruelly strip off the veneer of the Europeanizers to show them the profound depth of their Indoamericanism. However, although with less originality than might be supposed—if we make the examination of conscience which Arciniegas asks—Keyserling discovers in us the deep psychological secrets which everyone experiences in varying degrees, and hides and dissimulates better with the prodigal varnish of our habitual tendency to lie to ourselves.

Keyserling has made not a few Argentinian *porteños* angry by pointing out their Indian marrow. The colonialist intellectual groups of Buenos Aires have felt offended—those, who look unceasingly to Mother Europe and live attentive to her merest gesture so as to follow it. This indignation, in spite of being high-sounding, is artificial and snobbish. The Buenos Aires colonial elites and their literary flunkies—arrogant like good criollos—consider it ridiculous, abominable, and even indecent that a blue-blooded German gentleman should disclose the "Indian sadness" beneath their Parisian makeup and their bourgeois arts of dress. But the "Indian sadness" is in the Pampa—pampa, a Quechua name!—and even further within the true Indoamerican is Argentina, with its backbone in the Andes and lands attached to those that were the communitarian property of the Incas. "Indian sadness" is alive and profound like the bronze mark on so many Argentinian *cholos* whom I have seen in their villages of Humahuaca, of Jujuy, of Salta, and of Tucumán, where the imperial Quechua language still says its word as unifier of peoples in remote echoes which appear eternal.

Keyserling makes three assertions on the teluric transcendence of the Indian in our continent. He says that Indoamerican sadness "has nothing of the tragic." He demonstrates that in these peoples

---

* Residents of Buenos Aires.

"we encounter today indications of an autochtonous and original conception of the Universe." He recognizes that precisely the intellectualness and passivity of Indoamerica would confer on it in this juncture of history a transcendental mission for humanity, "because there already exist the conditions" and "the Indoamerican future appears assured." He deduces that "it is possible that the next renaissance of the spirit will arise in Indoamerica for the salvation of all men and for their redemption from brutality."

These are stimulating conclusions that are not based on a Europeanizing or colonial conception of Indoamerica, and that recognize the indestructible unity in our indigenous and teluric roots. Because our Indoamerican sadness, Keyserling says in perhaps the sharpest and most realistic of his theses, "contains more value than all the optimism of the North Americans and than all of the idealism of modern Europe."

That *optimistic sadness*—painful and ardent goad of our revolution—rises already cleansed and living in what there is of pure art in Indoamerica. It degenerates and is disfigured in the bad cabaret tangos and in all that poor jazz of colonial music which sullies the sadness with morbid sexual anguish. But it is strong and pure in the virile Quechua rhythms that do not sing of slavery—the *Kachampa* of Cuzco, for example—in more than one sweet and beautiful Maya song which I heard in Yucatán; in the mestizo music of contented peasants, such as the *pericón* and *santiaguenas* of the Gauchos, in the vibrant *zambas, zambacuecas,* or *zamacuecas* or *marineras* which with slight variations of emphasis are found in the Plata region, Chile, Bolivia, and Peru; in the *pasillos* of Ecuador and Colombia; in not a few Brazilian, Central American, and West Indian songs, and in the magnificent popular music of Mexico, full of grace and of vigorous resonance. This same optimistic Indian sadness arises also in the genial painting of [Diego] Rivera, [José] Orozco* and their disciples, and in the authentic Indoamerican rural poetry, ironic and agile, in the style of *Martin Fierro*,† because it is both sad and full of irony at the same time and is of firm Indian origin. In Quechua we have incomparable expressions of it.

---

* Rivera and Orozco were two of the principal figures in the great group of Mexican revolutionary painters which appeared in the 1920s.

† *Martin Fierro* is the great epic of the Argentine Gaucho written by José Hernandez in 1872.

For all of this announcing the spirit of what our great fatherland must be, *Indoamerican* is a name of total recovery, of an emancipating proclamation of national definition. Art has anticipated its
arrival, but through it is heralded the rebellion and the secret optimism which are bringing about a fundamental transformation of
our peoples.

That is the sense and the historical justification of the expression
Indoamerica. This involves and synthesizes, as has been said, all of
the rest: this continent was called *Indias* during three centuries by
our conquerors, and *America* is as European a name as ours. It is
Latin for Vespucio, or Hylacomylus, and for the Spaniards and Portuguese who accepted it. The word *Indoamerica*—we repeat—is in
any case of Iberian origin and is therefore of Latin extraction at the
same time it conserves the true denomination of the discoverer and
of its first defender, [Bartolome] Las Casas.** It also preserves the
same names which the basic institutions of the viceroyalty used, but
it goes beyond those allusions to the modern sense of the Indian
and of our America which is daily being transformed and defined in
the crucible of a new race and a new culture.

We are not ashamed then, to call ourselves Indoamericans. We
recognize that in the heart of our continent, as in each of our hearts,
is the Indian, and it must influence us even though it no longer shows
on the surface and sons refuse to admit it. Nevertheless, there is alive
what Arciniegas beautifully calls "la negacion agazapada," [the hidden negation], and it must flower in the fullness of its vitality some
day. Many times, voyaging through our lands, and hearing the speech
of our peoples, I have thought that the Indian is impressed upon us
even in the very intonations of our speech. The man of Mexico,
depending upon his region, gives Spanish an accent which is easily
perceived and distinguished when one also hears the Indian dialects
spoken there. Once I observed that there is a *Yankee* tone in the
slowness of the Aztec or Zapotec Northerns, in that of those of the
plateau and of the Maya-Quiche of Yucatán and Guatemala. Would
the Chibchas not speak with the Colombian cadence, and the Arau-
canians with the Chilean "sing-song?" The Andeans of Ecuador,
Peru, Bolivia, and the Argentine mountains have similar Quechua
inflections. The mochika "sing-song" is that of the coastal inhabitants

---

** De Las Casas was first bishop of Chiapas, Mexico, and carried on a long
campaign against the enslavement of the Indians.

of Northern Peru, and Guaraní is the intonation of Paraguay and
the Chaco. Where the Negro left his imprint, when he substituted
for the Indian, there is a peculiar manner of speaking the language
of Castile. We in Indoamerica do not speak, certainly, the Spanish
of Spain. We speak it with different tones. It is further worth observing that no one can hear his own accent. In each region of America
they say that the foreigners "sing."

The Indian "sings" in the phonetics of all, but we can only
recognize it in the foreigners! To know ourselves is perhaps the first
step towards what many times has been called the *rediscovery* of
Indoamerica.

II

THE POLITICAL SIGNIFICANCE
OF THE NAME

With respect to a prologue by D. Luis Jiménez de Asua: For some time I have owed to this illustrious intellectual of the new Spain a public response. In his book *Politica, Figuras y Paisajes,* a work full of interest and novelty, he has generously mentioned me. Now he does so again in the prologue to a book which I have just finished reading with great interest, written by Don Eduardo Bezo, under the title of *La Libertad de América.* It is in the third part of the prologue, a model of brevity and clarity, that Jiménez de Asua refers to "the three expressions which sum up the possible policy of the peoples of Spanish origin," without indicating if he includes generically in these peoples, Brazil and Haiti: "Pan Americanism, Latin Americanism and Hispano Americanism." Asua says, following this order, that the first represents "the imperialist menace of North America," the second "is of French and Italian invention and attempts to merge us in that imprecise kinship which the French revive when it is convenient to them and bury when it bothers them." The third "is a vague and sentimental expression and like every attitude of the heart, is felt or isn't." Then he refers, mentioning me, to our Aprista expression *Indoamerica,* which according to him "would be difficult to justify in countries like Cuba, in which the Indian no longer exists, or like Argentina, where he is not taken into account and is seldom thought of." For this reason, he doesn't feel inclined to accept this "partial word."

This question of the name of our America has, to my mind,

"Significado Politico del Nombre," 1930, published in *Construyendo el Aprismo.*

special interest. I don't believe in any of the expressions now used whether newly coined or of colonial origin. It seems to me that each of them corresponds to an epoch and form of political and social evolution of America, and has a historical content. . . .

It is true that the terms coexist: Some use Pan Americanism; others Hispano Americanism, others Latin Americanism, and still others Indoamericanism. But this usage has a social and economic significance. Still today, in our America, there also coexist and are juxtaposed various periods of historical evolution which succeed one another in other continents. In America we have simultaneously living together all forms of social organization and all grades of economic evolution, within the frontiers of our continent, and even within the frontiers of each country: savagery, barbarism, and civilization; primeval communal agriculture, feudalism, handicrafts, industrialism, and imperialism. Indians who have never known the use of a wheel, see crossing their mountain skies the airplane. The fancy young man of Buenos Aires, who dresses in fashion with London-tailored clothes, has as his compatriot and fellow citizen the half-clothed Indian of the Chaco. The same thing is true in Peru, in Mexico, in Colombia, and in Central America.

This lack of common definition, this contradiction, this historical juxtaposition, if these terms are adequate, form in large part the dialectic of our learning process. Our America has been and is the field of invasions, as Europe was. Since the immigrations and transmigrations of the pre-Colombian period, from Asia, from Indo-Europe and Oceania, from north to south and vice-versa, our America has been the field of unmistakable invasions and conquests. Three centuries of Spanish domination represent in our history a long period which appears to us as almost forever because it is so recent. But it is shorter in time than the eight centuries of the Arab domination of Spain, for example. The Arabs left Spain a great civilization and established a southern race or mixture, leaving an imprint in word derivations of about ten percent, according to the philogists. The Arabs have the right to the expression of the gratitude of the Spaniards in a new name, Ibero-Arabia or something of the sort. But the Arab invasion was an invasion, and historically determined, a movement of independence in which many Hispano-Arabs fought to free themselves from the tutelage of the ancestors of their race. A religious factor entered into this struggle and was less defined than the Indian struggle against Spain. In both conquests or "reconquests," however, can be seen the economic causes which are the root of all great historical phenomena.

In our America, after suffering the invasion of feudalism and mercantilism, with the Spanish conquest, we see it suffering the invasion of industrialism, or of capitalism, begun by England, particularly, and intensified and surpassed by North America afterwards. It could be that the new invasion will be less prolonged in this accelerated epoch, but it is an invasion with its own characteristics, with its own policy and with a formidable social impact. The future alone knows whether we shall suffer others. Beneath these outside conquering influences, there persists an economic fact: the object of the conquest is always wealth and this wealth is always worked principally by the Indian or his descendant. Qualified experts calculate the number of Indians of our America at seventy-five million; that is to say seventy-five percent, approximately, of our total population. Those Indians, with their own traditions, with their own languages, with their own pains and aspirations, with their own essential being, constitute in their immense majority the labor force, the "productivity," the hand creating the riches. Until now, from the social point of view and within the relativity of all things, that is what is eternal in America.

I do not agree with Count Keyserling's total philosophy, but he has brought together in his analysis of the United States, the observations of the Swiss psychoanalyst Jung, that expert investigator of the subconscious life of the Yankee. For those of us familiar with North America, there is something singularly interesting in the observations of Keyserling and in the studies of Jung. Both recognize the power of the conquered Indian environment over the conquering peoples, "to the point of putting them at the level of the aborigines." For this reason, says Jung with Keyserling's approval, "the national idea of North America is almost purely Indian, as is shown by the North American image or representation of the hero, the North American idea of sports, which are Indian and not European, as is also their tenacity and concentration on a determined objective." This influence, which I have noted for some time, I have seen defined and made concrete in Keyserling's study and in Jung's analysis, presented to the Preudencia School of Darmstadt. In 1927, speaking at the Institute of Political Science of Williamstown, Massachusetts, I stated similar concepts in a speech on the Central and South American Indian. The *New York Times* published a synthesis of these ideas.

For me the North American Indian head engraved on some of the money of the United States has always been more than a simple decoration, it is a symbol. The influence of the Indian on the white man of the Americas is indisputable. The Indian subconscious lives in all of us. Between the North American and the Englishmen there exists, in my opinion, greater psychological differences than between the North American and the redskin. I won't mention, for example, the case of the Vice President of the United States, grandson of Saxons and Indians.* Thus it is in our America. It doesn't matter that the Indian no longer exists in Cuba or that "he is seldom thought of in Argentina," an idea which Jiménez de Asua could rectify by talking to Ricardo Rojas or reading some of the modern, neo-Inca Argentine literature, including an interesting recent book of legends by Ernesto Morales.

It is true, and it is quite evident, that the modern idiosyncrasy of these peoples has much which comes from the aboriginal inhabitants of America. The Chilean of today is not as energetic or strong as the Araucanian of yesterday. The same is true of the Mexican. Nor is the Peruvian as pacific (Bolivian, Ecuadorean, North Argentine, and South Colombian). In Costa Rica there are few Indians, but there exists much Indian psychology, true and pure. Once I observed that Yucatecans and Guatemalans in both countries speak Spanish "with a Maya accent and intonation." Neither the virtues nor the defects of the Indians have died among us. Racial mixture has naturally brought promiscuity. The Negro, who constitutes another of the post-Colombian invasions coming to America, has had an enormous influence, both in the United States, as Keyserling and Jung note, and in the tropical regions of America below the Rio Bravo. After all, Haiti was the first independent state amongst us.

It appears to me that Waldo Frank has spoken the truth in his latest lectures at the University of Mexico, when he affirms that the European is being sublimated and transformed in America, as occurred to the Asian and the Aryan in Europe. England is increasingly further from North America, as Spain is from us. In those of our countries where progress is the greatest, Hispanicism is least. It is the least developed peoples and regions of ours where the Spanish tradition lives and where there abound people who wish to eternalize

---

* Haya refers here to Charles Curtis, Vice President under Herbert Hoover, who was part Indian.

the influence of colonialism. For this reason, Jiménez de Asua well says that Hispano Americanism is "a vague, sentimental expression," because, as he was able to see, it is only nourished thus, vaguely and sentimentally, particularly among conservatives.

Is Latin Americanism "a Gallic invention" as Jiménez de Asua affirms? I wouldn't agree with his claim. Historically, Latin Americanism appears to me a "Renaissance" expression. America, encircled by the Inquisition, lived intellectually in the Middle Ages. France brought us as *contraband* a projection of the Renaissance, of paganism, in the full meaning of the word, of resurrected classical thought in Europe. It is undeniable that our revolution against feudal Spanish imperialism has intellectual French liberal roots, a Latin essence. Our paradoxical republicanism is woven largely "a la francesa." Bolívar was a brilliant Latinist and swore romantically to struggle for the independence of America, while on the Aventine, facing the ruins of Rome, birthplace of the classic conception of the rights of the *demos*. The Encylopedists, the French Revolution, and the Napolenic legislation of Latin inspiration molded our America. Independence was inspired in France, and various countries, among them Peru, adopted even the political division and bureaucratic names of the French Republic. Haiti, a French-speaking Negro republic, became independent before us. Its treasure greatly aided Bolívar, protected by the Alexandre Petion plan,* and when Mexico asked for economic aid in the struggle against Spain, the Haitians had no funds left. (Alexandre Bonneau, *Haiti, ses progres, son avenir,* Paris: 1867.)

The expression *Latin Americanism* corresponds, then, undeniably, to our republican epoch and corresponds more to it than the restricted and colonial *Hispano Americanism*. The exploitation which the French can make of that word is as secondary in importance as that which the imperialist Yankees and Spanish monarchists make of one or another of the possible words. The three have historical significance.

Jiménez de Asua writes in his prologue that "every decision would be premature" in determining whether we are Hispano Americans or not. I believe that he is very correct and that his attitude is the only one possible for a Spaniard who has seen something of America and who is not stubborn. He must accept the historic truth

---

* Petion was the President of Haiti who gave refuge to Bolívar, and otherwise helped his cause.

that the influence of the *conquerors* is extinguished and transformed in the conquered peoples. Neither race nor language has any historic guarantee of eternity in the evolutionary process. Many undertake to preserve the purity of the Spanish language which is itself formed of other languages, a product of their obsolescence and transformation. Every attempt to conserve the purity of races and languages is, as we know, anti-scientific. The only reason that the English language is more expressive than Spanish is its freedom to develop, without academies or inquisitions, as a direct product of the economic and social evolution of a people, while ours is restricted. For that reason, in peoples undergoing great economic development, such as the Argentines, one sees that the old ways of expression are broken by the force of new needs. One could go on at length about this point.

Not being a devotee of heroic, episodic history, I believe in the economic determinism of all our historical phenomena. Thus, I permit myself this interpretation of the discovery and conquest of America, colonialism, the Negro invasion, as well as independence, the republic, dollar imperialism, European and Asiatic emigration, the Mexican Revolution, our anti-imperialist movements, etc. Economic causation does not exclude the heroic or the impact of individuals; there remain the Columbuses, Pizarros, and Bolívars of yesterday, and our Zapatas and Sandinos of today. I believe that they are not the causes but are the instruments or interpreters and guides of the movements and events.

From the economic point of view, I cannot be a Hispano Americanist. I believe that that would be to engage in "vague sentimentalism." The economic phenomenon of today is not Hispano Americanism. Our peoples have before them the great problem of the fight between imperialism, the result of the dominant organization and capitalist system in the United States, and the great national masses of workers in our countries, who are in their majority Indian. It is the world social problem, which in our America takes on very special characteristics, its own features, complexity, and transcendence, which are "very American." Because our reality is so much ours, I am frankly against all kinds of tropical, pseudorevolutionists who repeat European speeches as solutions for our problems.*

Now, then, what role does Spain have in all this? I see none.

---

* The reader will recall that by such references as this, Haya generally means the Communists, and to a lesser degree the Social Democrats, of Latin America.

However, the question is interesting and tends to clarify useful concepts for the ideological definition of the new America. The Apristas defend the expression Indoamerican as a name for our great renovating, unifying, and anti-imperialist movement. The debate, however, remains open.

I write this with public testimony of admiration and sympathy for this great Spaniard Don Luis Jiménez de Asua, who because he is an advanced liberal, sage and just, has been proscribed from his professional posts in Madrid, as in the times of that Holy Inquisition which in Spain appears undying.

Bibliographical Note

BY PROFESSION, VÍCTOR RAÚL HAYA DE LA TORRE MIGHT WELL BE labelled a journalist. Since the earliest years of his first exile, in the middle 1920s, Haya has been writing articles for daily papers and other periodicals, principally in Latin America, but also in the United States and Europe. One result of this has been that virtually all of the books which Haya has published consist of compilations of these articles. Some have been collections of disparate pieces and have little internal unity. Haya's only books written as single volumes are *El Antimperialismo y el Apra* and *Treinta Años del Aprismo*.

Haya de la Torre has published at least nineteen books. In chronological order, these have been the following:

Por la Emancipación de América Latina. Buenos Aires: Editorial Gleizer, 1927.

Teoria y Táctica de la Juventud Antimperialista. Buenos Aires: Federación Universitaria Argentina, 1928.

Ideario y Acción Aprista. Lima: Editorial Cahuide, 1930.

Teoria y Táctica del Aprismo. Lima: Editorial Cahuide, 1930.

Manifesto a la Nación. Panamá: 1932.

Impresiones de la Inglaterra Imperialista y la Rusia Soviética. Buenos Aires: Editorial Claridad, 1932.

El Plan del Aprismo. Guayaquil: 1932.

Política Aprista. Lima: Editorial Cooperativa Aprista Atahalpa, 1933.

El Proceso Haya de la Torre. Guayaquil: Partido Aprista Peruano, 1933.

Construyendo el Aprismo. Buenos Aires: Editorial Claridad, 1933.

A Donde Va Indoamerica? Santiago, Chile: Editorial Ercilla, 1935.

El Antimperialismo y el Apra. Santiago, Chile: Ediciones Ercilla, 1936.

Ex-Combatientes y Desocupados. Santiago, Chile: Ediciones Ercilla, 1936.

La Defensa Continental. Buenos Aires: Editorial Americalee, 1946.

Y Despues de la Guerra, Que? Lima: Editorial P.T.C.M., 1946.

Espacio-Tiempo-Histórico. Lima: Ediciones La Tribuna, 1948.

Treinta Años del Aprismo. Mexico: Fondo de Cultura Económica, 1956.

Mensaje de la Europa Nórdica. Buenos Aires: Editorial Continente, 1956.

Toynbee Frente a los Panoramas de la Historia. Buenos Aires: Compañía Editora y Distribuidora del Plata SRL, 1957.

The most significant books in this list are *El Antimperialismo y el Apra, Espacio-Tiempo-Histórico,* and *Toynbee Frente a los Panoramas de la Historia.* The first of these presents Haya de la Torre's fundamental political and economic theses and his ideas concerning how the society and economy of the Latin American countries should be reorganized. In the second and third, one can trace the evolution of the philosophical basis for Haya's ideas. I have borrowed heavily in the foregoing pages from these three volumes. In addition, I have taken appropriate articles from various of the other collections in the above list.

One other collection of Haya de la Torre's ideas is of considerable importance. This is a five-volume selection of Haya's writings made by Luis F. Rodríquez Vildosola, Carlos Manuel Cox, and Andres Townsend Ezcurra, and published under the title *Pensamiento Político de Haya de la Torre* (Lima: Ediciones Pueblo, 1961). This collection is divided as follows:

　　　Volume I　*Indoamérica*
　　　Volume II　*Ideología Aprista*
　　　Volume III　*Aprismo y Filosofía*
　　　Volume IV　*El Plan de Acción*
　　　Volume V　*Nuestra América y el Mundo*

Haya de la Torre and his ideas have been the subject of commentary since the early days of his career. Among the books sympathetic to him are the following:

　　　Alberto Hidalgo. *Haya de la Torre en Su Víspera.* Lima: 1931.

　　　Luis Alberto Sánchez. *Raúl Haya de la Torre, o El Politico, Crónica de Una Vida Sin Tregua.* Santiago: 1934.

Felipe Cossio del Pomar. *Haya de la Torre, El Indoaméricano.* Lima: Editoria Nuevo Día, 1946.

Harry Kantor. *The Ideology and Program of the Aprista Movement.* Berkeley: University of California Press, 1954.

Eugenio Chang-Rodriquez. *La Literatura Politica de Gonzalez Prada, Mariategui y Haya de la Torre.* Mexico: Ediciones de Andrea, 1957.

The Communists have been bitter opponents of Haya de la Torre, and of his party, for more than four decades. One of the most interesting and important critiques of Haya from the Communist point of view is Rodney Arismendi's *La Filosofía de Marxismo y Sr. Haya de la Torre* (Montevideo: Editorial America, 1946). Arismendi has for several decades been one of the principal leaders of the Uruguayan Communist Party, and in recent decades has been perhaps the outstanding ideologist of the Latin American Communists. The volume by Eudosio Ravines, ex-Aprista and founder of the Peruvian Communist Party (which he left in 1942), *The Venan Way* (New York: Scribners, 1953) is also of some interest.

In spite of Haya's long-time importance in Latin America, surprisingly few book-length treatments of him and his ideas have appeared in English, particularly in recent years. An early sympathetic study of Haya and the Apristas was that of Carleton Beals, *Fire on the Andes* (Philadelphia: Lippincott, 1934). In a later book, *Latin America: World in Revolution* (New York: Abelard-Schuman, 1963), Beals, who in the meantime had become an admirer of Perón and Fidel Castro, took the position that Haya was a "traitor." Serafino Romouldi devoted one chapter of his autobiographical *Presidents and Peons* (1967) to Haya de la Torre.

I have devoted a chapter to him in my *Prophets of the Revolution* (New York: Macmillan, 1962). James Payne has written a book critical of the Apristas and of Haya, *Labor and Politics in Peru* (New Haven, Conn.: Yale University Press, 1965), as has Frederick Pike, *The Modern History of Peru* (London & New York: 1967).

Numerous other writers have made passing reference to Haya and the Apristas in general volumes on Latin America. In addition, there have been a fair number of articles published in United States periodicals.

DATE DUE